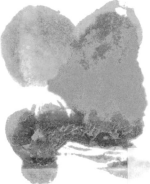

THE
TRANSFORMATION
OF THE
CHINESE EARTH

中國土地的演變與形成

THE TRANSFORMATION OF THE CHINESE EARTH

Aspects of the Evaluation of the
Chinese Earth from Earliest Times to Mao Tse-tung

KEITH BUCHANAN

Professor of Geography, Victoria University of Wellington
Wellington, New Zealand

LONDON: G. BELL AND SONS, LTD

The ploughing scene on the title page is taken from a carved brick of the Han dynasty

SBN 7135 1549 X

Printed in Great Britain by
The Camelot Press Ltd., London and Southampton

Remembering
the
Summer Palace

Foreword

PERHAPS THE origins of this book are to be sought a generation
ago when Professor R. H. Kinvig gave me my first insights into the
scope and the challenge of geography as a discipline; taught me, too,
that any real understanding of the geography of the non-Western world
called for what is surely the most difficult of all things to achieve—an
awareness of how the world, and the problems of their own homelands,
appear to the great majority of mankind who are heirs to a different
cultural tradition from that in which we of the West have our roots.
Five years work in Africa underscored the reality of what (heretical—or
perhaps farseeing—as it was in terms of the then fashionable geography)
I had been taught in Birmingham.   My years in Africa, in what were
then the Union of South Africa and the colonial territory of Nigeria,
were important, too, in another way for they demonstrated to me
at first hand the horror and hopelessness of life for those whom
Frantz Fanon has termed 'the damned of the earth'.   In the 'native
reserves' of South Africa, the slums of Lagos and the shanty-towns of
Morocco or Algeria I saw something of the subhuman and brutal
quality of existence to which two-thirds of my fellow men were condemned.   The grain ripened slowly, but by the time I was teaching in
New Zealand the condition of this submerged two-thirds of humanity
had become one of the central preoccupations of my working and my
thinking.   And it was thus inevitable that I should be drawn to an
increasing interest in what New Zealanders term their 'Near North'
(however remote it may be from their thinking or their concern), in
the gigantic experiment which the Chinese were making in an attempt
to wipe out the poverty and the wastage of human abilities and the
exploitation of man by man (and of woman by man), which, I had seen,
were the lot of so many of my fellow men.   There was no difficulty in
getting a Western view of what was going on; with a few honourable
exceptions most writers, most 'experts', condemned without under-

vii

standing; what I wished for was to see these 'deplorable' developments at first hand, to talk (even through an interpreter) with those who were being 'ground down under the iron heel' of the new society, to learn what *they* thought of the transformation of their land, to learn what *their* hopes and aspirations were, to learn what the world looked like from Peking. . . .

The opportunity came in 1958, again in 1964 and 1966. The China I discovered bore little relationship to that described then—and still today described in identical terms—by much of the Western press. I wandered around, following routes which I myself chose, and discovered a new world in the making. . . . And while travelling, and after returning, digesting the experiences of these journeys, I tried to relate what the Chinese were striving to do to the problems of that submerged two-thirds of humankind whose increasing relative and absolute poverty is the dominating human reality of our time. This volume gathers together both fact and interpretation and it attempts to see the Chinese experiment in both its historical and global setting; it attempts, too, to evaluate the human significance of the Chinese experiment—and I write here not as a detached and objective academic, for the ostentatious objectivity of many scholars is, as I point out later (p. 307), mostly spurious, and it is not possible to be, at one and the same time, both human and 'detached' when we are confronted with the tragic human conditions of today. And at a time when the greater part of humanity is being engulfed by a 'dark tide of violence', when those who dwell within the affluent societies of the capitalist and Communist blocs are being stifled by their alienating affluence, the Chinese preoccupation with the 'quality of life', their vision of a society in which human and economic relations are motivated not by considerations of material gain but by moral incentives, appear to me elements of decisive importance to humanity as a whole. . . . The view is heretical and time alone will make it possible to assess its accuracy—but—I write this on the eve of the American circumnavigation of the moon—I believe the 'Chinese experiment' to be a greater contribution to 'the creation of a more human world' than the most spectacular break-through in interplanetary navigation, than all the achievements of a technology which is bringing a progressive dehumanisation of the societies in which it flourishes and whose contribution to alleviating the lot of the damned of the earth is derisory. . . . 'China,' says the Greek writer Nikos Kazantzakis, 'the only land in the world that can give you the clues to the future, the more distant mankind. . . .'

The New Zealand Government does not recognise the government of the People's Republic of China; it would seem that similarly New Zealand librarians do not recognise the existence of China for there are great gaps in their book stocks. None of the larger atlases of China (not even those published in Taiwan) appear to be held here; there are major gaps as far as other source material is concerned though some of these were made good by colleagues in China and elsewhere overseas. An unevenness in the coverage of this volume was therefore inevitable though selective emphasis by the writer on particular topics must be held responsible for some at least of this unevenness. No volume of this size can adequately cover all aspects of the transformation of the homeland of almost one-quarter of humanity, especially when the historical span is extended over some five or six millennia. The picture is inevitably impressionistic and the author's attempt to correct the hazed or distorted images of reality purveyed by our mass media is in part responsible for an apparent preoccupation with some aspects of development in the most recent period. . . .

My debts to the writings of René Dumont, Charles Bettelheim, Paul Bairoch and Pierre Jalée will be evident in those sections where I attempt to set Chinese development policies into their global perspective; equally, in more specific sections of the work, my debts to the American Sinologists Herold Wiens, Edward Schafer, Ping-ti Ho and Yuan-li Wu.

The writer acknowledges with gratitude the warm help and guidance given by numerous colleagues of the *Academia Sinica*. Knowing how many urgent tasks they are preoccupied with, aware of the critical role many Chinese geographers are today playing in the transformation of their land, I am particularly grateful to them for the long hours they gave to me, in field work and discussion, during each of my three visits to China. Involved in a great variety of collective enterprises, dedicated to the uplifting task of creating a new earth, they would not wish for individual acknowledgement; I, a lone and individual wandering scholar, can only pay tribute to their selflessness and warm humanity. My 1958 visit was at the invitation of the *Academia Sinica* and my 1966 visit was made possible by a grant from the University of New Zealand Research Committee; to both bodies I would express my gratitude. And without the patience and hospitality extended to me by peasants, workers and cadres my field work would have been impossible.

I owe a heavy debt to all those who, here in Wellington, have made possible the preparation of the volume; to Mrs. Joan Elmes who, with patience and with skill, coped with hundreds of pages of pencil-written MS, much-amended and unpredictable in its appearance from month to month; to Mrs. Jean Benfield who transmuted my colour transparencies into half-tone photographs; to Miss Robin Somerville who drafted most of the maps; finally to Miss Ann Stewart who read the proofs and prepared the index. Without their help the final completion of this volume, whose preparation has had perforce to be fitted into the teaching commitments and other involvements of a university department, would have been impossible. And, last but by no means least, I am grateful for the tolerance and patience shown by Mr. M. H. Varvill and other friends at Messrs. G. Bell & Sons Ltd.; at times they must have experienced something of the frustration and despair I myself experienced at the slow progress of the work. Their help and their understanding has been warmly appreciated.

Feast-day of St. Thomas Didymus   KEITH BUCHANAN
1968

Contents

Maps and Cartograms

Plates

Tables

'A grammar of fate like the map of China . . .'
Lawrence Durrell,
Collected Poems, p. 24

'Ils vont leur chemin sans se soucier de ce qu'on en pense'
Robert Guillain,
Dans trente ans, la Chine, p. 8

'Les mécanismes d'une économie evoluée, qu'elle soit capitaliste ou socialiste, n'existent pas au départ. Il faut créer leurs conditions de jeu.'
Maurice Byé in Jacques Freyssinet
Le concept de sous-développement, p. ix

'We will realise that the accounts (and accounting symbolism) of different societies are not comparable; that we cannot compare separate accounting aggregates for one society with those relating to another with a different social and economic framework, and hence a different system of accounting values.'
S. H. Frankel,
The Economic Impact on Underdeveloped Societies, p. 53

CHAPTER 1

Introduction

'With Their Own Strength they made the Landscape . . . '

WE IN the West, who have spent much of our life in a country-side which has been slowly, laboriously, transformed over countless generations, whose soils and trees and hedgerows were cherished because they were the result of the labours of those who went before us and must be handed on as a legacy to those yet to come, we often forget how exceptional the humanised and domesticated land-scapes of our earth really are. . . . We regard such landscapes as the *normal* type of landscape and the values which go with it as the *normal* values. In fact, such intensely humanised landscapes exist on any scale in only two areas of our globe, at the two extremes of Eurasia, in the Mediterranean-derived culture world of Western Europe and in the Chinese culture world. Only in these two areas do we find landscapes that have been transformed by the labours of untold generations of men, men who were heirs to a distinctive and coherent culture, and who have left the signature of that culture on the earth's surface—in the shape of the medieval town patterns and the hedged fields of Western Europe, the hill-top village and the dry-stone terracing of the Mediterranean or the flowing lines and curving mirror-surface of the South Chinese rice-field. In these areas so pervasive and so profound has been the impact of man that the geographer is often at a loss to determine which elements of a landscape are 'natural' and which 'man-made'; how far can we regard the intensively-worked soils of lowland Britain or of the north Chinese lowland, transformed by centuries of manuring and cultivation, as elements in the 'natural' environment? how much of the vegetation of Western Europe or eastern China is a 'natural' vegetation? The countrysides of Europe, the countrysides of China, are like ancient palimpsests, manuscripts on which countless generations have inscribed the poetry—and the misery—of their daily lives and the writing they have left behind them is only partly effaced by the bolder characters inscribed by the latest arrivals in this unending succession of peasants and farmers, of village dwellers and city folk. . . .

Of the two great culture worlds of Eurasia, it is the Chinese that has left the most decisive mark on the landscape. It is true that the civilisations of the Mediterranean can rival the civilisation of China in terms of their antiquity, but the Mediterranean civilisations lack the continuity of Chinese civilisation; their cultural cohesiveness (with all that this has meant in terms of man's moulding of his environment) has been less; above all, the sheer pressure of human numbers, of countless millions draining and clearing and cultivating the land, has been less in western Eurasia than in the monsoonal lands of the continents eastern fringe. This long and cumulative humanisation has been sensitively portrayed by Robert Payne; the Chinese, he says, are a people

> whose dust was so intermingled in the soil that they perhaps alone of all nations do not feel themselves strangers to the land. They may curse their land at times, thinking how barren it is and how unprotected from invaders; but it is theirs by a greater right than ours is ours.[1]

And it is theirs because they confronted the impenitence of the land, its floods, its barrenness and its poverty, and with their sweat and their toil, with dogged determination and a millennial-old endurance, they made of it a grainfield, a garden and an orchard. 'With their own strength they made the landscape'[2]—as Robert Payne puts it—and in this phrase is compressed the last five millennia of Chinese history, no less than the profound transformations of the last two decades. . . .

One of the most striking features of contemporary China is the massive mobilisation of human muscle and human skills to transform their land, to create, if we may lapse into Western concepts and ways of speaking, a 'new Heaven on Earth'—and for the Chinese this means a condition where no one hungers, where the physical or mental potential of no child is wasted, where each and every citizen may expand to the full his or her capacity for selflessness, dedication and solidarity in the service of humankind. This mobilisation, this 'turning of labour into capital' to use the fashionable phrase, must be seen as a specifically Chinese attempt to solve the major problems of our century—and that is not the protecting or perfecting of the living levels of those who dwell within the handful of affluent societies which dominate the globe, but the creating of 'a more human world'[3] for the two-thirds or so of humanity which exist in degrading and increasingly impoverished subhuman conditions. Like the remainder of this great submerged mass of humanity the Chinese confronted the problem of development lacking the capital and the capital equipment on which the progress of the affluent nations has rested; they had little but the muscles and the

---

[1] Robert Payne, *The White Pony* (Mentor Books, New York 1960) p. xi.
[2] *Ibid.*, p. xvii.   [3] The phrase is Pope Paul VI's.

ingenuity of their people with which—and the phrase is used here both in its literal and metaphorical sense—to create a new world. The far-reaching and widespread transformation of the Chinese earth in the last two decades has been achieved by the mobilisation of these resources. . . .

Yet we do well to remember that, in many essentials, the momentous development of the last two decades does not represent a fundamental break with the past, that, plotted over time, the progress of development, the process of transforming the Chinese earth, might indeed resemble the graph of population change in China (p. 279), with a long, immensely long, period of consolidation, of advance and retreat in the face of natural or man-made calamity, followed by an almost vertiginous upward surge of the graph. V. A. Kovda, in a passage cited later in this work, refers to

> the far-reaching, pertinent and purposive effect of man on China's rivers, on the relief of the hilly and mountainous regions, and on the relief and soil blanket of the valleys, plains and deltas,[1]

and Joseph Needham stresses the antiquity of this human transformation of the land:

> The importance of irrigation channels for intensive agriculture, water conservancy for preventing floods, and canal transport for the gathering in of the tribute to the Imperial Court from the provinces, led to the establishment of a veritable tradition of great public works which is absolutely living in China today as much as it ever was in the Han or Chhing or Thang dynasties.[2]

He adds

> the role of the Communist Party there, in putting the accent on great public works, is something which is much less new to Chinese society than it might be to any other nation in the world, except, perhaps, the Egyptians and the Sinhalese.[3]

But while the contemporary transformation of the Chinese earth has its roots deep in history and continues an age-old tradition it is unique in both its pace and its extent. Its pace is illustrated by the Chinese claim that in 1957 and 1958 they brought more land under irrigation than in the whole of China's earlier history; its extent is indicated by programmes of agricultural development, industrialisation and mining development which extend from the rainforests of the south to the subarctic forests of the northeast and the red sand deserts of the far west. It is a transformation which is integrating formerly marginal areas such

[1] V. A. Kovda, *Soils & Natural Environment of China* (U.S. Joint Publications Research Service, Washington, 1960), p. 79.
[2] Joseph Needham, 'The Past in China's Present' in *Pacific Viewpoint* (Wellington), September 1963, p. 123.
I have left Needham's transliteration of dynastic names as in his original.
[3] *Ibid.*, p. 124.

as these into the Chinese *oecumene*, which is revealing their long-neglected potential, which is continuing the process of humanisation which began untold generations ago when the Chinese people began to disperse from their cradle area in the valley of the Yellow River and hesitantly, but with increasing assurance, to assess the potentials of the new environments into which they moved.

We have compared the Chinese earth to a palimpsest; today there is new writing on this ancient manuscript, writing whose characters are bold and clear and confident. The message it carries is equally bold and clear and confident and it is a phrase of Mao Tse-tung's 'The working people who live on the 9·6 million square-kilometres of the People's Republic of China have really begun to rule this land'[1]—and in this phrase Mao refers not only to political control but also to the increasing capacity of the Chinese to transform their environment, to their control over the Chinese earth. Standing today alone, standing self-reliant in a world which believes development without foreign aid is impossible, it is 'with their own strength'—and with this alone—that the Chinese people are engaged in the long, the immensely long, and arduous task of building a new world. . . .

[1] Mao Tse-tung writing in *Hung Ch'i* (1958) and quoted by Stuart Schram in *The Political Thought of Mao Tse-tung* (New York and London 1963), p. 253.

CHAPTER 2

The Occupation of the Chinese Land

PERSPECTIVE

THE HISTORY of China is the history of the Chinese peasant, of a people whose association with their cradle area was so intimate, so ancient, that they have been termed 'the Children of the Yellow Earth'.... A people who 'cared only for humanity', whose vision of happiness is captured in the earliest of their poems, *The Book of Songs*:

> *Rustling of the reaping,*
> *Plumping of fat sheaves,*
> *Piling like a heaped wall,*
> *Shaped like a toothed comb.*[1]

There are over 100 million peasant families in China. In the river-fretted alluvial lowlands of the east and on the dusty yellow plains of the north they are closely packed: two thousand, three thousand, five thousand people contrive with careful garden cultivation to wrest a living from each square mile, from an area which in New Zealand, even in many parts of Europe, might support a dozen families. In the hills of the south and west the farming population is much sparser—small clusters wherever a patch of level or gently sloping land can be cultivated —and in the far west the settlements of Chinese farmers string out like beads in the narrow zone where mountain meets desert and irrigation water is to be had.

This pattern has gradually evolved over many thousands of years and, indeed, the real history of China is not so much the history of the rise and fall of great dynasties as the history of the gradual occupation of the Chinese earth by untold generations of farming folk spreading out

[1] Robert Payne, *The White Pony* (New York 1960), p. 40.

southwards, westwards and northwards from an original 'cradle area' in the middle reaches of the Yellow River valley. And the real actors in the drama of Chinese history have not been the great emperors, nor the great generals, nor even the celebrated beauties, the 'flower-shadows behind the silken curtain' of imperial China, but rather the nameless peasants who set forth and carved out for themselves homes and tiny plots of beans or rice or sweet potatoes far from the villages where they were born. . . . And the most recent episode in the history of China—the establishment of a Communist régime—this represents perhaps the final stage in this peasant epic—the stage in which the peasant, after long centuries, finally establishes his control over the Chinese earth and, liberated from his old bondage, begins that re-appraisal of the environment which will make possible the creation of a new world of plenty.

BEGINNINGS[1]

The earliest stages of this immense drama are partially lost in the mists of time, in the uncertainty which, in spite of recent archeological progress, still envelops the prehistory of the East Asian mainland. As Watson has observed, the Chinese people 'has occupied the valley of the Yellow river from time immemorial. . . . The manner and time of the colonisation of the great Central Plain of north China, supposing such a thing were ever a definable historical event, is beyond know-ledge and conjecture alike'.[2] Thus the most ancient human remains, those of the pre-*sapiens* type known as Peking Man, date back perhaps half a million years and indicate the presence in North China of a Paleolithic population possessing rudimentary tool-making skills. This population belonged genetically to the species *Sinanthropus* yet shows some anatomical features similar to the modern population of the area; the deposits in what is known as Locality 1 at Chou K'ou Tien indicate, moreover, a stability of physical type extending over a period of hundreds of thousands of years. Towards the end of the Paleolithic period the remains of 'Upper Cave Man', who inhabited a cave towards the summit of the hill on the same site, belong to the modern type *Homo Sapiens*. The archaeological record suggests that, by this date, possibly some 20,000–30,000 years ago, deliberate burial of the dead had become established and that trade was carried on over considerable distances.

These remains may be taken to mark the end of the Old Stone Age in China. There then follows an inexplicable break in the continuity of the archaeological record. The Mesolithic and early Neolithic

[1] I have drawn on the excellent summary in Joseph Needham, *Science and Civilisation in China*, Vol. 1 (Cambridge 1954), and on William Watson's two studies, *China: Before the Han Dynasty* (London 1961), and *Early Civilisation in China* (London 1966).
[2] W. Watson, *China*, p. 11.

periods seem to have been periods of relatively abundant rainfall in North China and it would seem that the habitability of the area was then at its maximum. Yet while scattered finds (of as yet uncertain date) have been made in the desert and grassland margins of the northwest of China no archaeological finds that can be definitely attributed to this period have been made in North China proper. There are no apparent predecessors for the farming communities of the valley of the Yellow River, no sites which would enable us to fill in the gap between Upper Cave Man and the Neolithic villagers. Yet, suddenly, around 2500 B.C., the North China area appears to support a dense village-swelling population, with hundreds, even thousands, of villages. These village communities possessed an already complex culture, derived from several sources: their basic cereal was millet, supplemented later (as the impressions on pottery suggest) by rice from Southeast Asia; they had domesticated dogs and pigs, sheep and cattle; they possessed highly developed techniques of pottery-making. And in their pottery-making there is little evidence of outside influences filtering in from the West; indeed, the hand-painted pottery of Kansu, once regarded as evidence of such cultural transfer from outside, is now thought to be later than the pottery of the central plain of North China.

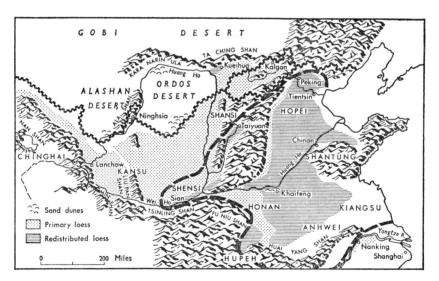

Figure 1. The Cradle Area of Chinese Culture.

Heavy broken line represents area controlled by the Shang Dynasty (c. 1300 B.C.) according to Herrmann; Paul Wheatley regards this as probably exaggerated and suggests the 'metropolitan core' area was centred around Loyang, west of Khaifeng.

The cradle area of these early Chinese, whose life and whose material culture are being increasingly illuminated by the progress of archaeology, lay in the basin of the Hwang Ho, an area of loess or loess-derived alluvium.   In early historic times it would have had an open landscape and fertile and easily-worked soils.   The 'islands' of harder rock protruding through the loess mantle were forested and provided timber and water.   Its climate five millennia ago was probably very similar to its present-day climate, though possibly wetter.   It was an area which possessed many attractions for early man—a rich and friable soil, stone, timber and water close at hand—and which was strategic-ally-located at the eastern end of the great transcontinental corridor zone which was subsequently to be known as the 'Silk Road' (Figure 17). Within this general area three subdivisions may be distinguished: the semi-desert margins of the northwest, the area of primary loess, extending through Kansu, Shensi, western Shansi and western-central Honan, and the area within which the loess has been redistributed in the form of alluvium, an area which includes much of Hopeh Province, the lowlands of western Shantung and parts of Honan Province (Figure 1).   These subdivisions appear to have been of some signific-ance in the early cultural history of North China.   Thus, the steppe and desert fringes appear to have preserved a pre-farming stage of culture

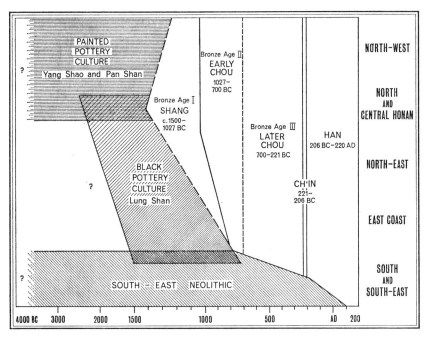

Figure 2.   The Chronological and Regional Pattern of the Early Chinese Cultures
(based on Watson).

Note the 'cultural lag' of South and Southeast China and the significance of the North and Central Honan region in the early development of Bronze Age culture (for the character of this development and the survival of Neolithic techniques see p. 12).

(using 'microliths' and roughly polished stone tools but with a knowledge of pottery) at a period when settled agriculture had become
established in the more humid lands to the south and east. And within
this more humid zone the area of primary loess coincides closely with
the distribution of the painted pottery culture known as the Yang Shao
culture, while the area of redistributed loess was the domain of the
black pottery culture, the Lung Shan culture. Some, it should be
added, are hesitant to accept this picture of two distinct Neolithic
traditions in China, one northwestern, the other northeastern in its
distribution, and claim that the Lung Shan culture was a later, more
developed, form of the Yang Shao culture. But, as Watson has
pointed out, the differences between the two cultures are such as to
'imply complex local influences';[1] if indeed there is no cultural dis-
continuity, it is hard to understand 'why the line of division between
them in stratified deposits should be as clearly marked as it is in most
instances'.[2]

The boundaries of this cradle area on the northwest were not clearly
defined; with decreasing rainfall there was a gradual transition into
the arid and semi-arid grasslands of Mongolia. These grasslands
represented an environment in which relict cultures could survive (as
demonstrated by the apparent persistence of a pre-farming culture and
a microlithic industry when the rest of North China was in the full
Neolithic) and which were subsequently to emerge as the domain of
the nomadic pastoralist; the building of the Great Wall may be regarded
as an attempt to establish a clearly defined boundary and a defensible
frontier in this direction. Southwards, the change was relatively
sharp, for the east–west trending ridges of the Tsinling-Tapa Shan
represent the southernmost limit of the loessial environments and
constitute the most clearly-marked physical and biological divide in
east Asia. To the south, the subhumid environment gives place to a
humid tropical environment. Temperatures and rainfall are high
most of the year and the growing season long. The natural vegetation
is luxuriant and includes bamboo, citrus fruits and palms, as well as
broad-leaved evergreen forests. A tropical fauna, including elephants,
monkeys, rhinoceros and water buffalo, replaces the northern steppe
and grassland fauna. Here were found a greater variety of environments—though none rivalling the North China cradle area—and a
greater variety of population groups than in the north, including
negrito peoples and proto-Malay seafaring folk. For long, however,
this southern area remained a backward area, outside the mainstream
of Chinese development and preserving, as in the Old Stone Age,

[1] W. Watson, op. cit., pp. 42–3.
[2] The application of carbon-14 dating techniques may push the origins of the pottery-
making Neolithic cultures of China back some millennia. As Watson points out, carbon-14
dating shows that the first pottery in Japan appears in the eighth millennium B.C. and 'it is
extremely unlikely that the first appearance of pottery on the mainland should be later'.
Early Civilisation in China, p. 43.

stronger cultural links with Southeast Asia than with the developing civilisation of the north.

The lowlands of Anhwei and Kiangsu and parts of the Yangtse valley in Hupeh serve as a corridor zone between north and south and while the dominantly agricultural civilisation of the Yang Shao and Lung Shan peoples was in full efflorescence in the loess-lands this zone was characterised by a distinctive pottery tradition and by an economy in which hunting and fishing were carried on alongside agriculture. And in the coastal lowlands of Fukien and the broad (and then probably marshy and forest-choked) alluvial valleys of Kwangtung the peoples of the so-called Southeast Neolithic culture possessed the techniques of pottery-making (the 'stamp-decorated' style) yet were largely food-gatherers who remained ignorant of farming until 'only a few centuries before the beginning of the Christian era'.[1]   Much of China's history, political or economic, is taken up with the gradual absorption of these southern lands into the expanding culture of the Han people.

FORMATIVE INFLUENCES

Watson places the beginning of the Bronze Age in China at 'somewhere between 2000 and 1500 B.C.'.   He adds, 'At some such date the Neolithic period of north and central China may be said to finish, as the country came under the domination of city-states where power was based on the possession of bronze weapons'.   Whether this technological revolution was the result of cultural diffusion from the Bronze Age civilisations of western Eurasia is as yet unclear; all that can be said is that there is to date little evidence of such outside influences.   Yet equally there are few signs in the archaeological record of North China which might indicate the early stages of bronze-working; rather does a technologically highly developed and artistically sophisticated bronze-using culture seem to spring fully-formed from the loess-lands of the north.

By 1500 B.C. the developed Bronze Age civilisation of the Shang was flourishing in the middle Hwangho region.   The area of this bronze-using culture was closely paralleled by that of millet and of wheat cultivation, the latter having spread apparently across Asia from the Middle East.   These people, like the people before them, do not appear to have ever passed through a pastoral phase; they had developed the art of writing, and the use of cowrie shells and the beginnings of the extensive use of bamboo suggest culture-contact with the tropical and subtropical south.   During this formative period several basic cultures contributed to the evolution of the Chinese culture-complex.   First, a northern group, typified by the neolithic culture of North China and sometimes termed 'proto-Tungusic'.   It brought to the Chinese

---

[1] W. Watson, *op. cit.*, p. 19.

culture-complex a matriarchal organisation of society, the use of pit-dwellings and bone arrow-heads, and the practice of a shamanistic religion. Secondly, a group of southeastern cultures, termed 'proto-Thai'. These were a complex group, partly maritime in character

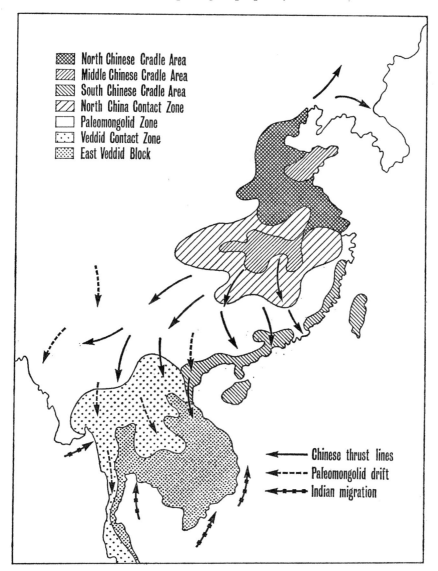

Figure 3. Dynamics of Early Population Movement in East Asia (second to third millennium B.C.).

Illustrating the overspilling and southward thrust of migration from the three Chinese cradle areas and the consequent pressures on the tribal peoples of subtropical China and on the darker Veddid peoples who occupied most of mainland Southeast Asia (after von Eickstedt).

and with some Indonesian affinities. Their distinctive features included the use of longboats; dragon myths and serpent-worship; the use of the crossbow and bark cloth, of bamboo, iron and lacquer work; the domestication of the water buffalo; milpa and terraced rice cultivation; finally, ancestor-worship.

The Bronze Age civilisation of the Shang resulted from a fusion of these two streams, though, obviously, environmental factors would significantly affect the areal extension of individual culture-elements; for example, terraced rice cultivation and the use of the water buffalo were of minor importance in the cooler lands of North China. Two other cultural streams have also influenced this emerging Chinese culture: a northwestern, proto-Turkic culture, derived from a nomad patriarchal society and bringing with it the use of mound burials and the worship of the heavenly bodies and a western, proto-Tibetan culture; the most distinctive elements derived from this culture were cremation and polyandry.

From its very beginnings, then, Chinese civilisation has been composite in character, integrating elements from many sources. And as the recent assimilation (and transmutation) of the basic concepts of Marxism-Leninism demonstrates, this capacity for synthesis is still a major feature of Chinese civilisation.

SOME EPISODES IN THE EMERGENCE OF THE CHINESE STATE

During the Chou period (*c.* 1100 B.C. onwards) North China was occupied by people from the west who carried still further the Bronze Age feudalism of the Shang. This Bronze Age civilisation and the use of bronze weapons was, as during the Shang period, confined to the ruling class of a series of city-states 'dotted about in a sea of neolithic barbarism', set in the midst of a countryside where the use of stone implements by the peasant communities seems to have survived well into the first millennium B.C.; the use of stone reaping-knives thus persisted until their replacement by *iron* sickles. And even among the ruling groups the use of bronze spread slowly; from the region of the lower Yellow River it spread south, reaching the Huai River by the seventh century B.C. and the Yangtse valley (the state of Ch'u) a century or so later.

There were some hundreds of these city-states, linked only by their loose allegiance to the dynasty of Chou. Their location was dependent partly upon environmental conditions; many were river basin units or were protected by marsh or river. The aims of their rulers were simple: defence against other states and against the aboriginal tribes; the possession of as much arable land as possible—since disposable grain supplies determined the size of armies and were thus the key to military strength; finally, the control of major trade routes. During this period the command of large bodies of forced labour made possible the beginning of those developments, such as irrigation and terracing, which eventually transformed China into a land of intensive cultivation and which called for much more than desultory local efforts. Ultimately, the development of irrigation on a large scale led to an increasing need to coordinate and unify water control over wide areas; by the seventh century the number of states had thus been reduced to a dozen and the Chou state was under increasing pressure from its vigorous neighbours: the state of Ch'i to the northeast, whose economic basis was represented by the lowlands of eastern Shantung and its control over the trade in salt and metals, the state of Ch'in in the loess country to the northwest and the state of Ch'u which was based in the lower and middle valley of the Yangtse, and whose rise was due partly to the extension to that area of sedentary irrigation-based agriculture and of a bronze-using technology.

The conflict between the various states between which the Chinese *oecumene* was divided reached a peak during the period known to Chinese annalists as 'The Period of the Warring States' (403–221 B.C.). It was terminated by the rise of the western hill-state of Ch'in and it was the Ch'in ruler Shih Huang-ti who finally accomplished the unification of the empire in 221 B.C., a success sometimes attributed to the equipment of his armies with the long iron sword which, following the Iron Age revolution, rapidly replaced bronze weapons.[1] This Iron Age revolution—which began in the seventh or sixth centuries B.C.—shows a remarkable parallel with the earlier Bronze Age revolution in the suddenness with which the new technology, and refined aspects of that technology, appeared. Thus the techniques of iron-casting which in Europe dates from the late Middle Ages dates back in China to the fourth century B.C.; there was not, as in Europe, a long time-gap between the development of iron-forging and the subsequent development of iron-casting. As Stuart Piggott comments: 'Technological innovation and refinement appears as a characteristic feature of Chinese culture from the beginnings of metallurgy.'[2]

Under Shih Huang-ti the discontinuous stretches of defensive wall which had been built by the earlier feudal states on the northwest fringe of the Great Plain were joined in a single defensive structure— the Great Wall. The state organisation was consolidated and the foundations of the tightly-knit bureaucratic system which was to be typical of China for the next two millennia were laid. Most important of all, the southward deployment of the Ch'in armies resulted in the incorporation of much of the area now forming the provinces of

[1] See, for a partly fanciful—but convincing—account of the role of the new metal in Chinese economics and politics, Ronald Fraser's elegant novel, *Lord of the East*, and Leonard Cottrell's study *The Tiger of Ch'in*.
[2] Preface to William Watson, *Early Civilisation in China*, p. 8.

Fukien, Kwangsi and Kwantung into the Chinese state and in the extension of Chinese influence beyond the low hills which fringe the Si Kiang lowland into the adjoining Red River lowland of Tongking. The Ch'in dynasty, however, did not long survive its founder whose death in 210 B.C. was followed by widespread revolts and by the emergence, in 206 B.C., of the Han dynasty. Seen in its wider perspectives, the rise of the Han dynasty was, in Lattimore's phrase, 'a reaction of the South against the North'. The triumph of Ch'in over Ch'u had been the triumph of wheat-eating chariot-fighters from the northwestern loess-lands over the rice-growing peoples of the southwards-oriented lands of the Yangtse valley; the Han settlement, as Needham remarks, was a compromise, providing for 'a centralised

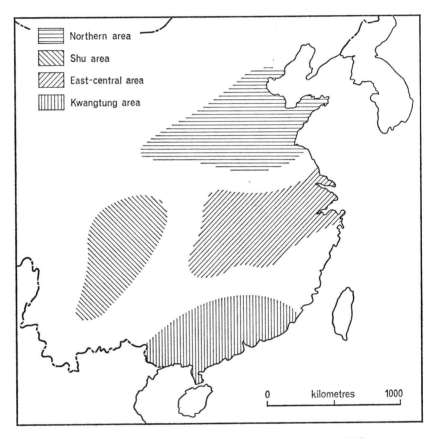

Figure 4. The Key Economic Areas (after Chao-ting Chi).
Primary centre on the loess and loess-derived alluvium of the north; later centres in middle and lower valley of Yangtse, in Szechwan and in the southern coastal plains and valleys. Note relationship of these key areas to the kingdoms of Wei, Wu and Shu (Figure 5) and to the major population concentrations of contemporary China (see pp. 28–29).

empire, but with due regard to the Yangtse provinces'.[1] In these events we find a pre-figuring of the rivalry between what have been termed 'the key economic areas' (Figure 4), a rivalry which has been an important theme in Chinese history and which has manifested itself at periods of disintegration such as the period of the Three Kingdoms (A.D. 220–65).

Between 200 B.C. and A.D. 200 the Han dynasty was responsible for the expansion of Chinese culture over a great deal of what constitutes modern China, an expansion accomplished, in the words of J. E. Spencer, 'by military conquest and political expansion of the simplest imperialistic type'.[2] On the north and west encroachment by the nomads was arrested, a process which involved the extension of Chinese political power along the caravan routes of Central Asia where it came into contact with Imperial Rome. Southwards, the Chinese expansion tended to by-pass the forested upland country of South China, leaving scattered pockets of aboriginal peoples in these hill areas, occupying most of the lowland areas suited to intensive cropping and thrusting far south into the lowland of Tongking. This military conquest was followed by a process of establishing Chinese culture in the conquered area. A new administrative framework was set up with the county, the military corps area and the political district as the basic regional units. The walled city[3] became the pivot of this process of colonisation, for in times of war it offered a refuge while in peacetime it was a base from which the cultural and economic infiltration of the surrounding countryside could take place. In advance of the city the village became the normal unit, though in the Red Basin settlement, taking place under the protection of established walled cities, tended to be dispersed in character.

The non-Chinese groups of the south, including many non-Mongoloid peoples, were in some cases assimilated, in other cases forcibly transplanted. In still other, and possibly the most numerous, cases these tribal peoples avoided contact, moving into the remoter recesses of their forested hills, so that what Wiens terms 'a vertical migration' (i.e. to higher altitudes) was superimposed on this lateral movement, or drifting further to the south. And all the time the gradual process of colonisation began to fill in those areas by-passed on the earlier military conquest, a slow process and one still continuing. This process of Chinese expansion has been most continuous in the humid subtropical south; in the semi-arid west and northwest, by contrast, the last two millennia have witnessed a cyclical advance and retreat of the steppe and the sown, of pastoral nomad and sedentary cultivator, of Chinese

[1] *Science and Civilisation in China*, Vol. 1, p. 116; the views of Bishop and Lattimore on these aspects are referred to by Needham.
[2] J. E. Spencer, *Asia East by South*, pp. 306–10.
[3] On the role of the walled city and the small regional unit for which it served as the core, see L. Cottrell, *op. cit.*, pp. 70–1, drawing on Owen Lattimore.

c

and 'barbarians'. We may comment briefly on some aspects of this expansion.

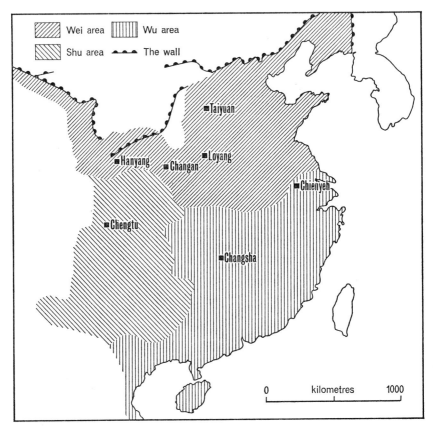

Figure 5.   China in the Period of the Three Kingdoms (A.D. 220–65). (Needham, after Herrmann)

'SO THAT WE MAY PLANT OUR MILLET'

If in the preceding paragraphs we have tended to emphasise the rise and fall of some of the early dynasties it is because these provide a convenient framework within which to consider the early spread of Chinese culture. Yet, as emphasised in the earliest paragraphs in this chapter, the most important theme in Chinese history has been the progressive extension of the Chinese living space by countless millions of peasant families, of pioneering groups. Indeed, altering our simile, we may say that, if dynastic conflict and the increasingly effective administrative organisation which emerged from this conflict shaped the skeleton of the Chinese state, it was the massive movement of peasants into the newly pacified areas, into the lands of promise in humid southern China, which clothed this skeleton with living flesh.

We can glimpse this process of colonisation from the folk-songs preserved in *The Book of Songs*:

> *Ah, they are clearing the land!*
> *Thousands of couples are digging up roots,*
> *Some in the lowlands, others in the high ground. . . .*
> *Why have they torn up the thorny brushwood?*
> *So that we may plant our millet.*

And, on the quality of this peasant life on the steadily expanding margins of this early Chinese society:

> *Work, work from the rising sun*
> *Till sunset comes and day is done.*
> *I plough the sod*
> *And harrow the clod. . . .*[1]

It is true that these songs may date from the early Chou period but it is also true that this pattern of life changed very little during the hundred generations which elapsed since they were first sung, somewhere on the margins of the yellow-earth landscape of North China.

The dynamics of this expansion, which transformed China south of the Yangtse from a dominantly T'ai land[2] into an integral part of the Han-Chinese culture-world may be glanced at briefly. Two of the outstanding features were the rapidity with which the Han-Chinese culture spread and the thoroughness with which peripheral groups such as the T'ai were assimilated. Wiens, following Eberhard, sees the syncretic nature of Chinese culture—or what he terms the 'superimposition' of varying cultures within it—as an important factor explaining the rapidity and thoroughness with which it assimilated marginal peoples. 'The peripheral folk', he comments, 'experienced the new culture not as an alien culture, but as a further extension of its own ancient culture. For this reason, they possess a great receptivity for this new Han-Chinese culture.'[3] Moreover, this culture, resting on a uniform written language for the numerous spoken tongues and on a highly sophisticated technology, possessed 'a unique power of resurgency and unexampled persistency'; as such, 'it did not engulf ruthlessly any more than it drew in its victims through fascination'.[4] It 'progressed relentlessly, proceeding peacefully for the most part, unobtrusively and below the surface'.[5]

In his discussion of the motive force behind population movement in east Asia von Eickstedt emphasises the role of what he terms the 'pressure chambers' of the Yellow River valley, the Yangtse valley and

---

[1] Quoted from the *She King* by L. Cottrell, *op. cit.*, pp. 72–3.
[2] 'For centuries China was actually the land of the T'ai.' Herold Wiens in *China's March into the Tropics* (Office of Naval Research, U.S. Navy, Washington 1952), p. 13.
[3] *Ibid.*, p. 22.   [4] *Ibid.*, p. 64.   [5] *Ibid.*

the valley of the Si Kiang. His general thesis is that pressures from the desert and steppe zone of the northwest act on the peoples in the Yellow River valley; their overflow in turn creates pressure on the Yangtse valley peoples and these overflow in the direction of the Si Kiang valley and the upland and basin country of southwest China. The result is a series of great racial 'ripples' which spread successively further south into the mainland and islands of southeast Asia. And in generating the initial pressures it seems (see below) that natural calamities and warfare were more important than 'over-population' in the plains of northern China

To these pressures Wiens adds the psychological attraction of the South which from early times has been regarded as a granary for the North. This idea of the South as a land of plenty (today it is responsible for 61 per cent of the country's total food production and contains 68 per cent of the country's pigs: see p. 180) must, he comments, 'have had the effect of strengthening the dynamic drive from the northern pressure chambers'. The result was a general southward progression of high population densities, a progression which can be indirectly measured by city-building and abandonment and also by census data indicating for each province the number of *hsien* with more than 10,000 registered people (this registration involved only Han-Chinese or groups more or less thoroughly Sinicised).

There were two periods of major population displacement;[1] these were superimposed on the general southwards drift as a result of war, political upheaval and natural calamities. The first of these mass migrations occurred towards the end of the third and beginning of the fourth centuries (*c.* A.D. 298–312); the second followed the Mongol invasion of the early twelfth century. In its early stages the first saw the mass displacement of some 300,000 people, moving from Kansu and Shensi towards Szechwan and Yunnan. This human tide was followed by mass movements from Szechwan towards Yunnan, Hupeh and Hunan totalling, according to Wiens, between 600,000 and 700,000 people; smaller migrations took place from Hopeh into western Shantung and northwest Honan. The total involved in these movements was probably of the order of two million people, representing over one-third of the recorded population of North China. Then, in A.D. 310, North China was ravaged by drought and famine and by the southward advance of the Tartar tribes. These pillaged the capital at Loyang, slaughtered hundreds of thousands of Han-Chinese and gave further impetus to the southwards flight of North China's population. Some 60–70 per cent of the Han-Chinese population of the central provinces fled south beyond the Yangtse and the southward displacement of the economic centre of the country is indicated by the facts that from A.D. 280 to 464 the Han population of the South increased

[1] Herold Wiens, *op. cit.*, pp. 100–4.

fivefold and that in the succeeding T'ang dynasty nine-tenths of the tax revenues came from Chiang-nan (i.e. the land south of the Yangtse). Eight centuries later this pattern was repeated when the Tartars captured the Sung capital in 1125; this intensified the southern thrust of the Han and marked the beginning of effective and solid Han occupation of Kwangtung, Fukien and Kwangsi.[1] The integration of the southwestern upland country of Yunnan was accomplished relatively late, in the early Ming dynasty. Prior to the Ming period, according to Wiens, 'only about 10–20 per cent of the Yunnan-Kweichow plateau was accessible to the Han-Chinese; by the time of the Second World War the figure was 60–70 per cent'.

These episodes involving mass displacement southwards of the Han people were superimposed on a continuous, millennial-old 'seepage' of Han peasants and Han culture towards the subtropical south. As a result of these processes the T'ai peoples, who had formerly occupied much of China as far north as Shantung and Kiangsu, were either absorbed or themselves displaced southwards. A sizeable bloc of such peoples, the Chuangs, survived in the area of Kwangsi, where their individuality is today recognised in the constitution of a separate Autonomous Region. Others, seeking the aquatic environments suited to their rice-culture, pushed towards the upper reaches of the Menam and Mekong, displacing the original Mon-Khmer peoples who had hitherto dominated this northern fringe of Southeast Asia. By contrast, many of the Tibeto-Burman tribal peoples, such as the Lolo and Maîo, were displaced vertically, taking refuge in the higher lands unsuited to rice cultivation, then, as these areas became 'saturated', moving southwards through the upland country of the Burmese-Indochinese borderlands.

NEW CROPS & NEW LAND

By the Han period some form of Chinese control had been established over much of the area we know as 'Agricultural China'. Since then, there has been a gradual process of 'filling in', a process initiated largely by the gradual build-up of population pressure (from a total of 60 million in 1290 the population of China rose to 179 million in 1750 and 430 million in 1850); speeded up by the periodical displacements due to various types of calamity; and facilitated by the introduction of new crops.

Such new crops provided the Han farmer with what we may term 'biological auxiliaries'; these enabled him to utilise more effectively

---

[1] In the latter part of the eleventh century 71·5 per cent of the households in Kwantung consisted of indigenous folk and only 28·5 per cent of Han folk. It may be noted that the heavily malarial character of the Canton lowland long deterred its occupation by the Han people and that the more favoured lowland of Tongking to the south was closely settled at a much earlier date.

his existing cropland and, even more important, to bring into cultivation land formerly marginal for agriculture.   Both these processes added greatly to the country's food supply and provided the basis for a continuing, if sometimes irregular, expansion of population.   Early Chinese treatises on agriculture indicate that the rices then used demanded some 180 days from sowing to harvesting; under such conditions a second crop was difficult to obtain and rice, up to the end of the first millennium A.D., remained largely confined to the aquatic environment of the Yangtse valley.   Then, at the beginning of the eleventh century, the Sung emperor Chen-tsung introduced into South China a rapid-maturing rice from the Indochinese kingdom of Champa. The new strain of rice (reputed to mature in a hundred days) was publicised by the government and new rapid-maturing strains were developed by Chinese farmers.   The Champa and other early-maturing rices not only made possible the double-cropping which is now a distinctive feature of the rice economy of South China, it also provided a 'fill-in' crop which ensured a steady supply of food throughout the year and, requiring less water than other rices, could be grown on higher and sloping land which had been unsuitable to the older rices.   The subsequent development of rices which would mature within as short a space as 30–40 days and of rices which could be harvested in late autumn or winter made possible the agricultural utilisation (and hence settlement) of a wide range of marginal environments.[1]   The revolutionary impact of these new rices has been stressed by Ping-ti Ho:

> Within two centuries of the introduction of Champa rice the landscape of the eastern half of China's rice area had already been substantially changed.   By the thirteenth century much of the hilly land of the lower Yangtse region and Fukien, where water resources, climatic and soil conditions were sufficiently suitable for the cultivation of early-ripening rice, had been turned into terraced paddies. The early ripening rice not only ensured the success of the double-crop system but also prolonged the economic hegemony of the Yangtse area.[2]

During the past millennium the rice area, and the food output, may well have doubled; this meant that the food situation—and the potential for continued population growth—was more favourable in China than in Europe which had to wait until the eighteenth century for *its* agricultural revolution.

The second group of 'biological auxiliaries' which made possible the more effective utilisation of the Chinese living space were the 'dry-land crops'—wheat, barley, sorghums—whose cultivation was

[1] See, on all this, Ping-ti Ho, *Studies on the Population of China 1368–1953* (Cambridge, Mass. 1959) especially Chapter VIII.   This is a fundamental work, much wider in scope than its title suggests; indeed, it is virtually a historical geography of rural China.
[2] *Ibid.*, p. 175.

extended southwards from their northern cradle area into the rice region of China.   At the beginning of the fourth century an imperial decree of the Ch'in emperor aimed at promoting the cultivation of wheat and barley in the lands of the lower Yangtse valley and the great population displacements of this period may have carried knowledge of the crops into this area and into Szechwan.   The Sung emperors in the late tenth century prescribed wider cultivation of dry-land crops in the provinces south of the Yangtse and, though the cultivation of these became established in certain area (e.g. Kiangsu, Chekiang), their widespread cultivation outside the North dates largely from the last two or three centuries.   And it was above all the possibility of the production of selected strains of wheat, barley or buckwheat in areas liable to heavy flooding that made possible the peasant occupation of these formerly marginal areas.

By the middle of the sixteenth century a third group of crops was becoming available to the Han peasant—the 'American crops' such as maize, sweet potatoes, Irish potatoes and peanuts.   These became of major importance in the eighteenth and nineteenth centuries, at a time when the momentum of what we may term the 'rice-growing revolution' was slackening and they either complemented or, because of their higher yields, competed with the traditional dry-land crops. Above all, they made possible the agricultural colonisation of those areas of upland China unsuited to rice.   As Ho puts it:

> American food-plants have enabled the Chinese, historically a plain and valley folk, to use dry hills and mountains and sandy loams too light for rice and other native cereal crops.   There is evidence that the dry hills and mountains of the Yangtse region and North China were still largely virgin about 1700.   Since then they have been gradually turned into maize and sweet potato farms.[1]

From the sandy river valley soils of South and central China, where peanuts became an important (nitrogen-fixing) crop in the rotation, to the higher and cooler parts of the loess plateau, Mongolia and the northeast, where the Irish potato became 'the mountaineer's staple' these 'American crops' played a major role in the transformation of the rural economy.   They complemented rice and the more exacting cereals and made possible the use—and settlement—of a wide range of environments; to quote a mid-nineteenth century local history:

> In the level area in the vicinity of the walled city rice is usually grown. In the comparatively shallow hills and mountains maize predominates.   In the lofty mountains where maize cannot be successfully grown the only source of food is the Irish potato.[2]

The new American crops and the extension of dry-land crops certainly added to China's total food output and were important

[1] *Ibid.*, p. 184.   [2] History of Fang-hsien cited by Ho, *op. cit.*, p. 150.

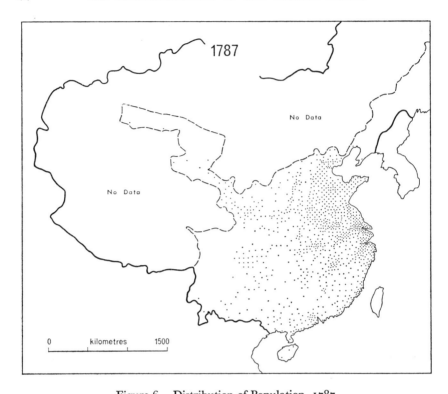

Figure 6. Distribution of Population, 1787.
Dot represents one per mille of the population at that date (i.e. 292,000). Major concentration in Yangtse valley and lowlands of North China.

factors in the more effective utilisation of the Chinese earth: as Ho observes, 'In the absence of major technological inventions the Chinese peasant's main weapon in his struggle with new land was crops'. Their extension had two other consequences which can be commented on but briefly. First, the extension of these crops to marginal environments in central and North China helped to redress the strong southward shift of the 'demographic centre' of the country which resulted from the extension in the South of the rapid-maturing rices. Secondly, the new crops were grown on easily erodible, originally forested, hill soils; these were deeply dug and planted in straight rows, and there was little attempt at rotations. This ruthless exploitation of fragile soils of low fertility was followed inevitably by declining yields and ultimate abandonment of the land as the farmer moved on to clear new land. There thus developed an almost cyclical pattern of colonisation, followed by the build-up of population, increasing deforestation, over-cultivation, erosion and abandonment. The ravaged vegetation and eroded soils of much of upland China are largely a legacy of this type of exploitation; so, too, is the silting of the rivers and the recurrent flooding which became increasingly serious menaces to the peoples of the plains.

THE LAST HUNDRED YEARS

Ping-ti Ho estimates the rate of growth of China's population as 0·63 per cent per annum between 1779 and 1850 and as 0·3 per cent per annum between 1850 and 1953. These figures suggest that the growth of China's population—and the potential flow of migrants[1] to the still relatively thinly-peopled regions of the country—must have been inhibited by increasing pressures during the nineteenth and early

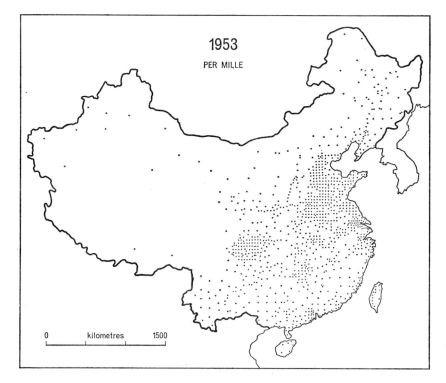

Figure 7.   Distribution of Population, 1953.

Dot represents one per mille of the population in 1953 (i.e. 583,000). Compare with Figure 6 and note the build-up of population in Szechwan and the southwest and the relative decline in the semi-arid areas of the northwest (regions 2C and 3C in Map 84).

twentieth centuries.   It has long been customary to regard these pressures as for the most part environmental pressures (using the term 'environment' in the sense of physical environment).   One of the great

[1] Migration certainly occurred, as from China's southeastern provinces, but largely owing to internal instability and civil war was directed chiefly overseas, towards Southeast Asia.

merits of the work of scholars such as Gourou, Dumont or Ho has been to focus attention equally on the institutional and political environment; indeed, as commented elsewhere (p. 117) these institutional and political factors have often exaggerated the impact of elements of the physical environment such as drought or flood. It is only in the light of these factors that we can fully understand the ills affecting Old China, the impasse in which rural society found itself—and with this the logic behind and the justification for the social and economic policies of the present Government.

Thus, increasingly during the last two centuries, the economic diversification which, by opening up new sectors of the rural economy, might have relieved population pressure had been impeded by institutional factors—by the greater profitability of monopoly trade, by the diversion of wealth to non-economic uses, by an educational system in which the study of moral philosophy dominated and the experimental sciences were neglected; a combination of lagging technology and increasing population led to a deterioration in living levels as the nineteenth century progressed. Political conditions were even more important than economic conditions. Under the enlightened rule of the early Manchus the population (and especially that of centenarians) increased rapidly in number. Conversely, during the nineteenth century, peculation, official extravagance and an increasing fiscal burden on the peasantry disrupted life and limited the expansion of population.

By the middle of the nineteenth century the process of agricultural colonisation had resulted in the occupation of most of the cultivable land of Agricultural China; by that date 'the Chinese people with the technological means then at their disposal, had probably approached a maximum in land utilisation in China Proper'.[1] During the early nineteenth century increasing pressure of population, building up within a stagnating and backward economy, contributed to a series of upheavals, culminating in the Taiping rebellion, probably the greatest civil war in world history. The appalling slaughter in this and subsequent rebellions reduced population pressure in the provinces affected and gave a short breathing space during which powerful currents of migration brought about a new balance between population and resources. The respite was, however, localised and temporary and for much of the next century Chinese society was to exist poised on the knife edge of starvation and tragically vulnerable to the 'catastrophic deterrents' of flood and drought. It was left to the present régime to tackle the underlying causes of population pressure and peasant poverty by removing the institutional barriers to increased productivity and by modernising and diversifying the old rural economy.

The pressures, both physical and institutional, to which we have

[1] Ho, *op. cit.*, p. 153.

referred expressed themselves globally, in the form of declining rates of population growth for China as a whole, and also regionally, in the form of the changing growth rates of various provinces or regions of China. This changing regional pattern reflects the varying regional impact of civil war and natural calamities, and the outflow or inflow of migrants to which these gave rise. Owing to the sometimes uncertain nature of the provincial population data for earlier periods any assessment of these changes must be tentative; the general pattern is summarised in Figure 8.

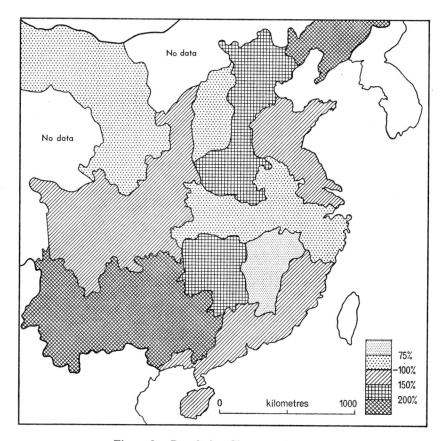

Figure 8. Population Changes, 1850–1953.
Note the relative depopulation of central China and parts of the northwest and the heavy build-up of population in southwest and northeast China (data from Ping-ti Ho).

The most striking feature is the apparent decline of the four Yangtse provinces—Chekiang, Anhwei, Kiangsi and Hupeh—whose aggregate population appears to have declined by some 36 million between 1850 and 1953. In part this may reflect the 'saturation' of the rice economy whose rise and expansion had provided the economic basis for the earlier expansion of population in this region, but in part only for these were provinces which were devastated during the Taiping rebellion; this led not only to great loss of human life but also to considerable out-migration and abandonment of farmland from which parts of the region had not recovered by 1953.   Equally striking is the marked increase in the provinces of Hopeh, Shantung and Honan in the North China Plain.   This increase was of the order of 50 million during the period 1850–1953; it was made possible (as was the increase in Hunan) by the relative freedom of the region from the civil wars which devastated other parts of China and also by the increasing intensification of agriculture in a region which, following the 'rice revolution', had tended to lag behind southern China.   In the northwest the provinces of Shansi and Kansu declined over the century before 1953, partly as a result of the Moslem wars of the latter part of the nineteenth century, partly as a result of the savage drought-famines which afflicted these provinces.   Shensi did not escape either war or famine but, because of its less marginal environment, more readily recovered as a result of in-migration.   The trends for the southeastern coastal provinces of Kwangtung and Fukien are distorted by the heavy overseas emigration from this area; by contrast, the increasing interior colonisation in the southwest, and above all the development of the upland valleys and basins of this region, is reflected in the growth in population in the provinces of Yunnan, Kweichow and Kwangsi.   These increased their population some two-and-a-half times over the 1850 total; in part this is due to the exclusion of non-Han groups from earlier enumerations yet, even allowing for this, the actual increase appears to have been considerable.

THE PRESENT-DAY DISTRIBUTION OF POPULATION

There are few areas in the world where gradients of population density are as steep as in east Asia.   Parts of China have been continuously occupied by man for some five millennia; over this immense period of time he has adjusted his pattern of land use and of settlement to an environment highly differentiated in terms of relief, of soils and of climate.   He has assessed this environment in terms of his culture—that of a farming group practising an intensive garden-style of cultivation based on grains and on vegetables—has selected certain areas and rejected or by-passed others.   The areas he has chosen have been those lending themselves to intensive use—the alluvial lowlands, the loessial plateaux and the gentle and easily-terraced slopes—and for over a hundred generations population has accumulated in these favoured areas.   Lacking techniques of upland farming and livestock rearing he has rejected the upland areas or has used them destructively, as a source of firewood or constructional timber and, where the forest vegetation has been destroyed, he has grubbed up the very grass roots to use as fuel.   The contrast between the closely settled meticulously cultivated flatlands and the empty ravaged uplands strikes the traveller again and again in China; the population map repeats in the finest

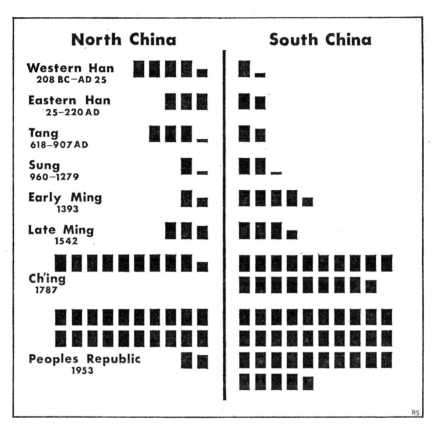

Figure 9.   Secular Changes in the Balance of Population between North and South. Each rectangle represents ten million people.   Illustrating the early dominance of the North, a dominance which lasted until the Middle Ages when the spread of Han settlement beyond the Yangtse and the introduction of new rice varieties (see pp. 19–20) resulted in a great increase in population. Subsequent partial recovery of the North, as a result of the Han colonisation of the Manchurian provinces and the recent concentration of industrial development in this region; the South, however, still remains the dominant area in terms of population as of food-production (see pp. 179–180).

detail the land-forms map or the soil map.   And the steady build-up of population in the lowlands has not greatly changed this picture, for once population pressure reached a critical point it was relieved, not by any overlapping on to the marginal uplands, but by the seeking out and occupation of neighbouring river basins and alluvial lowlands. From the North China cradle area, then, there has been a steady southward expansion of Chinese settlement, an expansion which followed selectively the pockets of 'good earth'. In this expansion the Red Basin of Szechwan and the lowlands or the Middle and Lower Yangtse were occupied, then, and further south, the old lake basins of the southwest, the valleys whose alluvial-covered floors probe deep into the uplands of South China, the pockets and occasional wider spreads of fertile soil which are closely hemmed in between the sea and the mountains along the whole of the southeast coast. . . .

Today, some nine-tenths of China's population live on one-sixth the area of the country. Densities within this 'peasant *oecumene*' exceed 250 persons per square kilometre or approximately 500 per square kilometre of cultivated land. These densities become more meaningful if compared with other parts of the globe; thus, in some villages of Yunnan 500–600 people may find a living on an area equal to that of an American family farm supporting 5–6 people. . . .

Some 500 million people—three-quarters of China's population—are concentrated into four major regions:

(a) The North China Plain. Here the loess and loess-derived soils support 'a dense mat of people', representing in the aggregate over one-quarter of China's population. Over large areas of the plain densities exceed 300 per square kilometre; this rises locally to over 400 and even in the rocky massif of Shantung densities are still above 200 per square kilometre. The western margins of this closely-settled zone are clearly defined and coincide with the rocky eastern slopes of the Tai-hang Shan.

(b) The Middle and Lower Valley of the Yangtse. This region contains one-fifth of China's population. Densities reach 550 per square kilometre in the delta area (40,000 square kilometres); 300 in the middle valley. They drop sharply in the salt marsh zone of the Hwai Plain and in the river-fretted upland margins of the main valley.

(c) The Red Basin of Szechwan. This is a zone of great population accumulation, with rural densities reaching the very high figure of 660 per square kilometre. In detail, the pattern is one of close settlement in dispersed dwellings, with a great number of small market towns. Some 12 per cent of China's population live in the Red Basin.

(d) South China. Here the high density areas form a series of scattered ribbons or islands along the alluvial floors of the valleys, in interior basins, above all in the delta region around Canton. In this latter area densities reach 400 per square kilometre, contrasted with densities below 50 in the uplands.

These major zones of population concentration coincide strikingly with what C'hao-ting Chi has termed the 'Key Economic Areas'—the Northern area comprising the lower valley of the Hwang Ho and with Sian and Anyang as capitals; the Shu area of the west, focused on Szechwan and with Chengtu as its centre; the East Central area of the Lower Yangtse centring on Nanking and Hangchow; and the Southern area centred on Canton. This historical continuity between these key areas of the past, where agricultural productivity and ease of transport permitted the accumulation of the grain surplus on which political and military power ultimately rested, and the high density areas of the mid-twentieth century underlines the remarkable stability of the major features of China's social geography. Above all, it emphasises the rigid control which, for long periods of Chinese history, a highly developed and specialised agricultural system has exerted on the distribution of population in the country.

THE STABILITY OF THE PATTERN

As seen above (pp. 20–22) the introduction of new food plants and new agricultural techniques during the period from the seventeenth century onwards certainly made possible some 'filling-up' of the Chinese living space and particularly an expansion into the marginal areas of north and west China. Otherwise, and with the exception of the great flow of migrants towards Manchuria in the 1920s and 1930s (with the industrialisation and agricultural development of that area acting as the magnet), the recent centuries of Chinese history have shown a remarkable stability of population pattern. Only natural or man-made calamities, drought and flood, civil war or banditry, brought about any major migrations—and these were often temporary so that when conditions improved the peasants returned to their village. This stability of pattern, this close crowding together of many men on little land, is due to many causes. Partly it is due to the fact that the level alluvial lowlands or loessial flats are margined abruptly by unproductive regions of difficult relief, poor soils or adverse climates, regions little suited to an intensive garden-style agriculture based on grains and vegetables. Partly the stability is due to cultural and social factors which have impeded long-range migration—the attachment to family and village, the veneration of the ancestors, the difficulties of language. Partly stability has been imposed by poverty, for the peasant lived close to the margins of existence, his savings were meagre and easily wiped out by natural or man-made calamities—and an impoverished family was scarcely likely to be tempted out into the unknown, to break in land of doubtful agricultural value. Famine might *force* a family out—but except when driven by iron necessity the peasant clung to his patch of land, to the known landscape he and his ancestors had created. . . .

The great social and economic upheavals of the most recent period do not appear to have greatly changed this stability of pattern. It is true that between 1949 and 1960 China's urban population increased by some 70 million, as a result of what has been described as 'one of history's largest population shifts in so short a time', but this migration appears to have been largely a *short range* migration; those involved have been largely peasants moving to the growing cities of their own province and there seems to have been no major inter-provincial shifts of population. And the introduction, early in 1958, of a system of population registration gave the Government the means to control this city growth and, above all, to avert the social and economic problems which a massive and uncontrolled migration to the cities might have created.

The policies of industrialisation and of development in the interior certainly brought some changes but, in spite of sensational reports of the movement of millions of Chinese settlers into Tibet, these have been on a limited scale. Some 55 per cent of the capital investment in the First Five-Year Plan was directed to the interior districts and industrialisation has been accompanied by a very rapid expansion of some of the cities of the interior—the population of Lanchow, for example, increased three and a half times between 1950 and 1956—but inter-regional migration contributed little to this expansion; rather has it been due to the influx of local peasants taking up unskilled or semi-skilled urban occupations. The movement of skilled workers has been on a very small scale for the *total* number of such workers in China is small. An American estimate of the numbers of migrants involved in this opening-up of industry in China's Far West puts the total at about one million; it will certainly increase as new resources and new industries are opened up but it is not likely to bring about any significant change in the broad pattern of China's population. The same general conclusion can be drawn from examination of China's agricultural development since 1949. New areas on the north and west fringe of 'Agricultural China' are being brought into production but the number of settlers involved is not large; between 1949 and 1957 a total of some 1·3 million are estimated to have shifted to these 'new lands' and present-day trends suggest that this flow of migrants is unlikely to exceed half a million annually in the measurable future. If the figures cited above are seen in perspective, against a total Chinese population of over 700 million and a yearly increase of some 15 million, it will be apparent that the changes in the spatial pattern of China's population since 1949 have been slight indeed.

CHAPTER 3

The Unity and Diversity of the Peoples of China

'A COMMONWEALTH OF POVERTY'

IN HIS study of the community of Ch'uhsien, in the Yangtse delta east of Nanking, Morton Fried observed that every one, with the exception of the school teacher:

> seems to be on roughly the same low economic level, evidenced by thinness of body, if not emaciation, and by poor and ragged clothing. The numerous beggars are clearly in the worst condition, but the differences, which at the first casual glance separate them from the working population, seem, to the untutored Western eye, to be quite superficial.[1]

It was a society, mirroring that of the larger Chinese society of which it was a tiny part, which lived within 'the tightest of closed economies, that of misery'. We may be familiar with some of the contours of this larger society from the novels of Pearl Buck or the short stories of Lu Hsun[2] but we do not always bear in mind that some 85–90 per cent of the population of China lived at the level of those whom Fried passed in the streets of Ch'u, at the very margins of human existence, citizens of what can only be described as a 'commonwealth of poverty', members of 'a fellowship of the dispossessed'.[3] We are aware of the artistic and

---

[1] Morton H. Fried, *Fabric of Chinese Society* (London 1956). The field work was completed before the Communists came to power. In his introduction Julian Steward comments: 'Unfortunately for western social science research in China, the nation was swept by the Communists just at the time when interest in the area had reached significant proportions.' It somehow doesn't seem to occur to Dr. Steward that what may be a Western social scientist's paradise may be a hell to those who have to live their whole lives in such a society, with only an occasional sociological expedition descending on them to break the deadly monotony of their lives. . . .

[2] *Selected Short Stories of Lu Hsun* (Peking 1956–).

[3] As was the outlaw band in the great Chinese novel *Shui-hu Chuan* (*Water Margin*) translated by Pearl Buck as *All Men are Brothers* (New York 1937).

literary achievements of Old China, less aware perhaps of its scientific achievements, and our vision—and the 'norm' against which we attempt to judge contemporary China—is couched largely in terms of these achievements. Yet the exquisite water-colours or jade carvings, the perfection (so simple yet so sophisticated) of a fragment of poetry, the pottery and the architecture and the formal gardens which the word 'China' calls to our mind, these were the work of, or designed for the delight of, a small and privileged class. The Chinese system of examinations may, indeed, have meant that this class was open to all men of ability (at least in theory) but the privileged nature of the class remained. And we must, if we would understand contemporary China, bear in mind that this privileged group was like the sunwashed tip of a great iceberg, buoyed up by an immense and submerged mass beyond our sight.

The quality of life of these peasant masses has been described by Jack Belden in the following terms:

> Have you ever considered what it means to be a Chinese peasant in the interior of North China? Almost completely outside the influences of modern science and twentieth-century culture, the peasant was a brutal, blundering backwoodsman. He had never seen a movie, never heard a radio, never ridden in a car. He had never owned a pair of leather shoes, nor a toothbrush and seldom a piece of soap. And if he was a mountain man, he perhaps bathed twice in his life—once when he was married and once when he died—not because he so much enjoyed wallowing in the dirt, but because water was scarce and could be spared only for drinking.
>
> Consider the immense implications of such a materially impoverished life. Consider what you as a human being would value most of all in such an environment as this. Is not the answer obvious: food, clothing, shelter, but above all food.[1]

And the level of such a life is indicated by the figures cited by Belden for the *per caput* consumption of essentials in North China: between two and four-fifths and four bushels of millet a year, about one and one-third pounds of meat a year, in cotton-producing areas two and two-thirds pounds of cotton cloth and the same amount of raw cotton. . . . 'Figures', says Belden. 'But those figures spelled tragedy for the peasant'.

There were, of course, variations upon this general pattern even in the rural areas. There was the variation through time which manifested itself in the cyclical pattern of family fortunes: a family with energy, frugality and shrewdness began to accumulate land and perhaps add to their wealth by participating in commerce; the wealth accumulated was dissipated by the next generation, their lands were sold and they fell back into poverty. There was the spatial variation manifesting itself in the contrast between the poorer communities in the environ-

---

[1] Jack Belden, *China Shakes the World* (London 1952), p. 129.

mentally marginal areas and the rather more fortunately-placed communities in the more productive lowlands,[1] between areas where peasant ownership was typical (as in the Spring Wheat zone of the northwest) and those areas more solidly dominated by the landowner (such as the rice-growing South). But the situation was rarely static; during the Japanese war the relative prosperity of the marginal hill areas and the richer lowlands seems to have been reversed, for the former escaped Japanese occupation and, especially in the Shansi-Shensi Border Region, production was expanded while the lowlands suffered the full impact of invasion and war. And, as the war dragged on, Kuomintang officers, accumulating land to offset the dwindling value of the paper money in which they were paid, began to emerge as a new landlord group,[2] a process accompanied by a sharp increase in the number of peasants dispossessed of their land. Land concentration meant growing poverty, 'it also meant thousands of souls for agrarian revolution'.

The impact of the 1911 Revolution on the broad mass of society had been slight but the growing Western penetration of the coastal areas of China through the Treaty Ports had a profound effect. In these areas—and Shanghai is the outstanding example—there emerged a class of entrepreneurs, landlords or bureaucrats or both, who acted as cogs in the Western exploitative machinery.[3] This was the comprador class, a class of merchants, bankers and industrialists—in short, a nascent bourgeoisie. With the rise of this group in the cities came the rise of a lower middle class group—clerks, teachers, shop-owners and the like—and, with the depression of the handicraft industries and the process of land concentration, there was a growing flow towards the cities of impoverished peasants who formed the lowest stratum in the hierarchy—a proletariat of factory workers, coolies, beggars. . . .

These processes seemed to be introducing into Chinese society the sort of class stratification which had emerged in the West. The role of these classes was, however, rather different from their role in the West. The proletariat was, for example, much smaller and weaker than its counterpart in Europe (some two and a half to three million workers in modern industry) and was geographically much more localised (mainly in the coast belt). And while the industrial bourgeoisie in Europe had played an important role in initiating social

---

[1] The average grain production *per capita* in the Spring Wheat region in the early 1930s was 220 kg., as against 712 kg. in Szechwan. J. L. Buck, *Land Utilisation in China* (second printing, New York 1964), p. 286.

[2] 'In Szechwan, it was estimated that during eight years of war anywhere from 20 to 30 per cent of the total landlords were new landlords who occupied 90 per cent of the land owned by the old landlords.' Jack Belden, *op. sup. cit.*, p. 151.

[3] 'By the first decade of the twentieth century, the various types of foreign economic domination cost China an annual loss of well over a thousand million dollars.' Ping-chia Kuo, *China: New Age and New Outlook* (Harmondsworth, 1960), p. 25. See also Mao Tse-tung, 'The Chinese Revolution and the Chinese Communist Party' in *Selected Works*, Vol. 3 (London 1954), pp. 78–80.

change and breaking the hold of the landlord group it could not fulfil such a role in China. It was relatively small, for investment in land remained more attractive than investment in industry, and it was closely linked with the landlord class and so opposed to any form of change in the traditional landholding system. In short, as Belden points out,[1] the bourgeoisie was caught in a double set of contradictions, being tied both to the landlord group and to the outside interests which had called it into being. And because of this involvement of outside interests the Chinese proletariat—and the Chinese peasantry—had, if it wished to create for itself the conditions in which even minimum levels of human decency were to be attained, to eliminate the power of both its internal and external oppressors. It was these factors that shaped the character of the Chinese Revolution.

THE CONDITION OF THE CLASSES

The forces of conservatism in China, represented by the landlord and comprador classes and backed up by foreign influences, succeeded for many decades in maintaining China in a feudal[2] and pre-industrial condition. The economic profile of this pre-industrial society is summarised by Rostow:

> Agriculture, accounting for 75 per cent of the population, contributed 40 per cent to the national product, while the urban sector, with only 15 per cent of the population, made roughly the same contribution. At least an additional 10 per cent of China's people lived in rural areas, engaged mostly in non-farm tasks and producing about 20 per cent of the total national output.[3]

The figures may be a little too precise but Rostow's *schema* gives us a general picture of the economic structure. The social structure which resulted—and whose lineaments are fundamental to an understanding of recent Chinese history and of the changes in China's countryside—was delineated by Mao Tse-tung in his 'Analysis of the Classes in Chinese Society' (1926) and his study of 'The Chinese Revolution and the Chinese Communist Party' (1939).[4]

The two major groups opposed to social change were, Mao pointed

---

[1] Jack Belden, *op. sup. cit.*, pp. 141–3.

[2] The alliance between the local bourgeoisie and outside interests was illustrated by the crushing of the Taiping rebellion by troops partly supplied by the British and French governments and led by General Gordon; see C. P. Fitzgerald, *China: A Short Cultural History* (London and New York 1965 ed.), pp. 578–85 for the character of the rebellion. For 'feudal remnants' in Chinese society (China wiped out *formal* feudalism two millennia ago) see Jack Belden, *op. sup. cit.*, pp. 139, 154–7.

[3] W. W. Rostow, *The Prospects for Communist China* (New York 1954), p. 224.

[4] For the first see *Selected Works of Mao Tse-tung* (Peking 1964), Vol. I, pp. 13–21 or Ann Fremantle, *Mao Tse-tung: An Anthology of his Writings* (New York 1962), pp. 51–9; for the second, *Selected Works of Mao Tse-tung*, Vol. 3 (London 1954), pp. 72 sqq. For background, see Stuart R. Schram, *The Political Thought of Mao Tse-tung* (New York and London 1963).

out, the landlord group (approximately 5 per cent of the population) and the comprador group.   The former he saw as 'the principal social basis for imperialist rule over China', as a group using the remnants of the feudal system to oppress and exploit the peasantry and to obstruct the political, social and economic progress of the country.   The comprador group, called into existence by overseas interests, served these foreign interests and was in turn supported and 'fed' by them; since, however, several foreign powers were involved, the attitudes of the comprador class were not always cohesive—thus during the Japanese invasion pro-Japanese elements collaborated with the invaders while those elements aligned towards Britain or America were more vacillating.   The group as a whole had strong ties with the landlord class; together they constituted an extreme counter-revolutionary group.

This comprador group, or 'big bourgeoisie', is to be distinguished from the 'middle' or 'national bourgeoisie'.   The latter, consisting of the emergent indigenous capitalist groups, found itself oppressed by both feudalism and imperialism; smarting under this oppression, it tended to favour the revolutionary movement directed against its oppressors.   At the same time, the carrying-through of real social and economic change would threaten its position. . . .   In consequence, as Mao foresaw, there was no room for such a group to remain 'independent'; sooner or later it would disintegrate, with some sections throwing in their lot with the revolution, others aligning themselves with the forces of reaction (this, indeed, began in 1927).

The petty bourgeoisie as defined by Mao is a heterogeneous group. It included the middle peasants (the 'owner-peasants', making up some one-fifth of the rural population) and the handicraftsmen, the intellectuals, and the professional men and the tradesfolk whose numbers grew with the expansion of the 'big' and 'middle' bourgeoisie.   Though all these strata had somewhat the same economic status, three major subdivisions might be distinguished: first, those who earned, in the shape of money or grain, more than they consumed; secondly, those who in normal years were self-supporting but who were aware 'that the world is no longer what it was', and who were becoming increasingly aware of the pressure and exploitation of the upper groups; thirdly, those whose life was becoming more and more difficult, who 'shudder at the thought of the future'.

Yet lower still in the scale but much more numerous were the members of the 'semi-proletariat'—the peasants who owned land but whose property was insufficient to support them, the poor peasants (70 per cent of the rural population) who owned no land and were 'tenant-peasants exploited by the landlords', the small handicraftsmen, the shop assistants and the pedlars.   These were all marginal or submarginal groups whose only hope of improved living conditions lay in the complete remoulding of the social and economic order; they, and especially the poor peasants, represented, in consequence, 'the biggest motive force of the Chinese revolution'. . . .

Finally, there were the groups created by the two processes of rural impoverishment in the hinterland and industrial development in the coastal cities. The modern industrial proletariat, the factory workers, railway workers, miners, were estimated by Mao to total between two-and-a-half and three millions in 1939; there were in addition some twelve millions employed as labourers in small-scale industries and handicrafts in the cities and as shop assistants and the like. These groups were the victims of a three-fold exploitation—they were exploited by foreign interests, by the reactionary and feudal elements in Chinese society and by the bourgeoisie. They experienced a degree of oppression scarcely paralleled elsewhere; they possessed in consequence a revolutionary drive unmatched in any other social class. Moreover, their potential as an agent of social and political change was enhanced by their close ties with the peasantry since their own origins were to be found in the disintegrating rural society of China.

Within what we have termed the 'commonwealth of poverty' in China there were thus subtle but significant diversities in the conditions of existence. It was the awareness of these diversities, of the pressures upon, and the aspirations of, each group that enabled the Communist Party to consolidate its position and to shatter the old order of things. And it is their awareness of what the conditions of life were like in the past for the submerged masses of China that today sustains the Chinese people in their long struggle to perfect 'a new man'—and create a new earth.[1]

THE PATTERN OF LANGUAGES AND CULTURES

As a result of the processes of historical development sketched earlier, China is a multi-national state and the old flag of the Republic emphasised this ethnic diversity, its five bars representing the five major groups—Chinese, Manchu, Mongol, Mohammedan and Tibetan. The non-Chinese groups, it is true, make up only 6 per cent of the total population but their absolute numbers are impressive—some 35–40 million in 1953—and they occupy about two-thirds of the area of the Chinese state. Their importance has been stressed by Mao Tse-tung in a saying written on the wall of the Central Institute for National Minorities in Peking:

China has a large territory, abundant material resources and numerous population. Of these three the Hans possess one, namely, they are

[1] See, for example, C. Bettelheim, 'The Quality of China's Socialism' in *Monthly Review* (New York), June 1965, pp. 45–9; L. Huberman and Paul Sweezy, 'The Cultural Revolution in China' in *Monthly Review* (New York), January, 1967, pp. 1–17; E. L. Wheelwright, 'The Cultural Revolution in China' in *Monthly Review* (New York), May 1967, pp. 17–33.

many in number; minority peoples possess two, namely, they have vast territories and rich resources.[1]

The Chinese, or Han group, occupies a fairly compact area, coinciding broadly with Agricultural China (Figure 51). In the southwest,

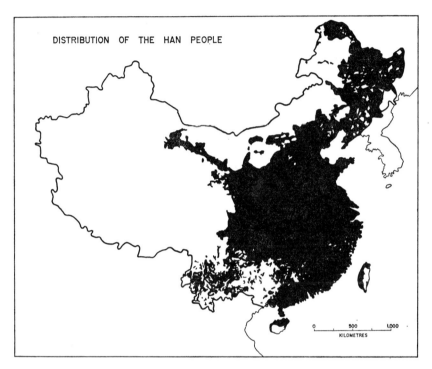

DISTRIBUTION OF THE HAN PEOPLE

Figure 10. Distribution of the Han People.

The Chinese, or Han people, are concentrated in the eastern, largely lowland two-fifths of China. In the northwest Chinese farmers have long been installed along the line of the Kansu Corridor; in the southwest, Han and minority peoples are complexly intermingled.

however, there has been a complex interpenetration of Han and minority peoples; here the Chinese occupy the river lowlands and lake basins, the other groups the intervening upland areas. Towards the northwest Chinese influences have extended far west, through the 'sub-oases' of Kansu and along the line of the old Silk Road, so that the Great Wall does not form an effective human barrier.

The Han group itself is by no means homogeneous linguistically and may be broken up into eight major groups:[2]

[1] Quoted by Josef Kolmas, 'The Minority Nationalities' in *Contemporary China*, ed. Ruth Adams (New York 1966), p. 51.
[2] Yuen Ren-chao, 'The Languages and Dialects of China' in *Geographical Journal*, August 1943, pp. 63–6.

1. Northern Mandarin
2. Southern Mandarin
3. Southwestern Mandarin
4. Wu group
5. Foochow group
6. Amoy-Swatow group
7. Hakka
8. Cantonese

There is a striking contrast in linguistic geography between North and South China. The North is a more or less solid area of Northern Mandarin speech; the South by contrast, approximately to the south of the Tapa Shan divide, shows a great complexity of Chinese dialects as well as large pockets of non-Chinese speech. Broadly, the three groups of Mandarin dialects may be regarded as one language; they are as close to one another as, for example, the languages of the various English-speaking nations. The other groups of dialects are about as

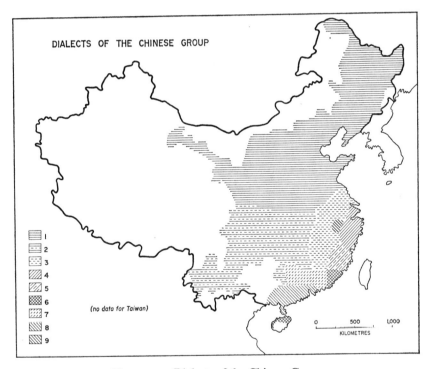

Figure 11.   Dialects of the Chinese Group

Major contrast between the uniformity of the north (solidly Northern Mandarin in speech) and the complexity of the south.

KEY: 1. Northern Mandarin.   2. Southwestern Mandarin.   3. Southern Mandarin.
4. Wu Group.   5. Foochow Group.   6. Amoy-Swatow Group.   7. Hakka.
8. Cantonese.   9. Anhwei Group.

far from Mandarin as, say, Dutch or Low German is from English. Most educated people whose home tongue is a non-Mandarin dialect will acquire sufficient Mandarin to obviate linguistic difficulties; consequently, at public meetings language difficulties arising from dialect differences are negligible, except in the case of the illiterate or those who have little contact with speakers of other dialects.

The Han people, we have seen, developed in a cradle area in the Middle Hwang-ho valley and, as their numbers grew, they progressively extended their influence over the lands to the south and the west. We may distinguish two trends in this expansion: first, in the subtropical lands of the south, the massive displacement of pre-Chinese groups followed by large-scale agricultural colonisation by Chinese settlers; secondly, in the deserts and high plateaux of the west, the extension of Chinese political influence over extensive areas inhabited by non-Chinese groups. The minority of peoples of China[1] today fall into three broad groups, and this grouping reflects the character of this early expansion.

1. A northern or Altaic group, including Turkic, Mongol and Tungus elements. These peoples occupy their historic homelands, having been incorporated in the Chinese state as a result of the political expansion of China during the Han dynasty. Some Chinese-speaking groups have established themselves among these peoples, mainly along the trade routes and in the oases of Central Asia.

2. A Tibetan group, speaking a Sino-Tibetan language; in contrast to other groups of the southwest this group is occupying its historic homeland.

3. A southern group, speaking languages of the Sino-Tibetan or Austro-Asiatic families and today represented by peoples such as the Yi, Miao, Yao and Kawa. These peoples were displaced southwards by the expansion of Chinese settlement and are now found in the broken upland country of south and southwest China.

These groups differ from the Han people, and differ among themselves, not only in cultural traits such as language, religion or social organisation, but also in their racial characteristics. Thus, the Turkic-speaking peoples of Kansu and Sinkiang are basically White or Caucasoid in race type, belonging to the Alpine branch of the White race. Many of the minority peoples of the southwest, too, show Caucasoid features, particularly in character of hair and facial features; these groups are of hybrid origin, resulting from mixing between the Mongoloids and primitive Caucasoids, related on one hand to the Mediterranean peoples of Europe and on the other to the peoples of Indonesia.

[1] Wu Wen-tsao, 'Facts on National Minorities' in *China in Transition* (China Reconstructs, Peking 1957), pp. 184–9.

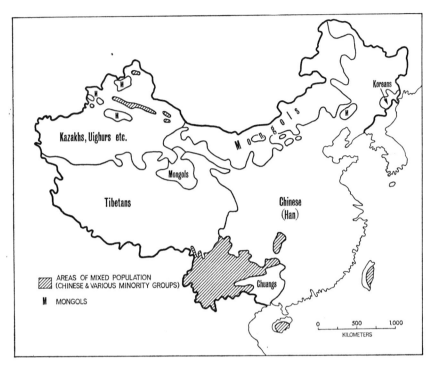

Figure 12. Major Ethnic Blocs.

Showing the Han bloc of Eastern or Agricultural China, the Mongol and Kazakh-Uighur blocs of the northern and northwestern arid regions, the Tibetan bloc of the western high plateaux and the bloc of complexly intermingled peoples in the plateau-and-basin country of the Southwest.

The linguistic diversity is very great and languages belonging to three of the world's major linguistic families are spoken by these people.[1] In the Far West the languages belong to the Ural-Altaic family; they include the Turkic (4·3 millions), Mongol (1·5 millions) and Tungus groups. These groups comprise a number of languages; thus the Turkic group includes Uighur (3·6 millions), Kazakh (0·47 million), Kirghiz (0·08 million) and Uzbek (0·01 million). These languages are written, not with the ideographs used by the Chinese, but with alphabets derived from the Koranic or Arabic script, though since 1955 the Cyrillic alphabet has been used by the Mongols. This Northwestern region contains 16 separate nationality groups, of which 12 are located in Sinkiang. In the Southwest, a population of some 21 millions is divided between 20 separate nationality groups. Most of the minority peoples of the Southwest speak languages belonging to the Sino-Tibetan family. These include the Thai-Chuang group, some

[1] Wu Wen-tsao, *op. sup. cit.*, and Ma Hsueh-liang, 'Many Languages' in *China in Transition*, pp. 190–7.

10 million strong (Chuang 6·6 millions, Thai 0·6 million); the Miao-Yao group totalling over 3 millions (Miao 2·5 millions, Yao 0·64 million, Li 0·33); and the Tibeto-Burman group totalling 7·5 millions (Yi 3·2 millions, Tibetan 2·8 millions, Kachin 0·11 million). In this South-western area a small number of peoples speak languages of the Mon-Khmer group, belonging to the Austro-Asiatic family; the largest group are the Kawa (Wa of Burma) totalling one-third of a million. Of the Sino-Tibetan and Austro-Asiatic languages, Tibetan has a script of Indian origin; the other groups either had no written language or scripts little suited to present-day needs. Under these conditions, the creation of new scripts for these minority groups has been a task of major importance. These new scripts are being devised by experts of the Institute for National Minorities and are usually based on the Latin alphabet. A new world of literacy is thus being created for many millions of formerly illiterate people and an increasing flow of political and technical literature is being turned out by the State publishing institutions to satisfy the craving of these people for the new knowledge which is now within their reach.

The relationships and distribution of some of these linguistic groups is summarised in Table 1; the distribution of some of the major groups is shown in Figure 12:

TABLE 1

THE MINORITY LANGUAGES OF CHINA

Family	Group	Branch	Area
Sino -Tibetan 75 per cent	Thai-Chuang	Chiang Thai	Southwest China
	Miao-Yao	Li Miao Yao	West and Southwest China
	Tibeto-Burman	Tibetan Yi Kachin	West and Southwest China
Austro-Asiatic	Mon-Khmer	Kawa and Palaung Pu	Western Yunnan
Altaic 24 per cent	Turkic	Uighur, Uzbek Kazakh and Kirghiz	Sinkiang and Kansu
	Mongol	Kalmuck Buryat	Inner Mongolia and Sinkiang
	Tungusic	Tungus	Inner Mongolia, Sinkiang and Lower Sungari Region
Indo-European	Iranian	Tadjik	Southwest Sinkiang

Source: Ma Hsueh-liang: *China in Transition*, p. 193.

The religious diversity, too, is great. The most important and most widely distributed religion among the minority peoples is Islam. This is the faith of ten million people belonging to ten different nationality groups. The Tibetans and Mongols are Lamaists. Other groups are Buddhists, Taoists or polytheists whose religion is shot through with primitive survivals. All groups appear to be free to practise the religion of their choice.

Finally, there is great social and economic diversity. The peoples of China's Far West are nomads or oasis cultivators; until recently they lived in a feudal type of society which had changed little since the Middle Ages. The Tibetans were mainly pastoralists, who lived in one of the few surviving theocracies and were dominated by a small serf-owning class totalling possibly 50,000. The people of the south-west were primitive farmers, many of whom practised a bush fallow system of agriculture. Tribal or clan organisation of society was common; some groups, such as the Yi, were virtually a slave people.

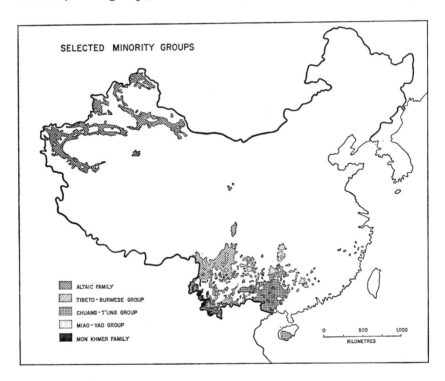

Figure 13.   Selected Minority Groups.

Showing major population concentrations only. Note 'corridor' pattern of Altaic-speaking peoples (e.g. Uighurs, Kazakhs) in better-watered piedmont zones of west, and complex mosiac of peoples in the uplands of Yunnan and in the adjoining province of Kwangsi. Note, too, how the former extent of these groups (see pp. 17–19 is indicated by 'outliers' far to the north of their present homelands.

A. Palát, a Czech Sinologist, classifies the minority peoples into four categories on the basis of their social organisation; his classification is summarised by Josef Kolmas as follows:

(1) Nationalities with a rather developed system of feudal landlordship, sometimes interwoven with certain elements of capitalist economics. Such was the case with the Huis, Chuangs, Manchus, Uighurs, and most of the Mongols. (2) Nationalities with a prevailing system of feudal serfdom. The Tibetans are an example. (3) Nationalities where slavery still existed as a system. This

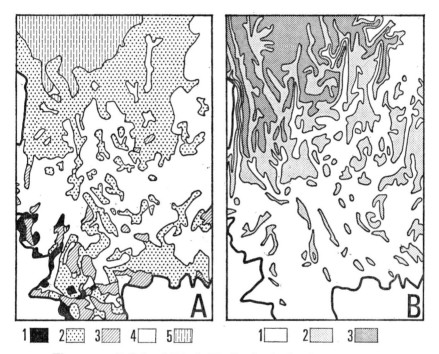

1 ▓▓ 2 ░░ 3 ▨ 4 ☐ 5 ▥   1 ☐ 2 ░ 3 ▒

Figure 14.   Relief and Ethnic Distribution in Southwest Yunnan.
KEY: Map A: 1. Mon-Khmer people.   2: Yi and Ha-ni.   3. Thai.   4. Han peoples.
5. Tibetans.
Map B: 1. below 1,500 m.   2. 1,500–2,000 m.   3. above 2,000 m.
Note the concentration of minority peoples in the hot and humid valleys of the South (Mekong or Lan Tsang valley) or in the uplands fringing the Tibetan massif. Han settlers have filtered in from the northeast, occupying intermediate levels.

category includes the Is (i.e. Yi) of the Yunnan-Szechwan marches. (4) Nationalities living in primitive communes as well as in various stages of transition between primitive communism and class society. They live mainly in the border regions of Yunnan, on Hainan island and in northern parts of Inner Mongolia.[1]

[1] Josef Kolmas, *op. sup. cit.*, p. 55.

In the case of all these groups social structures were such as to perpetuate poverty (at least for the masses) and under-utilisation of the resources of their homelands; only with a drastic remodelling of society could a fuller utilisation of the environmental and human resources of these minority regions become possible. This aspect has been emphasised by Victor Purcell; in Purcell's words:

> There can be no doubt that there is enormous scope for the economic development of these minority regions. Tibet, for example, is a land of glaring contradictions. While it abounds in iron ore, its people, with very few exceptions, cooked their food in crude stone pots. Though research has proved that the soil is suitable for a very wide variety of grain and vegetable crops, only a few crops such as huskless barley, spring wheat, turnips, peas and broad beans used to be grown. Sinkiang affords another example. The province is rich in natural resources, but because the old irrigation systems had been allowed to break down, only 18 per cent of the arable land was cultivated. Sinkiang's pasture land extends over wide areas, but only a small part was used for grazing herds which were actually diminishing in size. The rich resources of oil, coal, metals, and the virgin forests of the northern part of the province remained almost completely untapped.[1]

It is in situations such as this that the significance of Sauer's concept of natural resources as 'cultural appraisals' becomes evident; it is no less clear that the progressive social and political transformation of these minority regions after the People's Government came to power would have a major impact on the land-use pattern, both in the agricultural and industrial sectors.

MINORITY POLICY: Repaying Old Debts

To integrate the wide diversity of minority groups into the Chinese state, socially, politically and economically, to wipe out the suspicion and fear and memories of exploitation from which many of the minority groups suffered, and—an important but often neglected motivation— to repay the debts the Han people owed to groups who had formerly been the victims of 'Great Han chauvinism'—these have been major challenges to the People's Government. These challenges have been met, and with a large measure of success. The old policies of assimilation and of 'divide and rule' have been rejected and the present constitution makes punishable 'discrimination against, or oppression of, any nationality, and acts which undermine the unity of the nationalities'. The music, art and other cultural attainments of the minority groups are widely popularised and contribute to the cultural richness of the Chinese people as a whole. At the political level, the policy is

---

[1] Victor Purcell, *China* (London 1962), p. 196.

to grant a measure of autonomy to the larger and more clearly defined groups, within a tiered structure of administrative units.   The basic units in the Chinese system of autonomous administrative units is:

1. The *Autonomous Region*.   There are now (1968) five of these: the Sinkiang Uighur A.R.; the Inner Mongolia A.R.; the Ningsia Hui A.R.; the Kwangsi Chuang A.R.; and, the most recently-established, the Tibetan A.R.

2. The *Autonomous Chou*.   There are some thirty of these, providing a measure of autonomy for smaller national groups within the framework of either the province or the A.R.;[1] examples are the Yen-pien Korean A.C. in Kirin province, the Lin-hsia Hui A.C. in Kansu province, or the Kizil-su Kirghiz A.C. in the Sinkiang Uighur A.R.

3. The *Autonomous Hsien* or *Autonomous Ch'i*.[2]   These represent the lowest-level units in the administrative hierarchy of minority groups.   Examples are the autonomous *hsien* within which the smaller minority groups within the Kwangsi Chuang A.R. are organised, e.g. the Pa-ma Yao A.H. or the Cheng-pu Miao A.H. or the autonomous *hsien* of the Northwest, e.g. the Mu-lei Kazakh A.H. within the Chang-chi Hui A.C. of Sinkiang or the Tung-hsiang A.H. within the Lin-hsia Hui A.C. of Kansu province.

These minority groups receive a generous allocation of seats in the National People's Congress.   In this body, the supreme political body of China, they occupy 14 per cent of the seats, though they make up only 6 per cent of China's population.

Economically, a determined effort is being made to raise the level of living in the minority regions and to eliminate the long-standing differences in degree of economic development between the Han group and the minority peoples.   The fact that the latter inhabit environments long regarded as economically marginal, whether because of their coldness (as in Tibet) or their aridity (as in the Northwest) or because of the broken nature of their terrain which rendered them little suited to the traditional intensive cropping of the lowlands (as in the South China hill country) poses major problems.   On the other hand, as we have suggested, one of the most important obstacles to economic and social progress lay in the character of traditional society which, as in the lowlands of Eastern China, rendered the peasant virtually helpless in the face of environmental difficulties, whether seasonal drought, soil poverty or inadequate and uncontrolled water supplies.   Today, as in the great plains which are the major zones of

[1] Franz Schurmann observes: 'The autonomous *chou* are national minority regions set up in areas of mixed population.   Though technically under provincial jurisdiction, Party organisation appears to have some independence from provincial control.' Schurmann, *Ideology and Organisation in Communist China* (Berkeley and Los Angeles 1966), p. 152.

[2] The *ch'i* is the *banner*, the unit of social organisation among the Mongols.

Figure 15. The Contact Zone between the Minority Regions of China and her Southern Neighbours.

Stippling indicates those regions within which minority peoples possess some degree of autonomy. *Dark stipple:* Autonomous Regions within the Chinese People's Republic and the Democratic Republic of Vietnam and non-Burmese States of the Union of Burma (1 = Special District of the Chins). *Light stipple:* Autonomous *Chou* or Autonomous Area within the Chinese People's Republic.

This administrative patchwork reflects the great diversity of minority peoples in this 'ethnic crossroads' of East Asia. Both Thailand and Laos contain sizeable minority groups in their northern districts and there is no clearcut ethnic division between China and her southern neighbours.

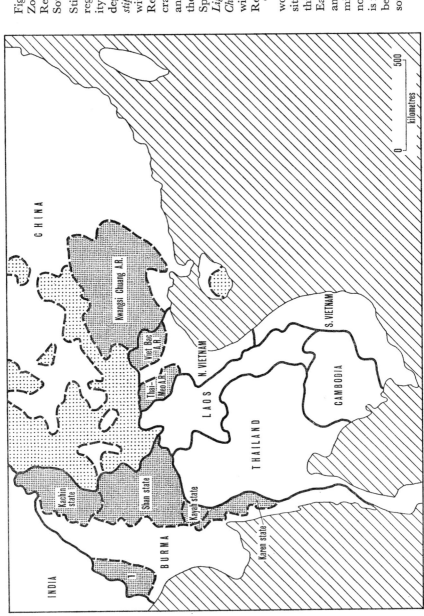

concentration of the Han people, the transformation of the social and political structures of the minority groups is making it possible for these groups to confront and overcome many of the apparent limitations of their homelands. Moreover, the introduction of new technologies has made possible, first, a reappraisal of the mineral and other resources of these regions; secondly, the development of extractive and manufacturing industries based on local resources. And the trading relations between the Han and minority peoples have undergone a profound transformation; formerly trade had been a technique of colonial-style exploitation of the weaker groups; today, operated by

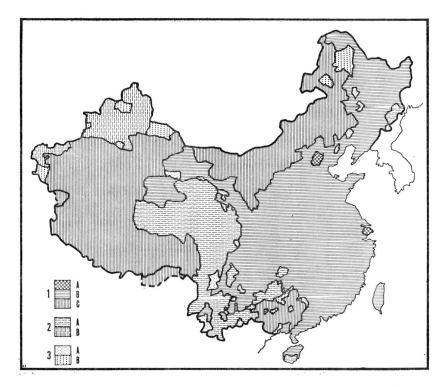

Figure 16.   The Administrative Structure of China.

Showing the three-tiered structure of administration.

KEY 1: Units of the first level:
   A: Centrally-governed municipalities
   B: Provinces
   C: Autonomous regions
   2: Units of the second level:
   A: Autonomous *chou* in province
   B: Autonomous *chou* in autonomous region
   3: Units of the third level:
   A: Autonomous *hsien* or autonomous area in province
   B: Autonomous *hsien* or autonomous *c'hi* in autonomous region

E

State trading organisations and sometimes at a loss, it has become rather a form of help which makes it possible for the minority peoples to make good their colonially-induced backwardness.

The acceleration of *overall* economic development in these regions is illustrated by the ten-fold increase in the industrial output of the national minority districts in the first ten years of Communist rule. And, as *specific* examples, the development of the Karamai oil-field in Sinkiang, of the steel centres of Hami and Ti-hua (also in Sinkiang), of Liu-chow or Nanning in the Kwangsi Chuang A.R., or of Paotow in the Inner Mongolian A.R., illustrates this increasing economic diversification which is transforming China's national minority regions.

The flow of trade, and especially the importation into the minority regions of Chinese-made factory goods, coupled with the increasing impact of the mass media (both reflecting the breaking down of the old isolation), is undoubtedly leading to a measure of non-coerced Sinicisation of the minority peoples. At the same time, there is no obvious pressure to adopt methods of production or new social systems *against the will of the majority*; the official policy is 'to give whatever help the nationalities may require in moving forward at their own pace and under their own leaders'. But this process of change is by no means a one-way process, for, as noted earlier, the culture of these groups has its impact on the Han majority and, to a greater degree than ever before, the minority peoples 'are co-shapers of the great Chinese civilisation'.[1]

THE INSTITUTES OF NATIONAL MINORITIES

In the implementation of Chinese minority policies the Institutes of National Minorities, as at Peking, Lanchow and Chengtu, are playing a major role. The staff of these Institutes is carrying out fundamental research into the social organisation, the economic problems and the history of the minority peoples. They have created new scripts for those who had no written language. Above all, they are training carefully selected students, drawn from some dozens of minority groups, not only in the fundamental principles of Marxism-Leninism but also to become doctors and veterinary surgeons, teachers and administrators, agricultural scientists and technicians, who will return to work among their own people.

The layout of these Institutes is impressive, the staffing generous, the library and other facilities are excellent. The students are young and enthusiastic; they will return to their remote villages, professionally skilled and ardent supporters of a régime whose resources are marshalled to wipe out the poverty and exploitation from which their parents suffered, which has given them opportunities undreamed of by their parents. In assessing the significance of the frequent reports of unrest

[1] Josef Kolmas, *op. sup. cit.*, p. 61.

or revolt among the minority peoples of China it is well to bear in mind the increasing effect of China's minority policy. It has created—for perhaps the first time in history—a real and living unity between the many peoples of China. Victor Purcell's assessment is very relevant here:

> On balance, and not forgetting Tibet, it seems clear that the Chinese Communists have been rather more successful to date in associating 'minorities' and 'ex-subject peoples' with themselves than have most of the European nations in Asia and Africa. It is one thing to declare that minorities, or ex-colonial peoples, are equal: it is another to persuade them that you really mean it. There is evidence that the Chinese Communists have, to a considerable extent, been taken at their word.[1]

The importance of this achievement is clearly not confined to China and it has major implications for China's southern neighbours who face the same problem of racial and cultural fragmentation.

---

[1] Victor Purcell, *op. sup. cit.*, p. 198.

CHAPTER 4

The Diversity of the Chinese Earth

TO UNDERSTAND the significance of the Chinese earth, the full significance of its diversity to those who occupied it, who shaped it and who were sometimes shaped by it, we have to strive to see the land as it must have appeared to the Chinese themselves. Almost two decades ago K. G. T. Clark underlined that:

> at supra-biological levels of interpretation men react to external things not in terms alone of the objective characteristics of these things, which are to be understood in physico-chemical terms, but also according to the ideas they have in their minds concerning these external things.[1]

Only if we 'know something of the men and the furniture of their minds', he stressed, will we attain any real understanding of the human geography of the region we study. And this is doubly true in the case of China, the majority of whose people possess an old and highly-specialised food-getting economy and who have over the millennia been confronted with the need to adjust to or to transform a wide range of environments. In the first sections of this chapter we shall be concerned with the Chinese appraisal of the various elements of their environment and with the diversity of these elements—relief and climate, the soil-vegetation assemblages and the biological complexes—that characterises the Chinese living-space.

FROM THE YELLOW RIVER TO THE WESTERN REGIONS & NAM VIET

The historical background to this evaluation of the Chinese earth has been sketched in Chapter 2 above. In the broadest of outline, three main processes have been involved: first, the development of a

[1] K. G. T. Clark, 'Certain Underpinnings of our Arguments in Human Geography' in *Trans. and Papers, Institute of British Geographers*, Number 16 (1950).

distinctive and coherent society, based on a distinctive agricultural economy, in the Chinese 'cradle-area'—the yellow-earth country of Northwest China; secondly, the slow, discontinuous but increasingly effective assertion of Chinese control over the nomad peoples who ranged the subhumid or arid lands to the northwest of Agricultural China and over the corridor of oases which, to the north of the Tibetan plateau, linked China with Central Asia and the West; thirdly, the southward extension of Chinese power and settlement into the sub-tropical region of red and yellow soils south of the Yangtse, an extension which by the seventh century brought the fertile lowland of the Red River into the Chinese culture world.[1] To these ancient processes we may add two more recent processes: the massive agricultural colonisation of the cold grasslands and forests of the Northeast (Manchuria) and the diffusion, in the last century and a half, of several million settlers into the Nan-yang, the lands of Southeast Asia and of the Southern Ocean.

The advantages of the yellow-earth lands lay, as Lattimore has emphasised,[2] not so much in their richness as in the fact that they were easy to work. Moreover, the structure of the loess lent itself admirably to the construction of cave-style dwellings; these were cut vertically into the soil in the earliest period but later were excavated horizontally from the vertical faces of the cliff-like valley sides. Rainfall variability was a problem to the farmer but drought was never so severe as to drive out the population and it could in any case be offset by the development of simple irrigation techniques using the network of small tributary streams which flow into the Yellow River as it swings eastwards towards the sea. And having adopted a system of irrigation-based agriculture in such an environment Chinese society was, in this formative stage, 'predestined to a certain evolutionary bias'.[3] For, while the individual family might carry out successfully the rudimentary irrigation and cultivation of its own small plot:

> Beyond that, the control of soil and water in combination lay only within the reach of groups of people, helping each other to dig larger channels and perhaps to build embankments that would keep flood water out of the bottom lands. Communal labour probably required, at this primitive level, communal ownership.[4]

Progress in land utilisation then, as in China today, 'made collective action unavoidable' and the mobilisation and control of labour—and the possibility this gave of making maximum use of all water—was more important than the ownership of land.

This was demonstrated by the expansion of settlement on to the

---

[1] The Protectorate of Annam (i.e. the 'Secured South') was proclaimed in A.D. 679.
[2] Owen Lattimore, *Inner Asian Frontiers of China* (Boston, paperback, 1962), p. 30.
[3] *Ibid.*, p. 32.
[4] *Ibid.*, p. 33. Most of this section follows Lattimore's account.

loess-derived alluvial lowlands of the North China Plain, an area notoriously prone to flooding by the silt-laden waters of the Yellow River. Here settlement and permanent agriculture depended on dyking and the techniques of water control evolved to irrigate the valleys of the loess-lands and, above all, the technique of labour mobilisation provided the technological basis for the construction of the large-scale flood-control works which were necessary. Once this break-through was achieved, however, 'both the land and its tribes could be brought within the scope of the expanding Chinese culture and made Chinese'.[1] And, as Lattimore observes, with reference to the semi-mythical labours of Yü, 'when the Chinese passed from the primitive working out of their agricultural technique to the wider territorial application of it, "history" became necessary'.[2] The expansion of 'China' is, therefore, largely the history of the expansion of a specialised agricultural economy, an economy whose technological roots go back to the first elaboration of a 'hydraulic civilisation' in the loess highlands some four millennia ago. It is often tacitly assumed that this 'Northern' agriculture is much less intensive than the agriculture of the South. The differences between North and South are, however, differences in degree rather than in kind, for the agriculture of the North, relying on water from wells where river water is unavailable, is 'as intensive as the social organisation of the Chinese can make it'.[3] With the development of a stronger and more organised rural society in the last two decades there has, indeed, been an intensification of agriculture based on an expanded programme of well-sinking (see pp. 149, 151); this has been facilitated by subsoil conditions, for in many areas the water-table is sufficiently high to be tapped by shallow wells.

From the yellow-earth country of the North the Chinese spread westwards and southward. The basic contrast between the two types of environment encountered—the subhumid or arid grassland environment of the northwest and the humid forest environment of the sub-tropical and tropical South—was reflected in the contrasting agri-cultural history of the two regions. Moving westwards, the Chinese found themselves occupying an environment where increasing aridity translated itself into diminishing returns; they moved, in Lattimore's phrase, towards 'a margin of differentiation and limitation'.[4] South-wards, by contrast, the Chinese settlers moved towards an environment whose long growing season and 'moist aquatic fringes' promised increasing returns for their efforts; they were moving towards 'a margin of indefinite expansion'. Climate and soils were certainly very different from those of the North; there was a difference of scale, for the lake-stippled lowlands of the Yangtse valley could not compare with the level loess plains and sweeping loess plateaux of the North and in

---

[1] *Inner Asian Frontiers of China* p. 35.   [2] *Ibid.*, p. 34.   [3] *Ibid.*, p. 36.
[4] *Ibid.*, p. 38.

the extreme south—in Nam Viet—the cultivable land consisted of mere ribbons of alluvium along the valley floors and coastal fringes (though climate, by making possible an increasing number of harvests south-wards, offsets this increasing paucity of level land); nevertheless, the 'evolutionary bias' which, as we have seen above, typified early Chinese agriculture ensured that the development of farming techniques was in the direction of uniformity rather than diversity. Within Agricultural China, from the steppe margins of the Northwest to the jungles of Nam Viet, the techniques of food-getting showed a remarkable homogeneity:

> In the North, as in the South, the determining consideration is the farming of the best land, the concentration of the most people on the most productive land, and multiple cropping in order to keep the land and the people busy.[1]

It is through the gradual extension of this farming system that China as we know it today emerged for China, to borrow Paul Mus' vivid evocation of the emergence of Vietnam, was:

> a manner of being and of inhabiting, whose expression and instru-ment of expansion are the village, then the multiplication of villages, and, finally, a uniform sheet of rice-growing villages, enveloping a countryside which had to be seized either from a state of nature or from other peoples.[2]

The expansion towards the Northwest, towards 'the margins of differentiation and limitation', had rather different consequences. Attempts to extend irrigated and intensive agriculture in this direction met with progressively diminishing returns as the irrigable valleys grew smaller and smaller and rainfall scantier and less dependable. By the third and the fourth centuries B.C. the limits of expansion had been reached and the process of differentiation began to manifest itself. Less developed groups, originally of Chinese stock, were progressively 'extruded' from those environments suited to the increasingly intensive and specialised agriculture which had become the basis of Chinese life; they moved into a land submarginal for agriculture but offering considerable potential for a pastoral way of life and, the evaluation of the new environment having been made, they began to evolve into an independent—and alternative—type of society, that of the pastoral nomad:[3]

> Tribes along the margin of the steppe, which until this time had been neither exclusively agricultural nor exclusively pastoral, began to take up 'for good' an unmistakable steppe nomadism. They established a sphere of activity of their own, eccentric to the sphere of 'civilized' society in China.[4]

[1] *Ibid.*, p. 37.   [2] Paul Mus, *Viet-Nam: Sociologie d'une guerre* (Paris 1952), p. 20.
[3] Owen Lattimore, *op. cit.*, pp. 408–9.   [4] *Ibid.*, p. 63.

This process took place along the whole of the northwestern edge of subhumid China and in the 'sub-oases' of Kansu and Ninghsia which were isolated by intervening zones hostile to intensive farming. The 'frontier problem'—the problem of whether the mobile society of the steppe or the earth-bound society of China was to prevail—had emerged. Because of the difficulties of fully integrating these Western Regions, because of the need to protect the vulnerable northwestern flank of the Empire, China was drawn deeper into the steppes and deserts of the west, towards the Dzungarian Basin and the Takla Makan. Effective control of these Western Regions was discontinuous—for Kashgar it has been estimated at about 425 years out of some two millennia—and the pattern was one of control from afar and both armed force and trade were employed in an attempt to integrate these peripheral areas into the Chinese state.[1]

GOLDEN PEACHES & VERMILION BIRD

The ebb and flow of these seemingly endless frontier wars and the steady pulsing of trade along the lonely caravan routes of the Western Regions left an enduring mark on the Chinese character. Speaking of the frontier wars, Robert Payne says:

> these places on the edge of China have a significance for the Chinese that it is impossible for any foreigner to grasp. Those wars fought thousands of miles away, in a strange savage country, are indelibly impressed on their minds. We had no wars like this until recently. The images of splendour and desolation are nearly always images that arise from these far-flung territories—the green grave in the northwest where Chao Chun was buried, the yellow sands of the plains, the snows and the Yin mountains. . . . In some place unknown, along the shores of the Tsinghai or in distant Fergana, the hearts of the Chinese have their home.[2]

The harshness and hostility of the 'strange savage country' which lay beyond the Great Wall and the Jade Gate permeates much of the poetry of medieval China. Ts'en Ts'an (mid-eighth century) writes, in a song of farewell:

'*The north wind sweeps over the land, twisting and breaking off the hoary grass.*
The barbarian weather brings the fluttering snow of early August.
As though overnight a small wind came to make thousands of pear trees
blossom . . .'[3]

Wang Chi-wen, in the ninth century, writes of the land beyond the Jade Gate Pass:

[1] Owen Lattimore, *op. cit.*, pp. 169–76.
[2] Robert Payne, *The White Pony* (New York 1960), p. xi.　　　[3] *Ibid.*, p. 180.

Figure 17. The Silk Road. Illustrating conditions at the height of the Roman Empire in the West and the Han Dynasty in China. Major land routes linking China and the west of Eurasia are indicated. These, passing from Chang'an through the oasis zone of the Tarim basin towards what is today Soviet Central Asia, were the lines along which the land-trade in silk was carried on; it was also the route along which travellers and new ideas penetrated into China from the West. Sea-routes are indicated very diagrammatically.

Note the dominating role of Kushan and Anhsi as intermediaries in this critically important traffic.

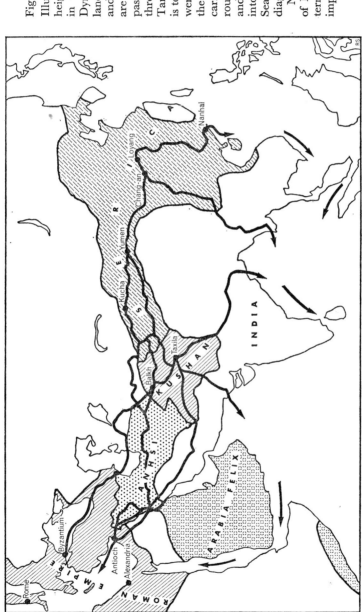

> *The Yellow River climbs amid the white clouds;*
> *A lonely city stands and heaven-piercing peaks.*
> *Why should the Tartars complain of the willows?*
> *The wind of spring never crosses the Jade Gate Pass.*[1]

An alien world, dominated by mobile nomadic tribes, and contrasting in virtually every respect with the garden-cultivated world of eastern China with its earth-bound peasant society. . . . And because of the specialised character of Chinese intensive agriculture the boundary between Chinese peasant society and this pastoral society of the steppes (today dominantly Mongol in its ethnic character) is almost dramatic in its sharpness. No important and independent society based on extensive agriculture or on a combination of cropping and livestock production emerged, for, as Lattimore has pointed out, the elaboration of the intensive irrigated economy of China demanded a plentiful supply of cheap labour and diversification and the development of a secondary economy would have had the effect of reducing such a supply; consequently,

> political tradition had from the very beginning to be hostile to any diversification of the basic intensive agricultural economy, and to treat as recalcitrants any marginal communities whose local interest would otherwise have prompted them to farm extensively, to multiply their livestock, and to make themselves individually independent by eliminating idle time and engaging in the maximum number of different kinds of activity.[2]

This sharp differentiation—and with it the unending strife between the nomad and the settled cultivator—persisted into the mid-twentieth century. But with the emergence of the Chinese People's Republic these northwestern regions were firmly integrated into the political structure of China as Autonomous Regions and with political change came economic change. Edgar Snow, writing in 1960, described the growing 'agrarianisation' of Mongol life in those areas more favoured environmentally;[3] elsewhere, if the pattern remains one of nomadism, the quality of this has changed; more and more Mongols become settled, permanent winter houses replace the *yurt*, the seasonal movement of flocks and herds is reduced to movement within the limits of the livestock commune.[4] And the communes supply not only beef and mutton and dairy products to the population of North China but also the livestock whose introduction into the agricultural economy of the communes of this latter area marks the beginning of the diversification and intensification of the old grain-specialised economy. The sharp differentiation between the world of the nomad and the world of the cultivator, a differentiation first imposed then maintained by political

---

[1] Robert Payne, *The White Pony*, p. 233.   [2] Owen Lattimore, *op. sup. cit.*, p. 325.
[3] Edgar Snow, *The Other Side of the River* (New York and London 1963), p. 60.
[4] René Dumont, *La Chine surpeuplée* (Paris 1965), Chapter VI.

forces, is being attenuated as a result of a change in the character of these forces. . . .

At an early stage in Chinese history the need to protect this vulnerable northwestern flank led, as we have seen earlier, to an increasing Chinese preoccupation with this Western Region. The basis for control lay in the oases which stretch, like a necklace of jade, along the narrow zone where the mountain ranges meet the desert floor. But such control, involving campaigns against a mobile and elusive enemy, in a hostile terrain which lay many weeks of marching from Chang'an, or involving costly subsidies or tribute, meant a continuous drain on funds; moreover, once the oases and the surrounding countryside *were* subjugated, revolt was easy. It is against this background that Lattimore sees the rise of trade, and especially of the silk trade, in the Western Region; this trade

> arose in the course of an adjustment of the activities of the Chinese to an environment akin to that of China in some respects but different in other important respects . . . it suited Chinese policy because it gave the native rulers of the oases an interest in political affiliation to China.[1]

It was along this trade route—the route which became known as the Silk Road—that much of the trade (including the trade in ideas as well as goods) between China and western Eurasia flowed. In the east the route was protected by the Great Wall and this protective 'screen' was continued westwards by the Chinese frontier posts of the Tarim region and the walled oasis-cities of Turkestan and Persia and, beyond Persia, by the Roman garrisons of the Euphrates valley. The volume of trade reached its peak during Roman times as a result of the Roman demand for silk (of which China then had the monopoly) and it was a trade whose balance was strongly in favour of China and the cities such as Balkh which acted as intermediaries; there was little the West could send in return (dancing girls and Roman glassware were major items) and there was a continual draining of wealth eastwards, mainly in the form of silver, and estimated at some £1 million sterling annually.

The westward expansion of Chinese power and the development of trade beyond the Jade Gate resulted in the establishment of sizeable Chinese communities in the oasis zone of Central Asia in areas suited to the intensive land use of the Chinese or critical for trade (Plate 16); it had, in addition, a major psychological impact. This has been described by Samuel Merwin in his novel *Silk*[2] and, with all the scrupulous care of a culture historian, by Edward Schafer in his volume *The Golden Peaches of Samarkand*.[3] The infusion of exotic

[1] Owen Lattimore, *op. sup. cit.*, pp. 174–5.
[2] Samuel Merwin, *Silk* (Harmondsworth, 1942).
[3] Edward Schafer, *The Golden Peaches of Samarkand* (Berkeley and Los Angeles 1963).

elements into the civilisation of China which took place along these
trade routes is typified by the import into T'ang China of musicians
from Kashgar and Bukhara and dancing girls from Sogdiana and
Tokhara and regions far to the west ('the western houris' of Li Po's
poems), by the mingling of art styles (the girls' slippers ornamented with
a mingling of Chinese and Middle Eastern motifs found in a plundered
building in the Tarim desert, or the Greco-Buddhist Gandhara art of
Central Asia); by the spread of new ideas and new religions (Nestorian
Christianity, Buddhism, Zoroastrianism, even Manicheism which had
been adopted by the Uighurs).   Above all, it is typified by the Golden
Peaches of Schafer's essay, 'as large as goose eggs and with a colour
like gold', sent to Chang'an as formal gifts from the kingdom of
Samarkand and which came to symbolise 'all the exotic things longed
for and unknown things hoped for' from the oasis-cities and the trade
routes of these Western Regions.

Southwards, beyond the Yangtse, Chinese settlers (and Chinese

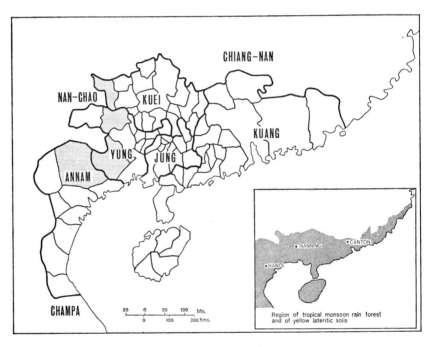

Figure 18.   Nam Viet.

China's tropical South, consisting of Lingnan to the east and Annam to the southwest,
showing the administrative pattern of the T'ang period (after Schafer). Stippled
areas are 'Haltered & Bridled' counties, i.e., counties with a predominantly non-
Chinese population governed by a system of indirect rule. Note the former extent of
Chinese control along the coastlands of what is today Vietnam.

Inset: the tropical zone of China, as defined by the ecologist (after Hou, Chen
& Wang)

civilisation) moved towards 'a margin of indefinite expansion'; they moved towards the province of Chiang-nan, the subtropical transition zone south of the Yangtse River, and, beyond that, to the tropical zone of Nam Viet, consisting of Lingnan to the east and Annam to the southwest. The frontier of the South, continuously extended equatorwards by Han settlers and exiles, soldiers and administrators, was an unstable frontier; in Schafer's words it was:

> a wavering, shadowy fringe rather than a clear demarcation. It was a chronic ulceration for which no medicine could be found, differing from the northern frontier of the pastoral nomads in that here we have no 'gentleman's' agreement.[1]

And, of the character of much of the Han migration into the South, Schafer says

> [The Chinese] . . . moved into the rich valleys of the south in 'pools' —dense aggregations of hopeful humanity, supported by troops who killed those natives bold enough to resist, leaving the survivors to be indoctrinated, exploited or enslaved by Chinese agents and their aboriginal collaborators. The infiltration has gone on to the present day.[2]

The area was assimilated into the Chinese state over two millennia ago (in 111 B.C.); Nam Viet was then organised into nine provinces. The adjustment of the Chinese to the alien environment of the South, however, was to prove by no means an easy process. The world of Nam Viet, to the Chinese accustomed to the (to him) ordered and harmonious landscapes of the North, to landscapes 'stern, sober and correct', was an 'abnormal' world, a world more fertile, more hot and humid, and whose wealth of plants and animals, of strange diseases and strange supernatural beings, was overwhelming. And it was a world, too, whose forest-dwelling and water-dwelling peoples, set apart by their speech, their customs and their colour, were at first regarded as at the best semi-men, folk who were labelled with the stereotyped adjectives all colonising groups apply to those they overrun or displace— they were 'cruel', 'treacherous', 'volatile', 'lacking all moral standards'. It was not until the early Middle Ages that this phase passed; by then the South had become the land of attractive landscapes and of seductive women, and the most celebrated beauty of ancient China, Hsi Shih, was, we may recall, 'a woman of the streams of Viet'.

The immigrants, moving into a tropical land, found themselves missing the seasonal changes and the autumn colourings of the North; in the words of Sung Chih-wen:

---

[1] Edward Schafer, *The Vermilion Bird: T'ang Images of the South* (Berkeley and Los Angeles 1967), p. 34.   [2] *Ibid.*, p. 14.

The southern country has neither frost nor graupel;
Year in and out you see the florescence of nature.
In the blue forest—dark changing of leaves,
With red stamens—constant opening of flowers.[1]

It was a land whose equatorwards margins were still under dense tropical forest, where:

'*Wild creepers in a shadowy jungle intertwine to cover the sun;*
Pendent snakes and knotted vipers seem to be grape vines.[2]

It was at first a hostile land, with a strange climate and vegetation, with strange animals and poisonous reptiles, a land of malaria and beri-beri, of cholera and typhus, 'a land', as one exile put it, 'of barbarians and infidels, herded together with trolls'.[3]   These 'trolls' or 'mountain imps':

are single-legged, reverse-heeled, and their hands and feet are triple branched. . . .   They make their nest on great trees out in the open. These have wooden screens, wind canopies, and curtains, and are very well furnished with things to eat.[4]

Here, as Schafer suggests, we may see a composite vision in which the shadowy outlines of three denizens of the forests of the South are merged—the pile-dwelling pygmies, the gibbons and the ghosts. . . .

Eventually, a more precise picture *did* emerge—of peoples whose diet consisted of those typical Southeast Asian staples, rice and fish, of peoples planting in irrigated ricefields (especially the Thai peoples) and of upland peoples whose economy was based on a slash-and-burn agriculture:

'*Wherever it may be, they like to burn off the fields,*
Round and round, creeping over the mountain's belly.

    .   .   .   .   .

They drop their seeds among the warm ashes;
These, borne by the 'essential heat', burst into buds and shoots.
Verdant and vivid after a single rain. . . .'[5]

By the T'ang period a new appreciation of these Southern landscapes was showing itself in the works of the literary men and minor function-aries and the administrators who came into contact with the area. This appreciation of what had been at first so hostile and so alien an environment, peopled by hostile and alien folk, was perhaps made easier by the Chinese experience of, and literature about, their sub-tropics during the fourth, fifth and sixth centuries; it was also facilitated by the 'creoles', Chinese born among the aborigines of the South, and who served as an intermediary between the Han (or Hua) world of the North and the Man world of Nam Viet.   And, inevitably, with this

[1] Edward Schafer, *The Vermilion Bird*, p. 126.   [2] *Ibid.*, p. 168.   [3] *Ibid.*, p. 111.
[4] *Ibid.*, p. 113.   [5] *Ibid.*, pp. 54–5.

new attitude there came the beginning of an appraisal of the resources of these tropical frontier regions. These included resources precious and strange: coral and crystal, gemstones and pharmaceutical minerals; aromatic timbers and new flowers—cinnamon, camelia and hibiscus; magical and poisonous plants (and also useful plants such as the banana, the lichee and various palms); cowries and pearls, rhinoceros horns and ivory. . . . And by the tenth century, as the T'ang empire was crumbling, the area of Nam Viet:

> began to acquire a new and unconventional romantic aura. . . .
> Only then were the old images transformed and given new life:

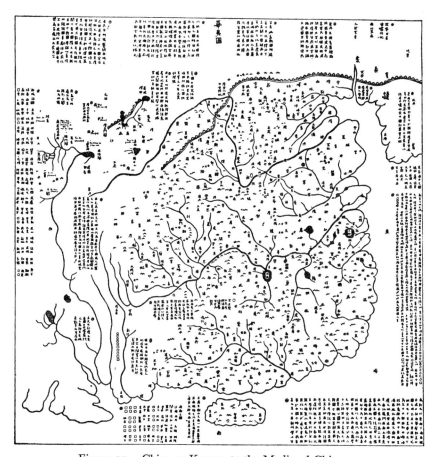

Figure 19. China as Known to the Medieval Chinese.

This map, the *Hua I Thu* (Map of China and the Barbarian Countries) dates probably from the middle of the eleventh century and gives us an indication of the extent of Chinese knowledge of China at this early date. The map shows a remarkable precision in its delineation of the major features of eastern China but the Western Regions are clearly little known at that date. The detail of the eastern half of China indicates, indirectly, the extent of effective Chinese control. (After Joseph Needham.)

the Vermilion Bird became incarnate in the red-sleeved girls of Nam Viet. . . .[1]

Although the tropical Eden was only tentatively and partly realised, a steady stream of new metaphors and mental pictures flowed northward to enrich the language and the thoughts of the Chinese. The dusty, conservative land-lubbers were steadily being transformed into men ready for any kind of world and every rare experience.[2]

Meanwhile, from North and Central China, a growing stream of peasants flowed towards the rice-bowls of China's tropical fringes . . . 'dense aggregations of hopeful humanity', whose settlement in the lowlands and the valleys added yet another element to the many-coloured ethnic pattern of the South.

THE FOUR QUARTERS OF CHINA: Structure and Surface

Let us now look, in generalised fashion and employing some of the concepts of the modern physical geographer, at the environments of China, of the Chinese 'core', which came to comprise most of humid eastern China, and of the peripheral zones of the west and the south.

In the title of this section we speak of 'the four quarters of China' and, indeed, in terms of its topographic features the Chinese culture world does comprise four more or less equal areas; eastern humid and sub-humid China (the area referred to by many writers as 'Agricultural China') breaks up naturally into the plains of north and northeast China and the southern hill country; western arid and subarid China ('non-agricultural China' or 'Outer China') into the mountain-girdled basins of the northwest and the high plateau of Tibet to the southwest. The original Chinese cradle-area lies, it may be noted, at the meeting point of these four major regions. This broad contrast is illustrated, more effectively than it can be described in words, by the relief diagram (Figure 20).

The pattern of the Chinese subcontinent is best understood, not in terms of a catalogue of regions but rather in terms of the tectonic forces of which its mountains, plains and plateaux are the expression. The Russian geologist V. M. Sinitsyn[3] provides one such interpretation distinguishing a series of old and resistant Pre-Cambrian massifs, often slightly warped and, as in the lowlands of north and northeast China, with a sedimentary cover, separated by zones of complex and intense folding (Caledonian, Hercynian, Indo-Sinid, Tienshanid and Hima-

---

[1] Cp. Li Po:

> The jade faces of the girls on Yüeh Stream,
> Their dusky brows, their red skirts,
> Each wearing a pair of golden spiked sandals.

Robert Payne, op. sup. cit., p. 168. The Yüeh seem to have been the northern Viet people, of Thai stock.

[2] Edward Schafer, The Vermilion Bird, pp. 264–5.

[3] V. M. Sinitsyn in Voprosy Geologii Azii, ed. N. S. Shatskii (Moscow 1955).

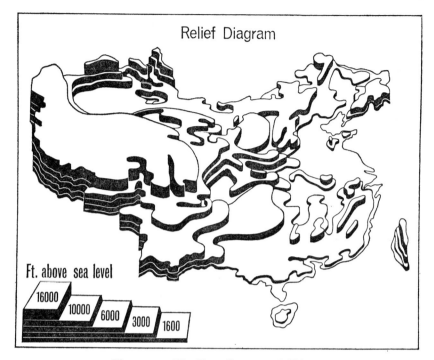

Figure 20. The Four Quarters of China.

Illustrating the contrasts between eastern, Agricultural China and western or Outer China and, within these two areas, the contrasts between the plains of North China and the hill country of the South and between the Tibetan-Chinghai Plateau and the basins and ranges to the north.

layid). The northeast quadrant of China, north of the Tsin-ling-Tapa Shan Line, in this interpretation, forms part of the Chinese Shield; locally, as in the Great Plain, Manchuria and the Ordos region, it is mantled deeply by sedimentary rocks. A similar massif underlies much of South China; this massif shows a series of great upfolds and down-folds as in the lower Yangtse region and is margined to the west by the resistant sediment-covered mass of Szechwan and to the east by the great upfold termed the 'Katasiatic geoanticline' which gives rise to the hills of the east China coast and of Korea. In the west of China Sinitsyn distinguishes a series of sediment-covered blocks lying at various elevations (Tarim Basin, Dzungaria, Chang-tang and Tsaidam) separated or margined by zones in which intense folding has taken place giving rise to some of the loftiest mountain ranges on earth (Altai, Tien Shan, Himalaya). . . .

An older but more useful explanation of China's structure has been given by Li Ssu-kuang (J. S. Lee);[1] this recognises three main elements: the NE–SW fold zones; the E–W zones of mountain ranges and,

[1] J. S. Lee, *The Geology of China* (London 1939).

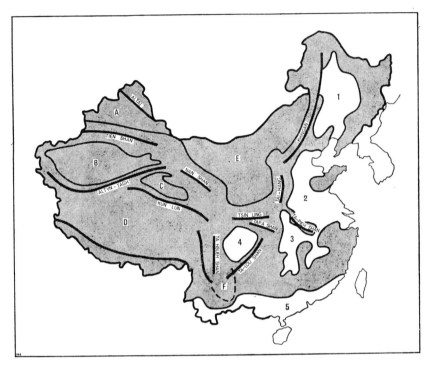

Figure 21.   Major Lineaments of Relief.

Showing, in much generalised form, the main upland areas (stippled), the main ranges (named) and the southern and eastern lowlands (white).

KEY to upland plateaux and basins: A. Dzungaria; B. Tarim; C. Tsaidam; D. Tibet; E. Mongolia; F. Kweichow.

KEY to lowlands: 1. Manchuria; 2. Great Plain; 3. Middle and Lower Yangtse; 4. Szechwan; 5. Southern marine amphitheatres.

superimposed on this already complex 'lattice' structure, a series of gigantic 'shear-folds'.   The first element, the fold-zones, consists of an alternation of upfolds and downfolds—the downfold represented by the Pacific Deep; the upfold which runs through Japan, the Liuchu Islands and Taiwan; the downfold of the Straits of Taiwan and the Korea Straits; the great upfolds represented by the mountains of the South China coast (Kwangtung, Fukien, Chekiang), extending northwards to Korea, and the upfold which runs from the Sikhota Alin of eastern Manchuria through the Liaotung Peninsula into Shantung. To the west this zone of upfolds is flanked by the great downwarp (or trough) to which Li gives the name 'Neocathaysian geosyncline'.   This downwarped zone is a zone of accumulation of younger sediments and it is here that many of the 'key economic areas' of Chinese history are to be found—the Great Plain of North China, the Manchurian Lowland, the Central and Lower Yangtse Valley.   The fringing uplands, however, isolate most of it from the coast and indeed, as Joseph Needham points out, this downwarped zone has contact with the sea at two points only—in the province of Hopeh in the North and in the coast zone of Kiangsu. It is bordered on the west by two series of steps leading up to the high plateau of Tibet. These, according to Li, form part of a geoanticline which begins in the north with the Great Khingan Range, is continued by the Taihang Shan and the Gorge Mountains of the Yangtse into the eastern Kweichow Plateau and the Yaoshan range in Kwangsi.[1] The highest step in the series is formed by the margins of the Tibetan Plateau with the Ta-hsueh Shan running along the west of Yunnan, the Taliang Shan along the upper Yangtse and the Nan Shan in the north; these ranges all present their steepest face outwards, to the east and to the north.[2]

Cutting across these longitudinal zones are the latitudinal fold zones. Three major zones can be distinguished, framing the basins of Shensi and Szechwan, the Kweichow Plateau and what Needham terms 'the southern maritime amphitheatres', e.g. Kwangtung. The most northerly of these is the Yin Shan, running E–W above the great northward loop of the Hwang Ho and dividing Mongolia from the self-contained world of Kuanchung.[3] The biggest of these E–W zones is that of the Tsinling, continuing the line of the Kun Lun, dying away to the east and separating the Kuanchung area from the Red Basin of Szechwan to the south. The southernmost zone is much shattered and is represented by the Nan Ling which separates the southern and marine-oriented Kwangtung lowland from the main trough of the Neocathaysian geosyncline.

The third element in China's structure is a series of 'shear-folds' superimposed on the gridded pattern described above. The most important of these types of fold is represented by the ε type, so named because in plan it resembles this letter. The broadest of these is in the north; here the western half of the 'bow' is the Nan Shan, the centre the Tsinling Shan, the east the Lüliang Shan; the 'backbone' is the N–S-trending Liupan Shan. An even larger—though more debatable example—is the Yunnan arc whose western arm is the Sikang Mountains and whose eastern arm divides into the Ta-liang Shan and its extension north of the Red Basin and the Ta-lou Shan to the southeast of the basin; the backbone is represented by the high ranges, such as the Ta-hsüeh Shan, which culminate in Minya Konka (24,900 feet).

One point may be stressed here—and that is that though geologists may differ in their interpretation of the structure of China, of the relations of the various tectonic units to one another, all interpretations

[1] J. S. Lee, *op. cit.*, p. 232.
[2] For an impression of the contact zone between High Asia and the Mongolian region see Pierre Teilhard de Chardin, *Letters from a Traveller* (London 1962), p. 178–9.
[3] I.e. the area 'within the passes' and consisting of eastern Kansu, northern Ninghsia and central Shensi.

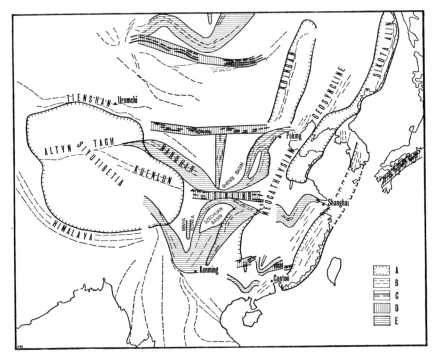

Figure 22.   Major Structural Elements.

KEY: A = old massifs and modern geanticlines   B = structural axes of various ages
      C = axis of East and West tectonic zone   D = East and West tectonic zone
      E = ε type of shear-form

(After Li Ssu-kuang (J. S. Lee))

emphasise the compartmentalised character of the Chinese land.   The
picture which emerges is of a series of core areas—alluvial plains,
coastal lowlands or interior basins—cut off from one another (and
often from the sea) by high and broken mountain chains or elevated
plateaux.   Four-fifths of the country lies above the 500 m. contour
and the height of many of the mountain chains leads to a marked
zonation of vegetation types and to wide expanses of poor and shallow
montane soils—thus accentuating the compartmentalisation of the
country.   Needham underlines the contrast with the much more
favourable, because accessible, structure of Europe[1] and draws attention
to the immense difficulties of holding together a country so sundered by
its physical conditions.   To these difficulties we may add the difficulties
which arise from hydrographical factors.   The deep down-cutting of
many of the major rivers results in a low base level for tributary streams
and thus predisposes much of the country to soil erosion.   Elsewhere, in
the lower reaches of the rivers, where their momentum slackens and
transporting power diminishes, the deposition of eroded materials

[1] Joseph Needham, *Science and Civilisation in China*, Vol. I (Cambridge 1954), pp. 66–7.

builds up the river-beds above the level of the floodplain and, though
the river may be contained by dykes, the draining-off of surplus water
from the land presents the peasant with a major problem.   And in the
West huge areas are without any drainage to the sea, consisting of arid
mountain-rimmed basins in which for millennia mechanical and chemical sediments accumulated . . .(Figures 23, 24).   The thorough and
pervasive Sinicisation of so much of China in the face of these difficulties

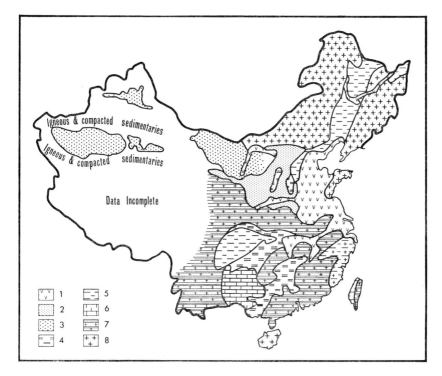

Figure 23.   Surface Geology.

Showing, in generalised fashion, the major rock types.

KEY: 1. Alluvium; 2. Loess; 3. Desert sands and gravel; 4. Old (Paleozoic) marine
    sediments; 5. Younger (mesozoic) sediments; 6. Major karst region; 7. Com-
    pacted and metamorphosed sedimentaries; 8. Igneous and metamorphic
    rocks (associated with 5 in Fukien and Chekiang).

Data for western China is too incomplete or uncertain for a map such as this. (Based
partly on *Oil and Natural Gas Map of Asia and the Far East*, E.C.A.F.E. 1962.)

was an achievement with few parallels elsewhere in the world; it was
carried through by what Teilhard de Chardin has termed 'an enormous
mass of concentrated peasant'.[1]

    The geologic make-up of China is shown in very simplified form in
Figure 23.   In this map the various geological formations are classified

[1] Pierre Teilhard de Chardin, *op. cit.*, p. 130.

in terms of their lithology (the actual character of the rock, whether igneous or metamorphic, compacted and partially metamorphosed sedimentaries, relatively undisturbed sedimentaries and the like) rather than by geological age.   Shown on the map also are the major areas of superficial deposits—the desert sands, the loess and the alluvium.   The data for parts of Tibet and the West are insufficient to permit mapping on the scale adopted.

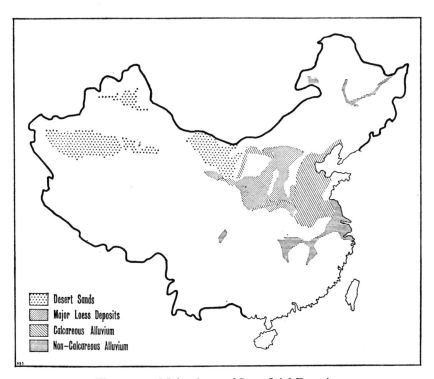

Desert Sands
Major Loess Deposits
Calcareous Alluvium
Non–Calcareous Alluvium

Figure 24.   Major Areas of Superficial Deposits.

Showing the major spreads of shifting desert sands in the arid and semi-arid North-west; the major loess deposits (note the interruption of the loess mantle by ranges such as the Taihang Shan); the area of calcareous alluvium, consisting largely of loess redistributed by the Hwang Ho; and the alluvial deposits of rivers such as the Yangtse and the Sungari.

The most resistant rocks are represented by the igneous and meta-morphic masses which fringe the Manchurian lowland to west and east —the Khingan and Tungman Shan—and which extend southwards into the Shantung peninsula.   The mountain belt of Central China— the Tapa Shan and Tapieh Shan for example—consists of sediments compacted and often metamorphosed under the stress of mountain-building movements and similar rock types occupy much of the upland country of southeastern China and the eastern periphery of the Tibetan-

Himalayan mass. Relatively undisturbed and geologically old sediments (Paleozoic) occupy two broad southwest-northeast trending zones of the South China hill country and similar little-disturbed sediments of much younger age (Mesozoic) floor the lowlands of Manchuria and the Szechwan basin; in the former they are terrestrial in origin, in the latter marine. Similar marine sediments floor the basins of western China—the Tarim, Tsaidam and Dzungarian basins; these basins are framed by the igneous rocks and the compacted sedimentaries of the Kuen Lun and the Tien Shan. The karst limestone zone of the Yunnan-Kweichow plateau constitutes a distinctive and unique environment; all stages in the dissection of the limestone mantle, from deep valleys and swallow-holes to isolated residual peaks rising from the level clay-floored lowland, are represented and can be seen as one flies south from Chengtu to Kunming.

Approximately one-sixth of the surface of China is veneered by superficial deposits; this excludes the deep laterite deposits developed by millennia of weathering in the tropical South. The major superficial formations are the dune sands and gravels of the arid Northwest (Takla Makan, Tsaidam, Ala Shan and Ordos deserts); the deep loess deposits of Shansi, Shensi and Kansu; and the great alluvial sheet of the North China Plain (consisting mainly of redistributed loess and hence calcareous) and of the middle and lower valley of the Yangtse. It is the loess and alluvium, including the innumerable alluvial plains too small to be shown on the map, and the relatively undisturbed and young sedimentary rocks of the Szechwan basin and the Manchurian lowland that form the 'key areas' in the Chinese agricultural economy. The desert sands and gravels and the upland masses of igneous rocks and compacted or metamorphosed sedimentaries represent, by contrast, pioneer fringe zones for which the techniques of optimum utilisation are still being elaborated.

Figure 25. Deposits of water-rounded boulders, I-Shan, southern Shantung.

Figure 26. Rejuvenation of a valley, Kuang-wu Shan, northern Honan.

CHINA'S PHYSICAL GEOGRAPHY AS SEEN BY ITS ARTISTS

From Joseph Needham, *Science & Civilisation in China*, Vol. 3 (by permission).

Figure 27. Plain of marine denudation with wave-cut arch, near Tsingtao, Shantung.

Figure 28. The Permian basalt cliffs of O-Mei Shan in western Szechwan.

CHINA'S PHYSICAL GEOGRAPHY AS SEEN BY ITS ARTISTS

Figure 29.   U-shaped glacial valley with dipping strata to right, northern Szechwan.

Figure 30.   Karst topography in Kwangsi.

CHINA'S PHYSICAL GEOGRAPHY AS SEEN BY ITS ARTISTS

PERPETUAL SUMMER TO PERPETUAL WINTER:
Climatic Diversity

The great latitudinal and longitudinal extent of China, together with the great diversity of topographic conditions and an extreme vertical range from over 29,000 feet in the Himalayas to below sea-level in some of the basins of Central Asia, are responsible for a great diversity of climatic conditions. The higher parts of the Tibetan-Chinghai plateau have a perpetual frost climate while even in much lower mountains such as the Great Khingan Range the climate is sufficiently severe for permafrost conditions to prevail in the more elevated sectors. By contrast, the extreme south, and especially the islands of the South China Sea, is a land of perpetual summer, with high year-round temperatures and humidities. Between these extremes there is a wide range of combinations of temperature and humidity conditions. These, by the limitations they may place on the length of the growing season (limitations due to insufficient moisture or insufficient heat—or both), directly influence the farming pattern; moreover, since they play a major role in the evolution of the soil-vegetation complex, they exercise an important indirect influence on farming. And the variability and the extremes of the climatic elements are an important challenge to the Chinese in their attempts to build a stable and high-yielding agriculture on which a modern economy can be based. . . .

In very general terms, the country falls into four major climatic regions; each of these occupies approximately one-quarter of the area of China. These major regions are: the cold high plateau of Tibet-Chinghai; the cold-winter hot-summer deserts of the Northwest; and the Eastern Monsoon sector (as Chinese geographers term it) which can be subdivided into the temperate and cold region of the Northeast and the subtropical and tropical region of Central and South China. Let us look briefly at the various elements—temperature and humidity being the most important—which constitute the climatic environment.[1]

Winter temperatures in eastern China range from $-10°C$ north of Peking to $0°C$ south of the Shantung Peninsula and $16°C$ in the extreme south; Shanghai has a January temperature of $6°C$ but Chengtu, in the sheltered and cloud-blanketed Red Basin, is $4°C$ warmer. In summer the temperature gradient is less steep; in the South and over much of Central China July temperatures are of the order of $30°C$ as compared with $20°C$ north of the Great Wall. The length of the growing season reflects these contrasts; it is less than 200 days north of Peking, 250–300 days in Central China and is virtually year round in Szechwan and the

---

[1] Based on Huang Ping-wei, 'The Complex Natural Zonation of China' in *USSR Academy of Sciences: Geographical Series* (Moscow), 1961, Number 1, pp. 25–39 (in Russian) and V. A. Kovda, *Soils and Natural Environments of China*, U.S. Joint Publications Research Service (Washington 1960).

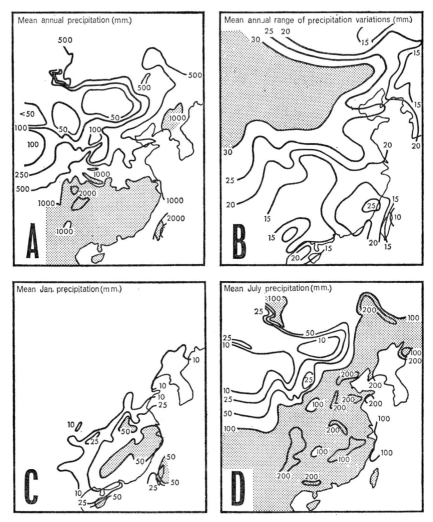

Figure 31.   Some Elements in the Climatic Environment in Eastern China (I).

A. Mean annual precipitation (mm.). Illustrating the rapid decrease in total rainfall northwest of the Great Plain and the patchy pattern of precipitation in South China, reflecting the orographic effect.

B. Mean annual range of precipitation variation (mm.).   Highest degree of variability in the northwest, i.e. the regions of lowest mean annual rainfall.   Relatively high range of variation in the southeast coastal provinces, though this must be seen against a much higher mean annual rainfall.

C.   Mean January rainfall (mm.).   Emphasising the contrast between North China, with its dry cold winters, and the South with cloudier conditions and limited but significant precipitation caused by depressions moving down the Yangtse valley or, in the extreme south, northeasterly winds which have picked up moisture in their passage across the Yellow Sea.

D.   Mean July rainfall (mm.)   Marked contrast between North and South; in the former area mountain barriers confine the influence of the rain-bearing on-shore monsoon to the Great Plain.   Strong orographic effect evident in South China.

South. Chinese scientists have distinguished six major temperature belts (excluding the Tibet-Chinghai plateau):

(i) *Cold-temperate belt.* Accumulated active temperatures[1] are below 1,700°, winters are severe and prolonged, the soil is frozen in part for some 6–8 months and scattered patches of permafrost occur at high elevations. Crops such as rice, kaoliang or the various temperate fruits cannot be grown and even hardy crops such as buckwheat, potatoes or millet mature only with difficulty. The plant cover consists of coniferous forests growing on slightly acidic brown podzolised soils.

(ii) *Temperate belt.* Accumulated temperatures range from 1,700° to 3,200°. Winter temperatures are very low (coldest month ranges from −8° to −24°) and the prolonged frost season rules out cotton and winter crops and confines temperate fruits to the warmer southern margins of the belt. Summer temperatures are, by contrast, high so that heat-loving crops such as rice, maize, kaoliang and castor-oil plant can be grown, in addition to wheat, soya beans and sugar beet. In the moister areas the vegetation consists of mixed forests; in the drier areas desert or steppe. Soils range from podzolised brown forest soils through chernozems to grey and brown desert soils.

(iii) *Warm-temperate belt.* Accumulated temperatures range from 3,200° to 4,500°. Winters are cold (temperature of the coldest month from 8° to 0°) but summer temperatures are almost as high as in the subtropical belt. Two crops a year, or three crops in two years can be grown; autumn-sown wheat and temperate fruits such as apples, pears, persimmons and grapes as well as heat-loving plants such as cotton are typical of this belt. More exacting crops such as citrus fruits, tea or tung are, however, absent. The dominant vegetation in the humid areas consists of deciduous broad-leaved forests; soils vary from brown forest soils to 'Heilutu'[2] and brown desert soils in the drier areas.

(iv) *Subtropical belt.* Accumulated temperatures range from 4,500° to 8,000°. Winter temperatures are relatively low (temperature of coldest month from 16° to 0°) and this excludes the truly tropical crops. Two crops of rice a year can be grown and other crops include winter wheat, citrus fruits, tea and tung, with bananas, pineapples, lichees and similar heat-loving crops on the southern margin of the belt. Dominant natural vegetation consists of 'monsoonal' evergreen and mixed evergreen and deciduous forests growing on leached red and yellow soils.

(v) *Tropical belt.* Accumulated temperatures range from 8,000° to

[1] I.e. the sum of the air temperature on days when the average 24-hour temperature is above 10°C.
[2] I.e. the so-called 'chestnut chernozem' soils as developed on the loess-lands.

9,000°; temperatures are high throughout the year and mean temperatures of the coldest month are above 16°, with an average absolute minimum over a period of several years of not lower than 5°. Lowland vegetation consists of tropical 'monsoon' rain-forests growing on lateritic soils. Three crops of rice can be got and other crops include such heat-demanding tropical crops as sugar cane, coconut palm, rubber and coffee; winter wheat is ruled out by temperature conditions.

(vi) *Equatorial belt.* This lies south of the maximum winter extension of the polar front and has accumulated temperatures in excess of 9,500°; the temperature range is small. This belt is of insignificant importance, and includes the scattered Chinese islands of the South China Sea, e.g. the Nangsha archipelago.

It is to be noted that severe winter cold extends far towards the equator in East Asia as a result of the outpouring of cold air from Inner Asia. There is thus a general southward deflection of climatic boundaries; Peking, which is closer to the Equator than Naples, may as a result experience winter freezing of the soil to the depths of up to 50 cm. and over much of eastern China, where latitudinal considerations might lead us to expect a subtropical climate, temperature conditions are either temperate or warm-temperate.

In eastern China precipitation, like temperature, increases pro-gressively southwards; the Tsitsikara-Shenyang region receives between 380 and 660 mm. of rain, the Shanghai region between 750 and 1,250 mm. and subtropical China between 1,500 and 2,000 mm. This increase in temperature and humidity southwards leads to a speeding-up of the chemical and biochemical processes associated with soil formation. It leads also to an acceleration of the processes of plant growth and this shows itself in the increase in multiple cropping towards the tropics. Inland, precipitation diminishes sharply owing to distance from the sea and the sheltering effect of the great mountain ranges; in the Tarim and Turfan basins of the northwest it drops to below 20 mm.

The relationship between evaporation and precipitation is of critical importance to the farmer and, on the basis of this relationship it is possible to distinguish four major zones: humid, semi-humid, semi-arid and arid:[1]

(a) *Humid areas.* Index of dryness (i.e. ratio of evaporation to precipitation) is less than 1·0. Rainfall is relatively dependable, deviations from the mean annual norm being less than 20 per cent. Typical vegetation is forest; soils have a low humus and plant nutrient content. Given favourable conditions of warmth, drain-age and topography, dependable levels of crop production can be

[1] V. A. Kovda, *op. cit.*, pp. 51, 54, distinguishes *five* zones (a) extremely arid (E:P>3·4); (b) dry 3·4–2·0; (c) balanced 2·0–1·0; (d) moist 1·0–0·5; (e) extremely moist E:P<0·5; this classification is perhaps an example of what S. Potter terms 'One-upmanship'.

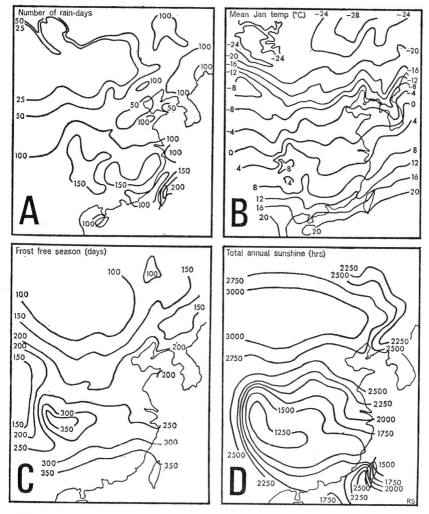

Figure 32.   Some Elements in the Climatic Environment in Eastern China (II).

A.   Number of rain-days: Major divide (isopleth of 100) follows Tsin-ling-Tapa Shan range; highest totals recorded over the upland regions of the South, with a relatively steep 'gradient' on the northwest fringes of Agricultural China.

B.   Mean January temperature: Major divide (isotherm of 0°C) again follows Tsin-ling-Tapa Shan divide.   Contrast of almost 50°C between the winter-warm southern fringes (Hainan 20°C, i.e. 68°F) and the 'poles of cold' in the Mongolian steppes.

C.   Frost-free season: The extreme south (Lingnan) is virtually frost-free; by contrast the frost-free period is barely four months at Peking, a little over three months in parts of Inner Mongolia.   Note the anomaly of the Red Basin of Szechwan; the heart of the basin, shielded by the surrounding mountains and blanketed with cloud, is virtually frost-free.

D.   Total annual sunshine: Heavy cloud cover reduces the annual amount of sunshine to less than 1,250 hours in Szechwan and adjoining regions.   The climatic individuality of the North, with its relatively small number of rain-days and clear cold sunny winter, is suggested by the very high annual amounts of sunshine recorded; parts of the Peking lowland, for example, receive almost two-and-a-half times as much sunshine as Szechwan.

attained.   These humid areas occupy 32·2 per cent of China and
stretch through all six thermal belts.   Their most important extent
is in the subtropical belt whose humid sector occupies 26·1 per cent
of the territory of China, the humid areas of the cold temperate,
temperate, warm temperate and tropical belts containing respectively 1·2 per cent, 2·5 per cent, 0·8 per cent and 1·6 per cent of the
country's area.

(b) *Semi-humid areas*.   Index of dryness is between 1·0 and 1·5.
Under favourable conditions of site and soil a stable agriculture
is possible, though year to year variations are much higher than in
the humid areas and frequently exceed 20 per cent and spring
drought is a recurrent danger.   Vegetation ranges from dry forest
to meadowland and steppe, with mixed meadow-forest or meadow-
steppe in the Chinghai-Tibetan highland zone.   The humus and
nutrient content of the soils is high and salinisation is sometimes
found.   These subhumid areas make up 15·3 per cent of China and
rank with the humid areas as the major agricultural areas.   Forestry is less important than in the humid areas; animal husbandry is
an important aspect of the economy.   The semi-humid areas of
the warm temperate belt represent 6·9 per cent of the area of
China, those of the temperate belt and of the Chinghai-Tibet
highland zone 4·4 per cent and 4·0 per cent respectively.

(c) *Semi-arid areas*.   Index of dryness may reach 2·0.   The typical
vegetation form is dry steppe, with mixed forest-meadow and
steppe meadow in the upland regions of western China.   The
soils have a marked zone of lime-accumulation and are easily
eroded; in consequence, while dry-farming is possible in some areas,
the dominant type of land use is animal husbandry.   These semi-
arid areas make up 21·7 per cent of the area of China; the semi-
arid area of Chinghai-Tibet alone represents 13·3 per cent of the
country's area, the semi-arid areas of the temperate belt 5·9 per
cent and those of the warm-temperate belt 2·5 per cent.

(d) *Arid areas*.   Characterised by a desert-steppe or desert vegetation.
Agriculture is virtually impossible without irrigation and stock-
rearing is developed chiefly on the margins of these areas, and in
the foothills and mountain country.   Arid areas occupy 30 per
cent of China, 13·1 per cent in the temperate belt, 8·3 per cent in
the warm-temperate belt and 9·4 per cent in the Chinghai-
Tibetan sector.

These contrasting conditions of humidity, then, have a direct effect
on land utilisation; they have also an indirect effect through their
influence on soil-forming processes for while zone (a) is characterised
by the dominance of humid weathering and leaching (with the relatively infertile yellow and red podzolic soils and the lateritic soils of the

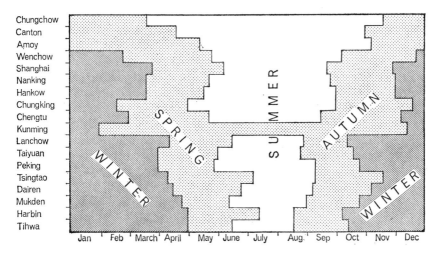

Figure 33. The Seasons in China.

Illustrating the absence of winter in the South, the almost 'perpetual spring' of Yunnan and the very reduced growing season of the Northeast. Winter is here defined as the period in which the 5-day mean temperature goes below 10°C (50°F); summer as the period in which it is over 22°C (72°F). (Based on Chi-yun Chang.)

South as typical end products) zones (c) and (d) are characterised by salinised and lime-accumulating soils. And in both humid and arid/ semi-arid regions destruction of the vegetation accentuates these physical processes . . .

The combination of temperature and humidity data makes possible a division of China into eighteen areas or sub-areas; this initial stage in the regional subdivision of the country is illustrated in Figure 83 C. The pattern is most complex in the northeastern sector where seven areas are distinguished, in contrast to the three major regions of the subtropical and tropical southeast; the northwestern arid sector is subdivided into two areas on the basis of temperature and the Chinghai-Tibetan sector into three areas based on moisture conditions (as evidenced by the vegetation cover). We shall see below (pp. 316–17) how this classification of China into temperature and humidity provinces is used as the basis for one of the latest attempts to determine the basic units in China's natural environment.

So far, we have been concerned largely with the generalised pattern of climate, based on data averaged out over more or less lengthy periods of years. But man, it has been observed, does not live in this rather hypothetical set of average conditions which makes up one aspect of climate, rather does he live in a climatic environment where conditions may fluctuate greatly—and disastrously—from year to year. And the closer his ties to the soil and the greater his proximity to one or another of the critical climatic boundaries (whether it be the uncertain margin

G

separating an area whose average rainfall is just adequate for cultivation from an adjoining area where rainfall normally precludes cultivation— or the critical temperature limit for a crop) the greater is his vulner- ability.   For centuries scores of millions of Chinese have lived in such zones of climatic uncertainty.   In the humid south they have faced the possibility of floods, whether due to the typhoons of late summer or due to swollen rivers fed by heavy rain falling on steep and deforested hillsides.   In the subhumid and semi-arid north and northwest the greatest hazard—and the greatest killer—has been drought.   The variability of rainfall is of the order of 15 per cent in the relatively high-rainfall areas of Szechwan and South China but north of the Hwang Ho, where average precipitation drops below 500 mm. (20 inches), variability exceeds 30 per cent.   Moreover, in this northern region the fluctuations tend to be particularly marked in June, the critical month for the northern farmer; as an example, over a period of fifty-five years Peking had twenty-one years in which the June rainfall was below 50 mm. (2 inches) and, of these, five years showed June rainfall totals of less than 10 mm. (0·4 inches).   These are the fluctuations which caused the murderous drought-famines of the past, which decimated the peasant populations of entire regions (see below pp. 114, 116). Moreover, there is evidence that with increasing population pressure and increasing destruction of the vegetation cover, both flood and drought were tending to increase in frequency.   Co-ching Chu summarises the evidence for East China in the table below:

TABLE 2

EAST CHINA: FLOODS AND DROUGHTS RECORDED BETWEEN THE SEVENTEENTH AND NINETEENTH CENTURIES

PROVINCE	Floods			Droughts		
	17th C	18th C	19th C	17th C	18th C	19th C
Shantung	14	20	35	11	8	30
Kiangsi	28	37	41	11	5	24
Anhwei	15	31	42	9	5	22
Chekiang	13	16	27	20	8	15
Fukien	n.a.	n.a.	17	6	5	2

Source: V. A. Kovda, *op. cit.*, p. 55.

Man cannot change the climate but he can, by afforestation which controls run-off, by shelter-belt plantings which create a favourable micro-climate in arid areas, and by irrigation in areas of uncertain rainfall, attenuate, even eliminate, climate's disastrous and at times killing impact.   But just as an impoverished peasant on his own can do little against disease so, too, were the peasants of Old China helpless when confronted by the variability of China's climate. One of the major results of the social and political changes of the last two decades has been to create a new relationship between man and climate in China, a relationship in which man, as a member of a tightly-knit group possessed of increasing technological competence, has initiated a transformation of the vegetation cover and the hydraulic situation which is establishing him as an 'ecologic dominant'.

DESERT & TAIGA, STEPPE & JUNGLE: Soil-Vegetation Assemblages

An awareness of the importance of ecological conditions to the farmer extends back into the early history of the Chinese people. The *Huai Nan Tzu*, dating from the Han Dynasty, assembles a vast amount of such information, designed to make possible the fullest utilisation of the Chinese living-space:

> Lands whether fertile or poor, high or low, should be used to their best advantage. Knolls, hillocks, steep places and even cliffs, where cereals may not be grown, ought to be covered with bamboos or trees; thereby fallen and withered timber can be gathered in spring, melons and fruits in summer and autumn, and faggots and firewood in winter—all to provide for the people.[1]

The need for careful adjustment to local conditions so as to make the best possible use of the agricultural year is stressed:

> The sun and moon move around on their courses, time waits for nobody. Therefore the sages value a whole foot of jade less than one inch of sun-shadow. Time is easily lost and hard to get.[2]

A slightly later work, the *Hsiao Ching Yuan Sheng Ch'i*, comments on the suitability of certain soils for certain crops:

> Soils yellow to white, are good for spiked millets; black, for glutinous millet and wheat; red, for beans; marshy, for rice.[3]

And the cumulative impact of differing ecological conditions is illustrated from his own experience by Chia Ssu-hsieh, author of the sixth-century agricultural encyclopedia *Ch'i Min Yao Shu* (i.e. 'Essential Ways for Living of the Common People'):

> Common garlic cannot be maintained in Ping-chow, seeding bulbs have to be brought from Ch'ao-ko. But after one year's cultivation, the bulb becomes bulbil again. . . . Turnips of Ping-chow are as big as bowls. Even grown out of seeds from other districts, it will be so big in one year's time. . . . . Peas of Ping-chow, when planted east to Tsin-Ching-K'ou, and spiked millet of Shantung, when

[1] Shih Sheng-han, *A Preliminary Survey of the Book 'Ch'i Min Yao Shu'* (Peking, second edition, 1962), p. 14. [2] *Ibid.*, p. 13. [3] *Ibid.*, p. 15.

introduced (westwards) into Hu Kuan and Shang Tan, will not
seed. . . . These are the phenomena of different local adaptiveness
of living beings.[1]

Other differences had been noted by earlier observers: for example,
that the tangerine of the South gives place to the thorny lime in the
North, and were attributed to differences in the *ti ch'i*, the 'land
pneuma' or 'earth breath', as Schafer translates it.[2]

This accumulation of careful observations of natural phenomena
continued during succeeding centuries and by the fourteenth century
it was possible for a Chinese author to outline a classification of China's
soils into five major groups: black (i.e. chernozem), white (i.e. sierozem
or arid soils), blue (i.e. swamp soils), red (the red podzolic soils of the
tropical South) and yellow (i.e. the yellow-earths of the North); each
group was divided into three subgroups on the basis of fertility and each
of these into three types, giving forty-five soil types.[3]   This accumulation of empirical knowledge is important, and its importance is underlined by the extent to which modern Chinese scientists are drawing on it
in their schemes of land classification; it was not, however, until a
relatively recent period that the overall pattern—and the regional
interrelations—of the various elements in the environment—climate,
vegetation, soils—was delineated.   The spatial pattern of vegetation
and soils (these two elements being closely influenced by the conditions
of topography, geology and climate) provides the essential background
to any study of Chinese agriculture; man has, as we shall see, profoundly
modified both vegetation and soil in many areas but the extent of such
modification and the broad pattern of crop assemblages are governed
by the character of the soil-vegetation complex and by the factors of
which this complex is the expression.

The soil- and plant-assemblages of China[4] are most conveniently
considered together since, as elsewhere in the world, the soil mantle
is profoundly influenced by the character of the vegetation cover and
both reflect the influence of climate.   The same four-fold subdivision
we noticed in the case of climate can be distinguished: Western China
comprises the high alpine-tundra region of Tibet-Chinghai and the
desert-soils and cold desert type of vegetation of the Northwest,
Eastern Monsoonal China the coniferous and broad-leaved forest zone
north of the Yangtse, with its podzol or brown forest soils and steppe
margins, and the evergreen broad-leaved forests of the South, growing
on leached yellow and red podzolic or lateritic soils.   Each of these
zones contains approximately one-quarter of the area of China.

---

[1] Shih Sheng-han, *A Preliminary Survey of the Book*, p. 35.
[2] Edward H. Schafer, *The Vermilion Bird*, p. 119.
[3] Cited by V. A. Kovda, *op. sup. cit.*, p. 77.
[4] On these see the work of S. D. Richardson, *Forestry in Communist China* (Baltimore 1966)
and, for Eastern China, J. L. Buck (Editor), *Land Utilization in China* (Chicago 1937).

Much of the Tibet-Chinghai region lies between 4,000 m. and 5,300 m. It is characterised by a cold semi-arid climate; rainfall may be as little as 10 cm., winter temperatures as low as − 16°C and only on the southeastern margins do summer temperatures reach 10°C (50°F). Here, in a relatively favoured valley location, Lhasa has a growing season of some five mor. 'hs. In the deeply dissected, more humid, eastern borderlands there is a dense woodland cover, consisting largely of conifers (this zone contains the biggest reserves of softwood outside Manchuria) and a rich and complex local flora. These forests are associated with a dominantly podzolic soil and their upper limits lie between 3,800 m. and 4,300 m.; they pass, through a transition zone of rhododendron, into alpine scrub and meadow. The main plateau block (which has an area of 1·75 million square kilometres) is banded by forest (broad-leaved at lower levels, passing through conifers to birch and rhododendron scrub) only on its warmer margins; the main plateau surface has a thin salt-tolerant scrub or grass vegetation growing on alpine meadow and desert soils. The high plateau has only a sparse nomadic population; closer agricultural and pastoral settlement is largely confined to the southeastern margins towards the valley of the Tsangpo.

North of the Kun Lun Mountains an area of desert and semi-desert soils, occupying almost 2 million square kilometres, extends towards the Altai Mountains and the boundary with the Soviet Union. With the exception of the mountain ranges, which break the region into a series of basins, the area has a low precipitation (10 mm.–0·5 mm.); winters are severe, with a January mean ranging from − 6°C to − 20°C, but summer temperatures are high (24°C to 26°C, reaching 33°C or 91°F in the Turfan and Hami depressions). Sand and dust storms may occur at any season. The soils are unstable, with a low organic and high salt content; they are typically sierozems or desert sands, carrying a grass or scrub vegetation, sparse in distribution and drought- and salt-tolerant in the poorest areas. Along the fringes of the sand plains (e.g. Takla Makan) the junction of basin floor and fringing mountains is characterised by a belt of fluvioglacial gravels, carrying remnants of a relatively luxuriant broadleaf forest, with poplar and willow as typical trees. The mountains themselves (e.g. Tien Shan, Altyn Tagh) are characterised by a pronounced altitudinal zonation of soils and vegetation. Soils range from chestnut soils at lower levels through grey forest soils to alpine meadow soils above the tree-line, vegetation from steppe species and grass with broken patches of deciduous forest at lower levels through conifer and juniper forest to high-level moist alpine meadows. This close juxtaposition of contrasting environmental zones provides the setting for a transhumant economy which utilises the high level grazings during the brief summer period. These forested mountains have a considerable lumber potential but this is at present limited by inaccessibility and difficulties of extracting the timber.

Within Eastern Monsoonal China V. A. Kovda[1] distinguishes the following theoretical sequence of soils from north to south:

Permafrost soils (tundra or podzol)
Seasonally frozen brown forest soils
Seasonally frozen black carbonateless soils
Brown forest and leached cinnamon soils
Yellow-brown soils
Yellow and red podzolic soils
Lateritic soils

This idealised pattern is, of course, modified by such conditions as nature of relief or of soil-forming rocks; moreover, superimposed on this sequence is the vertical zonation of soils in high mountain areas, a zonation which repeats the main features of the horizontal zonation set out above. The general distribution of soil-vegetation assemblages in eastern China can be considered most conveniently in terms of the two major sectors into which the area falls: the subhumid and semi-arid sector north of the Yangtse and the warm and humid South.

In the extreme north, parts of the Khingan Range and the mountains fringing the Amur valley have a mean annual temperature below zero, with winter temperatures of −25°C, dropping in extreme cases to −50°C; rainfall is between 35 and 60 cm. annually. Soils are dominantly podzolic (with permafrost soils at higher levels) and carry a coniferous forest cover (larch and various pines with an undercover somewhat similar to that of similar forests in Europe or North America); the tree-line is reached at some 1,100 m. Most of this area must be regarded as agriculturally marginal. To the east and southeast, with milder climate, this assemblage gives place to a zone of mixed coniferous and deciduous broadleaf forest. Mean annual temperatures may reach 5·5°C and the growing season is in excess of 125 days; climatic factors are not the major limiting factor in land use (as in the coniferous belt), rather do soil factors become more important. This region is dominated by trees such as the Korean pine, larch, birch, poplar and maple, growing on soils ranging from thin leached podzols on the mountains to brown forest and alluvial soils on the lower slopes. With increasing temperatures deciduous broad-leaved forest becomes the dominant formation. Over much of southern Manchuria, in Shantung and (conjecturally) on the Great Plain the tree cover consists of an oak-birch-elm assemblage, growing on the brown forest soils of the lower slopes and hill margins and with conifers dominant on the areas of drier and thinner soils. This whole region is much more favoured climatically than the areas to the north; the mean annual temperature varies

[1] V. A. Kovda, *op. sup. cit.*, p. 692.

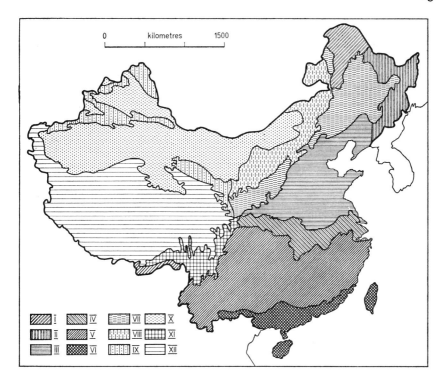

Figure 34. The Vegetation-Soil Regions of China.

   I Coniferous forest-podzol region
  II Mixed coniferous and broadleaved forests—podzol and brown forest soils
 III Deciduous broadleaved forest—brown forest and Korichnevie soils
 IV Mixed deciduous and evergreen broadleaved forests—yellow podzolic and yellow Korichnevie soils
  V Evergreen broadleaved forest—yellow and red podzolic soils
 VI Tropical monsoonal rainforest—yellow lateritic soils
 VII Forest steppe—chernozem and siero-Korichnevie soils
VIII Steppe—chestnut soils
 IX Mountains of northwest China
  X Semi-desert and desert—sierozem and desert soils
 XI Mountains and plateaux of eastern Tibet
XII Tibetan plateau

between 7°C and 16°C and the growing season is from 150 to 240 days, i.e. sufficiently long in the south to permit two crops a year. The most important sector of this region is represented by the Great Plain, floored by calcareous alluvium brought down by the Yellow River and dominated by the alkaline or neutral soils termed Korichnevie (i.e. cinnamon) soils. What the original vegetation of these loess-derived soils was is conjectural, for over wide areas there has been a complete humanisation of the plain which expresses itself in a man-maintained 'climax' vegetation of grain crops, soy beans and vegetables.

Forest remnants (e.g. around temples) and historical evidence suggest the plain may originally have supported a deciduous forest vegetation; the problem, it may be stressed, is no mere academic one, since the determination of the character of the original plant cover would provide an important guide to the tree species most likely to be of use in the extensive protection and shelterbelt plantings which are one of the key elements in the present programme of agricultural development.

With decreasing humidity these forest zones, with their podzol or brown earth soils, merge through the transitional zone of forest-steppe into true steppe. In its northeastern sector the forest-steppe is characterised by areas of open woodland, on grey forest soils or leached black earth soils, set amid extensive grasslands on calcareous chernozem or solonchak soils; the wooded areas seem of limited agricultural value but the grassland areas are now almost entirely cultivated. In its northwestern sector the forest-steppe zone is characterised by a sparse grass or scrub flora, growing on calcareous loess-derived soils (the so-called siero-Korichnevie soils). With lower rainfall these give place to chestnut and saline soils supporting a grass vegetation; except on the occasional upland areas or close to the desert margin woody vegetation is absent. This steppe zone has played an important role in Chinese history; it has also, as C. W. Wang points out, offered an ideal of feminine beauty—the 'agile and rather generously-proportioned horsewoman'—rather different from the willowy beauty of later Chinese tradition. Since 1949 Chinese agriculturalists have given a good deal of attention to the problems, notably water conservancy and protection forestry, and the pastoral potential of this steppe zone; one incidental result of this, suggests Richardson, is that 'the buxom horsewoman may again become the symbol of pastoral productivity'.[1]

The southeastern quarter of China consists of a region of evergreen broadleaved forests and of soils which are dominantly red or yellow podzolic soils. Between this region and the region of deciduous broad-leaved forests to the north there is a transitional belt running broadly from the Han River to the valley of the lower Yangtse. It is warmer and moister than the region to the north; growing season is between 230 and 280 days, January mean temperature 2–5°C and the July temperature some 25°C higher and rainfall some 120–200 cm. The northern limit of the belt is the northern limit of many evergreen species; within the belt there is a highly diverse forest cover of broadleaved trees and conifers (50 species of broadleaved trees and a dozen of conifers) with a rich understorey. Relict species of an earlier and warmer period (e.g. *Metasequoia*) are to be found. Soils are diverse—

---

[1] S. D. Richardson, *op. cit.*, p. 40. Richardson adds that Wang's description is 'a Gargan-tuan understatement' and that 'cursory examination of the art of the Han dynasty reveals proportions that would have delighted both Rubens and a twentieth-century film producer'; for the proportions sought by the latter see Geoffrey Wagner, *The Parade of Pleasure* (London 1954).

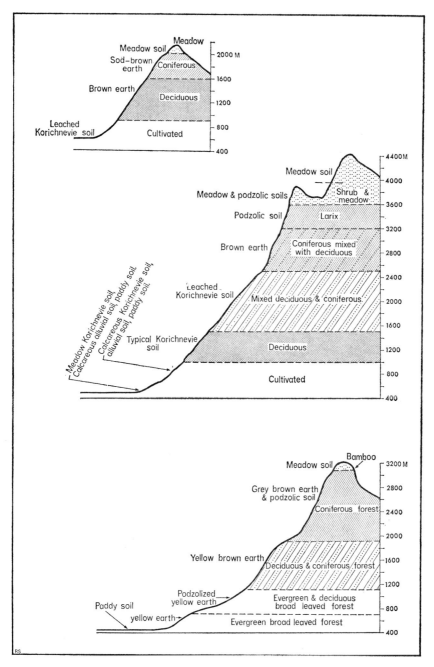

Figure 35. Altitudinal Zonation of Vegetation and Soils in North and Central China.

(a) Liaoning-Hopeh borderland, 40°20′ N lat.   (b) Tapa Shan, Shensi, 34° N lat.
(c) O-Mei Shan, Szechwan, 29°30′ N lat.

(After Wang Chi-wu, 1961.)

brown forest soils in the west, yellow podzolic soils on the foothills and the lower Yangtse hills, neutral cinnamon-brown soils where the parent material is calcareous. It was in this zone of middle China that the Han people gained their first experience of the subtropical and tropical South and it is an area which became at an early period one of the great 'bread-baskets' of China. Largely because of this only small remnants of the original vegetation survive; over wide areas the forest has been felled to make way for food production or has been replaced by a cover of secondary growth.

Most of the South is dominated by a great bloc of evergreen broad-

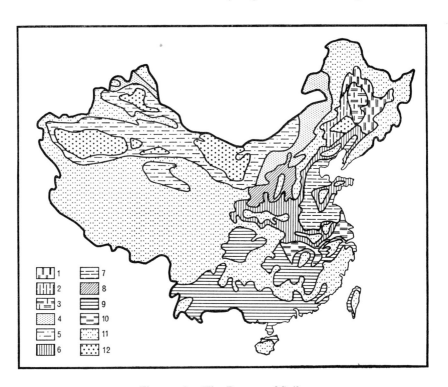

Figure 36.   The Pattern of Soils.

KEY: 1. Grey forest soils.   2. Leached chernozems.   3. Chernozems.   4. Chestnut soils.   5. Semi-desert and desert soils.   6. Brown forest soils.   7. Calcareous alluvial soils.   8. Grey-brown loessial soils.   9. Yellow and red lateritic soils.   10. Non-calcareous alluvial soils.   11. Mountain soils.   12. Desert sands.

Note the wide extent of mountain and semi-desert and desert soils (which together occupy some two-thirds of China) and that eastern China falls into three broad regions: the chernozem, degraded chernozem and grey forest soils of the northeast; the brown forest and grey brown loessial soils (and calcareous alluvium) of the north and centre; and the red and yellow soils of the south which include the lateritic soils of the tropical zone. Chinese expansion has been found from the original cradle area on the brown soils towards the red soils of the south and, later, the chernozems and leached soils of the northeast. (Generalised from map by Guerassimov 1957.)

leaved forest; this occupied some one-and-three-quarter million square kilometres, though much has been cleared and replaced by either cropland or grass and fern. Botanists distinguish an eastern and a western subregion, differing somewhat in climate and soils but with many common plant species. The eastern subregion has. a higher rainfall (120–220 cm.) and a temperature range of from 3–6°C in January to 21–31°C in July; at least ten months are above 10°C and in the heart of the Red Basin there is no winter interruption to the growing season. The soils are generally leached podzolic soils, yellow in the north and passing into red podzolic soils ('red earths') to the south and east and into purplish *rendzina* soils on calcareous parent materials in Szechwan and Kweichow. The evergreen cover includes evergreen oak, laurel and magnolia and the forest is characterised by a great diversity of species. Widespread human interference with the plant cover has resulted in considerable areas of more open secondary forest, with open mixed stands of oak and Masson's pine and xerophytic trees, shrubs or grassland. The western subregion is drier (mean annual rainfall 50–150 cm.) and more diverse topographically. Its climax vegetation is either broadleaved evergreen forest with conifers dominant at higher elevations or secondary forest. Soils are diverse—ranging from tundra- and meadow-soils at high elevations to purple-brown forest soils in parts of Yunnan, *terra rossa* on limestone parent materials and acid red or grey-brown podzolic soils merging into yellow podzolic soils in the east. Climatic conditions, which make possible rapid tree growth, and the hilly nature of the terrain both favour forestry and some 85 per cent of China's production afforestation is concentrated in the lands to the south of the Yangtse.

The extreme south—the 'southern maritime amphitheatres' of Needham—is the region of tropical monsoon forest, distinct physiognomically and generically from the evergreen broadleaved forest, and of lateritic soils. This is a region of a quarter of a million square kilometres overlapping the Tropic of Cancer. It has a rainfall of from 130 to 350 cm. and, though winter is the dry season, no month is rainless. January mean temperatures range from 13° to 21°C and frost is virtually unknown. Leaching and the breakdown of soil humus is rapid and uninterrupted and the typical soils are either poor or of only moderate fertility; this is especially true of the red earths and the yellow lateritic soils. The forest is largely evergreen, and is characterised by a great multiplicity of species yet considerable floristic homogeneity. In its unmodified state it is the tropical forest of popular imagining— dense, with a great profusion of lianas, climbing palms and epiphytes[1] yet, because of the multiple cropping which this southern climate makes possible, the greater proportion of the area has been cleared and the forest is replaced by an artificial climax vegetation of crops. These

---

[1] See page 60 above for early Chinese impressions of the area.

include tree crops such as mulberry, lichee, citrus with, in more recent years, rubber, cacao and coffee and, for timber production, trees such as the eucalyptus or the poplar which, in this hot, humid, environment, show phenomenal rates of growth.[1]

We have in an earlier section emphasised the imensely long history of man in China and in this section have drawn attention to some examples of man's modification of the vegetation pattern.   Old China, as the character of many soil profiles attests, was a land of forests but these have been destroyed over extensive areas and even the shrub and grass vegetation which succeeded them in the hilly areas has been cut and grubbed for fuel or for fertiliser.   The result was that, by 1949, only one-tenth of the country was forested; major reserves were confined to the less accessible areas, and in the densely-settled provinces of the east (Kiangsu, Shantung and Hopeh) and the developing provinces of the Northwest forest occupies less than 0·5 per cent of the land area.

The soil pattern has been similarly transformed by man who has altered the nutrient status or texture of many soils and, by terracing, has transformed the country's micro-relief. V. A. Kovda, in his account of the soils of China, stresses this 'far-reaching, pertinent and purposive effect of man on China's rivers, on the relief of the hilly and mountainous regions, and on the relief and soil blanket of the valleys, plains and deltas'.   This cumulative impact of countless millions of peasants, extending back some four millennia in some regions, has profoundly transformed the soils of the country.   The most obvious manifestations of this is to be seen in the zones of high soil fertility surrounding all the great cities of China.   This is a result of 'the continuous transfer of fertility' from often distant hinterlands supplying the urban populations with food; the organic and nutrient content of this food, in the form of human excreta, is eventually returned to the soils of the peri-urban area and these soils show a high humus, nitrogen and base content which makes possible very high and stable yields. This use of nightsoil diminishes sharply with increasing distance from the cities so these are surrounded by concentric zones of diminishing fertility; as a corollary of this it is evident that the remoter food-supplying regions must be undergoing a continuous depletion of fertility as a result of this outflow of nutrients (including the phosphorus loss due to export of animal products).

Many observers have commented on this phenomenon but there are other and equally significant changes in the soil mantle resulting from human activity.   The major rivers can be seen as agents of soil redistribution, removing great quantities of soil by erosion in their upper reaches and transporting it, as a silt load, towards the alluvial lowlands of the east.[2]   Part at least of this load is further redistributed by the

[1] S. D. Richardson, *op. sup. cit.*, p. 35.
[2] The Pearl River, it is estimated, transports some 28 million tons of silt annually, the Hwang Ho some 1,450 million tons. Kovda, *op. cit.*, p. 63.

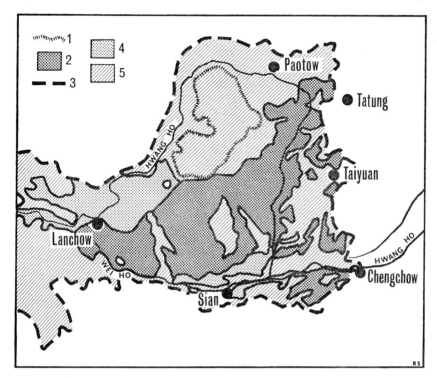

Figure 37. Soil Erosion in the Middle Valley of the Hwang Ho.

Illustrating the major problem area on the friable grey-brown loessial soils which occupy a SW–NE-trending zone across the great northwards loop of the Hwang Ho. These soils, which have been intensively cultivated for some four millennia, are particularly vulnerable to gully and wind erosion. Present policy aims at stabilising these soils by protection-planting of trees and by contour-farming (see Plate 26). The success of the ambitious plans for hydro-electric development on the Yellow River depends largely on reducing erosion and hence the siltation of reservoirs. Key: 1. Area of internal drainage. 2. Very heavy erosion. 3. Watershed. 4. Moderate erosion. 5. Slight erosion.

canal systems which, over the centuries, have been elaborated in the alluvial plains. In these alluvial lowlands the processes of soil-formation have thus been influenced by man's 'hydro-technical activities', i.e. dyke-building and irrigation. The deposition of silt during irrigation leads, according to the character of the silt-load, to acidity, salinisation or leaching; excessive irrigation may lead to the development of water-logged soils and the use of acidic spring-water or rain-water for irrigation (as in the loess area) to an increasing leaching-out of nutrients. In the coastal lowlands irrigation has the dual function of maintaining high ground-water levels in the dry season and of draining off excess water in the wet season. Ground-water levels—and thus the conditions of soil-formation—are, in consequence, largely man-controlled; the best example of this is the Grand Canal which plays a major role in

regulating the water-régime over much of the East China Plain. A
more direct and obvious transformation of the soil pattern is the piling
up on the fields of earth or mud derived from the digging or cleaning of
canals; this creates what are in effect artificial meadow soils often some
50–100 cm. above the original soil. The addition of sand to heavy
clay soils and, in Szechwan, the working into the soil of the local
purple shales which have a high phosphate and potash content similarly
create a specific 'cultural layer' whose thickness may vary from 20 to
50 cm. And the remodelling of the surface to convert even gentle

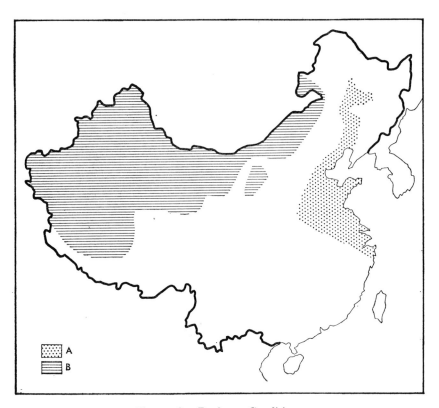

Figure 38.   Drainage Conditions.

A indicates areas of difficult drainage in the North China Plain and the Manchurian
lowland. B indicates areas of internal drainage. Almost one-half of China, it
will be seen, suffers from drainage conditions which pose problems to man.

slopes into a series of horizontal micro-plains separated by the vertical
terrace edges and the parapets of retaining walls creates, under irrigation, conditions for the development of a distinctive 'meadow-bog' soil
type.   Such terrace-systems are most strikingly developed in Szechwan,
the valleys of South China and the loess regions of the Northwest; as
Kovda comments:

On such terraced mountainous and hilly expanses and in the river valleys, the runoff is virtually completely regulated, soil erosion is halted, the fine earth transported from the overlying sectors is accumulated . . . the original undulating relief of the great delta-alluvial plains of China has been transformed into an ideally flat relief suitable for irrigation.[1]

PLAGUES, PESTS & PARASITES: *The Biological Environment*

We are all aware that man has to adjust his life to a particular *physical* environment, to a particular pattern of mountains and plains, of climates, vegetation types and soils. We have indicated the broad pattern of these elements in China in the preceding sections. We often ignore, because it is for the most part unseen, man's *biological* environment as represented by the great complex of diseases and parasites which consume his energy, eat away his flesh, and perhaps ultimately kill him. Yet especially in Asia it is impossible to ignore this biological factor in any real evaluation of the environment for there are few regions where the biological elements in the environment are so rich—or so hostile. Asia, and especially tropical Asia, has always been one of the great areas of endemic malaria, of plague and typhus, an area of infestation by a terrifying range of intestinal parasites and of disfiguring diseases such as yaws and leprosy. These drag down the efficiency of the peasant; if you are sodden with malaria or bloated with intestinal worms you are not likely to be able to put in a productive day's work however urgent your food needs. A great deal of the listlessness and apathy of many Asian peoples—and this included the Chinese—is explicable in terms of these diseases. Disease, then, reduces agricultural efficiency, lowers output and at the same time initiates a vicious circle. For, because you suffer from malaria or hookworm, your output as a farmer is low; because your output is low you and your family are inadequately fed; because you are undernourished you have lowered resistance to malaria or to any other disease. Yet there is no inevitability about this pattern for most of these diseases can be controlled, and given the technical know-how, a favourable socio-economic organisation (making possible, where necessary, mass mobilisation of the population) and the resources necessary in the shape of drugs or prophylactics, the biological environment can be reshaped as dramatically as the physical environment. And, as will be seen in a later section (pp. 202–5), for almost two decades the Chinese have been busy with the transformation of their biological environment.

Sorre, in his map of major disease realms,[2] distinguishes China as a subdivision of his Pacific Region. It is a region characterised by

---

[1] V. A. Kovda, *op. cit.*, p. 81.
[2] Max Sorre, *Les fondements de la géographie humaine: Tome 1, Les fondements biologiques* (Paris 1943), map on page 377.

cholera and plague, by malaria, kala-azar and leprosy and by a variety of parasitic worms. Even on the literary evidence alone it appears that many of these diseases have a long history in China. A treatise on typhus (which did not, however, recognise that it was a lice-borne disease) was compiled in the Han dynasty and the symptoms and treatment of Asiatic cholera were described by T'ang pharmacopoeias.[1] Malaria had long been recognised as a disease of Central and South China; in the words of the poet Tu Fu, writing twelve centuries ago:

> '*South of the Chiang is the land of malarial pest,*
> *Pursuing travellers without wane or gain*'[2]

though these distant Chinese, like the nineteenth-century travellers in Africa, were inclined to regard it as a product of local miasmas or effluvia rather than the insect-transmitted disease it is. It is impossible to give any detailed picture of the early distribution of these major diseases though it is possible to set some of them into perspective in the light of modern conditions.

There are three major insect-borne diseases, each with differing distributions depending on the ecological preferences of the vector: malaria, typhus and plague. Malaria, transmitted by the anopheles mosquito, is a characteristic disease of the warm and humid South. Here it was relatively early observed that its incidence was heaviest in the wooded hills, where ecological conditions were at their optimum for the mosquito, which prefers to breed in the water of upland streams, and relatively unimportant in the delta-lands whose saline or muddy water was a less attractive habitat. Its importance as a geographic factor can be measured by the fact that in the 1930s some two-thirds of the population of Central China was affected and throughout history it has undoubtedly been a factor explaining the aversion of the Han people to the upland areas. Kala-azar (a Leishmaniasis leading to spleen and liver changes and to growing emaciation) is transmitted by the bite of an infected sand-fly. It is as northern in its distribution as malaria is southern and before 1949 was endemic in twelve provinces north of the Yangtse, affecting some 600,000 villages, of which one-third were in Shantung. Typhus was early recognised and from its cool-weather incidence was known as 'Wounding Cold'; this seasonal incidence is linked with the fact that it is a lice-borne disease and that the close crowding together of impoverished peasants in squalid living conditions, which was inevitable as winter set in, provided ideal conditions for its spread. And plague, transmitted by fleas from infected rats, is equally a disease of poverty. . . .

The Chinese peasant has always suffered from a variety of parasitic worm infections, in part a reflection of poor living conditions, the moist

---

[1] Edward Schafer, *The Vermilion Bird*, pp. 133–4.
[2] Edward Schafer, *op. cit.*, p. 132.

soils and open channels inevitable under a system of irrigated agriculture and the universal use of human excreta to maintain soil fertility.[1] Schistosomiasis, an infection caused by a trematode which uses a fresh water snail as an intermediate host, is typical of central and South China. Surveys in the 1950s showed that some 10 million people were infected and a total of 100 million were in potential danger, that 'the situation was a burden on the country's economy and was affecting the labour situation'.[2] Hookworm, like filaria, is again a disease of the humid South and East, affecting between 50 and 100 million people. All these diseases, like the cholera which is transmitted by infected water, may be classed as environmental diseases in that they are associated with miserable living conditions, poor sanitation and a general ignorance of hygiene among the peasant masses. As such, they could be rapidly eliminated—and the biological environment transformed—once the causes of poverty and squalor were removed and the rudiments of hygiene were disseminated throughout the country by cadres, by medical technicians and by the health centres which, after 1958, became an essential element in the new agricultural system.

[1] On these, and on their agricultural setting, see G. Winfield, *China: The Land and the People.*
[2] Pierre Huard and Ming Wong, *Chinese Medicine* (London, 1968), p. 167.

CHAPTER 5

Under-development and Development in China

W E HAVE seen above how the nineteenth century was marked by an increasing pressure of peasant numbers on the Chinese earth and how the industrialisation which, by diversifying the economy, might have offered some relief was hamstrung by China's semi-colonial status. The century was therefore marked by declining rates of population growth (1779–1850 0·63 per cent annually, 1850–1953 0·3 per cent) and these reflected the impact of peasant rebellions and of disastrous floods and drought famines. The scale of these is indicated by the Taiping rebellion which may have cost 30 million lives, by the famine of 1877–78 which caused between 9 and 13 million deaths in the northern provinces, or that of 1928 which caused 3 million deaths in Shensi alone.

The collapse of the Manchu Empire and the establishment of the Republic in 1911 did little to cure the sickness of the Chinese State; the country was ravaged by warlordism and its economy warped and plundered by outside interests (based on the Treaty Ports) and their local collaborators. By the 1930s administrative corruption and incompetence, the ravages of civil war and of the Japanese invaders, the strangling hold of the landlord group on the peasant masses and of Chinese capitalists and outside interests on the truncated economy of the coast cities—all these combined to plunge the Chinese masses— one-quarter of mankind—into a nightmare existence of hunger and impoverishment. These were the days when the Chinese earth was littered with the bodies of those dead from cold and starvation, when the peasant who survived did so by eating roots and grass and selling the children he could not feed. The point reached by the great majority of China's people was the level of mere survival, a subhuman level far below anything ever experienced in the West in the darkest and hungriest days of the Great Depression. It is a level vividly portrayed by Hsü Chih-mo's description of a beggar:

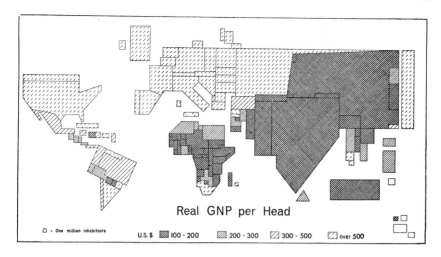

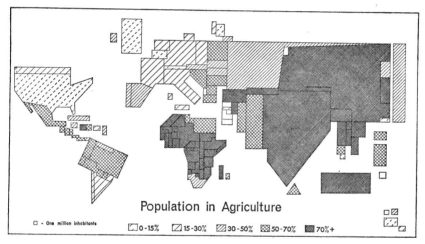

Figure 39. China in Relation to the Third World.

The Third World is that great bloc of 'under-developed' territories, including most of Latin America, Africa and Asia, characterised by disarticulated economies (see Figure 41), and by very low *per capita* GNPs and dominantly agrarian populations. Chinese development since 1949 increasingly sets her apart from these countries; because she confronted the same problems as they confront, her experience may be more relevant to them than that of the developed nations of the European capitalist or socialist blocs.

> '*I am but a pile of black shadows, trembling,*
> *Lying like a worm on the frontage road of humanity;*
> *I wish only a bit of the warmth of sympathy*
> *To shelter what's left of me, after repeated carving . . .*'[1]

by Wang Tu-ching's poem 'Sorrow of Shanghai':

[1] Kai-yu Hsu, *Twentieth Century Chinese Poetry: An Anthology* (New York 1963), p. xxvii.

*'Men's shadows huddle on the ground in front of the doors
—Ah, men? Are they human beings? It's but a cluster—
Squirming a little, and faintly groaning a little . . .'*[1]

or by Tsang K'o-chia's bitter poem on 'a society where man eats man'
entitled 'The Zero Degree of Life'.[2]

It is against the conditions of these days, this 'zero degree of life',
that we should attempt to measure the achievements of the present
government. Moreover, if we are to understand at all the present
situation in China we must go beyond *describing* the symptoms of a sick
society—the wealth of the few, the brutish quality of life of the masses,
starvation, men living as half-men, unemployed, illiterate, reduced to a
life which was no more than an animal struggle for survival whatever
the cost. We shall have to comment, even if briefly, on the causes of
this sickness—and in the policies of the People's Government we shall
see not only policies designed to cure the sickness but also designed to
wipe out its causes. . . .

GLOBAL PERSPECTIVES

In earlier sections we have sketched in, in the broadest of outlines, the
emergence of the Chinese people as a distinctive cultural group. We
have seen that their material civilisation rested on a distinctive base—
that of an intensive garden-style agriculture. We have seen how they
progressively occupied—and transformed—a highly differentiated
environment. Such an approach helps us to understand some of the
specific features of the 'Chinese experiment'. However, to attain a
fuller understanding of the changes of the last two decades in China
we have to broaden our viewpoint and see the Chinese experiment in its
global context—for the significance of this experiment is not confined
to China but is relevant to all those countries which face the same
problems as China faced in 1949, to the countries hopefully referred to
as 'the developing countries', the countries which French geographers[3]
group together as the 'Third World' (Figure 40).

Peter Worsley has pointed out[4] that while human society might be
objectively a single coherent unit it for long consisted *subjectively* of a
series of more or less isolated 'culture-worlds'—those of China and
India, of Black Africa and Meso-America, of the Middle East and the
Christian West. The unification of the globe as a single social system
was, he points out, the achievement of European imperialism. As the
critical date in this process of unification he selects 1885, the year of the
Congress of Berlin; this represents the high tide of imperialism and

[1] Kai-yu Hsu, *Twentieth Century Chinese Poetry*, p. 198.   [2] *Ibid.*, p. 290.
[3] See *Le 'Tiers-Monde': sous-développement et développement*, ed. Alfred Sauvy (Paris 1961).
[4] Peter Worsley, *The Third World* (London 1964), p. 10.

imperialism, he stresses, is not merely 'the highest stage of capitalism' but an entirely new phase in human social development: 'Imperialism brought about the consolidation of the world as a single social system.'[1] And, by a paradox, in the very act of achieving this unity it brought about a new and more significant division of the world into the rich nations and the poor nations, into a developed Euro-American core and an impoverished, because exploited, zone of tributary states; these include true colonial territories such as the African colonies of Europe and semi-colonial territories such as Thailand or China, Russia or the East European countries.   This simple duality created in the process of achieving unity was shattered by the emergence of Soviet Russia in 1917, then further shattered by the withdrawal of the Eastern European states from the world shaped by imperialism; the 'forced march' of this group of countries created a second—and socialist—group of developed and industrialised societies.   There thus emerged a pattern of three worlds, two dominantly industrial and, perhaps because of the over-riding importance of a common technology (and perhaps because they were both offshoots of the old Europe), tending to assimilate more and more common features,[2] the third remaining a dependent and satellite zone within which the two developed blocs manœuvred for position. By the early 1950s, however, Communist governments had come into power, along the eastern periphery of Eurasia, in China, North Korea and North Vietnam.   Today this East Asian sector of the Third World is dominated by a communism which is strongly 'national' in its character.   Its features are strongly influenced by the specific human geography of the area; its emergence has shattered the monolithic character of world communism—and its model of economic develop-ment offers to the rest of the Third World a 'Third Way', different from the model of the free enterprise system of the West or the 'classical' Communist system of the Soviet Union and her satellites.[3]   Let us glance at the problems facing the Third World countries.

The French sociologist Georges Balandier has commented:

The centres of power [i.e. the Euro-American bloc. KB] can main-tain their dynamism only by accentuating the 'depressed' character of the weaker zones to which they are related; this is evident within the limits of national frontiers where there emerge regions whose backwardness is increasing, and in the field of relationships between nations of unequal power.[4]

---

[1] *Ibid.*, p. 14.

[2] David Granick, *The Red Executive: A Study of the Organization Man in Russian Industry* (New York 1961).

[3] See for example, Gilbert Etienne, *La voie chinoise* (Paris 1962) and K. S. Karol, *China: The Other Communism* (London 1967).

[4] George Balandier, 'La mise en rapport des sociétés différentes' in *Le Tiers-Monde*, ed. A. Sauvy, p. 121; see also A. G. Frank, 'The Development of Underdevelopment' in *Monthly Review* (New York), September 1966, pp. 17–31 and Gunnar Myrdal, *Economic Theory and Underdeveloped Regions* (London 1963).

This 'depression' of the weaker zones (which, on a global scale, are represented by the countries of the Third World) is the result of the continuing exploitation by the advanced societies of the colonial or semi-colonial territories. It was this exploitation that reduced previously developed societies to the condition we now describe as 'underdeveloped'; it is on this exploitation that the well-being of the worker (including the left-wing worker) in the industrialised societies in part rests; it was this exploitation which created—and widened—the gap between the industrialised nations and the nations of the Third World.[1] And just how wide this gap is, is indicated in the table below:

TABLE 3

DISTRIBUTION OF WORLD WEALTH IN THE 'SIXTIES

	% of Population		% of World Income	
Developed countries	30·2		75·5	
Western bloc		19·7		58·7
European Communist bloc		10·5		16·8
Third World*	69·8		24·5	

* Including Asian Communist countries.

Source: Michel Bosquet in *Le Nouvel Observateur* (Paris), 21 Dec., 1966.

These statistics are conservative; according to an Italian source,[2] 85 per cent of the world's wealth is controlled by 15 per cent of the population and, failing any revolutionary change in the situation, the proportions twenty years from now are likely to be 90 per cent and 10 per cent respectively.

The processes of exploitation—or of economic development if we wish to use a less controversial language[3]—have thus created:

a relationship of subordination and dependence of the underdeveloped areas . . . with respect to those that are developed, a structure of superordination and subordination that is typical of a system of social stratification.[4]

This 'satellite'[5] quality of their economies and societies is the major distinguishing feature of the countries of the Third World and it is in this satellite status that most of their geographic problems are (and those of China were) rooted. Here attention may be focused on some of the major problems.

First, the countries of the Third World must confront not only a

[1] Pierre Jalée, *The Pillage of the Third World* (New York 1968).
[2] *L'Unita*, 15 February 1966.
[3] Though as Peter Worsley reminds us (*op. cit.*, p. 47) 'to utilize or valorize resources, colonialism has to exploit men'.
[4] Gustavo Lagos. *International Stratification and Underdeveloped Countries* (Chapel Hill, 1963), p. 6.
[5] B. F. Hoselitz, *Sociological Aspects of Economic Growth* (Glencoe, 1960), p. 93.

colonially-induced retardation of their technical progress but also the fact that their attempts at accelerated development are conditioned by the capitalist system within which, with few exceptions, they operate. Aid is conditional and must be devoted to building-up the free-enterprise sector of the economy; the development of this sector prejudices attempts to create a viable State sector, as in India; may, indeed, be diametrically opposed to the real interests of the emergent country. Moreover, the effectiveness and scale[1] of technical or financial aid can scarcely fail to be reduced by the White North's fear that massive development in the Third World:

> would in effect be creating a future world in which their own peoples would become progressively smaller minorities, and possess a progressively smaller proportion of the world's wealth and power.[2]

Secondly, coming relatively late on to the international scene, the emergent nations face the problem of establishing themselves within a structure of trading relations (and a system of prices) created and now controlled by the affluent nations. The discussion of price levels for primary produce at recent United Nations Conferences on world trade has revealed the extent of the cleavage between the views of the affluent nations and the proletarian nations; it emphasised the solidarity of the former wher t came to defence of their own interests; above all, it underlined the extent to which the possibilities of self-sustaining economic development in the majority of the Third World countries (with their dominantly export-oriented economies) are controlled by the affluent nations of the White North.

Thirdly, even though the conditions under which a breakthrough from stagnation and squalor to at least minimum levels of human decency and comfort can be achieved are becoming increasingly clear (these conditions include a high degree of central planning to allocate scarce resources, a restructuring of society including real and not token land reform and the massive mobilisation of the country's human and material resources to obviate a crippling dependence on external aid) this path can be adopted only at the risk of the hostility and probable active intervention of the West. The bitter opposition to China and other East Asian countries who have chosen this path; the economic blockade and armed invasion which aimed at preventing Cuba's restructuring of her society; the military intervention designed to prevent the Vietnamese from reshaping their society—all these illustrate the determination of the wealthy nations to maintain the countries of

---

[1] According to Mohammed Said Al-Attar this, between 1950 and 1961, averaged some 4,000 million US dollars yearly (the current American expenditure on the Vietnam War is over seven times as great); moreover of the aid, 45 per cent was returned to the donor countries in the shape of profits, interest and repayment of loans, 37 per cent was wiped out by deteriorating terms of trade, leaving some 28 per cent or slightly over 1,000 million US dollars for 'development.' *Développement et Civilisations* (Paris), June 1967, p. 22.

[2] F. Notestein in *Demographic Studies of Selected Areas of Rapid Growth* (New York 1944), p. 156.

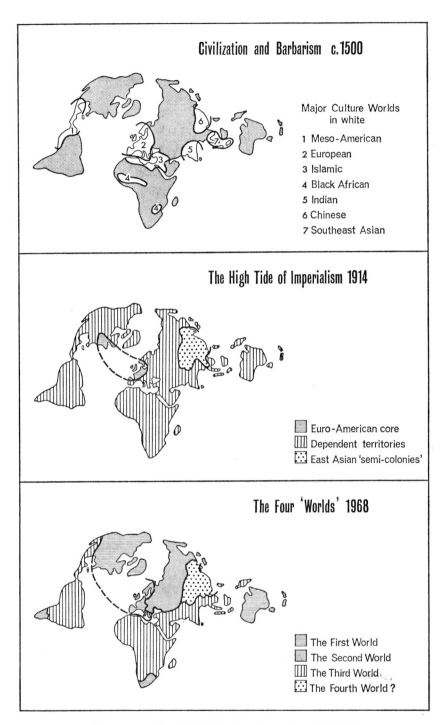

Figure 40. The Third World and the Fourth World.

Showing the major culture worlds at the beginning of the great period of European expansion; the high tide of imperialism, with most of the world constituting dependent territories of the developed Euro-American core, and with only China and Thailand preserving a tenuous independence as 'semi-colonies'; and the 'four worlds' of 1968 which have resulted from the breaking-away of the Soviet-bloc countries (beginning in 1917) and the subsequent split within the socialist camp, with China and the East Asian socialist countries (together with possibly Cuba) constituting the 'Fourth World'.

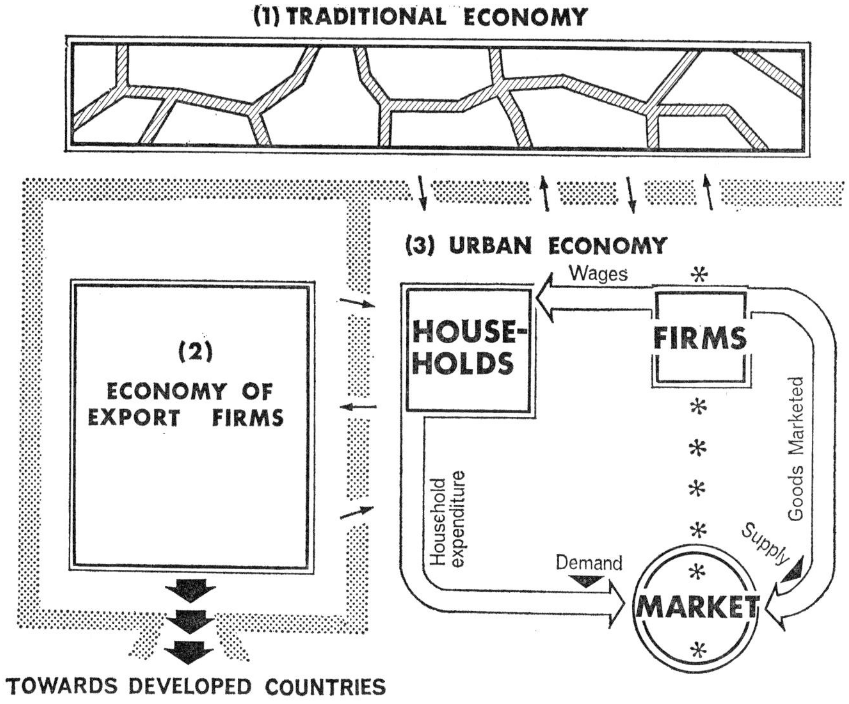

(1) TRADITIONAL ECONOMY

(3) URBAN ECONOMY

(2) ECONOMY OF EXPORT FIRMS

HOUSE-HOLDS

FIRMS

Wages

Household expenditure

Demand

Goods Marketed

Supply

MARKET

TOWARDS DEVELOPED COUNTRIES

Figure 41. Schema of a Typical Under-developed Economy (after J-M Albertini). Note the disarticulation of the economy into three major components: (1) the traditional agricultural sector, folded in on itself, lacking coherence and with few links with the rest of the economy: (2) the economy of the big firms, foreign or part foreign, and constituting an export-oriented enclave: (3) the urban sector, largely externally oriented but with limited links with (1), and (2) (e.g. flow of labour or funds), and with a 'decultured' way of life strongly influenced by foreign styles of life. The outlines of this general schema apply to pre-1939 China; the peasant economy was self-contained, isolated and seemingly unchanging, the Japanese economy in Manchukuo represented a typical enclave economy, and Shanghai and the other Treaty Ports were typical of most Third World urban sectors, dominated by foreigners or foreign-oriented groups (the comprador class) and only minimally integrated into the economic or social life of China.

Only by complete restructuring was it possible to begin to create a national economy and initiate nation-wide development. This involved the creation of a nation-wide infrastructure (transport network, educational and health services and political encadrement) and a planned economy characterised in the rural sector by the development of the people's communes, in the industrial sector by a dualistic structure comprising on one hand the (largely capital-intensive) State-controlled large enterprise, on the other by the smaller (largely labour-intensive) locally-controlled enterprise. It is to this dualistic pattern of development that the Chinese apply the phrase 'walking on two legs'.

the Third World in a subordinate—and exploitable—status. To repeat an earlier quotation: 'The centres of power . . . can maintain their dynamism only by accentuating the "depressed" character of the weaker zones to which they are related. . . .'

To these problems we may add the problems posed by low agricultural productivity and by population growth. Before the developments associated with the industrial revolution in Europe became possible the agricultural base on which the new economy would rest had to be assured. It appears that the level of productivity in Europe before the *agricultural* revolution was slightly above that of the Third World today but that in the forty to sixty years preceding the *industrial* revolution agricultural productivity increased by some 40 per cent.[1] This was of fundamental importance in assuring the food supplies of the emerging industrial population and, by expanding purchasing power, in providing a market for the developing industrial sector. Today, in much of Africa and Asia, levels of productivity are some 45 per cent below those of Europe on the eve of the industrial revolution; there seems a desire in many Third World countries to somehow skip the phase of expansion in the rural sector. The Chinese, as we shall see, came to recognise the importance of the agricultural base and, according to French estimates, their recent emphasis on agriculture has brought productivity to the level at which a sustained policy of industrial development is possible.[2] The relevance of this to other under-developed countries will be commented on later.

The demographic situation is important because it largely determines the choice of developmental models open to a backward country. The rate of population growth in Western Europe when this region began the process of economic 'take-off' seems to have been about 0·5 per cent annually; in the under-developed countries today it is around 2·2 per cent (China *c.* 2·0 per cent). Lack of agricultural development means that a stagnating agriculture has somehow to support increasing numbers of under-employed workers; on the other hand, to maintain the *status quo* in agricultural employment (assuming that four-fifths of the population is in agriculture and that the population growth is 2·6 per cent) would call for a 10 per cent annual increase in non-agricultural employment—an increase which would involve a rate of industrial growth virtually unrealisable. The Western tendency is to see the answer to this problem in terms of population control but this ignores the fact that the size of the younger age-groups in the under-

[1] Paul Bairoch, *Diagnostic de l'évolution économique du tiers-monde* (2nd edition, Paris 1968), p. 61. Bairoch uses in his analysis the concept of 'productivity units', a unit being a net production of one million calories per annum. With this as the basis he devises various 'thresholds', viz. the 'minimum physiological threshold', which makes adjustment for a non-agricultural sector and various types of loss, is a production of 3·8 units per active worker in agriculture; the level at which a country is potentially beyond the famine risk is 4·9 units. Europe's productivity on the eve of the Industrial Revolution he estimates at *c.* 7·0 units; China has today a productivity of 6·1 (or 5, depending on the data used), India of 4·1.

[2] Paul Bairoch, *op. cit.*, pp. 56, 213.

developed countries is now so large that even with smaller families the *absolute* growth rates will continue very high.   Population control thus offers no short-term solution and the only policy which offers any hope of absorbing a high growth rate of population and of providing a stable basis for industrialisation is an accelerated programme of agricultural development (see pp. 191–2, 285–6).

OLD WINE IN NEW BOTTLES: *Western and Soviet Development Models in China*

It is against this background that we have to set the development programme of China during the last two decades.

China, like all countries facing the problems of poverty and under-development, had three options open to it: it could follow the Western pattern of free-enterprise development, it could follow the Soviet model of development or, alternatively, it could pioneer a 'Third Way', drawing on the experience of other countries but modifying these models in the light of the social and economic conditions specific to East Asia.

Free enterprise, capitalist-style, development had no great appeal to the Chinese; the tradition of State participation in economic life has, as Joseph Needham has shown,[1] a very long history in the country and, in any case, many of China's problems—the festering slums of Shanghai, the exploitation of child labour and of the working class as a whole, the gap between a small 'elite' group and the great mass of the population, between the cities of the coast and the rural stagnation of the interior—had (or so it seemed to many) their roots in the free-enterprise system.   Moreover, the preconditions for the successful functioning of the free enterprise model of development—the existence of a class of trained entrepreneurs, the availability of capital derived from commerce or land, the existence of potential markets (internal or overseas) were largely lacking.   To these limitations must be added the low productivity of the traditional farming system (and in the West, it should be recalled, industrial development was not possible until agriculture had been rationalised and productivity greatly increased) and the sketchy character of the infrastructure in the shape of roads, railways, ports, educational facilities and the like.   China was faced, as are so many emergent countries, with the need to carry through simultaneously an agricultural revolution and an industrial revolution, and to create, virtually from zero, the whole technical and social infrastructure on which a modern nation depends.   And under such conditions, where the overwhelming need was to carry through in decades a social and economic transformation which had extended

[1] Joseph Needham, 'The Past in China's Present: A Cultural and Social Background for Contemporary China' in *Pacific Viewpoint* (Wellington), Vol. 4, Number 2, September 1963, pp. 124–5.

over centuries in Europe, the free enterprise system was irrelevant; as Robert Heilbroner observes:

> Every emergent nation, in beating its way to progress, must adopt a greater or lesser degree of centralised control over its economy, and the lower on the scale is its starting point, the greater does that degree of control tend to be.[1]

Given the pressure of time (constantly aggravated by the increase in population numbers) the free enterprise system seems incapable of handling problems as complex and deep-rooted as those faced by China or, indeed, any major developing country.

The second development model is that offered by the Soviet Union. This is more relevant to many under-developed countries than the Western development model, partly because the Soviet planners faced the same problem as many Third World countries, the problem of carrying through the modernisation of a backward peasant society, partly because of the speed at which this transformation has been carried through. The implementation of the policy has been on authoritarian lines and the 'forced march' towards an industrialised— and socialist—society has been characterised by an enforced austerity, by the deliberate holding-down of living levels while the resources needed to create a modern industry were accumulated and by the systematic exploitation of the peasant sector. The human cost of development has undoubtedly been high, though whether it was higher than the human cost of the West's much more protracted industrialisation is debatable. And, as Robert Heilbroner emphasises, to 'those below', to the impoverished masses, 'it may not be the *price* but the *promise* of rapid advance which exerts the most powerful sway'.[2]

The achievements of the Soviet Union in the technological field are, viewed from the standpoint of a Third World observer, undoubtedly impressive; from being a largely agrarian country, well behind the rest of Europe in its level of technology, the USSR has now reached the point at which she rivals the USA in the space race and she has achieved a level of economic growth well above that of the USA. Allen Dulles, sometime chief of the CIA and presumably therefore not disposed to exaggerate the Soviet achievement, has commented:

> Whereas Soviet gross national product was about 35 per cent of that of the United States in 1950 ... by 1962 it may be about 50 per cent of our own. This means that the Soviet economy has been growing and is expected to grow through 1962 at a rate roughly twice that of the economy of the United States.[3]

[1] Robert Heilbroner, *The Future as History* (New York 1959), p. 82.
[2] Robert Heilbroner, *op. cit.*, p. 89 (emphasis in the original).
[3] Quoted by Robert Heilbroner, *op. cit.*, p. 88.

To nations seeking a short cut out of poverty, seeking, too, to assert their national dignity (which has become indissolubly—and unfortunately—linked with the possession of modern iron and steel plants, skyscrapered capital cities and modern weaponry) these achievements had an obvious appeal; the negative side of the picture—the slow pace of growth in the agricultural sector, the increasing preoccupation of workers in a technologically-developed society with material possessions, the emergence of new and privileged classes—these were overlooked.

Other even more important factors were also overlooked: the fact that in 1917 the emergent USSR already possessed at least the beginnings of an industrial economy and an infrastructure (in the shape of communications, trained managers and the like) not matched in the majority of emergent countries today; the fact that the man/land ratio was much more favourable than in, say, the Asian countries; the fact that population growth was not pressing as heavily on resources as in much of the contemporary Third World. It is the limitations of both capitalism and of Soviet-style socialism that prompt J. L. Sampedro's remark:

It is clear that the more orthodox form of Marxism and the present capitalist ideology make equal claims as the only systems to emerge from social evolution, but circumstances do not favour the adoption of either and further variations can be expected.[1]

The Sinicised form of Marxism which has emerged in China as a response to the sociogeographic problems of East Asia and which bears the strong imprint of Mao Tse-tung's teachings[2] is an example of such a 'further variation'.[3] It is rooted in the fact that the classic dichotomy of bourgeoisie and proletariat, which has tended to dominate Western Marxist thought, has little relevance in China owing to the overwhelming importance of the peasantry; in Sampedro's words, 'the basic fabric of the model clearly differs from the Russian'.[4] And when, in 1949, peasant armies and a peasant-based revolution established in Peking the first Asian Communist government, the People's Government was able to extend to the whole of the country the techniques of social and economic development which the Communists had been testing out in their base regions in the Shansi-Shensi Border Region. The last two decades have been decades of trial and experiment, of bold advance on the economic front, followed by temporary retreat and renewed advance, of the continuous and at times painful working out of what Gilbert Etienne has called a 'Chinese Way'[5] in the field of

[1] José Luis Sampedro, *Decisive Forces in World Economics* (London 1967), p. 202.
[2] The 'Sinicisation of Marxism' is discussed by Stuart Schram in *The Political Thought of Mao Tse-tung* (New York and London 1963), pp. 111–15.
[3] Other variations include the communisms of North Korea and North Vietnam and the 'Buddhist socialisms' of Southeast Asia.
[4] José Luis Sampedro, *op. cit.*, p. 207.
[5] Gilbert Etienne, *La voie chinoise* (Paris 1962).

economic development.   And, though this is to anticipate later sections, one of the most striking features to emerge is that Chinese development planning appears concerned less with production as an end in itself than with the potential role of economic development in creating a 'new socialist man';[1] this preoccupation alone is sufficient to mark it off from both the Western and Soviet models of development.

Let us examine the broad lines of China's development since 1949. It will be convenient to distinguish two major phases: first, from 1949 to the 'Great Leap Forward' in 1958; secondly, the period from 1958 to the present day, a period marked by an increasing divergence from the Soviet model of development, a divergence emphasised by the so-called 'Sino-Soviet split', and, more recently, by the social, political and economic ferment of the Cultural Revolution.

THE CHINESE WAY

We can obviously, in the space available, do no more than emphasise some of the salient features of 'the Chinese Way'; these general remarks are intended to set into perspective the character of rural development, leaving to later sections the question of economic planning as it affects industry (see pp. 215–24).

The model is based on the doctrine of Marxism-Leninism and it mobilises all the energies and resources of the country to achieve a single goal—the wiping-out of poverty through the building of a socialist society.   It is a doctrine which incorporates a whole political, social and economic methodology and which became increasingly sophisticated as the result of Soviet experience during the inter-war and post-war years.   It was this model, which gave top priority to the rapid creation of a heavy industry sector, that provided the initial model for Chinese development; during the period of rehabilitation and during the First Five-Year Plan Chinese planners drew heavily on Soviet technical aid and on Soviet concepts of economic planning and, in the words of Alexander Eckstein:

> The First Five Year Plan, both in its conception and execution, bore all the earmarks of a Stalinist strategy of economic development with local adaptations.   High rates of saving and investment institutionalised through agricultural collectivisation; heavy emphasis on the development of those industries producing raw materials and investment goods; reliance on large-scale and capital-intensive technology in industry; and relative neglect of investment in agriculture, in consumer goods industries, and in social overhead represent the principal features of this Stalinist prescription.   It is a pattern of

---

[1] Charles Bettelheim, Jacques Charrière and Hélène Marchisio, *La construction du socialisme en Chine* (Paris 1965), esp. pp. 149–56, 166–8.   A convenient but brief summary is given by Charles Bettelheim in 'The Quality of China's Socialism' in *Monthly Review* (New York), June 1965.

economic development which is bound to produce rapid industrial expansion at the expense of agriculture, i.e. at the expense of agricultural productivity and of rural standards of living.[1]

This copying of the Soviet system was undoubtedly 'simpler and quicker than working out new forms and methods all at once'; nevertheless, the Soviet system was extravagant with educated man-power and, more important, its adoption meant a struggle 'against well-tried patterns of organisation more suited to the existing level of the economy'.[2]   The very originality of Chinese civilisation, the very size of the country (measured in terms of population) and the overwhelming preponderance of the peasant sector, the low level of development (which, measured in terms of industrial development or development of the infrastructure, was below that of the USSR in 1917)—all these things had to be conceded an increasing weight by Chinese planners. And, in any case, the relatively slow expansion of agricultural production was in danger of creating a bottleneck since agriculture supplied the bulk of the exports which made possible the import of capital goods as well as the raw materials for the domestic textile and food-processing industries.   The problem appeared increasingly as one of boosting the productivity of the rural sector without reducing the flow of investment towards (and thus the growth rate of) the industrial sector; in other words, the need was for the simultaneous development of both agriculture and industry, for a policy which would provide both bread and steel. . . .

The initial phases of the new strategy became evident during 1958; the Soviet emphasis on industry was retained but in all other respects there was a sharp break with the Soviet model of development.   The most striking feature of the new strategy—the mass mobilisation of the peasantry—was not new to China; it goes back far into Chinese history but what was novel was the scale of the mobilisation.   The aim of the mobilisation was to substitute abundant labour for scarce capital in the rural sector, indeed, *to turn labour into capital* in the shape of public works programmes (such as expansion of irrigation), agricultural intensification and the widespread development of small rural industries. Thus economic development became 'dualistic' with, on one hand, a modern, large-scale, capital-intensive sector and, on the other, a more or less traditional labour-intensive sector represented by agriculture and by the widely-diffused small industries; this is the policy termed by the Chinese 'walking on two legs'.   And with this mobilisation of labour and development of a 'dualistic' economy was associated a much greater degree of economic decentralisation which placed part at least

[1] Alexander Eckstein, *Communist China's Economic Growth and Foreign Trade* (New York and London 1966), pp. 29–30.   See also A. G. Ashbrook, Jr., 'Main Lines of Chinese Communist Economic Policy', in *An Economic Profile of Communist China* (Joint Economic Committee of U.S. Congress, Washington 1967), pp. 21–2.
[2] Audrey Donnithorne, *China's Economic System* (London and New York 1967), pp. 509–10.

of the statistical and planning machinery under local party control.[1] This last development was aimed at stimulating development from below through the medium of the 'mass line' which, it was believed, would make possible the release of the 'spontaneous initiative of the masses'.

Even a decade later, opinion is still divided as to the success of this strategy or the extent to which the difficulties of the early 'sixties were due to the policies of the 'Great Leap Forward' or to the severe climatic conditions during the years following 1958. American experts describe the developments of 1958 as 'a man-made disaster', adding, 'the formidable economic momentum built up during the first eight years of the Communist régime was lost. The Leap Forward had no redeeming economic feature. . . .'[2] Such an evaluation may have propaganda value but is no easier to sustain than the erroneous production figures released by the Chinese during the closing months of 1958. The material achievements of 1958—the expansion of irrigation, of energy output, of industrial production—cannot just be wished out of existence any more than the social and educational achievements of the commune system; we shall have occasion to comment on some of these later (see below, pp. 132-4). Moreover, Western preoccupation with purely economic criteria has tended to obscure the fact that, as Charles Bettelheim stresses:

> What the Chinese are trying to do is not only to develop their productive forces but, at the same time, to create a new man.[3]

Or, in the words of Barry M. Richman:

> The Chinese do not seem nearly as concerned as the Soviets about economic inefficiency at the factory level resulting from state planning and resource allocation problems. For the Chinese enterprise is not viewed as a purely economic unit where economic performance clearly takes priority. In fact, Chinese factories seem to pursue objectives pertaining to politics, education, and welfare as well as economic results. . . .[4]

The 'Great Leap Forward', no less than the current 'Cultural Revolution', must thus be evaluated not in Western terms, not in strictly economic terms, but in terms of the type of society the Chinese are striving to create. And the material achievements of twenty years of Chinese planning, coupled with the profound transformation of

---

[1] Alexander Eckstein, *op. cit.*, p. 36. For a fuller discussion see Gilbert Etienne, *La voie chinoise* (Paris 1962).

[2] A. G. Ashbrook, Jr., *op. cit.*, p. 32.

[3] Charles Bettelheim, 'The Quality of China's Socialism' in *Monthly Review* (New York), June 1965, pp. 48-9.

[4] Barry Richman, 'Capitalists and Managers in Communist China' in *Harvard Business Review*, Jan.-Feb. 1967, p. 61. Richman is Chairman of the International Business Program at the Graduate School of Business Administration, University of California, Los Angeles.

ways of thinking and behaving which has been accomplished, suggest a balance sheet much more positive than that put forward by American experts; indeed, the present writer has found it virtually impossible to believe that the China described in the United States *Economic Profile of Communist China* and the China he saw are one and the same country.

Gilbert Etienne[1] sees as the distinguishing feature of 1958—and in it a major explanation for the difficulties of the three subsequent years—a lack of moderation and an exaggeration in the application of fundamentally realistic principles; this represents a departure from the principles of moderation, of prudence, stressed as of fundamental importance in the project for the Second Five-Year Plan and by Mao Tse-tung in his work *On Contradictions* in 1957. By 1961 the Chinese had returned to the prudence and the sense of proportion of the earlier period; the economy went through a period of readjustment and consolidation and out of this emerged the present-day policy of 'agriculture as the base and industry as the leading factor'. And, looking at the most recent stage of Chinese development in the most general terms, five major features stand out as of critical importance.[2]

First, the flexibility of Chinese planning: the Chinese have been experimenting, have undoubtedly made mistakes, but have been able to rectify these mistakes; repeated Western claims that the economy was collapsing,[3] have been largely wishful thinking. Secondly, industrial development has been increasingly adapted, in its rhythm and its internal proportions, to the products offered by agriculture and the labour available once rural needs have been met; the concentration of this development in small and medium-sized cities avoids the creation of *megalopoli* (see below, pp. 216, 272, on the dispersion of development after 1957). Thirdly, in industrial development special weight is given to the needs of agriculture and heavy industry is called on to stimulate and sustain agricultural development. This means an emphasis on the production of agricultural equipment (electric pumps, tractors and the like), of fertilisers and insecticides. At the same time, development in agriculture, in the shape of the creation of an increasingly sizeable marketable surplus and in the freeing of labour, is essential for the development of the industrial sector. Fourthly, for the present, industrial progress will depend on increasing labour productivity; this explains the heavy emphasis given to renovation and technological improvement (which between 1960 and 1964 absorbed one-quarter of all industrial investment) and to quality. The aim appears to be to expand output without unduly increasing the scale

[1] Gilbert Etienne, *La voie chinoise* (Paris 1962), pp. 233–5.
[2] See Charles Bettelheim, 'Les cadres généraux de la planification chinoise' in *La construction du socialisme en Chine* by Charles Bettelheim, Jacques Charrière and Hélène Marchisio (Paris 1965), esp. pp. 37–40.
[3] See, for example, Joseph Alsop, 'On China's Descending Spiral' in *China Quarterly* (London), No. 11, July–September 1962, pp. 21–37.

I

of urban employment; more intensive rural development must therefore play the major role in absorbing population increase. Lastly, there is a basic contrast with the Soviet pattern of development; in this pattern, industry is the 'leading link' whereas in China this role is now allotted to agriculture. Some measure of year-to-year fluctuation in the output of the agricultural sector is, however, inevitable; in consequence, after the Second Five-Year Plan Chinese planning was largely on a year-to-year basis.

THE LESSONS OF THE CHINESE EXPERIMENT

We have stressed earlier that, because of their low level of agricultural productivity and the very high rate of population growth, the countries of the Third World face immeasurably greater difficulties than those faced by the developed countries (capitalist or socialist) when they began their 'economic take-off'. It is one of the strengths of the Chinese that they have recognised these difficulties. We may add also that they recognise implicitly that for the measurable future the great mass of their population will be peasants; Western 'spokesmen' and Western experts seem always to imply that the attainment of some semblance of Western levels of living is, as far as the 'developing nations' is concerned, just around the corner, an attitude which is, on the most charitable interpretation, unrealistic; interpreted less charitably, it is little better than 'sales talk' and hypocritical sales talk at that.[1]

The Chinese experiment has demonstrated the critical importance of the role of 'human investments', that the need is less for bulldozers or other costly equipment or for foreign aid than for a well-trained labour force with a strong sense of motivation; this has a relevance in many other parts of the Third World (e.g. India) which face problems of unemployment, under-employment and lagging economic growth. It has demonstrated the critical need to harmonise agricultural and industrial development and has shown that, until the agricultural base is firmly consolidated, rapid expansion of industry may prove premature; this is a lesson which might be heeded by India, by Pakistan or by many young African nations. It has shown the value of harmonising large-scale modern enterprises and smaller traditional enterprises, channelling scarce resources into the development of the former and relying on labour investment to expand the productivity of the latter; here again is a lesson which has relevance in both Southern Asia and Africa. It has shown, as Japan did under the Meiji dynasty, how rural taxation can take the place of foreign aid in getting economic develop-

[1] Paul Bairoch, op. sup. cit., p. 115, estimates the gap between the 'developing countries' and the West, 'expressed in terms of time and the rhythm of development of the West', at over 200 years for Africa and 150 years for non-communist Asia; at 1953–65 rates of growth, it will take 110 years for the Third World as a whole to reach the *present* level of development of the West. *Ibid.*, p. 204. See also Robert Heilbroner, *The Future as History*, esp. pp. 84–5.

ment under way; it may be that the Chinese level of taxation (or of forced saving) is too high but there is clearly a middle level between the Chinese figure (some 15 per cent) and the ridiculously low levels of India and Pakistan (*c.* 2 per cent).[1]

The basic patterns of economic planning the Chinese are evolving have a relevance not only to China but to much of the Third World; they are certainly more applicable to this latter group of countries than either the capitalism or the socialism of the developed world.   This does not mean they can be transplanted wholesale; as we have seen, the 'Chinese Way' has evolved out of *specifically* Chinese conditions and one of the strengths of Chinese planning lies precisely in this fact.   Moreover, Chinese development has been favoured by the existence of factors not always present in other emergent countries—the calibre of the leaders, the degree of disintegration in Kuomintang China, the dedication and drive of the masses, the high densities of rural population and the immensely long peasant tradition—all these, to cite but a few examples, gave China an incontestable advantage.   Adoption of the 'Chinese Way' *in toto* is unlikely—but many of the development techniques such as labour investment, 'walking on two legs', decentralisation of decision-making, above all, the psychological drive designed to show the peasant that he can initiate development himself, that he need not limp along supported by the twin crutches of outside expertise and outside aid, all these have a direct applicability to the majority of Third World countries.   And, as the limited achievements of their present development policies become evident, an increasing number of Third World countries may be drawn towards the lessons of the Chinese experiment, interpreting these lessons in the light of their own historical, geographical and social heritage. . . .

Meanwhile, it is within the framework, the always elastic framework, of the concepts sketched above that the 750 million people of China are carrying out their transformation of the Chinese earth.

[1] Gilbert Etienne, *op. sup. cit.*, pp. 273–4.

CHAPTER 6

The Rise of the People's Communes

BACKGROUND

THE BACKGROUND necessary to understand the processes of change in the countryside since the People's Government assumed power in 1949 will be found in almost any novel set in Old China. For a personal account, however, we must turn to Jan Myrdal's *Report from a Chinese Village*; in this volume the villagers describe, in a language as sparse and as bare as the Shensi landscape in which they live, what the Chinese Revolution meant at the grassroots level. And in the accounts of the older peasants we get a vivid picture of 'the point of departure'. The beginning of Fu Hai-tsao's account of his life, for example:

> We came to Yenan from Hengshan when I was five. That was during the great famine of 1928. We had been thrown out. My father brought the family with him here. Father starved to death the next year. We went about begging in 1929. We had nothing to eat. Father went to Chaochuan to gather firewood and beg food, but he didn't get any. He was carrying elm leaves and firewood when he fell by the roadside. . . . He was lying on his face and was dead. The elm leaves and the firewood were still there beside him. No one had touched a thing. The elm leaves were for us to eat. He wasn't ill; he had just starved to death. . . . That is my earliest memory; of always being hungry, and of Father lying there dead in the road.[1]

Or the episodes in the life of Tu Fang-lan, now a woman of fifty-six:

> . . . some years we were given to eat what the animals had. We even had grass to eat. I was with child eight times in that marriage. Four died. The first three were boys. They survived. The fourth

[1] Jan Myrdal, *Report from a Chinese Village* (London 1965), p. 135.

and fifth were boys too. They fell ill when they were four and died. . . . The sixth child survived. The seventh and eighth were miscarriages.[1]

Or the memories of Li Yiu-hua:

1928–9 was a period of famine. The 1928 harvest was bad and, in the spring of 1929, the slave dealers began coming to the villages of northern Shensi. They were out to buy children, and many were sold then. . . . The boys went to childless families which wanted their name to continue, and the girls were sold as brides or to the towns. When girls were sold, the slave dealers just took them away, and we did not know what happened after that. Most were never heard from again. There was just silence.[2]

These stories, multiplied by the tens of millions, give us some understanding of what it was like to live in Old China, of the living which was a kind of dying. . . . They underline the marginal quality of life for the rural masses, of life balanced always on the knife edge of starvation; they focus attention on the poverty which was the product of an undiversified and highly seasonal agricultural system with its inevitable under-employment or unemployment; they emphasise the power of the landlord group which, through its control of much of the country's arable land, possessed the power of life and death over the peasant. Above all, such fragments of autobiography illustrate the vulnerability of the individual peasant family confronted by natural disasters such as drought or flood. And unless we understand this marginal and precarious quality of existence we will find ourselves unable to understand the transformation of the rural scene since 1949, above all, the complete restructuring of rural society which has taken place and the preoccupation of the new society with peasant welfare and peasant security.

ENVIRONMENTAL PROBLEMS

The Chinese earth, even that limited portion in the humid or subhumid area we know as 'Agricultural China', offers no easy home to man; as Robert Payne puts it:

War and the terror of war have left their mark on the Chinese race, but even more merciless than war has been the poverty of the people. They will not speak about it often in their poems, but it is always there. The threat of starvation is eternally real in this country, where floods and barren fields are as common as thieving officials, where life must be fought for and every grain of rice is precious. . . . And because there was poverty, because death stood before them eternally like a threadbare ghost, they contrived all the more to

[1] *Ibid.*, p. 208.　　[2] *Ibid.*, pp. 335–6.

enjoy the sparse beauty of life, and sharpened their senses until a single peach blossom could shine with the glory of a king's ransom.[1]

The geographic 'roots' of such an attitude have been commented on above.   The greater part of the North China Plain and the Loess Plateau has a subhumid climate; rainfall totals are low and the year-to-year variability is very high.   In consequence, the history of the area is patterned with droughts of varying intensity, followed by famines which killed off millions by starvation; the 1878–9 famine in the loess region resulted in between 9 and 13 million deaths, while that of 1928 caused 3 million deaths in Shensi alone.   If deficiency of water caused death or, at the very least, a poverty-stricken and marginal existence in the north, central and south China were cursed by an equally unpredictable excess leading to widespread and protracted flooding.   In the south this excessive rainfall was often due to the tropical cyclones of summer and late autumn and when these coincided with high spring tides (as in mid-June 1959, when 578 mm. fell in the Canton region between 11 and 14 June) major flooding became inevitable.   And in the most recent centuries of Chinese history there is evidence that the deforestation of the hill country of south and central China aggravated the flood menace for it led to more rapid runoff and to erosion which provided the silt and mud which built up the beds of rivers such as the Hwang high above the level of the surrounding lowlands.

A second major group of factors contributing to the poverty of rural China are those which are biological; this includes both the animal and insect pests and the rich complex of diseases which flourish in a tropical or subtropical environment.   These include not only the diseases born of poverty (and which contribute to perpetuating poverty) such as tuberculosis, dysentery or typhus but also the 'five plagues' as the Chinese term them: hookworm, filariasis, kala-azar, malaria and schistosomiasis.   This latter group of diseases was particularly prevalent in the warm and humid South; five per cent of China's population (some 25 million people) were afflicted by malaria and some 10 million were victims of schistosomiasis. Both the poverty-born diseases and the 'tropical' diseases dragged down the efficiency of the peasant who was caught in a vicious circle in which disease led to undernourishment and undernourishment made its victims yet more vulnerable to disease.

Yet it cannot be overemphasised that this vulnerability to disease and to calamities such as drought or flood is not a constant, that it varies according to the degree of organisation, the technology and the resources of the human groups concerned; men, in short, are not only unequal in life but are also unequal in death, in the way in which they

[1] *The White Pony* (Mentor, New York 1960), p. xi.   Payne is writing of pre-Revolutionary China.

confront the threat of death. Pierre Gourou comments that it is virtually impossible to establish direct links between the physical and human elements in any environment and goes on: '[these links] exist, but they come about through the medium of civilisation, that distorting prism which, in accordance with the laws peculiar to each civilisation, transmits the influence of the physical environment to the human elements of a landscape.'[1] If the nature of the prism is changed, if a people's civilisation undergoes a transformation, then the character of the relationship between a society and its physical environment is changed too; the significance of the various elements in the environment may undergo a profound alteration. And this, indeed, is what has happened in China since 1949.

The outstanding elements of Chinese rural civilisation in 1949 were, first, the isolation and the helplessness of the individual peasant family; secondly, the monopolisation of land and other productive resources by a corrupt and rapacious landlord group. These were part of the 'prism' through which the influence of the environment impinged on the peasant community; together, they magnified the impact of natural calamities, for each flood or drought presented the individual family with problems that were insuperable in the context of the old society and if the family survived it was only to find itself yet deeper in debt to the landlord group. To this situation there was one solution and one solution only and that solution was propounded and then tested out in the Shansi-Shensi Border Region by the CCP; the solution was a complete restructuring of rural society through land reform and the creation of new forms of peasant organisation which would overcome the powerlessness of the individual peasant family. And these things could not be done without a drastic agrarian reform.

AGRARIAN REFORM: Its Varieties and the Chinese Model

The phrase 'land reform' covers a wide variety of sins of omission and commission; to avoid an oversimplified picture and to put the Chinese agrarian reform into some sort of perspective it is important to sketch in something of this variety.

In discussing the topic Andrew Gunder Frank[2] suggests that land reform is 'not so much an administrative, or even an economic, as it is an essentially political process'. On this basis of land reform as a *political* process, he distinguishes three major types of 'land reform'. First, there is the land reform without any significant political change, the type of 'land reform' carried through by conservatives. It is initiated by legislatures often controlled by the landowners themselves; it may integrate

---

[1] Pierre Gourou, 'Notes on China's Unused Uplands' in *Pacific Affairs*, September 1948, p. 237.
[2] 'The Varieties of Land Reform,' *Monthly Review* (New York), April 1963, pp. 656–62. The general discussion here draws extensively on Frank's analysis.

voluntary donations of land by the church or the landowners themselves. Every protection is afforded to the landowning groups whose
basis of power remains intact, and it is the last resort of the landowners
in their attempt to retain this power. Such reforms are typified by the
'land reforms' carried out by the Diem régime in South Vietnam and by
the abortive attempts at reform in Old China; such programmes are
usually fraudulent (as in South Vietnam) or mere paper exercises (as in
pre-1949 China). The second type of reform proposes to integrate
the peasantry into the existing socio-political community of the nation
by a process which mobilises all the progressive forces against the
conservatives but leaves the basis of their power intact. The reform is
spread out over a relatively long period—a decade or so—and attempts
to channel aid into the rural areas so as to benefit the rural population
as a whole and not merely the medium or large-scale landowners. This
type of reform presents two problems: first, by leaving intact the
economic and political power of the conservative or bourgeois group,
opposition to, slowing down of, or sabotage of, the whole reform
programme becomes a possibility. Secondly, with reform spread out
over a long period, there emerges the possibility that new groups will
acquire a vested interest in maintaining their newly-acquired advantages, allying themselves with conservative groups to oppose the
extension of the benefits *they* had gained to yet other groups. The drag
on the extension of agrarian reform programmes exerted by these
'new conservatives' was a feature of the agrarian history of Eastern
Europe in the inter-war years; it appears in a classic form in Mexico.
The third type of reform, and the only one to have achieved any
considerable measure of success, is that in which the entire structure of
society was changed at the same time as the land reform was carried
through. The change was effected by the mobilisation of the peasants
themselves and the ability of conservative groups to stage a come-back
was eliminated by depriving these groups of all effective power. This
has been the pattern of agrarian reform in Cuba and in China and the
other Asian socialist states. No reform can at one stroke eliminate the
reactionary or bourgeois attitudes whose roots may go deep into the
earlier history of a peasant society and that such attitudes may persist
as a problem even in a socialist society is indicated by the current (1966)
'cultural revolution' in China; nevertheless, a drastic and thorough-
going reform of the Chinese type does mean that the struggle to consolidate and perfect the new society is confined to a relatively narrow
front and is in the nature of a 'clearing-up of the dust' left behind from
an earlier period.

The development of the agrarian situation in China was strongly
influenced by Mao Tse-tung's short study *Analysis of the Classes in
Chinese Society*; this dates from 1926 and is concerned with the two
questions: 'Who are our enemies? Who are our friends?', in other

words, with evaluating the revolutionary potential of the various classes in pre-revolutionary China; the rural aspects of this study were carried further by Mao's *Investigation of the Peasant Movement in Hunan,* completed a year later. These studies made it possible for the CCP to formulate an agrarian policy that was both realistic and flexible. The role of the poor peasants is fundamental: 'Without the poor peasants there would be no revolution. To deny their role is to deny the

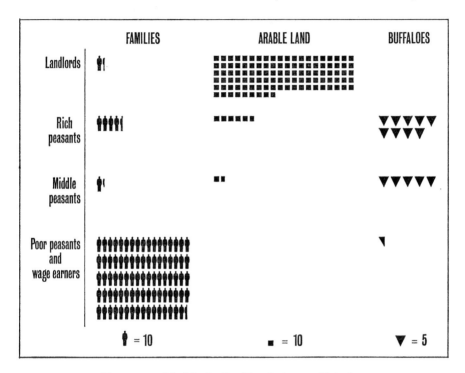

Figure 42. Model of a Pre-Revolutionary Situation.

Cartogram illustrating the extremes of inequality in the means of production (land, work-animals) in a north Kiangsu community. This type of concentration of the means of production in the hands of a very small group of landlords and the desperate quality of the life of the great mass of the landless peasants was to provide an important motive force in the Chinese Revolution. (Arable area in acres)

revolution';[1] at the same time careful analysis of the economic pressures on other groups in peasant society provided a basis for Communist policy to each group and from this emerged 'The Class-line of Agricultural Co-operation', that of 'resolutely relying on the poor peasants and firmly uniting with the middle peasants'. Chinese agrarian policies thus rested on a basis of careful analysis which was largely lacking in the USSR when it carried out *its* land reform; the Chinese

[1] *Selected Works of Mao Tse-tung* (Peking 1964), Vol. 1, p. 33.

policy was, in consequence, not only less ruthless and heavy-handed but also (and perhaps because of its sociological realism) more successful. To these general remarks we may add the fact that, when the Communists came to power in 1949, they had had many years' experience of handling peasant problems, experience acquired during the implementation of agrarian reform in their base region in Shansi-Shensi.

Except in this region, where reform of rural structures had followed the establishment of a Communist administration in the late 'twenties, and in the regions inhabited by national minority groups a complete reform of the agrarian system was carried out between 1949 and 1952. The landlord group was dispossessed and in many cases physically eliminated; the numbers killed are hard to establish, totals ranging from the 'countless millions' of the Western press to the 800,000 of Edgar Faure and the 50,000 of C. P. Fitzgerald (against this we may set the 12,000 workers killed in the space of three weeks of 1946 by Chiang in Shanghai alone or the 100,000 'communist sympathisers' slaughtered indiscriminately in the single province of Kiangsi). The first stage of the reform was to give the land to the tiller and this was done, not by simple legislation, but by a process of class struggle, guided in part by cadres who went to the villages, as Fitzgerald puts it, 'to instruct people in what were now their rights, to arouse them to demand land reform as their due, to denounce their landlords and if these had been oppressive, to demand their public trial'.[1] The peasants were thus encouraged to participate in the implementation of the land reform and this gave them a heightened political awareness and involved them in the policies of the CCP as active agents who struggled, *in co-operation with the government*, against the reactionary groups who supported the KMT. But, given the land pressure in Old China and given the scarcity or unequal distribution of means of production (including draught animals and farm tools), a simple policy of 'Land to the tiller' was only the first step in what was to be a continuous process of experimentation, advance and consolidation. For the initial phase of land reform resulted in a situation in which some peasants had adequate land, others draught animals, and yet others farm tools such as ploughs which could not be effectively utilised for lack of either land or animals. The development of the mutual aid team, grouping between six and fifteen households, pooling labour, animals and farm tools, but retaining individual ownership of the land, was a logical answer to this situation; such teams were initially seasonal and the individual peasants retained ownership of land, animals and tools. The development did, however, come up against one basic contradiction, the contradiction between the collective nature of work and the individual ownership of the means of production; this showed itself in the demand of each peasant that *his* land should be ploughed first or *his* crop harvested first. The next step was therefore

[1] C. P. Fitzgerald, *Floodtide in China* (London 1958), p. 103.

to move to what the Chinese term 'the Lower Stage' of agricultural co-operation; in this the administration directs the planned utilisation of the individual plots of land and, after the needs for taxes, welfare and accumulation had been met, production was shared on the basis of the labour and the land furnished by each member. Centralised direction of agriculture by the co-operative became possible, production expanded and with this the amount distributed to the peasant and the amount set aside for equipment and improvement could be increased, demonstrating clearly to the peasants the advantages of this next step towards collectivisation.

This expansion of production, however, revealed a new set of contradictions. In part, the expansion of production was made possible by more effective water control; this depended on irrigation ditches and pumping stations built by the collective but sited on individually-owned land. Moreover, mechanisation was becoming feasible in some areas and the boundaries of the individual peasant plot presented major problems to efficient use of machinery. A third problem lay in the system of remuneration, for the income of an individual or a family group who contributed much labour but had little land tended to be less than that received by a family or individual contributing much land but relatively less labour; such a state of affairs seemed an undesirable hang-over from the old system. It was an effort to resolve these contradictions that the advanced co-operatives came into being; in them, to quote C. P. Fitzgerald: 'All land is pooled; all boundaries are removed, all visible record of separate ownership or individual holdings disappears. The owners, now members, retain title to an equal share in the co-operative's joint property, but not a share proportionate to the smaller or greater holding they have pooled in the new organisation.'[1] And by substituting payment on the basis of work-days or work-points the link between level of living and ownership of land was finally broken. The new units of organisation, which had become the norm by 1957, grouped together an average of 168 households, as against 32 in the lower form of co-operative; each of these new units consisted of some five original co-operatives which constituted sub-units or 'brigades', though in some areas this phase was by-passed. By 1957 the greater part of China's rural population had been organised into some 740,000 advanced co-operatives.

As a result of this step-by-step process of change, with each advance followed by a period of consolidation and preparation for the next stage, the Chinese peasant, so conservative and individualistic according to some writers, 'became socialist without knowing'. Whether at any stage the CCP faced local peasant resistance, what were the scale and the intensity of such resistance—these things are virtually impossible to ascertain. René Dumont sees in the apparent stagnation of

[1] C. P. Fitzgerald, op. cit., p. 107.

agricultural production in 1957 an indication of peasant opposition and sees the rapidity of the transition to the next stage—that of the people's commune—as in part a response to this stagnation.   This, however, is merely a hypothesis and yet to be demonstrated false or true.   What is more certain is that an immense programme of political education, of self-education within the peasant masses, was preparing the way for yet a further remoulding of Chinese rural society, the institution of the commune.

'ONE STEP IN A TEN THOUSAND LEAGUE MARCH'

At this point we may pause and attempt to assess the specific characteristics and the achievements of this initial eight years of development in the Chinese countryside; they are summarised by Isabel and David Crook in their study *Revolution in a Chinese Village* which describes how a backward village was built into 'a revolutionary bastion'.

They stress that while local conditions varied, the central task—the overthrowing of feudalism—remained the same and so, too, did the main steps in this process.   These steps were the reduction of rent and interest which weakened the economic power of the landlord and rich peasant groups; the land reform which broke their political and economic power; and the gradual and pervasive process of reshaping social customs and ideology in a peasant society of some half a billion members.   Behind all these changes 'the mass line'—that everything is for the masses, that the CCP assumes full responsibility to the masses, that the masses alone can achieve their own real emancipation, and that one must learn from the masses before one can educate or lead them —remained the basic guiding principle.

The experience of the CCP in the Northwest Border region had given the Chinese authorities an extensive and first-hand awareness of the problems and the techniques of land reform and this was incorporated in the Agrarian Law promulgated in 1950 by the People's Government.   It also emphasised to them the extent to which success in any programme of rural reconstruction was dependent upon education, and especially political education, of the peasant masses.   This process of education was, moreover, a two-fold one, for in the process of carrying it through the cadres themselves gained a sharper awareness of the realities of peasant life; they learned from the peasant masses, gained an understanding of their fears and their aspirations and of the problems specific to the region in which they worked and by their dedication earned the respect of the local people, something that was essential if the transformation of rural society were to continue.

The process of political education in the countryside has been described by Liu Shao-chi:

In carrying out the land reform our Party did not take the simple and easy way of merely relying on administrative decrees and of 'bestowing' land on the peasants. For three solid years after the establishment of the People's Republic of China, we applied ourselves to awakening the class consciousness of the peasants. . . . We consider the time spent was absolutely necessary. Because we had used such a method the peasant masses stood up on their own feet, got themselves organised, closely followed the lead of the Communist Party and the People's Government, and took the reins of government and the armed forces in the villages firmly into their hands. . . . The broad masses of the awakened peasants held that exploitation, whether by landlords or by rich peasants, was a shameful thing. Conditions were thus created which were favourable to the subsequent socialist transformation of agriculture and helped shorten to a great extent the time needed to bring about agricultural co-operation.[1]

Citing this, the Crooks stress that the socialist transformation of agriculture and other aspects of economic development in China are not merely technological processes:

They are both technological and ideological. And the collective outlook on life and way of work associated with both agriculture and industry in China today have roots in the relations of mutual aid forged in the villages.[2]

Indeed, we are making a fundamental error which will prevent us from attaining any real understanding of the last decade of development in the Chinese countryside if we persist in regarding the whole process of agricultural change as a purely material, technological, process. It is much more than that; in the words of an experienced and perceptive French observer:

The essential factor is man and his improvement. No system of remuneration, however good, can replace education. This priority given to Man is in our opinion the key to the success of the communes.[3]

And, if we may anticipate somewhat, the changes which are today taking place in the Chinese countryside, the controversy and the animation which marks the so-called 'Cultural Revolution', the remodelling of the education system so that study and practice are integrated, the diversification of the commune's activities in the various sectors of life, all these reflect this preoccupation with 'man and his improvement' and with the drive to create a new 'socialist man'.

[1] Speaking to the *Eighth National Congress of the CCP, 1956*, and quoted by Crook, *op. cit.*, pp. 174–5.
[2] Crook, *op. cit.*, p. 175.
[3] Hélène Marchisio in C. Bettelheim, *La construction du socialisme en Chine* (Paris 1965), p. 99.

THE PEOPLE'S COMMUNE: Emergence and Evolution

René Dumont, as noted above, sees in the rapid transition from the advanced co-operative to the people's commune an attempt by the Chinese to overcome what he describes as the semi-stagnation of Chinese agriculture in 1957; perhaps more convincing is the argument that the rise of the commune is a manifestation of the chain-reaction quality of institutional and environmental change which has been a feature of Chinese development since 1949. Social change, and notably land reform, made possible the shaping of a new environment but at the same time the very process of re-modelling the environment itself stimulated further institutional change. As one Chinese writer put it at the time: 'As men transformed nature their own way of thinking was transformed too.'[1] There emerged, as Hélène Marchisio has shown, a whole series of contradictions: contradictions *between* co-operatives in the carrying out of major schemes of water conservancy and irrigation; contradictions *within* the co-operatives between the unit for accounting and the unit of production; contradictions between the economic unit and the administrative unit.[2] These contradictions were largely solved by the creation of the people's communes.

By late 1958 the 174,000 co-operatives had been merged into 26,000 communes. The average commune thus consisted of some six to seven advanced co-operatives; its population was of the order of 20,000 people, as compared with somewhat under 3,000 in the average advanced co-operative. Its area was usually co-extensive with that of the county or *hsiang*; under these conditions the contradiction between the economic unit and the administrative unit disappeared, for the administration of county and commune could be merged. Even more important, however, was the fact that these bigger units, with bigger resources of capital and manpower and often taking in the whole of a small river basin or catchment area, were able to confront far more effectively than the individual co-operative the more ambitious schemes of water conservation, irrigation or afforestation which were clearly the next tasks which the peasant masses had to undertake if they wished to create a solid basis for rural development. The people's commune was thus born in the countryside, from the experience of the peasant masses; its origin is to be sought in the determination of these masses to transform their environment so that the old spectres of insecurity and famine could be banished. It did not, as some commentators have suggested, represent an arbitrary form of economic and social organisation imposed on an uncooperative peasantry by some edict from Peking. The writer's own observations in China in the autumn of 1958 left him in little doubt as to the 'grassroots' origin of the

---

[1] Yang Min in *Peking Review*, 21 October 1958, p. 12.
[2] Marchisio, *loc. sup. cit.*, p. 99.

commune and, indeed, it is only in the light of this 'grassroots' origin of the system that its enthusiastic adoption by the peasants through the length and breadth of China can be appreciated.   And it may be added that any policy of *imposing* a new form of agricultural organisation in the rural areas would be completely at variance with Chinese agrarian tactics as expounded by Liu Shao-chi in the passage cited above.

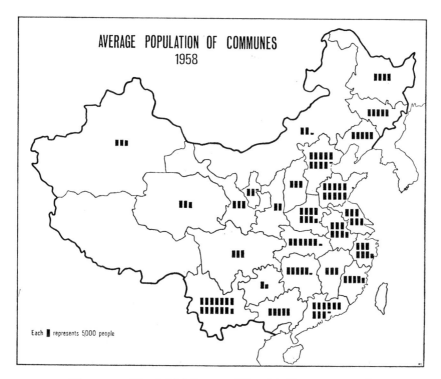

AVERAGE POPULATION OF COMMUNES
1958

Each ▮ represents 5,000 people

Figure 43.   The Initial Pattern of People's Communes, 1958.
Showing the average population, by province, of the original communes.   The provinces with the largest communes (average population over 40,000) were those of the North China Plain and the subtropical and tropical South.   Average populations were much smaller in the climatically marginal areas of the Northwest (Kansu 16,000, Shensi 11,000, Sinkiang A.R. 14,000). The very high figure for Yunnan appears to result from the fact that the very sizeable groups of tribal peoples in this province were not organized into communes at this date; their numbers thus inflate the average for the province.
The early 'sixties saw a subdivision of many communes into smaller units.   This trebled the number of communes so that there are today some 78,000 in the whole of China; on this see pp. 130. (Commune totals from Chiao-min Hsieh, 1967.)

Viewed in a narrow economic perspective the commune represents a means of mobilising the enormous latent productivity represented by the under-employed masses of rural China.   The huge population of China, long regarded as a major economic burden, has become 'an

enormous source of capital accumulation [devoting] part of its labour
. . . to the increase of the productive potential of the country'.[1] The
possibilities of mobilising this immense potential in Monsoon Asia as a
whole was recognised by René Dumont as far back as 1954; his words
have a prophetic quality: the main cause of Asia's backwardness was,
he wrote:

> The inefficient employment of the labour force. . . .   Even without
> modern equipment, the resumption of certain types of work by the
> peasants during the seasons of underemployment on the land would
> represent a net gain and a productive exploitation of a natural source
> of wealth.[2]

The tapping of this reservoir of under-employed labour presented
major problems however.   Much was of a seasonal character yet this
seasonal variation did not mean that over the slack period fewer men
were working but rather that most of them were working fewer hours
per day.   The surplus labour, under these conditions, could not
readily be 'invested' in capital formation.   Before this labour surplus
could be so utilised, a radical reshaping of the institutional pattern was
essential.   It is in this context that the development of the co-operative
and above all of the commune was so important for these made possible
the beginning of a rational use of labour.   Farm work could be
attended to by fewer workers, working full time, and with some
specialisation, and the labour of the remainder was made available, if
only seasonally, for long-term improvements such as irrigation,
terracing or the creation of rural industries, all of which represented
increases in the productive potential of the countryside.   By 1958 this
under-employment had been virtually wiped out and in parts of China
there was the paradoxical situation of a supposedly 'over-populated'
countryside suffering from a labour shortage and seeking a solution to
this through mechanisation and electrification.[3]

With the increase in the size of the peasant collective following the
emergence of the commune, a policy of 'turning labour into capital'
by seasonal 'investment' in public works projects such as dams
and irrigation systems or in the beginnings of rural industrialisation
became a possibility.   Moeover, the greater area of the new units
made possible the physical planning and the implementation of those
projects such as flood control which could not be tackled successfully
within the restricted area of the co-operative.   It would, however, be
misleading to lay the stress solely on the *economic* advantages of the com-

---

[1] C. Bettelheim in L. Huberman and P. Sweezy, *China Shakes the World Again* (New York 1959), p. 20.

[2] René Dumont, *Types of Rural Economy* (English translation, London 1957), pp. 162–3.

[3] In this context C. Bettelheim comments that 'in spite of the existence of an apparent labour surplus the maximum number of workers able to move to the cities, without compromising agricultural production . . . is in the last resort much smaller than might at first have appeared'. *La construction du socialisme en Chine*, p. 36.

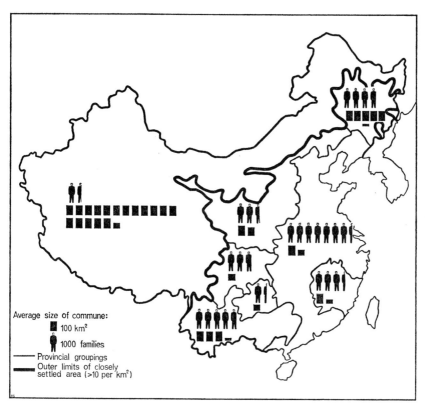

Figure 44. Contrasts in Size of Communes (by regional groupings), 1958.
Illustrating contrast between communes of the arid and subarid West (average area, 1,741 km.², with an average population of 1,613 families) and those of Eastern or Agricultural China (average area 155 km.², with an average population of 2,909 families). In Eastern China contrasts in size and population between communes of the lowland and basin zone stretching from Peking to Canton and those of the western hills and plateaux or the microthermal regions of the Northeast. (Figures from G. W. Skinner.)

mune; the commune, as has been suggested, is only a means to an end and that end is the increase in peasant well-being and the gradual transition to 'a new type of socialist man'. Only if we keep clearly in our mind the fact that it integrates the totality of elements making up peasant life—production, welfare, education, administration and defence—can we understand the scale of the changes which transformed an almost atomistic structure of isolated peasant communities into the tightly-knit interdependent complex of 'cells' which is Chinese rural society today. For, in addition to providing the framework within which the cadres and peasant masses can apply improved farming techniques and lay the foundations of a widely-dispersed rural industry, it is also a social unit organising welfare and education services. Its

K

network of hospitals and health centres make possible a frontal attack on disease, inculcate the basic elements of hygiene and are playing a critical role in that 'medical revolution' whose impact is to be seen in sharply declining child mortality rates, a longer expectation of life and the elimination of that dragging burden of ill-health which was a major factor in limiting peasant productivity in the past.   Its schools and its technical institutes, rudimentary perhaps to the eyes of an observer coming from an affluent society, are making possible that marriage of modern science and traditional peasant wisdom, of theory and practical work, which is one of China's most original and important contributions to the elimination of rural under-development, while its machine shops and construction teams provide a channel through which the techniques of modern industry can be disseminated deep into the countryside.   And, last but not least, its laundries and communal grain mills and provision of basic services such as water supply or electricity release tens of millions of women from many of the back-breaking chores of peasant existence so that, emancipated, they can participate along with their men-folk in productive work in field or factory.

These very real social and economic advantages of the commune, together with its 'grassroots' origin, help to explain the swiftness and ease with which the peasantry carried out 'this second revolutionary advance in ten years'.

THE COMMUNE: *Eight Years of Development*

At this point it must be emphasised that it is quite misleading to regard the people's commune as a static form of rural organisation, unchanged since its inception in 1958 and uniform in characteristics such as size, administrative structure and levels of remuneration from one end of China to the other.   There is—and this might be expected given the size and diversity of China—a wide variation in size and in population, in the structure as expressed in the number of brigades and teams and the functions of these, in degree of specialisation and industrialisation, and in wage levels both between communes and within one single commune; this geographic diversity is examined in a later section. There has also been a process of evolution and adjustment; this has been going on since the early 1960s and there is no reason to assume that the system of today will remain unchanged.   Chinese leaders have, indeed, recognised that change is inevitable and given the size of China's rural population, the diversity of forms which under-development took, and the entirely new—and therefore untested—character of China's rural development policies such change was to be expected. It is unfortunate that some Western observers have tended to regard every change, even those whose long-term effects were to make the system more viable, as a sign of the imminent breakdown of the system. . . .

The first years of the new system were, it is now admitted, years of excessive optimism, years in which the caution and the good sense which had characterised earlier Chinese rural development were abandoned. The system of free food supplied to families regardless of their earnings proved wasteful and probably weakened the incentive to earn; it was abandoned after a couple of years. The pace of development was at times excessive for it was geared to the unreal slogan of overtaking Britain in fifteen years; excessive demands on the labour force seem to have left a hang-over of weariness. The proclaimed intention of moving swiftly to a communist type of society (organised on the basis of 'to each according to his needs') is now recognised as premature and based on an underestimation of the problems yet to be overcome. The rate of investment in both the agricultural and the industrial sectors was very high and, as Professor Joan Robinson has pointed out, 'put the economy into an unbalanced position'.[1] It is perhaps still too early, and the documentation available is too thin, for a final judgement to be passed on the causes of this temporary throwing of cautious realism to the winds, though the excessive zeal of young and not over-experienced cadres is cited by many as an important element in the situation.

Nevertheless, in spite of certain 'economic excesses', the achievements of this initial phase in creating the infrastructure for subsequent development in the countryside can scarcely be exaggerated. These achievements are commented on more fully later; here we need only draw attention to the massive extension of irrigation, drainage works and terracing; to the extension of the electric power network which made possible a great surge forward in the field of rural industry and to the expansion of education and of welfare services. Given normal climatic conditions, indeed, it is probable that the initial 'growing pains' of the new system might have been speedily overcome. This, however, was not the case for, following 1958, there were 'three bitter years' of flood and drought and these natural catastrophes were added to the problems created by human errors. The result was a period of major difficulties on the food front, a period during which some areas, to use Edgar Snow's phrase, 'brushed close to famine'. But though there was hardship and shortages these were shared; the spectacle so common in Old China, of peasants dying by their millions while the wealthier classes continued to live, unregarding, in ease and opulence, was not repeated. There was austerity—but it was a shared austerity; there were shortages of grain but no one starved. It was a period during which the new Government demonstrated its capacity for organisation

[1] Joan Robinson, 'A British Economist on the Chinese Communes' in *Eastern Horizon* (Hong Kong), May 1964, p. 6.

and its concern for the masses; above all, it was a period which sub-jected the system of the people's commune to the most exacting of tests—its capacity to confront and overcome the millennium-old problem of flood, drought and famine.   And because it confronted these calamities with success, because its organisation made possible the rational deployment of the country's labour resources in a vast campaign of well-digging, irrigation and drainage and the imple-mentation where necessary of relief measures, the commune emerged strengthened and more flexible.   Strengthened because its obvious advantages as a form of agricultural organisation were driven home forcibly to the peasant masses, even those who may have been hesitant; for the first time in the memory of even the oldest peasant China *on her own* had been able to emerge unbroken from a protracted period of natural catastrophes.   More flexible because, confronting the rural situation with realism, the Chinese introduced into the system of people's communes those modifications necessary to correct some of the extravagances of 1958.

These modifications took three forms: first, modification in size—and hence in total number—of communes; secondly, structural changes within the commune; thirdly, limited concessions which incorporated a small individual sector into the economy of the commune.

The changes of 1958 had merged some 740,000 advanced co-operatives into 26,000 people's communes.   The experience of the next two or three year's demonstrated that some of these were too large for successful operation; many were in consequence subdivided to give units of a more manageable size.   By 1966 the total had risen from 26,000 to approximately 78,000.   The data indicates that the trend towards smaller units has been most marked in the 'regions of difficulty' such as the uplands and in such environments, where settlements and arable land are isolated by topographic barriers, this seems a rational development.   On the other hand, where environmental conditions are more favourable as in the double-cropping rice region of the south or the loessial plains of Hopeh the commune remains a large unit, at least in terms of population; thus the average population of a commune in Kwangtung is over 30,000, as against an average for China as a whole of between 7,000 and 8,000.

The structural changes resulted similarly from the experiences gained in operating the new units.   The size proved unwieldy for many purposes (the difficulties of organising a group of 50,000–100,000 people in an intensive and specialised agricultural economy need no emphasis) and to overcome this problem decentralisation of function within a tiered structure of which the component units were the people's commune, the production brigade and the production team was initiated.   The pattern of responsibilities has been described by Professor Joan Robinson:

On the one hand the staff of the commune has taken over the functions of the lowest rung in the old ladder of the administration —the *hsiang*. It is the channel through which the villagers deal with higher authorities for planning production, sales, purchases, taxation and so forth. On the other hand, the individual household is fostered and encouraged as the basic unit of economic life. (The propagandist stories about the destruction of family life are very wide of the mark.) A team consists of the workers of twenty or thirty neighbourhood families. The land allotted to them is, in the main, the land that their forefathers worked, with some modifications for convenience in cultivation. Eight or ten teams are grouped in a brigade. In the plains, where villages are large, the brigade usually comprises a single village. There is emulation between brigades which enlists old village rivalries in a constructive cause.[1]

The incorporation of a small individual sector in the commune's activities is the third major development. On the majority of communes each family has the right to a small individual parcel of land; in the aggregate these individual parcels represent between 3 per cent and 7 per cent of the total cultivated area of the commune. They are usually devoted to the production of vegetables needed by the household; some will include a fruit tree or some vines, others may be devoted to grain production. The role of this private sector is especially important in the field of livestock production. Most of the poultry production (excluding specialised products like Peking ducks) is in the hands of individual peasant families and a sizeable proportion of the pig-rearing is carried on by the private sector. Any crop or livestock products which are surplus to the family's needs may be sold at the local markets; these are held at regular intervals on most communes and in them the level of prices is determined by the conditions of supply and demand. Together with the sale of manure to the collective and with 'side occupations' such as peasant handicrafts this individual production of crops or livestock products may add between 10 per cent and 25 per cent to the income the peasant receives from the collective.

This is the general picture, though there is no single pattern to which all communes conform; rather is there a considerable measure of diversity within the general pattern, a diversity derived partly from environmental conditions, partly from human conditions and the varying levels of development attained by the earlier co-operatives, partly from the fact that the whole system is still evolving, with local diversities within the general pattern resulting from the initiative and the experiments of the peasant masses. And, far from sounding the knell of the commune as many outside observers hastened to assume, the changes introduced during the early 'sixties, with the new flexibility

[1] Joan Robinson, *op. cit.*, p. 7.

they meant and the recognition of the need, at this stage, for various types of incentive, have consolidated the system and created conditions in which continuing development and experimentation are possible.

THE COMMUNE: 1966 (a) Reshaping the Social Fabric of Rural Life

We have stressed above that it is misleading, when considering the processes of rural change in China, to regard these processes as exclusively material in their aims; their preoccupation with the human condition, with the drive to create a new socialist man, is an overriding preoccupation in China today. In his discussion of the bases of socialist planning in China, Charles Bettelheim stresses that 'the unit of socialist production has a fundamental extra-economic role, that of becoming the basic social group in the new society'.[1] This applies to the commune no less than to the factory; it is based on the belief that the optimum development of each person can be achieved neither within the framework of a 'liberal' individualism, nor within that of the family alone but must be sought in some larger grouping, and the most obvious and promising larger grouping is the economic unit in whose activities an individual or a family participates. Within such an economic unit, extended to encompass the whole range of welfare and social activities needed in a healthy and developing community, many of the problems and conflicts of the old type of society disappear or can be resolved: the conflict between worker and capital; discriminations based on sex; the separation between mental and manual work or between the carrying-out and the control of a job; above all, the segregation of man's productive activities from those activities necessary for his development in the widest sense of the word.[2] We, conditioned to life in a highly individualistic society, may dissent from such a vision of life but we cannot ignore it if we wish to attain any real understanding of what the Chinese are striving to achieve.

Certainly, even the briefest period of field work in the Chinese countryside drives home to the observer the fundamental role of the commune as a social and welfare unit. It is the unit which organises relief measures should an area be hit by natural calamities of any sort. Its militia, incorporating men and women, constitutes the basic element in the military defence of the community's heritage. In the day-to-day life of its members it provides the five 'basic guarantees' which give peasant life a security it never before possessed; these are food, clothing, shelter, medical care and funeral expenses. Families which are in need because of illness, or because the labour force they can muster is limited, are assisted by the welfare fund of the team to which they belong; old people without relatives may be similarly helped or may be cared for in the old people's homes (the 'homes of respect for the aged')

[1] C. Bettelheim, op. cit., p. 44.   [2] Ibid.

established by many communes. In the field of education the commune runs secondary and primary schools, either relying on its own resources or partly assisted by the State or the county; within the commune the individual brigades or teams may themselves run evening classes or literacy classes. There is little uniformity in the pattern from commune to commune. From statistics collected in the field, the average large commune may boast a total of between one dozen and two dozen elementary schools, though in one case, a commune of 12,000 households claimed a total of sixty-six elementary schools with 11,000 students; this total of sixty-six included also schools 'run by the masses', a name which draws attention to the policy of self-help which extends even into the fields of education. An important development at the present time is the part-work, part-study schools, designed to integrate theory and practice (see below, pp. 303–5); many of these are new, their student numbers relatively low and the courses they provide range from the simplest elementary level to relatively ambitious middle school programmes. They may well emerge as the dominant educational medium in the countryside since their drastic pruning of all superfluous book-learning, their flexibility when it comes to the question of integration with the pressing seasonal or daily needs of agriculture and the fact that, through their production of crops or livestock products, they are virtually self-supporting, fit them admirably to the present-day economic situation of rural China. The nurseries which are provided by some communes—some three-score on a large commune near Peking—provide care and a communal environment for children of the youngest age-groups and, by so doing, free the women-folk for productive work; where, however, three generations live in the same dwelling the grandmother will often tend the younger children while the mother works.

The medical encadrement of the countryside which the commune makes possible has been of major importance in reducing the impact of formerly killing or crippling diseases; again there is a tiered provision of services. Many communes possess their own hospital, sufficiently sophisticated in some cases to possess X-ray equipment and to undertake surgical sterilisation of men or women if this is requested; the doctors will include both Western-trained doctors and those who practise traditional medicine. This medical infrastructure, with its clinics and its health centres, makes possible the dissemination into the countryside of modern concepts of hygiene. Below the commune level the brigade and team will have its health workers (somewhat analogous to the medical orderlies of the former Belgian Congo) who can treat simple complaints, cope with the simpler type of injury and whose number will include some trained midwives. But, as in the case of education, there is no cut-and-dried pattern, for each commune, or each brigade or team, does the best it can with the resources at its disposal and this results in a considerable variation in the level of services offered from one commune to another. What *is* common to the whole country is the striking improvement over past conditions and the continuing progress which each year brings.

This transformation of the *social* environment is reflected in the young people who are healthier, more aware of the opportunities life holds for them and of the responsibilities that will be theirs than possibly at any other period of Chinese history. The transformation of the *physical* environments in which they grow up—the houses, the schools and the like—has been less. That there have been dramatic changes as a result of large-scale rebuilding in the cities of China is obvious to the most hasty of observers; that the pace of change should be less in the countryside is nonetheless readily understandable. In the reconstruction of the countryside certain priorities had to be established; these included social priorities such as the establishment of adequate health and education systems and physical priorities such as the creation of an irrigation and drainage system which would counter the basic problems of drought and flood, the extension and consolidation of terrace systems, the control of erosion through terracing and afforestation and the improvement of the transport network. Without the laying of such an infrastructure real rural development was impossible. Given the limited supply of capital and the need to mobilise labour and materials to create this infrastructure the large-scale building of domestic quarters had to be given a lower priority. And the size of this problem of rural rehousing scarcely needs emphasising; what is involved is the rehousing of some 120 million peasant families, together with the construction of the buildings—the nurseries, the schools, the hospitals— needed to house the increasing range of social services being provided. There appears to be no overall data on the progress of rural rehousing and the general picture the traveller gets is that the extent of such rehousing varies so much from commune to commune that generalisation is virtually impossible. Thus on some of the communes in Kiangsu little in the way of rehousing was evident; the problems of flood control and drainage, and the building of pumping stations and the associated hydraulic works, appear to have absorbed any resources of labour and capital remaining after the needs of production had been met. By contrast, a good deal of solid building of peasant homes is evident on the prosperous market gardening communes around Peking and also in the poorer areas of Shansi and Shensi; in the former province the Tachai brigade has replaced the old village settlement of mud-brick houses and cave-dwellings by a new stone-built village, in the latter province the Ma-chi Village Commune (3,650 households) has built a total of 7,200 rooms since the inception of the commune. The pattern is thus one of great diversity with each commune contributing its share to the gigantic task of rehousing China's 500 million peasants as and when economic conditions are such that resources can be diverted to this task.

THE COMMUNE: 1966 (b) Wages

On the majority of the communes the peasants own their own houses, and the cost of the increasing range of welfare services (notably health and educational services) is negligible; where other amenities are provided charges for these are very low (e.g. electricity costs, on the basis of three light bulbs for a household, were approximately 2s. per month in 1964). The wide range of welfare services—and, behind these, the security which the peasant is now beginning to enjoy, at every stage of his life—must be borne in mind when we attempt to make some sort of comparison between real levels of income in China and the other emerging countries.

That the last decade or so has witnessed a steady rise in living levels is very clear to the author from comparing conditions in 1966 with conditions at the time of his earlier visits in 1964 and 1958; this increased well-being is attested to by the steady improvement in the social services sketched above and by such indices as peasant purchases of bicycles, wrist-watches and radios in recent years. Unfortunately it is not easy to adduce in support of these impressions the sequence of statistics on such things as *per capita* income levels or wage rates which are normally available in countries with a long tradition of statistical documentation; such data as *is* available is fragmentary and demands careful interpretation.

A study of the national income of China during the early years of the People's Republic has been made by Alexander Eckstein.[1] Most of his data refer to 1952 and the study gives a useful—and highly detailed—analysis of the contribution of the major sectors of the economy to China's national income. It is, however, of only limited value in establishing some sort of base-line against which to set more recent data on rural income; from his estimate of the gross value added by the agricultural sector[2] it is possible, by using estimates of the number of able-bodied workers engaged in agriculture (*c.* 170 million at that date), to obtain a crude *per capita* output figure of approximately 170 yuan per annum. The figure underlines the poverty of China (at 7 yuan to the pound it means an income of under 10s. per week) but is difficult to equate with later estimates collected *in the field*. Thus, René Dumont, who carried out a careful study of some two dozen co-operatives in 1955, quotes *daily* wage rates which vary from 0·7 yuan (*for a working year of 49 days*) through a rate of 1·0 yuan a day (for a working year of 190 days) to a rate of 1·7 yuan (for a working year of 62 days).[3]

[1] *The National Income of Communist China* (Glencoe 1961).   [2] *Ibid.*, Table A-1, p. 92.
[3] R. Dumont, *Révolution dans les campagnes chinoises* (Paris 1957), Table, pp. 456–7.

TABLE 4

TOTAL INCOME AND WAGES DISTRIBUTED ON SELECTED COMMUNES: 1966

	Total Income of commune (yuan)	Distributed to Members (%)	Average Wage per Worker (yuan)	Range of Wages (yuan)	% in Kind
PEKING AREA					
Commune 1	—	49	600	2–300/8–900	5–10
Commune 2	17·0 M.	50	330–360	highest >500	—
Commune 3	12·0 M.	45	380	350/500	—
SHANSI					
Commune 4	3·5 M.	51	246	200/500	17
HONAN					
Commune 5	2·3 M. (est.)	60	140	110/170	50
Commune 6	2·5 M.	65	200[a]	—	—
Commune 7	2·26 M.	60	122–141 (?)	100/700	all in cash
SHENSI					
Commune 8	6·0 M.	65	400	—	30–40
Commune 9	2·6 M.	63	340	250–500	20–30
Commune 10	3.0 M.	55	280–300	200–700	—
KIANGSU					
Commune 11	2·22 M.[b]	72	230–240	180–300	<50
Commune 12	2·28 M.	65	215	180–400	54
Commune 13	2·49 M.	66	256		50 catties of grain per head, rest in cash
Commune 14	6·76 M.	68	194	highest 480	17
SHANGHAI AREA					
Commune 15	8·16 M.[b]	52	382[c]	200–600	all in cash
KWANGTUNG					
Commune 16	11·0 M.[d]	55	280	200–400	45
Commune 17	9·6 M.	57	278[c]	200–500	50
Commune 18	3·24 M. (est.)	54	300[e]	250–370	<60

Notes: [a] Including side-line occupations. [b] Excluding industry. [c] Sideline occupations add another 15 per cent. [d] Industry contributes 45 per cent of this total. [e] Sideline occupations add 20 per cent.

Gilbert Etienne quotes[1] yearly *per capita* income figures for 1960 which range from 85 yuan (1957: 45 yuan), through 139 yuan (1957: 85 yuan) to 272 yuan (1957: 79 yuan). Hélène Marchisio[2] gives the range of *per capita* real incomes between various teams on a Hunan commune as from 44 to 85 yuan; for Kiangsi she quotes, for the commune studied, a range of from 42 to 111 yuan.

[1] Gilbert Etienne, *La voie chinoise* (Paris 1962), p. 187.
[2] In Bettleheim, *op. cit.*, Tables on pp. 100–3.

The general picture which the writer obtained from a detailed study of eighteen communes in 1966 is summarised in Table 4 above.

The figures in this Table must be regarded as, at the best, merely approximate orders of magnitude. Moreover, unless explicitly stated to the contrary, the data for income per worker excludes income from sideline occupations such as the rearing of pigs or poultry or the production of crops such as vegetables; Joan Robinson states these 'sales from households do not provide more than 10 per cent of total supplies in the nation as a whole',[1] an estimate which accords with the estimate the present writer made and with the statistics cited in Table 4 above. There is, it is clear from the Table, a great diversity of conditions as between one commune and another; nevertheless, some broad generalisations may be made. First, many of the communes are, in financial terms, very large units; five of those listed had gross incomes of over £1,000,000 and of these one (Number 2) was handling a budget of almost £2,500,000. The aggregate income of the communes in Table 4, excluding in many cases income accruing through the individual sector, is close on £14 million; many, but not all, were undoubtedly 'above average' but to get this figure into its Asian perspective it should be underlined that it is larger than the GNP of countries such as North Borneo or Bhutan and about one-half that of Laos. Secondly, the proportion of the communes' income which is distributed among its members varies considerably—from about three-quarters to, more usually, one half; the remainder is set aside, partly to meet operating costs, partly to finance activities, such as the construction of housing, schools, or power plants, which will contribute directly to raising the living level of the communes' members (to this extent the figures for average wages represent an understatement). Thirdly, there is a considerable range in average incomes between communes—for the group studied there was a ratio of some 4 : 1 between the highest and the lowest average wages; between the various teams on a commune the ratio was 2 : 1, between individuals 3 : 1. Fourthly, there is little uniformity in manner of payment, the proportion paid in kind (i.e. in grain, oil or cotton) varying from one-twentieth to close on three-fifths; generally speaking, it is lowest on the more specialised communes such as those in the intensive market-gardening zone around Peking and high in the double-cropping rice regions of the east and south. To this payment in kind must be added the vegetables and grain produced individually by the peasant; this grain may represent between one-fifth and one-sixth of the family's yearly grain supply. But perhaps the most significant, however, is the continuous investment of a sizeable proportion of the commune's revenues, represented by the amounts set aside under the headings of 'accumulation' and 'welfare'; this appears to range between 5 and 12 per cent and

[1] Joan Robinson, loc. cit.

this steady investment in the production and welfare infrastructure of the Chinese countryside is unparalleled in any other 'developing' country.

THE COMMUNE: 1966 (c) Allocation of Resources

The system of allocation of resources within the commune system has been analysed very fully by Hélène Marchisio in the study cited above. She points out that some 80 per cent of the agricultural production is absorbed in the countryside and only 20 per cent enters the market. This largely self-sufficient character of the rural economy is reflected in the system of allocating the resources of the commune or the team, since, as can be seen from Table 4 a sizeable proportion of the peasants' income is in kind. The accounting unit, in fact, works with two complementary systems of accounting: 'accounting in kind for the distribution of the basic food crops produced, and a second system, that of accounting by value, which makes it possible to evaluate the real income of the peasants and to calculate the revenue in terms of liquid cash'.[1]

(A) ACCOUNTING IN KIND

The distribution under this head is based on discussion between team members and is integrated into the plan; it comprises four elements—sales to the State, taxes, costs of production, and the share of the peasants themselves.

(i) Sales to the State

The volume of these is determined after discussion between the various echelons of the commune—the team, the brigade and the commune itself—and the State planning authorities; in such discussions the final word rests with the production team. The sales are fixed in absolute quantities, based on the preceding harvest; they appear to represent some 20 per cent of the food crop output. In the event of a particularly good harvest no increase in the volume of grain delivered is demanded; by contrast, if for various reasons the harvest is a poor one, the quota may, after investigation, be reduced so that the peasants' food supply is not threatened. The State guarantees a fixed price for these basic products and this price level has been maintained even in years of difficulty; this stability of prices has been an important factor in ensuring the success of Chinese agricultural planning and the well-being of the peasant masses.

---

[1] Loosely translated from Hélène Marchisio, *op. cit.*, p. 87. The paragraphs which follow are based on Mme Marchisio's analysis of the economic structure of the commune.

(ii) Taxation

Taxes paid by the rural collective to the State are generally paid in kind. The taxes paid were fixed in 1958 at 15·5 per cent of the commune's income for 'a normal year'; initially this was to apply for a period of five years but there appears to have been no modification of the system. The base figure—that of a normal year's income—was a purely hypothetical figure and seems in most cases to have been below the real income; moreover, with the increase in the collectives real income as a result of the agricultural progress of the last eight years, the proportion of the income absorbed by taxes has shown a progressive decline. As Table 5 indicates, of the communes visited only one cited a figure as high as 15 per cent for its tax burden (and this was a commune for which there appeared some uncertainty as to total income); in the majority of cases the proportion of total income deducted for tax purposes was 7 per cent or less, dropping as low as 3 per cent in some of the more progressive communes.[1]

This taxation system undoubtedly encourages peasant initiative for it leaves at the disposal of the collective a high proportion of the income accruing to the group as a result of increased productivity.

(iii) Production Needs

The third element in the system of distribution in kind is represented by the share which goes to the collective. This comprises the need for seed, products fed to the animals of the collective and those processed by the industrial sector of the commune, and the basic food supplies which the cadres of the brigade or team receive in return for the time they devote to the service of the collective (this occupies only part of their time since all administrative personnel are expected to participate in productive work also). The proportion of the total production which goes to meet this group of needs on the part of the collective is estimated by Hélène Marchisio at between 6·8 per cent and 10 per cent.

(iv) The share of the Peasants

Initially the basic food-crops were distributed among the members of the commune according to the number of people in each household; this was made possible by the unusually abundant harvest of 1958 which seemed to make possible the final elimination of the fear of hunger which has always haunted the peasant. The subsequent 'years of difficulty' demonstrated that this development was premature and resulted in a stricter application of the principle 'to each according to his labour'. This, as Hélène Marchisio comments, made it possible

[1] It may be noted that the relationship between 'normal income' and real income provides an indirect index of the success of the communes, those communes showing the lowest proportions of income set aside to meet taxation being the more progressive and prosperous units.

for each member of the collective 'to establish a close linkage between the result of his work and his own personal interest, between his personal interest and the development of production, between his personal interest and the interests of the collective'. The system of allocation of basic crops was supplemented by the 'five guarantees' referred to above and by a system of aid, in the shape of granting of basic foodstuffs, to families who, through illness or other causes, found themselves in difficulties; this aid is given after discussion of each particular case by the accounting unit, a system which avoids favouritism and which associates each member, in a positive fashion, with the decision and the scale of the individual sacrifice which each such decision involves.

Where part of the workers' wage are in kind (and, as Table 4 shows, this is not every commune) the amounts involved appear to be of the order of 50–70 per cent of the collective's output of such basic crops. The bases on which the amounts to be distributed to each family are determined varies from commune to commune though two main systems appear to be used. The first system is a simple distribution of the basic foodstuffs remaining after the needs of the State and the collective (i–iii above) have been met on the basis of the number of work-points achieved by each member of the production team. The second is the allocation of a basic ration of foodstuffs to each person, the remaining amount at the disposal of the collective being distributed on the basis of the work-points gained by each individual.

(b) THE CASH ACCOUNT OF THE COMMUNE

The data given in Table 4 for total revenue underlines that the rural collective rests its system of accounting also on a money base; such a money base is, indeed, essential if rural wage levels are to be compared with those obtaining in industry and to provide a common denominator which makes possible a comparision of the material progress of the peasant masses as between one region of China and another, or even between one commune and another.

The *gross revenue* (second column in Table 4) is obtained by evaluating at market prices—which, for basic crops, is the price paid by the State —the total crop output; to this is added the income from livestock rearing, forestry, fish-farming and the like. The *net income* is the sum remaining after the major charges on the collective's funds have been met. These charges include taxes to the State (usually paid in kind, as noted earlier); production expenses which Hélène Marchisio quotes as of the order of 20–25 per cent of the total revenue (our data shows a wider spread—from 18 per cent to 40 per cent); and the funds set aside for accumulation and welfare. On the basis of her 1962 data Mme Marchisio gives a range of 2–7 per cent for the rate of accumulation, adding that this maximum was considerably exceeded in 1964;

she observes that the rate of accumulation is closely linked to level of production, dropping to low levels during years of poor harvest and rising when the harvest is good. On the communes in our sample the proportion of the total income set aside for welfare ranged from 1–3 per cent; from this it can be seen that the rate of accumulation (column five, Table 5) in 1966 was generally towards the higher of the levels

TABLE 5

ALLOCATION OF RESOURCES ON SELECTED COMMUNES: 1966

| | Total Revenue (yuan) | % of Total Revenue | | |
		Taxes	Production Expenses	Accumulation and Welfare
PEKING AREA				
Commune 1	—	3	35	13
Commune 2	17·0M	7	23	15
Commune 3	12·0M	3	40	12
SHANSI				
Commune 4	3·5M	7	30	12
HONAN				
Commune 5	(2·3M)[a]	7–8	26–8	6
Commune 6	2·5M	7	20	8
Commune 7	2·26M	3	30	6
SHENSI				
Commune 8	6·0M	5	20	9–11
Commune 9	2·6M	7	20	7–10
Commune 10	3·0M	7	30	8
KIANGSU				
Commune 11	2·22M[b]	3·3	18	6·1
Commune 12	2·28M	4	—	—
Commune 13	2·49M	4·8	(21)[a]	6·6
Commune 14	6·76M	5	20·7	6·4
SHANGHAI AREA				
Commune 15	8·16M[b]	4	33	11
KWANGTUNG				
Commune 16	11·0M[c]	(6)[a]	30	8·7
Commune 17	9·6M	7	26	6–10
Commune 18	(3·24M)[a]	15	c. 20	7–11

Notes: [a] Estimate. [b] Excluding industry. [c] Industry contributes 45 per cent of this total. For members' share see Table 4.

Mme Marchisio cites, reaching 10 per cent in Commune Number 4 and 12 per cent in Commune Number 1. Such a high rate of accumulation provides indirect evidence of the striking recovery of Chinese agriculture from the difficult years of 1961–63; tangible evidence of this recovery is provided by the range of equipment such as small irrigation pumps purchased by these savings on the part of the collective.

These charges having been met, some 50–70 per cent of the gross revenue remains as *net income* for the members of the collective (column three, Table 4). Of this, as already noted, a portion is usually paid in kind, but the situation varies so much from one commune to another that generalisation is almost impossible.[1] One point emerging from Mme Marchisio's study is that the variation in income in kind between the various teams on a commune is relatively small and that the major differential arises from varying levels of cash income. She comments that even a team whose land had been badly affected by flooding was able 'to guarantee its members a basic subsistence level almost equivalent to that of the other teams', adding 'this is a remarkable achievement by comparison with what would have happened under similar circumstances before 1949'. One further point which was evident in 1966 was that the remuneration in kind had, over the last three years, been on a scale sufficient to make possible the saving of a sizeable grain surplus; this, on one commune, amounted to 1·54 million catties between 1963 and 1965, or some 100 catties *per capita*. In a society in which food shortages had been endemic, in which the loan of grain from the landlord to tide over the critical period before the new harvest had been one of the major causes of the semi-serfdom of the peasantry, it is difficult to overestimate the psychological influence of such food reserves. To the peasants such reserves, along with the welfare services provided by the collective, appear as a major vindication of the realism and correctness of the rural policy of the People's Government.

It remains to comment briefly on the contribution of the individual sector to peasant income; this sector is represented by crop production on the small individual plot, by the rearing of livestock and especially poultry, and by small-scale craft industries. From the communes studied the contribution of these 'side-occupations' is, as noted above, of the order of 10–25 per cent; a figure much in excess of this is regarded as undesirable for it indicates a disequilibrium between collective and individual activities. On some communes the individual craft industries may be partially integrated with the industrial sector of the collective; this is a development which may well indicate the future trend in this sector of the rural economy.

[1] See Table 4 for the variation on the sample communes studied. The computation of income is illustrated by Mme Marchisio using as example one family on a commune she studied in Hunan. In 1962 this family earned a total of 3,201 *work-points*. One *work-day* (10 work-points) is evaluated at 1·55 yuan, together with the right to 12·8 lb. of rice. The family's income was thus 321 × 1·55 = 497·55 yuan, to which must be added 23 yuan for the sale of manure to the team, i.e. a total of 520·55 yuan. The family received 4,110 lb. of rice for its work-points plus 575 lb. as bonus for sale of manure and 80 lb. as bonus for a loan of 40 yuan to the team, i.e. a total of 4,765 lb. of grain. The value of this grain was 397·85 yuan. The *actual cash income* is obtained by offsetting this figure against the *total income* of 520·55 yuan, which leaves a *cash residue* of 122·68 yuan. Marchisio *op. cit.*, p. 94.

CHAPTER 7

Contrasts in the Micro-geography of Selected Communes

BACKGROUND

IN THE preceding chapter we were concerned largely with the development and the functioning of the commune system. From the text and the tables the diversity within the system is immediately evident; this diversity is in part a result of man's appraisal of the differing environments within China and in part a result of the fact that the system is still evolving and the scope for experimentation (in the shape of new crops or the development of new sectors of the rural economy) remains large. It should be emphasised again that the unit integrates not only various types of agricultural economy but the whole of rural life; it is the basic cell in the economic and social organism devised by the people of the largest nation on earth. The diversity between communes and the way in which rural life has been structured in China can best be brought into sharp focus by examining selected communes, each as a whole and in more detail than is possible in the tabulated summary given above (pp. 136, 141). For three of the communes maps are given; these will enable the reader to visualise the spatial pattern of activities and, together with the photographs, to gain a clearer picture of this basic unit of Chinese rural society. The data refer to either 1964 or 1966; an appendix gives briefer summaries of a cross-section of communes visited in their initial stages of development, i.e. 1958.

AGRICULTURE ON THE METROPOLITAN FRINGE
The Peking Municipal Area

The total area under the jurisdiction of Peking Municipality is 6,500 square miles—in other words, an area approximately half that of Belgium or Holland. Within this area there are slightly under 300

communes. It is fitting that our examination of some typical communes should start in the Peking area for here the general lines of
development and the potentialities of the system can be seen most
clearly. It is true that less than two hours' drive towards the west or
north brings one into broken and rocky terrain of limited agricultural
value and that the climatic divide between the more humid summer-wet
climate of Peking and the drier country to the west of the Great Wall
is almost incredibly sharp. It's true that like most of the North China
Plain the Peking area has a climate characterised by a high degree of
year to year variability. Nevertheless, the soils in the lowland area
adjoining the city are good, easy working, soils of the yellow-grey-earth
variety, soils that are versatile and that lend themselves to various
forms of intensive agriculture. There are, moreover, surface water
supplies to be drawn from the surrounding hills and subsurface water
can be tapped at no great depths—and these resources, long latent, are
now being developed on a large scale so the drought hazard can be
minimized. Most important of all, the proximity of a market of some
3 million people has been an important incentive to the diversification and intensification of agriculture, aimed at providing the milk,
fruits and vegetables which, with rising living levels, are demanded in

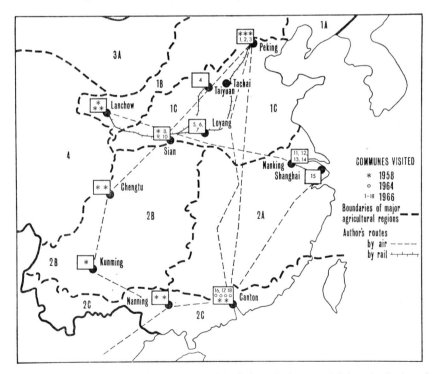

Figure 45. Location of Communes Visited in relation to Major Agricultural
Regions of Eastern China (for key to these regions see pp. 186–190).

increasing quantities by the population of the metropolis. And the development of these intensive branches of production has been facilitated by the careful organisation of Peking's food supplies through bureaux of the People's Council of Peking; these negotiate through the communes with the production brigades and teams, relating the needs of the city to the supplies offered, and are able to give the producer the advantage of stable prices fixed in advance.

The cumulative effect of all these factors is mirrored in the communes of the area, many of which bring together wihin one unit the intensive production of a wide range of foodstuffs—grain, vegetables grown in the open or under glass, an increasing range of fruits, milk and specialised items such as the Peking duck. This agricultural activity rests on a complex and developed infrastructure—drainage, irrigation, transport and the like—and the smooth integration of all these activities within one organisation and with the expanding food needs of a great metropolitan area demonstrate very clearly the full potential of the commune as a production unit. The details below of a representative commune underline the diversity of activities typical of these communes of the Peking area.

CROP-PRODUCTION, DAIRYING & JADE-WORKING: A SUBURBAN COMMUNE NEAR PEKING

This commune is situated some 20 kilometres east of Peking, on the yellow-grey loamy soils which are typical of much of the North China Plain. It occupies 9,390 acres, and has a population of 25,000, representing 5,400 households; the average density is thus about 660 persons to the square kilometre which, expressed in another fashion, means approximately 0·4 acres per person.

In its development it mirrors, on a small scale, the general pattern of development of Chinese agriculture described earlier. The land reform was carried out in 1950 and between 1950 and 1953 the poor and middle peasants organised themselves into mutual aid teams. These were units of 8–9 households; on them individual ownership of the land was retained but the means of production—tools, work animals and the like—were pooled. Between 1953 and 1955 the transition was made to elementary co-operatives; these were units of between 100 and 500 households and were merged subsequently into advanced co-operatives grouping between 800 and 1,800 families. Even these bigger units did not eliminate some of the basic problems in rural development; mechanisation had now become a possibility but the arable area controlled by each co-operative was too small to provide an economic unit of operation; the implementation of schemes such as water conservation or irrigation was impeded by the fragmentation of the land into numerous co-operatives; rational planning of land use which alone would permit the much-needed diversification of the economy similarly demanded larger units. It was considerations of this kind which lay behind the decision, taken in late 1958, to merge the co-operatives into a single people's commune.

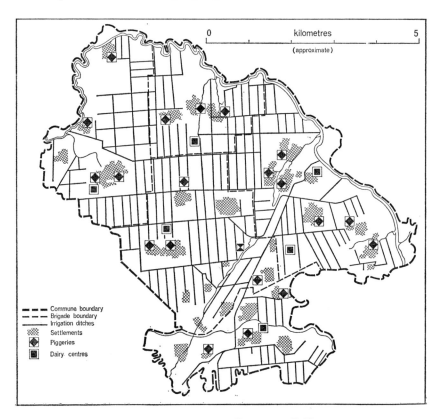

Figure 46.   Suburban Commune, Peking.

This commune has a population of 25,000 people and an economy which is highly diversified. Grain, cotton, vegetables, fruit, and livestock are produced, with vegetables and livestock products (including milk) going to meet the needs of the capital. Intensification in a climatically-marginal environment has been made possible by the development of irrigation; today more than nine-tenths of the commune area is irrigated.

Today the commune is organised into 5 production brigades and 55 production teams; of the latter, 14 are specialised teams concerned with such activities as fruit-growing, vegetable production or the rearing of ducks or pigs. The economy has become increasingly diversified: of the total area of 9,390 acres, 6,275 are under grain (wheat, maize, rice), 1,730 acres are under fodder crops and 1,385 are under fruit, cotton, oil-seeds or vegetables. The commune claims self-sufficiency in grain, cotton and oil. Livestock include 2,500 cows in milk, 14,000 pigs, 10,000 Peking ducks and 1,150 horses (half of these are high-quality animals used for breeding, the horses being sold to other communes in the Peking area). There are two large fishery stations and 35 smaller units while each family will own some 5–6 chickens and rear a pig or two each year. In addition to grain, the commune produces 17,000 tons of vegetables a year, 200 tons of fruit, 700 tons of milk and feeds 43,000 ducks.

A sharp rise in production (date supplied by the secretary of the commune suggested that grain yields had increased somewhat over two-and-a-half times since 1958) has been made possible by careful planning and technical developments which have eliminated some of the old hazards of agriculture in what is, in some years, a climatically-marginal environment. The levelling of the fields and the installation of three major and forty-eight small pumping stations now make it possible to irrigate 90 per cent of the commune's crop land; the critical importance of this high degree of water control was demonstrated in 1965, when, in spite of severe drought conditions (according to some the worst for forty years), a bumper harvest was reaped. Twenty-nine tractors make it possible to plough nine-tenths of the arable land by machine; one-fifth is harvested by the four combines the commune possesses. The creation of an electrical power grid (96 km. of cable) not only makes possible drainage and irrigation but also the milling of grain and the preparation of livestock foodstuffs are now done by machinery. Before 1958 the co-operatives were without electric power and, lacking pumping equipment, were 'dependent on Heaven for their crop'. The commune uses relatively large amounts of chemical fertilisers—the rate of application cited being 350–440 lbs. (ammonium salts and phosphates) per acre; a large experimental section of some 500 acres is used to ascertain the optimum ratio of organic to inorganic manures for various crops.

The most striking feature of the commune is, however, less its 'technical' development than the diversified character of the economy which is being built up. As the figure cited above suggest, the commune has an important livestock sector, including milk production (the expansion of milk production in suburban communes is one of the major changes in the suburban economy since 1958); it is an important vegetable producer and it supplies Peking with a wide range of fruit from applies and pears to strawberries and grapes.[1] This diversification is not only important as providing a more varied and attractive diet, it also provides a much more stable base for rural development than the old single-crop grain economy.

Industry employed an average of some 500 workers, with a marked peak of employment in the winter period when the needs of agriculture

---

[1] The plantations of fruit trees made in the early years of the people's communes are now coming into bearing, with the result that a wide variety of cheap fruit is available in the cities.

were less. The industries included basic industries such as brick-making and, an unusual industry to find in a rural setting, the manufacture from jade of *objets d'art*. Plans for 1966 included the establishment of an oil-mill, a blanket-mill and a small farm tools factory. Factory wages were generally similar to those obtaining in the farming sector, i.e. approximately 380 yuan (*c.* £54) per annum.

In the social field the commune is responsible for the running of three State-established middle schools with a total enrolment of 1,200 students; it also runs eleven primary schools with a total enrolment of 4,000. Medical services are provided by six clinics, staffed by forty-five doctors; three-quarters of these are Western-trained though their courses of training were much shorter than in the West (three years). There are, in addition, two nurses with midwives training for the commune and one for each production brigade.

This commune is not exceptional in its pattern of development; indeed, as the commune secretary pointed out, it ranked 56th among the 280 communes lying in the Peking administrative area. But in its progress towards 'the technical transformation of agriculture' through electrification, water conservation and irrigation and mechanisation, in the increasingly diversified character of its agriculture, it is fully representative of the general trends in the agriculture of this part of North China. And if one compares conditions on this commune and others in the Peking area which the writer visited in 1966 with those in the same area he visited eight years previously it is the progress made in the fields of water conservation and irrigation and in crop diversification which makes the most immediate impact. These developments, which are based in part on the heavy investment of labour, are making possible the emergence of a stable and highly productive agricultural system and this in turn, through the ploughing back of some of the profits by investment in machinery, fertilisers and improved social services, provides conditions for yet further progress. There are few better examples of the process of 'cumulative causation' as outlined by Gunnar Myrdal.

TRANSFORMING THE LOESS-LANDS: Two Communes in Shensi

The loess-lands of Shansi and Shensi have always been marginal areas for the agriculturalist. In seasons of adequate rain they were a great bread-basket, producing at the cost of a massive expenditure of animal and human muscle-power large crops of wheat and millet, beans and also cotton. But the climate, like most subhumid climates, is characterised by great year to year variability and by prolonged droughts which took a heavy toll of human lives. The heavy emphasis on water conservation in recent years, the sinking of thousands of deep and shallow wells, has begun to transform the situation; the old unpredictability of life has been replaced by a growing conviction that the environmental hazards can be attenuated or overcome and, though some of the communes are less wealthy than those in more fortunate areas, the gap between the levels of development here and in the rest of 'Agricultural China' has diminished.   Life is still hard perhaps—but no longer hopeless, for the peasant now feels himself increasingly master of his destiny; this conviction is strengthened by the much-publicised success of the people of Tachai, in one of the most impoverished and marginal areas of eastern Shansi, in coping with the problems posed by the loess-land environment.   General conditions and trends in this part of China can be illustrated by two communes in Shensi; the first is in the northern suburbs of Sian, the second, to the south of that city, may be regarded as typical of those communes which integrate alluvial lowlands and low loessial hill country.   Both illustrate the extent to which the development of water conservation and irrigation techniques has transformed environmental conditions.

(a) A Suburban Commune near Sian

This is a unit of 18,400 people, comprising 3,650 households and disposing of a labour force of 6,000.   It cultivates an area of some 4,660 acres.   Before 1958 the land was distributed between twenty-three co-operatives; today there are the same number of brigades, and these are subdivided into eighty-three teams.

One of the basic problems in the old days was ensuring an adequate and year-round supply of water.   The river was uncontrollable and the individual co-operatives were unable to solve the problem.   The irrigated area in pre-Liberation days was less than 100 acres; by 1957 it had reached a total of 700 acres.   Following the establishment of the commune there was a large-scale investment of human labour in flood-control and irrigation projects; in 1959, for example, some 100,000 man-days of labour were invested in such schemes.   River-fed irrigation is supplemented by irrigation using sewage water from Sian (there are two pumping stations to handle this) and by the digging of 400 shallow wells (15–30 metres deep) and 27 deep wells (200 metres deep).   As a result of this programme the entire cultivated area of the commune can be irrigated.

Almost seven-tenths of the cropland is devoted to grain and it is now possible to take two crops a year; the first is wheat, which is autumn-sown and reaped in early summer, the second is maize, beans or millet, crops which are summer-sown.   Approximately one-fifth of the land produces vegetables and 7 per cent is under cotton.   Here, as elsewhere in China, there has been increasing diversification of the economy.   This is illustrated not only by the vegetable production, which includes hot-bed production of cucumbers and egg-plants, but also by the new orchards (fifteen, with an area of 40 acres) and by the development of milk production (200 milk cattle).

The commune has a total of 1,200 large animals (horses and cattle, including the milk cattle referred to above). It also has 5,000 pigs; of these, 1,000 are reared by the brigades, the remainder by the individual peasants, giving an average of approximately one pig per family.

The beginnings of 'the technical transformation of agriculture' are clearly evident. Organic manures are used in large quantities on crops such as vegetables (for cucumbers the rate of application is from 18 to 30 tons per acre) but chemical fertilisers (rate of application between 1 cwt. and 2 cwt. per acre) are used on the grain and cotton. Thirty to forty per cent of the land is tractor-ploughed, the tractors belonging to a nearby State tractor station; the cost is one yuan per *mou*, or approximately one pound per acre. Electricity is now part of rural life; every household has electricity and much of the grinding of grain is now done by electricity. Industry employs approximately 300 men and 170–180 women throughout the year; the main branches are those closely dependent on agriculture, such as the manufacture of bean curd and noodles, the preparation of animal feed-stuffs, the manufacture and repair of agricultural implements and brick-making (there are seven brick-kilns).

The commune claims proudly that all its children can now read and write. It is responsible for four middle schools organised on the part-work, part-study basis while each brigade runs one or two elementary schools and one or two spare-time (evening) schools. The commune has four health centres and one mobile medical team.

One work-day (10 work-points) in an average brigade is worth 1·4–1·5 yuan; in the best brigades it may be as high as 2 yuan and under these conditions the best workers may attain wage-levels of 700–800 yuan (70–80 per cent of this is in cash).

(b) Loess-land & Alluvium: A Commune south of Sian (Figure 47)

This commune combines two contrasting types of terrain: rolling loess hills which are, because of their topography, unirrigated and devoted to grain, and an alluvial riverine margin under intensive and irrigated cultivation of grain and vegetables. Its population is slightly over 16,000, comprising 3,000 households and a work-force of 6,300; this population is organised into 16 production brigades and 74 production teams. The cultivated land totals 3,750 acres, or slightly under a quarter of an acre per head of population; most of this land is under grain, grown either on the unirrigated hill-slopes or on the irrigated valley floor, the only other major crop being vegetables which occupy 170 acres. Large stock (cattle and horses) number 600 and there are

2,000 pigs, 40 per cent of which belong to the collective, the remainder being reared by the individual peasants (i.e. an average of one pig to 2·5 households).

Measured against some of the communes visited this commune had progressed much less along the path of diversification. The commune members have, however, carried out a substantial modification of the environment and this process is continuing. The sinking of over 200 wells and the creation of an elaborate network of irrigation ditches on the lower land of the commune now makes it possible to irrigate one-third of the surface. Further extension of the irrigated area depends partly on levelling and terracing and this is now a major priority as on many other loess-land communes; almost 400 acres have been levelled and 60 acres terraced. Electrification of the commune facilitates the programme of agricultural development; there are three electrically-run pumping stations and 130 water wheels and this use of electricity has been extended to many of the commune's day-to-day activities such as threshing and grinding (there are forty electrically-operated grinding mills which, it is estimated, save the labour of 200 people and

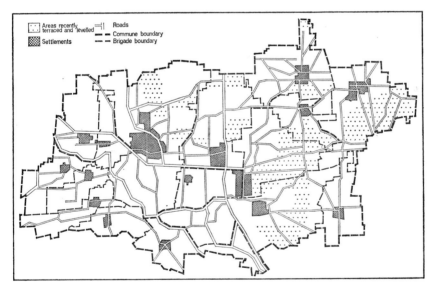

Figure 47. Commune in the Loess Area of Shensi.

Rolling loess terrain either levelled or terraced on the east, dropping down to more intensively-worked alluvial lands to the west (note the smaller area of the brigades in this area). The total area of the commune is approximately 4,000 acres.

300 animals). Seven-tenths of the land is ploughed by tractor, the tractors being hired from the county which charges 0·8–0·9 yuan per *mou*, and part of the wheat crop is mechanically harvested. In addition to possessing a wheat harvester the commune owns 34 threshers, 42

'ploughing machines' (12-tined scufflers), 157 spraying machines and 816 hand carts.   Chemical fertilisers are used, at the rate of 300 lb. per acre on grain crops and between 480 and 600 lb. per acre on vegetables; these supplement the 10–15 tons per acre of organic manures used. Industries are those which tie in closely with agriculture: six mills manufacturing bean noodles, three brick-kilns, cart-making and contructional teams and a tool-repairing shop; with the exception of the latter, which employs 27 workers permanently, these industries are seasonal, employing up to 800–900 workers in the slacker winter period.

In the field of education the commune runs two part-work, part-study schools, five State-provided elementary schools offering a six-year course and four offering a four-year course, and one middle school; in addition, each brigade runs a night-school for older members of the commune.   One small hospital run by the county is located within the commune and the commune itself has a health clinic and each brigade a health centre.   There is also a home for the aged which provides accommodation for those older members of the commune who have no relatives with whom they might live or who prefer to live a more independent existence.

Fifty-five per cent of the commune's income is divided among its members; this gives an average wage of some 300 yuan, of which 20–30 per cent is in kind, in the shape of grain, fruit and vegetables.

(c) A Note on the Tachai Brigade

In the development of the loess country of Shensi and Shansi the Tachai brigade, in the Taihang mountains of eastern Shansi, has come to occupy a critical role—that of 'pace-setter'. Since the brigade's achievements have been widely publicised in China as offering an example of how human determination and a correct application of political ideas can overcome apparently insurmountable difficulties, and since the drive and the dedication of the brigade are likely to set the pattern for development in many other parts of China, a brief comment on the experience of Tachai is relevant.

The brigade consists of 83 households, with an aggregate population of 370, and it farms some 500 acres, of which slightly over one-quarter are cultivated.   Its territory is hilly, with steep slopes and rock-strewn hill-tops where the older rocks pierce the loess cover.   The area, like the rest of loess-land, is one of great climatic variability, with protracted dry seasons broken by heavy downpours; high rates of runoff from the steep upper slopes have severely eroded the area, leaving deep steep-walled ravines and occasional isolated loess pillars.

The people of Tachai had long lived a marginal existence, seeing their laboriously-constructed loess terraces swept away by winter storms and their precious pockets of cultivable soil progressively reduced by erosion but after the floods of 1963 they decided the time had come to put an end to the problems of flood and erosion once and for all. They mobilised all their available labour and, relying solely on their own resources, they set about restoring and improving the system of terraced fields on which they depended for their livelihood. Rock outcrops were blasted away and the stone used in the construction of curving lines of terrace walls; these are some 2–3 metres high, with an additional 50 per cent of stonework below ground level to serve as a foundation. The tens of thousands of tons of rock used were largely moved by hand, as was the eroded earth which was carried up to reconstitute the ravaged fields. The lower and middle slopes of the hills were converted into stairways of stone-faced terraces; six irrigation wells were dug and a carefully constructed system of drainage and irrigation channels now effectively channels off flood-water and distributes the precious irrigation water during the dry months of spring and early summer. Meanwhile, time and labour were found for the rebuilding (in stone) of Tachai village and for the planting of shade and timber trees and extensive orchards on the lower slopes.

The major crops produced are grain crops, grown on a four-year rotation: maize (65 per cent), millet (20 per cent), wheat and beans (15 per cent). Organic manures are used at the rate of some 15 tons per acre, supplemented by slightly over a hundredweight of nitrogenous and phosphatic fertilisers. Small numbers of chickens and ducks are kept by the individual peasants, in all approximately 300 head, and the collective or individuals are rearing 190 pigs (i.e. 2·5 per household). There are no individual plots, these having been discarded by general agreement. The value of a work-day is quoted as 1·2 yuan; this, on the basis of 300 days employment per annum, suggests an average income (for a male worker) of some 360 yuan.

The rise in living levels which the data for the brigade indicates (a four-fold increase since the 1953–56 period) has been considerable but, impressive as this is, it is less impressive than the new stability and security of life which by their own efforts the people of Tachai have achieved in a traditionally marginal environment. Here, in one of the poorest areas of China's subhumid northwest, the harshness of nature tempered the spirit of the people; with spades and carrying-poles and dogged endurance and effort they demonstrated 'how a bad thing can be turned into a good thing'. And today in the loess-lands, and all over China, the drive to emulate this 'spirit of Tachai', the slogan 'Dare to think and dare to act' have become important motive forces in the transformation of the Chinese countryside.

INTENSIVE POLYCULTURE IN THE YANGTSE DELTA-LANDS
Two Communes in Kiangsu

The level lowlands of the Yangtse delta, gridded with dykes and closely set with villages, where only the feathery lift of the bamboo groves breaks the line of the pearl-grey misted horizon, contrast sharply with the thirsty and dust-hazed lands of the middle Hwang-ho valley. These delta lands are constantly moist, with hot humid summers (Köppen's Cwa type) and though the variability of rainfall or the liability to flooding or waterlogging was a constant menace in the old days, their climate suits them to a much wider range of crops than can be grown in the BSk climates of Shansi and Shensi; above all, in these regions the cropping programme based on a single crop a year, or on three crops in two years with which the peasant living in the areas to the north or northwest had to be content, can be here replaced by a much more varied programme. Two crops of grain, or several crops of vegetables are possible; sugar cane, silk and a wide range of fruits can be grown so that the typical economy is a true polyculture, based on the production of grain, vegetables, fruit, livestock products and fish. Such an economy can support very high densities of population, reaching on some communes the figure of six persons to the acre of crop land. Details are given below of two communes south of the Yangtse in southern Kiangsu.

(a) One-third Cultivated—and Six Persons per Acre

In the vicinity of Nanking the level surface of the alluvial lowlands is broken by low forest or scrub-covered hills; the paddy fields sweep up to their base but the hills themselves are of limited agricultural use. The details which follow are for a commune in this region; two-thirds of the area is occupied by uncultivated hill land under trees and used also for the gathering of medicinal herbs and for grazing.

The commune is sited 25 km. southeast of Nanking. It has a population of 14,000 comprising 3,081 households and a labour force of 6,900. This population is grouped into 65 'natural villages' and organised, for production purposes, into 9 brigades and 105 teams. Its cropland is slightly under 2,700 acres, giving a 'nutritional density' of almost six persons per acre or over 3,300 per square mile. Two-thirds of the cropland is irrigated, as against one-third in the days before the commune was formed. Eighty-seven per cent of the land is under rice, wheat, maize or sweet potatoes; the wheat is October-sown, reaped in early summer and followed by June-sown maize. Sesame and beans (for oil) occupy 170 acres; vegetables, including peppers, egg-plant, cabbages, onions and carrots, occupy somewhat over 80 acres. In addition, there are 250 acres of orchards (peaches, apples, pears) intercultivated when young, a small area of sugar cane and mulberry and an experimental plot of tea. The commune's livestock include 6,000 pigs (of these one-tenth belong to the collective, leaving almost two pigs per household in the individual sector), 523 cattle and some 30,000 individually-owned poultry. Pisciculture is an important sideline and there are eleven small reservoirs and 400 ponds used for fish-rearing.

The land is given heavy dressings of organic manure (figures of 45 tons per acre are claimed) and receives also approximately one cwt. of chemical fertiliser per acre. Water control is made possible by a network of twenty pumping stations and sixty small electric pumps. The commune is partially mechanised; it possesses eight tractors (of 15 h.p.) but these are found to be too heavy for use on the ricefields and experiments are being carried on in the use of smaller hand-tractors.

The industries of the commune include a tool-repairing shop, brick-making and the making of fans. The State has established two large factories, one for the manufacture of cement and one for glass-making, and these are operated by the commune. The total income from these industries, which offer seasonal employment to 500 workers, is some-what over £110,000 annually, which is about one-third the value of the output of the agricultural sector.

The social services the collective offers include a hospital and four health centres (towards the operation of which the peasants contribute three yuan (about 8s. 6d.) a year); three middle schools, of which one, run by the State, offers a seven-year course, two part-work, part-study schools, and eleven primary schools with a full-time enrolment of 2,200 pupils. There is, in addition, a theatre, a film group and a range of political clubs.

The average income is 115 yuan per head of *total* population; per worker it is of the order of 230–240 yuan with a range of from 300 to 180 yuan. Slightly over one-half the income is in cash. To these figures must be added the income derived from the individual produc-tion of livestock and from the individual holdings; these latter represent 5 per cent of the area of the commune (150 square metres for a typical family of five).

(b) Moving One Million Cubic Metres of Earth

East of Nanking the summer landscape is a water-dominated landscape, with wide stretches of paddy fields sweeping up to the foot of the high dyke which runs along the lower course of the Yangtse. Yet in spite of the apparently favourable conditions offered by the level terrain, the subtropical climate and the omnipresence of water, this was a region which had its full share of the natural calamities which ravaged the

Chinese earth.   On this commune, which lies some 50 kilometres east of Nanking, the peasants spoke of the old days as characterised by 'calamities in nine years out of ten': waterlogging affected wide areas in summer and autumn, typhoons, unseasonable droughts and unseasonal downpours—all these gave a marginal quality to existence and this marginal quality was aggravated by the depredations of the landlords who took one-half of the peasants' meagre crop, leaving them to eke out an existence on a diet which was half husks and half grain. Land reform made possible the beginnings of the transformation of life for these people; the large-scale physical remoulding of the landscape which, since 1958, has involved the shifting of a million cubic metres of earth has now basically solved the problem of water.

The commune has a population of 14,350 people, with 3,400 households and a labour force of 6,500.   Originally it consisted of seven advanced co-operatives; today it is organised into 10 production brigades and 136 teams.   The cultivated area is 5,000 acres, which gives a 'nutritional density' of almost three persons to the acre (c. 1,800 persons per square mile).

The development of the commune made it possible to carry through projects which had been beyond the scope of the co-operative.   In 1959 a major attack on the problem of water control was initiated by the digging of three major channels (18 metres deep) which were linked with 35 kilometres of ditches and controlled by seven locks. Five large pumping stations with a total power of 500 h.p. and thirty-three smaller pumps with a combined power of 566 h.p. now make it possible to irrigate 90 per cent of the paddy land by machinery and to replace the old single crop economy by an economy which gives two crops a year on three-fifths of the area.   Manuring is heavy.   Rice straw mixed with mud is applied at the rate of 24 tons to the acre; this is supplemented by one and a half tons of pig manure[1] to the acre and by night-soil brought by boat from Nanking (2,500 tons yearly). Approximately one cwt. of chemical fertiliser per acre is also used. Three-fifths of the cropland is tractor-ploughed (there is a State tractor station on the commune) and seven-tenths of the grain is machine threshed, the commune possessing twelve large threshing machines and a hundred small, locally-made machines.

The economy is highly diverse.   The basic crops are the food grains —rice, wheat, and maize—and other products include silk (two and a quarter tons) and fruit; the commune has a total of 50,000 fruit trees, mainly peaches and pears, some of which are still coming into bearing. There are 615 draught animals (including buffaloes), 255 sheep and 4,000 pigs; of the latter, 2,800 belong to the individual sector as do the 55,000 poultry on the commune.   150 acres were devoted to fish-

[1] The individual peasant selling pig manure to the collective is credited with one work-day for every hundredweight of manure delivered.

ponds, producing some 20–30 tons of fish annually, and, on the non-cultivable areas, 200,000 trees have been established.

Medical services are provided by a small hospital, three health centres and a mobile medical team. Each brigade has a 'health officer' and there are fourteen doctors or nurses on the staff of the commune. Eighty per cent of the school-age population, or a total of 2,360 children, are at school; the schools include twenty-eight elementary schools, forty-nine part-work, part-study schools and one junior middle school (110 pupils). For the older people, each brigade has a reading room and a mobile film unit shows one to two films per month.

The industrial sector consists either of 'servicing' industries, such as carpentry, blacksmithing, boat building, constructional work and quarrying or processing industries such as oil-pressing or flour-milling.

Income per worker ranges from 180 to 256 yuan; side-occupations may add as much as a third to this figure. This income includes 550 lb. of grain per head, to which the production from the private plots is said to add almost 100 lb. Today's *per capita* grain supply appears, from the data quoted, to be about double the supply before Liberation; in recent years it has been sufficient to enable almost one hundred weight of grain *per capita* to be saved and stored over the years 1963–65. The existence of this stored grain has an important psychological effect since it gives the peasant a very real sense of security; this is a relatively new experience for him and in his eyes is a powerful argument in favour of the commune system.

MARKET-GARDENING & INDUSTRY: *The Suburbs of Shanghai*

The railway from Nanking to Shanghai follows the line of the Grand Canal. It passes through a densely-settled countryside, a countryside of rice and vegetables and occasional orchards, for the most part intensively cultivated though with occasional areas where the appearance of the crops and of the villages suggests more marginal soil conditions. But in the vicinity of Shanghai, China's largest city (with a population of 6·2 million in 1953), the influence and the demand of this giant metropolis for foodstuffs shows itself in the closely-tended, multiple-cropped, vegetable fields and in the intensive utilisation of every inch of cultivable soil. In the suburbs agriculture penetrates deeply between the blocks of housing and the industrial zones and the commune described below is typical in this respect, being almost completely surrounded by urban and industrial development. As the details for this commune suggest, this region shows one of the most intensive agricultural economies in China; cropping is strongly market-oriented, the economy is based entirely on cash wages with none of the payment in kind we have seen on other communes, and the industrial sector is both sophisticated and highly developed.

(a) Eight People & Thirteen Pigs to the Acre: A Shanghai
   Commune

This commune is located in the northwest suburbs of Shanghai, 8
miles from the centre of the city, and is surrounded by residential or
factory development and crossed by the city's suburban rail lines.   Its
area is twelve and a half square miles; the cultivated land amounts to
2,700 acres and this, with the industrial sector, supports 23,700 people
or approximately eight persons to the acre.   There are 5,051 households and the total labour force is 11,000, organised into 14 brigades
and 111 teams.

The commune is highly specialised: 83 per cent of the area is under
vegetables and five crops a year can be obtained; small areas are under
grain for the animals and miscellaneous crops such as flowers and hemp.
Four-fifths of the crop area is irrigated (134 pumps with a total horse-
power of 1,800) and a third is tractor ploughed.   Manuring rates are
heavy: 30 tons per acre of night-soil or pig manure and heavy applica-
tions of river mud; these are supplemented by some 80–90 lb. of artificials to the acre.   It is of interest that this latter figure is one-half
the rate in earlier years, the decrease being due to the replacement
of artificials by pig manure which is now available in increased
quantities.

Linked with an intensive vegetable-producing economy is an
intensive livestock economy.   The commune has 75,000 poultry,
fattens each year 37,000 pigs and has 170 milk cattle whose milk is
destined for the Shanghai market.   Poultry pens, pig-sties and cattle
sheds are interspersed among the intensively-worked vegetable plots,
conveying the impression of a semi-industrialised agriculture.

There is a sizeable industrial sector employing 400 full-time workers
and additional seasonal labour at peak periods.   This sector includes
vegetable-processing (the most seasonal of the industries), tool-repairing and the manufacture of agricultural implements and bamboo-work
and a factory producing phosphatic fertilisers from State-supplied
phosphatic rock.   The gross output of the industrial sector is 2·5
million yuan.   Of this, 7 per cent goes in taxes to the State, 15 per cent
to the commune and 140,000–200,000 yuan is absorbed by wages (30
yuan per month); the remainder, after other operating costs have been
met, is ploughed back, providing the basis for a continuing expansion.

The income of the agricultural sector is over 8 million yuan, in
other words, over £1 million sterling.   Over half of this is distributed
and wages are entirely in cash.   Average wages are cited as 382 yuan
per worker per year, with a range between teams of from 300 to 450
yuan; to this total sideline occupations add another 15 per cent.   A
small number of commune members work in the city and their income
is pooled with the other earnings of the collective.

1. The enduring elements of China's history: rice, bamboo, water—and a child.

'THE CONTEMPORARY TRANSFORMATION . . . CONTINUES AN AGE-OLD TRADITION'

2. Changing elements in China's history: pavilions in the grounds of the Summer Palace, Peking, formerly an Imperial residence and now a park and recreational area for the people of the capital.

3. One of China's hundred million peasant families (Shensi).

'THE REAL ACTORS IN THE DRAMA OF CHINESE HISTORY...'

4. Vegetable-growing team in Kwangtung Province.

5. Children at a kindergarten in Peking. The kindergarten is attached to a large textile factory and represents one aspect of that provision of social services which is regarded as a basic responsibility of industry to its workers.

'THE MOST PRECIOUS OF CHINA'S ASSETS'

6. Children of factory workers in Peking. Children represent over one-third of China's population, and it is on the mind and muscle—and the dedication—of the young that the country's development depends.

7. The Northwestern minority peoples: girls in Sinkiang Uighur A.R.

'CO-SHAPERS OF CHINESE CIVILISATION'

8. The Southwestern minority peoples: Miao girls in festival dress (Yunnan).

9. Western sector of cradle area: loess landscape near Sian. Power-poles and distant grain fields of commune are the signature of the new society on a landscape whose grave-mounds and monuments are legacies from the old society.

THE YELLOW-EARTH 'CRADLE AREA'

10. Loess landscape in Shansi. A meticulously cultivated landscape in an environment of easily-worked soils and low rainfall: traditionally much of the settlement was in houses cut into the vertical face of valley walls.

11. The more humid eastern sector of the cradle area, floored by calcareous alluvium derived from erosion in the western loess country. A richer environment with more predictable climate but unpredictable rivers and with an economy dependent on careful dyking and water control.

THE YELLOW-EARTH 'CRADLE AREA'

12. Northern margin of cradle area where the man-made frontier of the Great Wall and the broken hilly terrain of the Taihang Mountains and their extension protected the rich agricultural lands of the Great Plain.

13. The rolling grasslands of Chinghai, home-zone of Altaic-speaking nomad peoples such as the Mongols and Uighurs, the 'containment' of whom gave rise to interminable frontier wars.

THE WESTERN REGIONS: 'MARGIN OF DIFFERENTIATION AND LIMITATION'

14. The deserts of the Far West. Trade and settled life was confined to the oasis-corridors which fringe these red sand deserts; only recently has man begun to shift from a passive adjustment to this desert world to an attempt to tame it through shelter-belt planting and dune stabilisation.

15. The 'sub-oasis' zone of Kansu. Here, in spite of semi-arid conditions, the waters of the Yellow River make possible irrigated agriculture and the extension of relatively dense settlement (see Map 10) far west along the Kansu corridor.

THE WESTERN REGIONS: 'MARGIN OF DIFFERENTIATION AND LIMITATION'

16. The oases of the Far West. Water derived from the snow- and glacier-fed streams of the western ranges combines with high summer temperatures to make possible an intensive irrigated agriculture in the piedmont zones of the Tien Shan and Kun Lan Shan. The dramatic contrast between the lush vegetation of the oases and the bare slopes of the adjoining ranges is illustrated by this view of the Turfan oasis.

17. 'South to a land of fragrant springs . . .' (*Li Yü*, tenth century). Terraced landscape in South China. (*Contemporary collective painting*).

THE RED LANDS OF THE SOUTH:
'MARGIN OF INDEFINITE EXPANSION'

18. Limestone crags, paddy fields, vegetative luxuriance and water. A Kweilin landscape contrasting sharply with the 'stern, sober and correct' landscapes of North China. (Contemporary painting by *Hu Jo-ssu*)

19. 'A world more fertile, more hot and humid . . .' Small alluvial lowlands set amid the red lateritic hills of Kwangtung Province. Vegetables, plantains and tropical fruits flourish in the warm, moist climate of the South.

THE RED LANDS OF THE SOUTH: 'MARGIN OF INDEFINITE EXPANSION'

20. Seventy generations of humanisation: part of the Pearl River lowland; two millennia ago, 'a waste of untamed waters populated by savages and wild beasts', now a carefully tended landscape dominated by wet rice and tropical crops such as plantain and sugar cane.

21. 'A complete recasting of the educational system.' The part-work, part-study school, integrating theory with practice, and, by its contribution to production, a largely self-supporting institution, is emerging as the distinctive Chinese medium of education. Illustrated is a veterinary class at a part-work, part-study school in Shansi.

THE PROCESS OF CHANGE: MOBILISING MIND AND MUSCLE

22. In the cities these schools give a theoretical and practical training in mechanics and engineering; their products are purchased for State factories. These girls are pupils at a part-work, part-study school in Peking.

23. The isolation and vulnerability of the individual peasant family is replaced by team effort mobilised within the commune framework: mother, children and grandmother harvesting the rice in the old style in Yunnan.

THE PROCESS OF CHANGE: MOBILISING MIND AND MUSCLE

24. Production team harvesting and threshing rice on a commune in Kwantung; the rice heads are beaten against the basket edge so that the loose grain falls into the shielded basket.

25. Terracing carried out in the vicinity of Lanchow during the winter of 1957–58. The terracing creates a series of micro-plains on which fruit and timber trees are being established. This terracing and afforestation, transforming the landscape, represent the creation, by labour-investment, of new capital in a climatically-marginal and formerly impoverished area.

'WITH THEIR OWN STRENGTH THEY MADE THE LANDSCAPE'

26. Levelling of fields on the uplands of this Shensi commune has created a new micro-relief, facilitating mechanised agriculture.

27. New stone-faced terraces at Tachai, on the margins of the loess country in Shansi. Here the labour-investment needed to create one acre of terraced land is between 1,200 and 1,400 man days: most of the walls have been built since 1963.

'WITH THEIR OWN STRENGTH THEY MADE THE LANDSCAPE'

28. Transforming the soil profile: mounds of calcareous concretions in the loess region. They result from the digging-out of the concretionary layer typical of many of China's subhumid soil types and which was found to be an impediment to the growth of fruit trees.

29. 'Hydro-technical' influences on soil formation. Dyking and irrigation modify the soil character over much of lowland China; here a team is opening irrigation channels on a commune in Anhwei.

'*WITH THEIR OWN STRENGTH THEY MADE THE LANDSCAPE*'

30. On a larger scale irrigation canals carry water from the uplands and make possible the maintenance of a high level of soil humidity in subhumid environments. This new canal supplies both irrigation and drinking water to the Peking lowland.

31. In areas of adequate rainfall storage reservoirs make it possible for man to overcome the problem of rainfall variability: the spillway of a storage reservoir built by a commune on the edge of the Canton lowland.

'WITH THEIR OWN STRENGTH THEY MADE THE LANDSCAPE'

32. With control over water supplies ensured, intensification and expansion of crop output becomes possible on the lower land of the commune.

33. The increasing diffusion of electric power through the countryside means that many jobs can be done by machinery. The use of electric pumps in irrigation is illustrated by this small pumping station on a Shensi commune. The increased availability of water means that cropping can be diversified and the cropping year extended.

THE TECHNICAL TRANSFORMATION OF THE COUNTRYSIDE

34. Construction of a new pumping station by members of a commune. An example of the investment of human labour to create the new capital equipment needed to boost production levels.

35. Large pumping stations, such as this one recently built on an Anhwei commune, now form an important element in the country's irrigation system.

THE TECHNICAL TRANSFORMATION OF THE COUNTRYSIDE

36. Pumping machinery, by contrast with the use of human muscle-power, makes possible the development of more elaborate irrigation systems: this intricate pattern of irrigation channels is part of a network supplying water to every field of this Anhwei commune.

37. The use of machinery reduces the need for heavy manual labour: a brick-cutting machine on a Kwangtung commune.

THE TECHNICAL TRANSFORMATION OF THE COUNTRYSIDE

38. And power-driven machinery can be utilised in a wide range of lighter tasks, such as pottery-making. This boy is turning out all the rice-bowls needed by the population of the commune where he lives.

39. Technical innovations go far to making each commune a self-sufficient unit, able to service and repair, and often to make, the basic agricultural equipment. This forge is on a Kwangtung commune.

THE TECHNICAL TRANSFORMATION OF THE COUNTRYSIDE

40. This girl, on a North China commune, is cutting the steel to build the mechanical seeder in the background. An increasing range of technical skills is one of the biggest assets to agriculture.

41. Cereal-growing finds its optimum topographic conditions in the wide, wind-swept plains of the North: hoeing of maize on the loess-derived soils of the Yellow River valley, in the cradle area of Chinese civilisation.

A FLAT-LAND, GRAIN-BASED TRADITIONAL AGRICULTURE

42. Chinese civilisation spread into the subtropical and tropical South. Here rice became the dominant crop and every inch of potential rice-land was brought under cultivation. These paddy fields are on the margin of the lake of Kunming, in Yunnan: settlement is on the lower slopes unsuitable for rice.

55. Traditional North Chinese-style housing: dwellings and outhouses with mud walls and tiled roofs arranged within a walled courtyard; suburbs of Sian.

REHOUSING ONE-QUARTER OF HUMANITY

56. The new suburban fringe of Sian. This ancient city and former Imperial capital has expanded greatly since 1949 and now has a population of one and a half million. New buildings—schools, research institutes and housing blocks— are set amid intensively cultivated fields and a bold road pattern is superimposed on the landscape.

57. Old and new in Peking. The buildings of New Peking rising above one of the remaining areas of semi-slum housing.

REHOUSING ONE-QUARTER OF HUMANITY

58. Housing the growing urban population. Workers' quarters in one of the older of the rehousing projects carried out in Peking by the People's Government.

59. New housing estate in Loyang. Multi-storey blocks of apartments, recently constructed and set among young trees to provide shade and coolness. Such blocks provide cheap and well-serviced accommodation for new families and for those displaced by slum demolition.

60. The development of the last two decades is illustrated by this sharp juxtaposition of old and new building styles. These examples taken in Kunming, Yunnan, are separated by a three-minute walk.

61. 'Travelling among the ice-capped peaks of the Tien Shan'
(*Hua Yen*, 1682-1786).

'*BEYOND THE FRONTIERS LIE THE HARD
WINTERS AND THE RAGING WINDS*'
(*Li Shih-ming*, seventh century).

62. 'Winter in the Taihang Mountains' (*Lu Tsun-pei*, contemporary).

'*AND ANXIOUS EYES THAT
WATCH EARTH'S BLOSSOMING*'
(*Li Yü*: Tenth Century)

63. Spring scene in South China: ripening rice in the middle distance, willows
and plum blossom, and the new season's ploughing under way; tractors, lorries, a
distant factory and a buffalo-drawn plough in the foreground—the new and the
traditional interwoven. (*Contemporary collective painting.*)

The social services available to members of the collective include seventeen elementary schools (of which twelve are run by the commune and five by the State) with a total enrolment of 6,300 students; one State-run middle school with over a thousand pupils and a small part-work, part-study school run by the commune. There is a small (45 cubicle hospital) on the commune and two clinics; each brigade and each team has one 'health officer'.

The density of population on the commune is almost 2,000 per square mile of total area or 5,600 per square mile of cropland. Full employment and a reasonable level of living (measured against other communes) have been achieved by a high degree of intensification of production. Present growth rates, however, indicate that the population can be expected to double in the next generation, to give a density of *11,000 people per square mile of cropland*. This single example illustrates the challenge posed by China's population expansion; this challenge, and the responses to it, are analysed in Chapter 13.

SECURING THE LOWLANDS & USING THE UPLANDS
Three Communes in Kwangtung

South China is exceptionally favoured climatically: it lies in the humid subtropical zone (the Cwa and Cfa types of the Köppen classification) and its climates are sufficiently warm and sufficiently moist throughout the year to make possible two to three crops of rice or up to eight crops of vegetables; tropical crops such as sugar cane can be grown and also a wide range of tree crops—lichees, persimmons, loquats, plums and bananas. Within this climatic zone, however, there is a considerable diversity of topographic and soil conditions, ranging from the bare karstic hills of Kweilin to the estuarine environment of the Pearl River delta. From the broadest possible view these environments can be grouped in two categories: first, the aquatic environments, sometimes coast-plains, sometimes estuarine flats where sea and land intermingle complexly, sometimes the alluvial-veneered floors of old lake basins; secondly, the upland environments, occasionally karstic in character as in northern Kwangsi, but more usually characterised by red or yellow lateritic soils of limited fertility. Historically, as we have seen, this contrast has been significant since it was towards the first type of environment that early Han settlement was directed, leaving to earlier groups the uplands which were little suited to rice cultivation or intensive cultivation of any sort. Today the two groups of environments present major but quite different challenges to the communes of the area and it is by reason of their confrontation of these challenges that the communes of Kwantung are of such interest to the geographer.

The basic problem of the lowlands is the control of water; this involves a system of water storage and control, extending into the uplands,

M

which makes available a regular supply of water; the construction of a
network of ditches and drains to distribute irrigation water and
draw off excess water; the construction, in coast plain areas such as the
Pearl River delta, of protective dykes sufficiently strong to withstand
the occasional combination of heavy rainfall, high tides and typhoon
conditions; the planning and the establishment of a grid of pumping
stations and the integration of all of these with the need to extend and
facilitate the use of the rivers and canals as a means of transport—
which involves the building of a complex system of locks.   Given a
solution to the water problem, the second problem in the lowlands
arises from the character of these alluvial soils.   While tractor cultivation appears cheaper than buffalo ploughing (a difference of 1:5)
many of the soils do not appear suited to the heavier type of tractor
which was fashionable when Soviet technology was providing the model
for Chinese development.   In this context the Sino-Soviet differences
of the early 'sixties may be seen in retrospect as blessings in disguise
since they forced many communes to a re-evaluation of their situation
and to the search for *Chinese* solutions to problems that were specifically
Chinese.   And, in evaluating the prospects for 'motorisation' on these
lowland soils, we may add two other considerations which are valid in
other regions of China: first, that a buffalo will give two tons of manure
a year (and hence, unlike the tractor, plays a double role as a source of
power and of nutrients), secondly, that with high densities of population
excessive motorisation may lead to a major problem of under-employment.

The uplands pose different problems and these were examined by
the French geographer Pierre Gourou almost two decades ago.   Looking at them in the context of China as a whole he suggested three
major lines of development: afforestation, fruit-growing and the development of a livestock industry based on improved pastures.   His
major concern was with the gross inequalities of population distribution, with virtually empty hill-lands fringing densely crowded lowland
areas, and he saw in the development of the uplands a means whereby
a more even spread of the population could be achieved.   Since 1949
some of the elements in his programme have been taken up, first by the
co-operatives and subsequently by the communes, as part of a prag-
matically-conceived development policy.   There has, however, been
little concern with the *spreading* of the population; indeed, while statistics
on the situation are not available, it appears to the writer that the old
gradients of population persist, may indeed have become sharper.
With the advantage of hindsight, it is now apparent that Gourou
neglected the possibility that technological change might bring major
changes in the lowland areas, and, by broadening the resource base
in these lowlands, alter completely the relationship between lowland
and upland.   The intensification of lowland agriculture and the

development of rural industries make possible the elimination of under-employment and provide conditions for the absorption of a greatly increased population in the lowlands.   There has certainly been development in the upland sections of many communes—extensive afforestation, planting of fruit trees, even the beginning, on a small scale, of an upland livestock economy.   But the most striking development of the last two or three years has been the use of the upland laterites for the production on terraced fields of leguminous green manure crops to be used on the lowland section of the communes.   These crops draw on the deep-seated nutrients of the upland soils (as well as fixing atmospheric nitrogen) and the accumulated nutrients locked up in their foliage are used to build up the fertility of the lowland soils. Such a system makes possible the increasing integration of the poorer uplands into the economy of the communes of which they form part; it also makes possible a steady build-up of fertility—and thus of population—in the lowland areas.

Details are given below of three communes in Kwangtung; the first is in the heart of the Pearl River delta, the other two overlap on to the hilly margin of the Canton lowland.

(a) Fruit, Flowers, Fish-ponds & Vegetables: A Delta Commune (1964)

This is a suburban commune, lying to the south of Canton in the midst of the complex maze of distributaries and islands which marks the mouth of the Si Kiang.   Its basic problems in the past were the result of this location; low-lying, the land around was especially vulnerable to the floods of May–June and, in fact, some seven-tenths of the commune's territory was flood-liable.   After the formation of the commune a coordinated attack on the flood problem became possible and between October 1959 and July 1960 the commune members undertook the construction of a major dyke along the Pearl River. This involved the shifting of almost three-quarters of a million cubic metres of earth and the construction of seven locks.   The total cost was one million yuan (c. £140,000) to which the State contributed one-fifth.   The work was carried further between 1960 and 1963 when forty-eight pumping stations with an aggregate power of 1,100 h.p. were installed.   Subsequently a hundred acres of very wet land was reclaimed by building another small pumping station (costing £2,000). Today, the problem of flood control, drainage and irrigation can be regarded as solved and, with this new security, commune members can concentrate single-mindedly on the intensification of production and the raising of the levels of rural life.

The commune is large.   Its area is 8,250 acres.   Its population is 45,000, consisting of 11,500 families and with a labour force of 20,000.

Formed by the merging of twelve co-operatives, it is today organised into 17 production brigades and 276 production teams. One-quarter of the land is under vegetables (and with more intensive production methods and better rotations it is now possible to get eight crops a year instead of five as previously; this means the effective crop-area under vegetables is 2,160 × 8 = 17,280 acres), one-third is under fruit, one-sixth under rice and one-tenth under sugar cane. There are also 330 acres of fish-ponds and 250 acres of flowers for perfume. Small areas are under a variety of other crops and there are 330 acres of individual plots. The commune has 620 milk cattle (200 before 1958), 1,500 groups of beehives and 5,400 pigs; an additional 4,000 pigs are owned by the individual peasants.

Expansion of production has depended ultimately on the water control measures described earlier; it has also depended on improved rotations, the use of improved seed strains and on minor changes in technique such as the change from the old 50:50 ratio between ridge and ditch (most of the vegetables are grown on ridges: see Plate 4) to a ratio of 60:40. The intensity of cropping calls for heavy use of manures: these include two-and-a-half hundredweight of chemical fertiliser per acre on vegetables, and some three-fifths that amount on other crops; the use of night-soil and sewage water from Canton; animal manure; river mud and vegetable wastes; bean-cake (especially for the sugar cane).

The industrial sector employs 250 people. It includes the manufacture of farm tools and the maintenance of the commune's mechanical equipment (pumps, lorries, etc.), brick-making and lime-burning and, as might be expected in the light of the commune's cropping programme, a wide range of food-processing industries; the preparation of dried fruit, the manufacture of soy sauce and pickles, the milling of rice and the distilling of wine are among the most important.

The commune has a ninety-bed hospital, fifteen health stations and eight maternity centres (maternity leave is fifty days). There are 110 crèches and 35 kindergartens and 80 per cent of the school-age population is at school, either in the middle school or one of the fifteen primary schools.

Average wages (1964) are 450 yuan and the range is from 100–700 yuan. From this it may be deduced that the total income of the commune is between 15 and 20 million yuan.

(b) Integrating the Uplands into the Agricultural Economy: A Commune northeast of Canton

To the north and northeast of Canon low lateritic hills finger south towards the level alluvial lowlands of the Si River delta. The higher and steeper of these are generally forested and the forests include extensive plantings of young conifers. The more subdued and gently-sloping hills, by contrast, have been the scene of what may prove to be one of the most significant developments in this region since 1949 and that is the use of these uplands for the production of a nitrogen-fixing green manure crop (*san-mao-dou*). Its use has spread remarkably in the last two to three years; it is grown on shallow terraces cut into the laterite slopes, often with fruit trees interplanted, and is cut three times a year and its foliage used as a green manure for the intensively-cultivated soils of the lowland. On this commune to the northeast of Canton almost one-third of the total area of 16,000 acres is mountainous. Of this upland area one-third is under fruit, some 1,000 acres are terraced for the production of green manures and on much of the rest the natural vegetation is cut and used for manuring the lowland sector of the commune. The draught animals of the commune are also pastured on the hills and a new development is the purchase of eighty young cattle to be reared for meat on the hill pastures. By extending this triple utilisation of the uplands—for fruit growing, green manure and livestock grazing—it is hoped to have 90 per cent of the commune area under some form of productive utilisation by the end of 1966.

The commune has a population of 22,000 which means it is below the average size for the province. The number of families is 5,000 and the labour force 8,000; there are 12 production brigades and 111 teams. The cultivated area (excluding fruit and green manure crops on the hills) is 5,330 acres; of this, almost 4,000 acres is under rice (two crops a year are obtained), 1,000 acres under groundnuts and smaller areas are devoted to maize, vegetables and fodder crops for the pigs. Ninety-five per cent of the cropland is irrigated. Between $2\frac{1}{2}$ and $3\frac{1}{2}$ tons of animal manure or night-soil is applied to each acre, supplemented with $7\frac{1}{2}$ tons of green manure and slightly under one hundredweight of ammonium salts; phosphatic fertilisers are used if necessary. Thirty per cent of the land is tractor-ploughed, the tractors being hired from the State which charges 5·4 yuan per acre for ploughing.

The livestock population includes 3,000 cattle and buffalo, 7,800 pigs (4,000 of which belong to the collective) and 70,000 poultry (40 per cent of which belong to the collective); there are 66 acres of fishponds and 100 acres of reservoirs which can also be used for fish production. Each pig, it is estimated, produces one ton of manure a year; those peasant families who possess pigs can sell the manure to the collective, a ton of manure sold having a cash-equivalent of about twenty-five work-days.

Industry does not represent a major component of the commune's activity. Some of the members are engaged in the transportation sector, others in the maintenance of the commune's two large pumping stations, but the major industries are those closely associated with agriculture. The commune has an agricultural engineering and maintenance shop and each brigade has a repairing unit; there are nineteen brick kilns and seven flour-mills (operated by the brigades) and the commune runs an agricultural processing centre which is concerned with such activities as the drying of lichees.

The commune runs a hospital and five clinics, and has a total of sixty-four doctors and nurses; the medical services seem sufficiently sophisticated to make possible population control through sterilisation and clinical abortion (though the rate of growth cited is still high— 3 per cent per annum as against 4 per cent in earlier years). Each brigade has a health centre and, in addition, the commune is able to draw on the advice and assistance of visiting medical teams from Canton. 4,200 pupils attend the 18 State primary schools on the commune, 550 attend the State middle school and 90 attend the part-work, part-study school run by the commune.

Average wage per worker is *c.* 300 yuan of which over two-fifths is in cash; to this the average family can add some 60 yuan derived from the sale of poultry, pigs and other items produced by the individual sector.

(c) Reservoirs, Melon-growing & Electro-plating

The development of a stable and intensive system of irrigated agriculture depends ultimately on the complete mastery of water-resources and this involves control of the whole of a catchment area, the stabilisation of the hill-slopes by afforestation and the creation of a system of reservoirs in the hill country which will make possible the storage of water and thus eliminate the danger of crop failure through deficient rainfall. This pattern of development is being followed on some of the communes on the northern periphery of the Canton plain; on these communes heavy investment of labour has made possible the building of a carefully-planned system of reservoirs, the realignment of some of the smaller rivers and the construction of a close network of irrigation channels which now permits the maximum degree of utilisation of the commune's lower-lying lands.

The commune shown in Maps 48 and 49 illustrates this pattern of development. Its total area is approximately 15,000 acres, of which the northern third consists of broken hilly terrain. Of the lowland area of 10,500 acres 98 per cent is irrigated, with rice as the major crop; 8,000 acres of early rice are grown, followed by almost 9,000 acres of late rice. Two crops of groundnuts are obtained (1,000 acres first crop, 350 acres second crop) and there are 350 acres of melons and slightly under 100 acres of lichees. Small quantities of other crops such as wheat or beans are also produced. Careful irrigation and heavy manuring make possible high and dependable yields; the manures include $2\frac{1}{2}$ tons of night-soil or pig manure, and 6 tons of green manure (grown partly on the terraced laterite of the hill slopes) to each acre; this

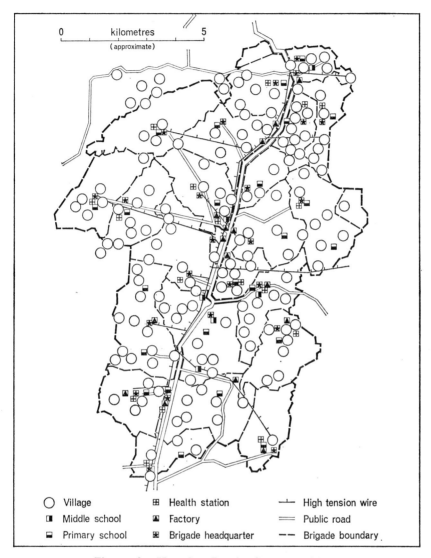

Figure 48. Hwa-shan Peoples Commune (I).

Illustrating the break-up into production brigade areas, the close settlement in small hamlets and villages and the distribution of social services. The electricity grid provides the basis for the beginnings of a diffused industrialisation.

is supplemented by up to 4 cwt. of nitrogenous and phosphatic fertilisers.

The commune has 3,750 cattle or buffaloes; 28,000 of the 43,000 pigs are collectively owned; 70,000 poultry are owned by the collective and there are 125 acres of fish-ponds.

There is a well-developed and varied industrial sector. This employs 830 people (at a monthly wage of 33·5 yuan) and the commune's *total*

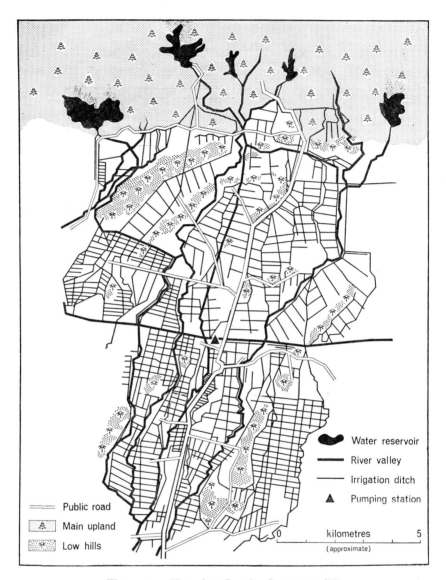

Figure 49.   Hwa-shan Peoples Commune (II).
Illustrating the close grid of irrigation ditches fed by recently-constructed reservoirs in the hilly areas to the north of the commune and by the diversion of river waters along the central east–west irrigation channel.

income derived from industrial sources is 1·7 million yuan, in other words, approximately £250,000; the *net* income (excluding wages) is 325,000 yuan.   There is the usual range of rural industries: agricultural tool repairing, lime-burning, brick-making, quarrying, and food-processing—and in addition relatively specialised industries such as electro-plating (carried out under contract to the State) and match-making. At the brigade level there are seasonally-operated brick-kilns and poultry hatcheries.

The total population supported by these activities is 50,000, consisting of 10,860 households and representing a labour force of 19,000. This population represents an increase of 8,000 over the 1958 figure; the 'nutritional density' is five persons per acre. A unit of this size can support a level of services not possible to the smaller or poorer unit. These include a hospital with X-ray equipment and operating theatre, twenty-four health centres, ten clinics and a medical staff of 117. This developed medical infrastructure has made possible control of population by the use of diaphragms, by clinical abortion or by voluntary sterilisation of either the wife or the husband; according to data supplied by the secretary of the commune 50 per cent of the 5,520 women of childbearing age were now practising birth control by one of the above methods, with a resultant decline in the rate of population growth from slightly under 2 per cent per annum to 1·5 per cent.

As on most communes, however, one of the most striking—and attractive—features is the swarms of young children. 10,500 are attending the twenty-seven commune-run elementary schools and 2,200 the four middle schools. Three of these are part-work, part-study schools and are run by the commune; the fourth is State-run and its curriculum includes English which is taken by all students.

The average wage is 278 yuan, with a range from 200 to 500 yuan. About one-half is in kind; an additional 25 yuan per head of *total* population is derived from the peasants' individual plots or from side-line occupations.

A BRIEF RETROSPECT: *The Communes Eight Years Ago*

Details are given below of five communes visited in 1958. The details are appended partly because the first four communes are in provinces in the west of Agricultural China which it was not possible to visit in 1964 or 1966; partly because they give a glimpse of the commune system at its point of emergence, at a time when certain social developments now largely discarded (such as communal dining halls) were being introduced and when the first phase of industrialisation, and particularly the peasant steel industry, was at its height.

(1) *Commune in Kansu.* Population 18,000, consisting of 3,000 households. Area approximately 4,500 acres (including some hill-land), most of which is now irrigated. Emphasis on production of vegetables and fruit, with some wheat and maize. Livestock includes 670 horses, donkeys or mules, 4,000 pigs, 3,000 sheep, 110 dairy cows (an innovation; it was hoped to quadruple the number in 1959),

20,000 poultry and 70 hives of bees. Small area of fish-ponds. Some 50 tons of sulphate of ammonia or bone-meal were used (i.e. about 15–20 lb. per acre) in addition to organic manures. Five tractors and one lorry. Commune runs twelve primary schools, one middle school and a veterinary school.

(2) *Commune in Szechwan.* Population 52,600, consisting of 14,560 households. 18,000 acres under crops, mainly rice, with wheat, vegetables, tobacco, potatoes, hemp and fodder crops. 35,000 pigs, 2,000 oxen and 15 dairy cows. Commune possesses five tractors and runs a wide range of small industries; it has 250 'factories' employing 3,750 workers. It runs 286 dining halls, 282 nurseries, 119 kindergartens, 39 primary schools (with a total enrolment of 2,630 pupils), 8 middle schools (with an enrolment of 1,070 students) and 4 clinics.

(3) *Minority (Yi) Commune in Yunnan.* Population 21,500, consisting of 4,800 households; labour force 9,100. Area 9,000 acres, of which one-third is irrigated lowland and two-thirds hill-land. Main crops rice and wheat on the lowland; maize, beans and vegetables on the hills. Livestock include 4,000 buffaloes and oxen, 6,300 sheep and 10,500 pigs. Commune runs 21 native-style blast furnaces, turning out some 20 tons of pig-iron weekly, 20 brick-kilns, lime-kilns and woodworking industries, including the manufacture of simple agricultural machinery. Formerly there was no doctor in the area and little schooling; by 1958 the commune could draw on the services of thirty State-trained health officers and schooling had been extended even to the girls who traditionally had never been educated (in 1958 half of those attending school were girls).

(4) *Commune in the Kwangsi Chuang Autonomous Region.* Population 2,014 households. Rice area 1,700 acres, vegetables 350 acres. Pigs, buffaloes and 100 dairy cattle. The industrial sector employs 350, the most important enterprises being coke-making (130 workers) and brick-making (107 workers); a sulphuric acid plant had been constructed and was shortly to begin production.

(5) *Commune near Peking.* Population 56,000 comprising 22,500 households, of which 9,000 are peasant households. Labour force 12,900. Crop area 10,000 acres. Some basic food crops (wheat, sweet potatoes, groundnuts) but main emphasis on vegetable production (tomatoes, cucumbers, peppers, cabbages, etc.), partly under glass. Fourteen tractors, with workshop for maintenance work and agricultural tools factory.

LIMITATION OF THE SAMPLE: Some Comments

The writer is only too well aware that the data presented in this and the preceding chapter give only a fragmentary picture of the complex and constantly evolving situation in the Chinese countryside. Given the size of the country, given the difficulties of access to many areas, given the difficulties of working through translators and the occasional problems posed by dialect, this is perhaps inevitable. A more serious limitation, at least at first sight, is the probability that many of the communes visited were above average, leading in consequence to some distortion of the picture built up from the impressions and the statistics collected. That this is a very real possibility cannot be denied. Indeed, the application of one or two quite simple tests *does* suggest that the group of communes discussed was somewhat above the average; thus, several communes cited chemical fertiliser consumption of over one hundredweight per acre, yet, assuming a level of fertiliser production in China of some 8 to 9 million tons, only 160–180 million acres out of the total cultivated area of (probably) 260 million acres could have received one hundredweight per acre. The same conclusion— that we are dealing largely with above-average communes in our sample—emerges if we consider data such as crop yields or wages.

Nevertheless, on reflection, the writer is inclined to the view that this is not necessarily a major weakness. In China today we are no longer, as was the case before the Second World War, dealing with a countryside, a whole rural society, held immobilised by the shackles of poverty and a stultifying social system. Rather are we concerned with a society in the process of rapid and radical change, not only in its social and political organisation but also in its technology and in the degree of industrialisation and the cropping systems and levels of production which reflect this technological change. The geographer must inevitably be concerned with such processes of change; as the writer put it some years ago 'the "sketching in of movement" is more real—and to us as geographers more rewarding—than the most careful but inevitably dated static description.'[1] Recent Chinese work on the division of the country into its basic agricultural regions underlines this for the classification is based, in part at least, on 'the direction of regional agricultural development' (see pp. 178, 185). In this context the more developed communes indicate clearly the *direction* of change in the Chinese countryside; they represent a prefiguring of the type of economy and the type of social system the Chinese are striving to achieve throughout the length and breadth of China. The best of them—and brigades like the Tachai Brigade—are models, or 'pace-setters', for those less developed; the techniques which made possible *their* development can be, and are being, adapted to their own conditions by the less advanced communes. And, as the experience of Tachai shows, it is not always the collectives in the more favoured areas which are remarkable for their progress; moreover, the more difficult the environment, the more significant to other poor areas is any 'breakthrough' in that environment.

[1] Keith Buchanan, 'West Wind, East Wind' in *Proceedings of the Third New Zealand Geography Conference*, August 1961, p. 20.

The communes analysed in earlier pages thus not only indicate the progress that has been achieved in many parts of China, they also provide us as geographers with a key to the understanding of the sort of countryside which is in the process of emerging—or, rather, *which is being consciously shaped* by half a billion peasant folk.   The data presented will, in spite of its imperfections, underline the immensity of this 'cultural reappraisal' of their resources on which the Chinese peasants have embarked.

CHAPTER 8

The Agricultural Regions of China

EARLIER CHAPTERS and maps will have indicated the immense diversity of the Chinese land. It includes some of the
highest mountain ranges on earth, some of the biggest alluvial lowlands,
rolling hill country and plateaux of varying geological composition
and great interior basins which sink, in the Turfan depression, below
sea-level. Its climates range from the perpetual frost climates of the
high Himalayas to the tropical climates of its southern fringe, from the
parched steppe or desert climates of its west to the humid mesothermal
climates of its eastern deltas. Parts are densely settled by Han Chinese
whose history in these areas (and whose appraisal of the potentialities
of the environment) reaches back several millennia; other areas, like
the Northeast, are areas of relatively recent settlement. Vast areas
are occupied by minority peoples whose food-getting economies are
quite different from those of their Han fellow-citizens. New technologies, largely in the form of new crops, have penetrated unevenly.
It is, therefore, inevitable that patterns of agriculture developed over
the centuries should vary greatly from one region to another and that
the resultant mosaic of agricultural regions should be one of very great
complexity; indeed, one of the most recent attempts at classification
yields a total of 129 minor regions. In the paragraphs below a brief
account is given of some of the attempts to delineate this regional
diversity.

A PIONEER CLASSIFICATION—THAT OF J. L. BUCK

The most outstanding pioneer work in this field was that of John
Lossing Buck, carried out in 1929–33 when Buck was Professor of
Agricultural Economics at the University of Nanking. It was based
on a study of 16,786 farms in 168 localities, within that eastern sector of
China sometimes termed 'Agricultural China', and covered not merely

land use but also such topics as size of holding, farm labour, marketing and prices and rural living levels. Within the area of 'Agricultural China' Buck distinguished two major regions: the Wheat Region and the Rice Region, and eight subregions or 'areas'. 'The boundaries of these regions and areas were determined by basic factors mostly physical, by factors affecting type of land use, and by factors affecting the success of the land use. . . . If there was doubt as to where the line should be drawn . . . differences of soil and topography were the deciding factors because these usually coincide with differences in success of land use.'[1] This regional classification rapidly became almost a 'classic' framework for studies of China; though Buck himself stressed that, as more data accumulated, revision of some of the boundaries would become essential and that, as with all systems of regional classification, the 'weight' given to the various factors was admittedly subjective. The regions were drawn up partly to provide a basis for the sample survey on which Buck's work rested; the detailed statistical material which the project provided was thus, in part at least, subsequent to, rather than a preliminary to, classification; what Buck presents us with is essentially a series of 'groups of localities in which sample studies were made and for which averages were computed'.

The general picture which emerges is shown in Map 50 and in Table 6.

The maps and statistics with which Buck illustrates his regional account of Chinese agriculture give us an excellent picture of the country's rural economy at the end of an era, an era which had lasted many hundreds of years, during which agricultural systems had become increasingly adjusted to the potentialities of the terrain—and increasingly fossilised. The tensions building up within Chinese peasant society rarely intrude into the pages of this meticulous and rigorously detached analysis—yet it was these tensions which, in the next two decades, were to shatter the old society and initiate a transformation of Chinese rural structures—and of the Chinese agricultural scene—which is still going on.

The basic themes of China's agricultural geography are clearly delineated: the relatively low proportion (25–27 per cent) of the total area cultivated, in spite of heavy and increasing population pressure; the contrasts in proportion of land cultivated between the Wheat Region and the Rice Region (the proportion being twice as high in the former); the low intensity of cultivation in certain areas, such as the Southwestern Rice Area which has only 7 per cent of its land under cultivation; the heavy emphasis on grain crops which occupy between three-fifths and three-quarters of the cultivated land depending on area; within this, the contrast between the heavier single-crop dominance of

[1] John Lossing Buck, *Land Utilisation in China* (reprint, New York 1964), pp. 24–5.

TABLE 6

SELECTED INDICES FOR THE EIGHT MAJOR AGRICULTURAL REGIONS OF CHINA (after Buck)

Percentage of Total Crop Area occupied by various Crops

	% Total Cultivated Land	% of Land Cultivated	Grains	Legumes	Fibres	Barley	Maize	Kaoliang	Rice	Wheat
WHEAT REGION	51	39	68·2	13·0	3·8	3·9	13·3	14·9	1·3	40·2
RICE REGION	49	18	68·7	7·6	3·5	11·7	5·5	2·5	58·9	17·1
WHEAT REGION AREAS										
Spring wheat	7	18	76·0	11·1	0·2	7·2	2·4	7·9	0·3	18·2
Winter wheat/millet	9	22	69·0	9·2	5·0	7·9	12·5	11·6	2·5	39·7
Winter wheat/kaoliang	35	68	65·1	15·7	4·3	0·8	16·3	18·5	0·7	45·5
RICE REGION AREAS										
Yangtse Rice/wheat	12	35	69·7	8·2	7·9	18·5	4·6	5·2	56·8	30·8
Rice/tea	12	18	70·1	8·2	1·0	11·2	3·4	1·2	67·7	15·3
Szechwan Rice	14	32	59·4	10·3	3·1	13·9	14·2	5·2	41·3	18·6
Double-cropping Rice	6	13	72·8	1·8	—	6·7	1·4	0·6	58·9	9·6
Southwestern Rice	5	7	65·1	8·0	0·1	8·3	13·6	2·2	58·7	10·5

Source: J. L. Buck, *op. cit.*, pp. 33, 209, 211.

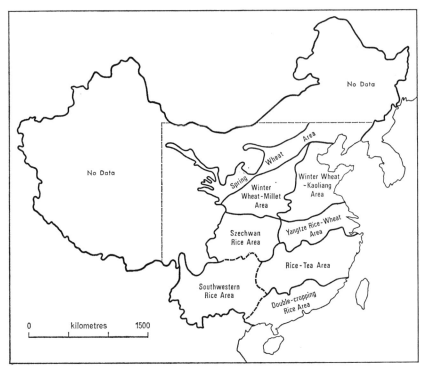

Figure 50.   Agricultural Regions of Eastern China (after J. L. Buck).
Basic contrast between northern wheat-millet regions and southern rice region.

the Rice Region (almost three-fifths of most areas under rice) and the
more reduced role of the dominant crop in the Wheat Region (two-
fifths of the cultivated area, dropping to one-fifth in the Spring Wheat
area).   The *effectiveness* of man's utilisation of the environment is
indicated by the maps showing distribution of cultivated land[1] and of
irrigated land.[2]   The areas of any considerable size where the proportion of cultivated land exceeds two-fifths of the total area are confined
(see Map 7) to the North China Plain, the Red Basin and parts of the
middle Yangtse valley; over much of the remainder of what is termed
'Agricultural China' the proportion drops to one-tenth once the narrow
ribbons of alluvial lowland and pockets of coast plain are left behind.
At the time the survey was carried out (over thirty years ago) less than
one-half of the crop area was irrigated and irrigation as a major feature
of the agricultural scene was virtually confined to the area of South
China, south of the Tsinling-Tapa Shan divide; 69 per cent of the land
in the Rice Region was irrigated, as against a mere 15 per cent in the
Wheat Region (where the major development of irrigation was to be
found on the sub-arid margins of the northwest).   The massive devel-

[1] J. L. Buck, *op. cit.*, p. 168.   [2] *Ibid.*, p. 187.

opment of various forms of irrigation in North China in recent years (pp. 193–8) has done much to blur this contrast between North and South; it is also introducing a new stability into life and opening up new possibilities of diversification into those areas of northern China traditionally scourged by drought and dominated by an impoverishing monocultural economy based on grain.

Some indication of the efficiency of the agricultural system is given by Buck's estimate of the production as measured by what he terms 'grain-equivalent per man-equivalent'. For China as a whole this works out at 1,400 kilogrammes. This is only one-fourteenth the comparable figure for the United States at this date but even this low figure drops to almost one-half (787 kilogrammes) in the Spring Wheat Area; the figure is highest in the Southwestern Rice Area, followed by the Yangtse Rice-Tea Area and Szechwan. The density of population per square mile of crop area shows a close relationship to this productivity gradient; the average for China is 1,485 with a range from 858 in the Spring Wheat Area to 2,636 in the Southwestern Rice Area and an extreme range, for the smaller statistical units, of from 212 persons per square mile in parts of the Winter Wheat-Kaoliang Area to 4,372 (i.e. *almost seven persons per acre of crop area*) in parts of the Southwestern Rice Area.

A NOTE ON A POST-WAR CHINESE CLASSIFICATION INTO AGRICULTURAL REGIONS

A rather more detailed classification of the agricultural regions of China—and one that, unlike Buck's, was not confined to eastern or Agricultural China—appeared in a textbook of economic geography published probably in 1956.[1] This includes a series of maps showing the major crop assemblages for each economic region of the country; it is from these that Map 51 has been compiled.

Some of the major divides distinguished by Buck two decades earlier are recognisable: the general western limit of more or less intensive agriculture, the northern limit of the Yangtse Rice-Wheat Area or the northern limit of the Double-cropping Rice Area, to take a few examples. Elsewhere, however, the pattern portrayed is a good deal more detailed and represents, in the light of the present writer's travels, a much closer approximation to reality. Thus the Wheat Region, which in Buck's study is broken down into three major subdivisions— the Spring Wheat Area, the Winter Wheat-Millet Area and the Winter Wheat-Kaoliang Area—is in this later classification broken up into seven regions: (4) the Wheat-Oil-seeds Region; (5) the Wheat-Miscellaneous Grains Region; (6) the Cotton-Wheat Region; (8) the Maize-Millet Region; (9) the Potatoes-Grain Region; (10) the Rice-

---

[1] *Kao-chung Chung-kuo Ching-chi Ti-li*, compiled in Canton and printed in Hong Kong.

N

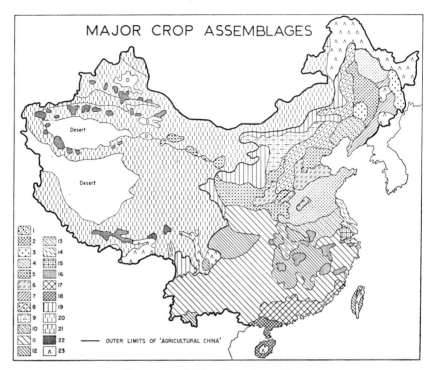

Figure 51.   Major Crop Assemblages.

KEY: 1. Cotton/Kaoliang; 2. Soybean/Kaoliang; 3. Kaoliang; 4. Wheat/Oil Seeds;
5. Wheat/Miscellaneous grains; 6. Cotton/Wheat; 7. Maize; 8. Maize/Millet;
9. Potatoes/Grain; 10 Rice/Wheat; 11. Rice/Maize/Timber; 12. Rice; 13.
Cotton/Rice; 14. Cotton; 15. Rice/Wheat/Silk; 16. Tea; 17. Rice/Sugar/
Tropical Fruits; 18. Rubber/Tropical Crops; 19. Semi-farming/Livestock;
20. Desert Grazing; 21. Mountain grazing; 22. Oases of West (including
agricultural area of Tibet); 23. Forest.

Wheat Region; (19) the Semi-farming-Livestock Region.[1]   In the
Rice Region of Buck's classification most of the rolling upland country
is placed by this 1956 classification in a single Rice-Maize-Timber
Region (11), from which the Rice-Wheat-Silk area (15) of the Yangtse
delta and the Tea Region (16) south of the Yangtse are separated.
The Double-cropping Rice Area of Buck is—and this serves to emphasise some of the secondary elements in its economy—divided into (17)
the Rice-Sugar-Tropical Fruits Region and (18) the Rubber-Tropical
Crops Region which takes in the southernmost tip of China and the
island of Hainan.   This rather more detailed break-up, together with
the recognition of transitional zones such as the Semi-farming-Livestock Region (19) of the Inner Mongolian fringe and the delimitation
of the forest zones (23), the various types of grazing country (20, 21)

[1] Numbers refer to the key on Map 51.

and the oases of the west (22) brings the diversity of the Chinese countryside into sharper focus and, even though the statistical bases of the classification are not indicated, it represents a step towards that demarcation of 'the smaller sub-agricultural areas' which Buck saw as the next stage in our understanding of the Chinese countryside.

TOWARDS A SCIENTIFIC CLASSIFICATION OF AGRICULTURAL REGIONS

The latest and most detailed classification of China into its basic agricultural regions is that carried out by the Chinese Academy of Science in 1962,[1] a classification which rested on a graded classification running from four major regions (or first category regions) to a total of 129 regions of the fourth category. The Academy was careful to stress that this was a tentative and preliminary classification, and that, given the vast area of the country and the inadequate statistical and research background, a rigorously scientific classification was not yet possible. Nevertheless, the classification was not only the most detailed to date, it was also the most objective so far attempted, integrating into the basis of classification both the existing land use and its trends and also the elements of the physical setting and the historical evolution of each area.

In introducing the classification the author stresses that future agricultural development must be based on practical foundations and that in contrast to some sectors of the economy agriculture has a very long history which is manifested in the pattern of agricultural regions; effective agricultural development must be based on these regions and their 'improvement in a definite direction'. This, in turn, demands a measure of 'scientific predictability' which is possible only if we know 'the objective regularity of the productivity of the different agricultural regions'. Moreover, it is stressed that the pattern of agricultural regions is not 'a simple, fortuitous and fixed division' but rather a stage in the process of agricultural development; as such, it calls for more than a superficial analysis and any changes in the present situation should be undertaken only after rigorous scientific analysis. A scientific demarcation of the basic regions, by highlighting the main issues and showing the direction of development, provides 'a better idea as to what future development is possible'.

(a) BASES OF CLASSISICATION

The classification is based, firstly, on 'regional land utilisation and the special characteristics of agricultural production'; these include the

[1] C. C. Teng, 'A Preliminary Study on the Demarcation of the Agricultural Regions of China' in *Acta Geographica Sinica* (Peking), Vol. 29, Number V, December 1963, pp. 265–78.

effectiveness of utilisation of heat, moisture and soil resources; the relative importance of the various agricultural products and their role in the national economy; the cropping and livestock system and other aspects of production techniques; the level and consistency of yields. Secondly, on the natural economic conditions under which farming is carried on; these include moisture conditions (rainfall and subsurface water); temperature, sunshine and growing period; land resources, including character of terrain, soil and vegetation resources; demographic aspects such as labour force, distribution of ethnic groups, historical development of agriculture, the level of economic development and the like.   Thirdly, the general trends and possible direction of future agricultural development; to the extent that the classification is based in part on regional trends and an evaluation of future potentialities it is a *dynamic* classification as opposed to the essentially static classification of earlier workers in this field.

The process of delimiting the regions is described by Teng.   The initial steps involved the compilation of maps based on national statistics; these showed the intensity of land use, the man-land ratio, the cropping systems, the types of agricultural products and of livestock, the distribution of commercial forest areas and the level of production.   Detailed field studies, where available, were used to make good deficiencies in the statistical coverage and in many areas fieldwork rather than statistical data provided the basis for the delineation of regional boundaries.   This agricultural data was supplemented by data on the 'natural geographic factors'—water, heat and soil conditions—which provide part of the basis for the understanding of regional agricultural patterns.   Such patterns when analysed show certain features which are common to most regions and also features which are specific to one region or group of regions; the differences between regions may be large or minute.   This aspect is recognised in the classification by a 'hierarchy' of regions, from four 'macroregions' which are progressively broken down by the application of more specialised criteria, into a total of 129 regions of the lowest order. This is indicated in the table below:

TABLE 7

THE HIERARCHY OF AGRICULTURAL REGIONS

Major (first category) regions	*Northeast*	*Southeast*	*Northwest*	*Chinghai-Tibet*	*Total*
Second category	3	3	3	3	12
Third category	13	18	10	10	51
Fourth category	44	47	24	14	129

Source: Teng, *op. cit.*, p. 267.

(b) Regions of the First Category

The greatest contrasts are to be found between regions in the first category. These contrasts arise partly from contrasts in environmental conditions, in the contrasting combinations of heat, moisture and soil conditions; partly from contrasts in the historical development of agriculture in the four regions.

The most basic environmental contrast in China is, it will be apparent from pp. 76–9 above, the contrast between the east and the west. The critical elements in crop production—heat, moisture, terrain and soils—are more favourably combined in eastern China. This area has a long history of agricultural development and a high population density. The intensity of land use is high and it is here that the greater proportion of China's crop output, her livestock and fisheries output, and her forestry resources are concentrated. Given its favourable environmental conditions, the basic problem is that of expanding still further and stabilising the agricultural output. Conditions in the west are rather different. The environmental complex—moisture-heat-terrain-soils—is far less favourable owing to such factors as deficient humidity or soil poverty. The population is much sparser, the majority of the population are minority peoples and the agricultural history of the area much shorter than in the east. Arable land is limited in extent and scattered in distribution; much of area is arid or subarid and the overall intensity of land utilisation is low. The potential for both agricultural and pastoral development is rated by Teng as high.

These two basic regions can each be subdivided into a northern and southern sector. In the more favoured eastern half of China, the northern region is characterised by dry-land arable farming with a significant development of livestock production; the southern region by wet-rice cultivation and by tropical and subtropical tree crops and forestry. In the west, the northern region is a vast arid region, with fragmentary patches of arable land where irrigation is possible and a considerable grazing potential; the southern region is represented by the Tibet-Chinghai area, a high pastoral area where lack of heat is the major problem. The significance of these four major regions in the agriculture of China as a whole is summarised in Table 8 overleaf.

Certain of the basic features of China's agricultural geography stand out even from this highly generalised table. Thus, the Northeast (i.e. the plains and plateaux of the northern sector of 'Agricultural China') contains over one-half of the country's arable land but accounts for only slightly over one-third of the total food output and supports approximately the same proportion of the total agricultural population. The Southeast, by contrast, has only 44·1 per cent of the arable land but produces three-fifths of the total food output, contains over three-fifths of the agricultural population and plays a role in the country's livestock

TABLE 8

CHARACTERISTICS OF THE MAJOR AGRICULTURAL REGIONS

	Northeast	Southeast	Northwest	Tibet-Chinghai	Total
Total arable land (%)	52·0	44·1	3·2	0·7	100
Wet-rice (%)	6·2	93·3	0·5	—	100
Vegetable oils (%)	45·2	52·5	1·9	0·4	100
Total food production (%)	35·8	61·2	2·5	0·5	100
Total cotton production (%)	57·0	39·5	3·5	—	100
Number of cattle (%)	30·1	53·6	4·6	11·7	100
Number of pigs (%)	31·5	67·7	0·5	0·3	100
Number of sheep (%)	36·2	8·1	27·0	28·7	100
Number of goats (%)	52·1	24·2	13·4	10·3	100
Agricultural population (%)	35·1	63·0	1·4	0·5	100
Land per capita (mou)	4·6	2·2	6·9	4·1	3·1

Source: Teng, *op. cit.*, p. 268.

economy that is not always appreciated—it contains over one-half of China's cattle and over two-thirds of the pigs. The two western regions—the Northwest and Tibet-Chinghai—are at present insignificant in the country's arable economy; together they have slightly under one-twenty-fifth of the arable area, contain 1·9 per cent of the agricultural population and produce 3 per cent of the total food output of China. The dominance of pastoralism in these subarid or arid regions is emphasised by the data for livestock distribution; the two regions contain approximately one-quarter of the goat population and over one-half of China's sheep.

(c) REGIONS OF THE SECOND CATEGORY

Regional variations in the pattern of agriculture, forestry and pastoralism due to environmental conditions and historical evolution, as well as regional differences in agricultural production, are the basis on which the twelve second-category regions are delimited. Within the agricultural area considerable emphasis is placed on what is termed 'the crop-maturing system', i.e. the number of crops it is possible to harvest over a given period of time; this reflects the intensity of land utilisation under varying heat conditions. The basic divides in the east are as follows (Map 52):

(1) The line demarcating those regions where it is possible to obtain only one crop a year, or three crops in two years. Low winter temperatures here rule out winter wheat which is either damaged by winter cold or else matures so late as to make the maturing of a following summer-sown crop hazardous. Thus, over much of the

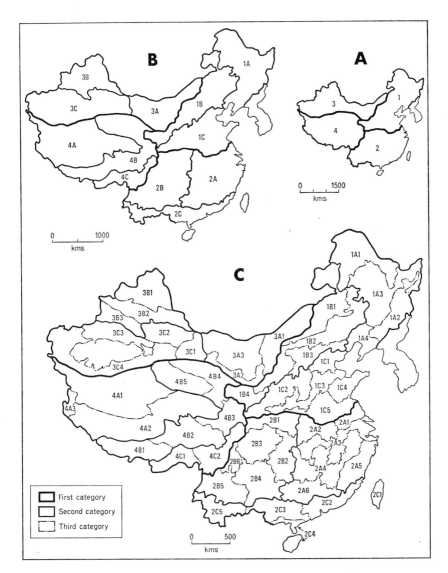

Figure 52. Stages in the Division of China into Agricultural Regions.
Showing regions of the first, second and third category.

area only one crop a year is possible; only on the warmer southern
margin is it possible to take two crops annually.

(2) The Wei River–Tsin-ling line marks the northernmost limit of
the zone in which two crops a year are possible; typically these
crops are either rice and wheat or cotton and wheat.

(3) The line Foochow–northern Kwantung–northern Kwangsi
represents the divide between that part of China where two crops a

year are possible and those subtropical areas where three crops can be produced.   To the north, the pattern is one of either two crops a year or five crops in two years; to the south, triple-cropping, based on two rice crops and a winter crop such as sweet potatoes, leguminous crops, oil crops or wheat, is typical.

The influence of altitude becomes important in the Szechwan, Yunnan and Kweichow regions; these lie within the central two-crops-a-year belt but variations in altitude, and hence climate, complicate the general picture.   Thus, on the lowlands two crops a year can be obtained but on the foothills the farming system may rest on a system of three crops in two years or one crop annually.   Moreover, although much of the lowland is irrigated, much of the remainder of the area is difficult to irrigate and dry-cropping is typical.   It is on this basis that the double-cropping wet rice and tree crop region of the south is sub-divided by a N–S line running through western Hupeh and western Hunan.

In northwestern China the 'lack of balance' in the heat-moisture-soil complex of southern Sinkiang marks this area off, in its environmental conditions, from northern Sinkiang.   In the Tibet-Chinghai region there is likewise a duality, the southeastern river valleys being warm enough for two crops a year (maize or barley) as contrasted with the single crop (usually millets) of the high plateau country to the north. What are termed 'natural economic and historical factors' are reflected in the other subdivisions of west and northwest China; the contrast, for example, between the purely pastoral region of the north Tibetan plateau and the agricultural-pastoral regions of Tibet-Chinghai; the contrast between the western Inner Mongolian and Ho-hsi irrigated agriculture and arid nomadic grazing country and the northern Sinkiang irrigated agriculture and mountain pastoral region; or between the Inner Mongolian one-crop-yearly agro-pastoral region and the remainder of North China.   These subdivisions are shown on Map 52.

(d) REGIONS OF THE THIRD AND FOURTH CATEGORIES

Further subdivision is based on: the combination of crops and of livestock; the methods of cultivation or the pastoral pattern; the level of production; and 'the key question of similarities and differences between the main branches of agriculture, pastoralism and forestry'. The third category reflects the common characteristics, the fourth the differences in the agricultural structure *within* the third category region.

The process of subdivision may be illustrated by reference to one of the second category regions—the North China three crops-biennally dry agricultural region; all the areas within this region are characterised by the general three-crops-in-two-years régime but between various areas there are differences arising from the types of crops, the level of production, and the environmental conditions. On the basis of these differences this second-category region may be subdivided into five third-category regions as follows:[1]

1C1 the wheat-millet-maize-wet-rice-fruit region
1C2 the wheat-maize-millet region of the plateau
1C3 the cotton-wheat region of the northern plain
1C4 the polycultural region of the Shantung Peninsula, with wheat, soya beans, peanuts, tobacco, fruit and fisheries
1C5 the wheat-soya bean-tobacco-sesame region of the Huang-Huai lowlands

Each of these five third-category regions possesses its own distinctive potential for agricultural development, its own distinctive characteristics and problems.

At the same time, within the relatively large area of these third-category regions there is frequently a considerable diversity; thus region 3 above, the cotton-wheat region (which is the largest cotton-producing region in China), shows an internal diversity which makes possible its subdivision into three fourth-category regions. This diversity manifests itself in several forms: in the degree of concentration on cotton, in the level of production of the crop and in the physical conditions favouring or impeding irrigation (the area west of Sian being less suited to irrigation because of soil and water conditions). The fourth-category regions distinguished on the basis of these contrasts are:

1C3(1) the cotton-wheat region of Shantung and adjoining Hopeh and Honan
1C3(2) the wheat-cotton region of the mountainous districts of the west
1C3(3) the cotton-wheat region of south Shansi, central Shensi.

Forty of the 51 third-category regions are thus subdivided into from two to six fourth-category regions. Eleven of the third-category regions, mainly in the west or the islands of the South China Sea, are, however, not subdivided, either because of their relative simplicity or because of the absence of sufficiently detailed data; these are regarded as both third-category and fourth-category regions. Effective agricultural development, including the raising of production levels, the adoption of improved techniques and the realisation of the full potential of each area must, as Teng stresses, be based on an awareness and understanding of the diversities of conditions which are brought out at the third and fourth stages of classification.

[1] The numbering follows that of the map on p. 184.

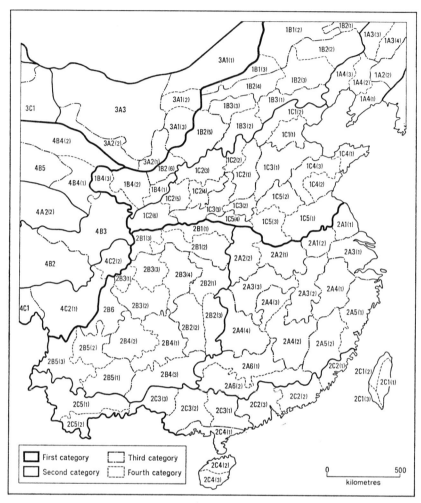

Figure 53. Agricultural Regions of Eastern China.
For the names of the regions see list pp. 186–90.

There is a total of 129 fourth-category regions[1] in China.   These are listed in the appendix to this chapter and the pattern in the eastern two-thirds of the country is shown in Map 53.

COMMENTS ON THE SYSTEM OF CLASSIFICATION

Given the size and complexity of China a single-factor classification into regions based simply on, say, the characteristics of agriculture is of only limited value as a basis for development planning.   Moreover,

[1] Incorporating presumably the grouping of the 298 'agricultural production types' (based on crops alone) which resulted from analysis of the 1957 data.   These 298 types comprised, in turn, no less than 2,188 'units'.

given the interpenetration of cropping, pastoralism and forestry in certain areas a broad classification into arable, pastoral and forest regions (comparable to some of the earlier systems of classifications in Europe) is scarcely practicable; even the west of China, usually regarded as a pastoral area, has an important arable component; cultivation has extended considerably in Inner Mongolia in recent years; forest areas are widely scattered throughout China. The first-category regions are for these reasons based on the characteristics of the crop land/forest/pastoral land complex, on the environmental factors which influence this, and on the historical development of agriculture. In defining regions of the second-category the emphasis, we have seen, is on 'the crop-maturing system'—the number of harvests which can be got in a given period. In many areas the *actual* number is less than the *potential* number of harvests; since this latter figure gives a better indication of the possibilities and limitations of future agricultural development it is the figure used in the demarcation of the regions.

The third- and fourth-category regions are based on the combination of crops and livestock, on the methods of farming and the level of production. The basic regional names are those of the major crop/livestock assemblages; such a system of nomenclature presents no major problems in areas such as South China (where 70–80 per cent of the crop land is devoted to rice) but elsewhere, owing to the complex intermingling of crops, the diversity of environmental conditions, the generally subsistent character of farming and the limited development of commercialised production[1] the system is less easy to apply. Under these conditions, emphasis is given not only to 'what is produced' but also to 'how is it produced?'; techniques of cropping, the organisation of the farming system and the efficiency of utilisation of water, heat and soil resources become important considerations. Field investigation must obviously be the basis for the initial delineation and increasing refinement of regional boundaries at this level. Finally, it must be stressed that existing conditions represent but one stage in the process of development of a region and that it is only in the light of this process of change that today's situation can be understood and the most promising lines for future development sketched in.

---

[1] In contrast to, say, Western Europe or the USA where the high degree of agricultural specialisation makes possible a division into regions based on dominant crops or stock.

PROVISIONAL LIST OF THE AGRICULTURAL REGIONS OF CHINA[1]

1 *NORTHERN DRY AGRICULTURAL AND PASTORAL REGIONS*

1A *Northeast one-crop-yearly dry agricultural and forestry regions*

1 Khingan Mountains forestry and agricultural regions

2 Chaingpai Shan agricultural and forestry regions
(1) Mu-tan-Kiang soya beans, maize, rice, spring wheat and forestry region
(2) Changpai Shan (mid-southern sector) soya beans, rice, maize and forestry region

3 Sungari-Nun Plain soya beans, maize, spring wheat, sugarbeet regions
(1) Plain of the Three Rivers soya beans, spring wheat, maize sugarbeet region
(2) Nun-kiang Plain soya beans, millet, maize, spring wheat, sugarbeet region
(3) Sungari Plain soya beans, maize, sugarbeet, flax regions
(4) Changpai Shan (west) soya beans, rice, maize region

4 Liaoning kaoliang, maize, fruit and aquatic products regions
(1) Liaoning hill country, maize, rice, groundnuts, fruit, silk and aquatic products region
(2) Middle and Lower Liao River kaoliang, maize region
(3) Liao Highland (west) kaoliang, millet, cotton, fruit region

1B *Inner Mongolia one-crop-yearly dry agricultural and pastoral regions*

1 Pastoral regions of Inner Mongolian Plateau

2 Agricultural and pastoral regions of southeast Inner Mongolia
(1) Khingan (east) maize, millet, grazing region
(2) Hsi-liao Ho kaoliang, maize, millet, grazing region
(3) Chi-je Mountain millet, oats, kaoliang, maize, grazing region
(4) Ta-ching Plateau spring wheat, oats, potatoes, sesame, grazing region
(5) North Shensi millet and grazing region
(6) Ninghsia (southeast) millet, spring wheat, sheep region

3 Agricultural regions of mountains along the Great Wall
(1) Chi-pei Shan millet, maize, soya beans, kaoliang region
(2) North Shansi oats, millet, hemp region
(3) Taching Shan oats, hemp region

[1] The author is grateful to Dr W. Jenner of the University of Leeds for checking and correcting the translation of this list.

4 Kansu-Chinghai Plateau semi-dry agricultural regions
   (1) Liu-pan Shan sesame, oats, sheep region
   (2) Lung-chung spring wheat, millet, potatoes, hemp region
   (3) Tao River spring wheat, barley, potatoes region

1C *North China three-crops-biennially dry agricultural regions*
   1 Hopeh wheat, millet, maize, rice, fruit regions
      (1) Central Hopeh wheat, kaoliang, rice region
      (2) Yen Shan millet, maize, wheat, fruit region
   2 Loess Plateau wheat, maize, millet regions
      (1) Southeast Shansi millet, wheat, maize, subsidiary forestry region
      (2) Central Shansi wheat, millet, kaoliang, region
      (3) West Shansi, North Shensi millet, wheat region
      (4) Wei River-northern Plateau wheat, soya beans, maize, millet region
      (5) King-ho wheat, millet, oats, sesame region
      (6) Upper Wei River wheat, maize, hemp region
   3 North China Plain cotton wheat regions
      (1) Hopeh-Shantung-Honan cotton, wheat region
      (2) West Honan wheat, cotton region
      (3) South Shansi-Kwanchung cotton, wheat region
   4 Shantung Peninsula wheat, soya beans, groundnuts, tobacco, fruit, fisheries regions
      (2) Tai-Yi Mountains wheat, sweet potatoes, groundnuts region
      (3) Central Lowland wheat, soya beans, tobacco region
   5 Hwang-Huai River Lowlands wheat, soya beans, tobacco, sesame regions
      (1) North Anhwei wheat, soya beans, tobacco regions
      (2) East Honan-West Shantung wheat, soya beans region
      (3) East Honan wheat, tobacco, sesame region
      (4) Fu-niu Mountain wheat, maize, sweet potatoes, subsidiary forestry region

SOUTHERN WET-FIELD AGRICULTURE AND COMMERCIAL FORESTRY REGIONS

2A *East and Central China double-cropping wet rice and subtropical forestry regions*
   1 Yangtse-Huai interlocking wet-field and dry agriculture regions
      (1) North Kiangsu plain rice, wheat, cotton region
      (2) Huai-nan (south of Huai River) rice, wheat, tobacco region
   2 Tapieh Shan wheat, rice and forestry regions
      (1) Foothills wet rice, wheat, tea and forestry region
      (2) Nan-yang basin wheat, wet rice, cotton, sesame region
   3 Middle and lower Yangtse Plain rice, cotton, silk, hemp and fish regions
      (1) Lower plain rice, cotton, silk, jute and fish region
      (2) Central Anhwei and Po-yang Hu plain double-cropping rice, wheat and fish region

(3) Tung-ting plain double-cropping rice, cotton, ramie and fish region

4 Chiang-nan rice, tea and commercial forest regions
   (1) Anhwei-Chekiang-Kiangsi border rice, tea and forestry region
   (2) Central-south Kiangsi rice, tea-oil, and forestry region
   (3) Hunan-Kiangsi-Hupeh birder double-cropping rice, tea and ramie region
   (4) Hunan (central-south) rice, sweet potatoes, tea and tea-oil region

5 Chekiang-Fukien hills rice, tea, fruit and timber regions
   (1) Chekiang-Fukien coastlands region of double-cropping rice, tea, oranges, fish and forestry
   (2) Fukien (western hills) rice and forestry region

6 Nan-ling hills rice, tea-oil and forestry regions
   (1) Northern Nan-ling rice, tea-oil and forestry region
   (2) Southern Nan-ling double-cropping rice and sub-tropical fruit region

2B *Southwestern highlands and basins double-cropping wet-field agriculture and forestry regions*
   1 Upper Han River maize, wheat, forestry regions
      (1) Southern Chinling maize, winter wheat and forestry region
      (2) Tapa Shan maize, winter wheat and forest]y region
      (3) Pailung Kiang maize, winter wheat and livestock region

   2 Szechwan-Hupeh-Hunan-Kweichow border rice, maize and forestry regions
      (1) Yangtse and southwestern Hupeh maize and forestry region
      (2) Southeastern Szechwan and eastern Kweichow rice, maize, tung oil and forestry region
      (3) Western Hunan rice, tung oil and forestry region

   3 Szechwan Basin rice, sugar cane, tung oil and pig-rearing regions
      (1) Changtu Plain rice, rapeseed and tobacco region
      (2) Southern Szechwan double-cropping rice, sugar cane, pig-rearing and citrus region
      (3) Northern Szechwan rice, sweet potatoes and silk region
      (4) Eastern Szechwan rice, maize and tung oil region

   4 Kweichow plateau rice, maize and forestry regions
      (1) Central Kweichow rice, tobacco and forestry region
      (2) Western Kweichow-northeast Yunnan maize and livestock region
      (3) Kweichow-Kwangsi-Yunnan border rice, maize and forestry region

   5 Yunnan Plateau rice, maize and forestry regions
      (1) Eastern Yunnan rice and tobacco region
      (2) Kinsha Kiang (upper Yangtse) rice and forestry region
      (3) Western Yunnan rice, wheat and forestry region

   6 Taliang Shan maize, forestry and livestock region

2C South China treble-croppping wet-field and tropical tree-crop regions

   1 Taiwan rice, sugar cane, tropical products and fisheries regions
      (1) Taiwan hills and eastern coast-lands rice, timber and fisheries region
      (2) Western and northern rice, sugar cane, tea, tropical fruits and fisheries region
      (3) Southern rice, sugar cane, tropical tree-crops and fisheries region

   2 Fukien-Kwangtung coast rice, sugar cane, tropical and sub-tropical fruits and fisheries regions
      (1) Southern Fukien rice, sugar cane, tea, fruit and fisheries region
      (2) Eastern Kwantgung rice, sugar cane, fruit and fisheries region
      (3) Central Kwantung rice, sugar cane, silk, fruit and fisheries region

   3 Kwangtung-Kwangsi lowlands rice, maize and tropical tree-crops regions
      (1) Kwangtung-Kwangsi rice, sugar cane and tropical tree-crops region
      (2) Central-southern Kwangsi rice, maize and tropical tree-crops region
      (3) Yunnan-Kwangsi border maize, rice, cattle and tree-crops region

   4 Western-Kwangtung-Hainan rice, sugar cane, tropical crops and fisheries regions
      (1) Western Kwangtung rice, sweet potatoes, sugar cane, tropical crops and fisheries region
      (2) Northern Hainan rice, sweet potatoes, tropical tree-crops and fisheries region
      (3) Southern Hainan rice, sweet potatoes, tropical tree-crops and fisheries region

   5 Southern Yunnan rice, maize and tropical crops regions
      (1) Southern Yunnan rice, maize, tea and tropical crops regions
      (2) Hsi-shuang Pan-na autonomous *Chou* rice and tropical crops region

3 NORTHWESTERN ARID & IRRIGATED AGRICULTURAL & PASTORAL REGIONS*

3A Inner Mongolia, Ninghsia, Ho-hsi one-crop yearly irrigated agriculture and pastoral regions

   1 Central and Western Inner Mongolia spring wheat, millet and arid pastoral regions
      (1) Siwu desert nomadic region
      (2) Hai-t'ao spring wheat, millet and sugar beet region
      (3) Western Ordos settled pastoral region

   2 Ninghsia-Ho-hsi spring wheat, rice, irrigated agricultural regions
      (1) Ninghsia plain wheat, rye and sheep region

* The smallest subdivisions (i.e. fourth category regions) are omitted in these western regions which lie outside the limits of Map 53.

(2) Ho-hsi corridor spring wheat and rye region

3 Ala-shan desert camel-rearing nomadic region

3B   *Northern Sinkiang-Tien Shan one-crop yearly irrigated agriculture and upland grazing region*

1 Altai spring wheat agricultural and pastoral regions

2 Northern Tien Shan spring and winter wheat, cotton and pastoral regions

3 Tien Shan spring wheat and upland grazing regions

3C   *Southern Sinkiang multiple-cropping irrigated agricultural regions*

1 Tunhuang-Yümen wheat-cotton region

2 Turfan-Hami spring wheat, cotton, melons and fruit region

3 Southern Tien Shan spring and winter wheat, maize and cotton regions

4 Northern Karakorum wheat, maize and cotton regions

4   CHINGHAI-TIBET HIGH COLD AGRICULTURAL AND PASTORAL REGIONS*

4A   *Northern Tibet high cold pastoral regions*

1 Chang-tang cold desert nomadic pastoral region

2 Northern Tibet pastoral region

3 Ari River valley barley and goats region

4B   *Chinghai-Tibetan plateau mixed agricultural and pastoral regions*

1 Valleys of southern Tibet barley and rapeseed regions

2 Northeastern uplands of Tibet barley, potatoes and goats region

3 Upper valley of Hwang-ho yaks and barley region

4 Chilien mountains and Koko-nor lake district barley and sheep region

5 Tsaidam basin spring wheat and sheep region

4C   *Southeastern Tibetan plateau warmer and humid agricultural and forestry regions*

1 Southeastern semi-tropical agricultural and forestry region

2 Chamdo-Szechwan border maize, wheat, barley forestry and pastoral region

* The smallest subdivisions (i.e. fourth category regions) are omitted in these western regions which lie outside the limits of Map 53.

CHAPTER 9

Agricultural Production in China

PERSPECTIVE

THE TRANSFORMATION of the Chinese countryside discussed in preceding pages and the priority now accorded to agriculture in Chinese planning derives not only from the need to provide food for a population of over 700 million, growing at the rate of some 2 per cent per annum and which in the past never knew security from famine. It derives also from the Chinese recognition of the fundamental importance of agriculture as the basic element in the Chinese economy, an element on whose development progress in the industrial sector is ultimately dependent. The emphasis on this latter aspect is sometimes regarded as a reaction against the Soviet model of development based on heavy industry, a model whose limitations in a Chinese context became apparent in the early nineteen-sixties; in reality, however, this emphasis pre-dates the 'Great Leap Forward' and it was spelled out most clearly by Mao Tse-tung as early as 1957. In the words of Mao:

As China is a great agricultural country, with over eighty per cent of its population in the villages, its industry and agriculture must be developed simultaneously. Only then will industry have raw materials and a market, and only so will it be possible to accumulate fairly large funds for the building up of a powerful heavy industry. Everyone knows that light industry is closely related to agriculture. Without agriculture there can be no light industry. But it is not so clearly understood that agriculture provides heavy industry with an important market. This fact, however, will be more readily appreciated as the gradual progress of technological improvement and modernisation of agriculture calls for more and more machinery, fertilisers, water conservancy and electric power projects and transport facilities for the farms, as well as fuel and building materials for the rural consumers. The entire national economy will benefit if we can achieve an even greater growth in our agriculture and thus induce a correspondingly greater development of light industry during the period of the Second and Third Five-Year Plans. With the development of agriculture and light industry, heavy industry will be assured of its market and funds, and thus grow faster. Hence what may seem to be a slower pace of industrialisation is actually not so, and indeed the tempo may even be speeded up.[1]

With regard to the first aim—that of freedom from famine—K. S. Karol observes: 'I had been told and had seen for myself that everywhere today the Chinese peasant eats his fill, which for him is the victory of victories'.[2] The country certainly experienced 'three bad years' in the early 'sixties but the food shortage and the significance of the subsequent import of food grains seems to have been carefully exaggerated by many Western 'observers'; in the words of René Dumont: 'people are dying of hunger in India every year, by the tens of thousands and even after good harvests. . . . However it was only the Chinese food shortage, a little too swiftly labelled "famine", that monopolised the headlines.'[3] And the reality of progress on the food front in China in recent years is driven home by a comparison of conditions in China and India. In the Chinese cities where food grains were rationed in 1966 the monthly rations ranged from 44 to 55 lb. for workers, 39 lb. for students and 35 lb. for cadres;[4] in India the grain ration is officially 30–32 lb. monthly, dropping to 20–24 lb. in states like Kerala where other foodstuffs are said to be available. This progress—and the implications of this progress for economic development as a whole—has been emphasised by Paul Bairoch in a recent study of agricultural productivity in the Third World. Says Bairoch:

In Asia the outstanding phenomenon is . . . the progress achieved by China since 1950, a progress which contrasts with the regression or stagnation of most of the countries of Asia. Even on the basis of Western estimates the annual increase in productivity has been 2·7 per cent per annum between 1946–50 and 1960–64; the index of productivity[5] has risen from 3·7 to 5·1. At this level China has passed the threshold of vulnerability to famine.[6] It is even possible that the [actual level of the] harvest lies between the estimate based on Western data and that based on official announcements. From this it can be postulated that the index of productivity lay, towards 1964, above 6. This would permit the country to embark on the process of industrialisation since at this level of productivity it

---

[1] Mao Tse-tung, *On the Correct Handling of Contradictions among the People* (Peking 1960), pp. 67–8; the speech was actually delivered to the Eleventh Session of the Supreme State Conference in February 1957.
[2] K. S. Karol, *China: The Other Communism* (London 1967), p. 189.
[3] René Dumont, *La Chine surpeuplée: Tiers-Monde affamé* (Paris 1965), p. 9.
[4] Quoted by K. S. Karol, *op. cit.*, p. 195.
[5] Measured in millions of net calories per male worker per year.
[6] This Bairoch places at a productivity level of 4·9 units.

becomes possible to draw off a significant proportion of the agricultural labour force.[1]

The statistical difficulties which confront any outsider who attempts to document *in detail* the trends in the Chinese economy since 1960 are referred to below; here it is sufficient to note that the assessment of foreign experts,[2] agronomists, economists and the like, who have visited China is very different from that of the 'China-watchers' in Hong Kong and that this assessment indicates that the physical and socio-economic transformation of the Chinese countryside in recent years has enabled China, alone among the major Afro-Asian nations,[3] to begin to emerge from under-development and to begin to eliminate the hunger and malnutrition which characterise all under-developed economies.

THE BACKGROUND OF RURAL DEVELOPMENT

This beginning of a breakthrough on the food front is of critical importance in a world menaced with the prospect of widespread famine in the next decade or so. What must be borne in mind, however, is that the expansion of crop production is but one part, albeit the most important part, of an integrated and overall plan of rural development and that achievements on the food front are intimately dependent on progress in other sectors. Three critically important facets of this rural reconstruction programme have been the increasing mastery of water resources made possible by recent developments in the fields of water storage and irrigation; the large-scale afforestation which is an essential component of any flood control schemes and which creates new resources in the countryside; and the increasing control over the biological environment as a result of the campaign against human diseases and plant diseases and pests. Each of these is commented on below.

(a) Towards the Elimination of Flood and Drought

The achievements of the Chinese in this field represent, in the words of René Dumont, 'the most positive result of the Great Leap Forward'.[4]

By 1949, and as a result of some three millennia of development, China had 53 million acres of irrigated land. By 1955–56 this had risen to 66 million acres. In the next year a further 20 million acres were added to the irrigated area, then, in the winter of 1957–58, a

---

[1] Paul Bairoch, 'L'évolution de la productivité agricole dans les pays économiquement sous-developpés de 1909 à 1964' in *Développement et Civilisations* (Paris), March 1966, p. 27.

[2] Notably René Dumont, Gilbert Etienne, Robert Guillain, Joan Robinson and E. L. Wheelwright.

[3] Emphasised by René Dumont, *Nous allons à la famine* (Paris 1966), p. 139.

[4] René Dumont, *La Chine surpeuplée: Tiers-Monde affamé*, p. 58.

further 80 million acres.   In eighteen months China brought more land under irrigation than in the whole of her earlier history.   At the end of 1958 it was claimed that 60 per cent of the crop land was irrigated; preliminary plans for 1959 aimed at increasing the irrigated area to some 250 million acres or 89 per cent of the crop land, while by the end of 1960 virtually the entire cropped area was to be under irrigation.   The fact that, at the end of 1965, some 43 million people were engaged in extending the irrigation system suggests that the targets for 1959 and 1960 were not attained; nevertheless, the immense labour-investment in water-control and water-storage schemes since the People's Government came to power certainly blunted the impact of the drought years in the early 'sixties.   In addition, it has been an important factor in increasing the labour-absorptive capacity of the countryside and in thus reducing or eliminating under-employment; in the humid areas more effective water control has made possible an increase in the number of crops that could be obtained each year while in the subhumid areas the availability of water, often from deep or shallow wells, has made possible the extension of cropping into what was formerly a 'dead' season agriculturally (for want of water) and the diversification of cropping (e.g. the addition of vegetables to the formerly single-crop grain economy of the loess regions).

The official policy for water conservation is described as a 'three-pronged' one; first, to build mainly small projects, supplemented by medium and large ones where necessary and feasible; secondly, to try to accumulate rather than divert water; thirdly, to rely on the people rather than on the Government.

The great proliferation of small-scale projects strikes the traveller all over China, and especially in the south; seen from the air the country-sides of Kwangsi and Kwangtung glitter with countless man-made water surfaces.   The projects take many forms, according to the nature of the terrain, ranging from the combination of drainage and water storage which has made possible the utilisation of the waterlogged lowlands around Tientsin, or the use of both deep and shallow wells, as in the Peking area or the loess uplands of Shansi, to the 'water melon' system of irrigation and water storage developed in the dry uplands of the northwest of Hupeh Province.   One of the most complex systems was that devised for the North Huai Plain.   This area, which supports some 12 million people, has always been a problem area: it 'suffered from big floods when there was heavy rain, small floods when the rainfall was low, and drought when there was no rain'.   Its problems have been solved by the creation of a complex network of canals, totalling some 85,000 miles in length; within this canal mesh are inter-spersed wells and storage ponds, partly nourished by underground water from North China.

The smaller projects are constructed by the commune which thus invests the formerly under-utilised labour potential of the peasant in increasing the productive capacity of the countryside.   Such a policy means that the Central Government's funds can be devoted to larger multi-purpose projects: thus, while Government expenditure on water conservancy in 1958 was as large as the total expenditure over the First Five Year Plan, the total constructional work done in this field was eight times that achieved over the earlier period.

These smaller projects are important in their own right as helping to expand crop output and reduce or eliminate the catastrophic impact of drought or flood.   They are, at the same time, vital elements in a boldly-conceived and nation-wide programme of water conservancy.

> Built along the course of a river above a big project, the small projects enable water to be retained for irrigation, reduce the volume of run-off and thus lessen the pressure on the big project.   Those built below the big project make it possible again to store water discharged from the power station and use it for irrigation.   Thus a complete system is formed of big and small reservoirs connected by the main river, its tributaries and canals.

The pattern of major water conservancy works is shown in Figure 54: it should be stressed that the effectiveness of these projects is intimately bound up with increasing control over runoff and soil loss in the upland country of the west and south and this is dependent on local water-conservancy schemes, terracing and afforestation.

The most advanced multi-purpose scheme is that for the control of the Yellow River.   Earlier schemes had attempted to cope with the problem of flooding by construction of embankments on its lower reaches.   Such a policy was obviously useless for it did nothing to reduce the heavy runoff and silting due to deforestation and destructive cropping in its middle reaches.   After 1949 a comprehensive plan for the Yellow River basin was worked out.   It envisages the transformation of the main channel into a 'water staircase' by the construction of forty-six dams, to be used for flood prevention, irrigation and power, and the application of soil and water conservation techniques to halt erosion of the loess country through which the river flows in its middle reaches.[1]   This is a long-term project, the first stage being originally for completion in 1967.   To date, five dams on the main river and four on its tributaries are under construction, among them the giant Liuchia Gorge and Sanmen Gorge projects, and by autumn 1958 some 200,000 square kilometres of eroded land had been rehabilitated. Nevertheless, it is obvious from the air that the problem of erosion in China's loess areas is far from solved; gullies are still cutting deep into the friable yellow-grey soils and rivers are heavy with silt, a feature

[1] Nine-tenths of the Yellow River's silt appears to originate in Kansu, Shensi and Shansi provinces.

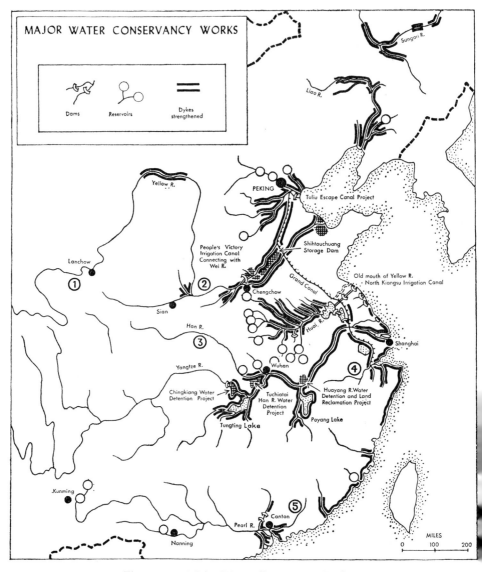

Figure 54. Major Water Conservancy Projects.

Illustrating the large-scale flood-control schemes and some of the more important
hydroelectric schemes completed or under way.

KEY: 1. Liuchia Gorge; volume 4,900 million cubic metres, power 1·05 million kW.
2. Sanmen Gorge Project; volume 64,700 million cubic metres, power 1·1
million kW.
3. Tanchiangkou Project; volume 51,600 million cubic metres, power 730,000
kW.
4. Hsinankiang Project; volume 17,800 million cubic metres, power 650,000
kW.
5. Hsinfengkiang Project; volume 11,500 cubic metres, power 290,000 kW.

Some four-fifths of the country's hydro potential is in the Yangtse, Tibetan or
Southern drainage areas; the major role of developments in the North is to control
flooding or soil erosion. Note how, from a power point of view, the southern
concentration of water power complements the northern and northwestern distribution of coal and petroleum (see Map 65).

which may explain some of the 'difficulties' encountered with some of the bigger schemes such as the Sanmen Gorge scheme.

Even more ambitious is the proposed redistribution of China's water resources by diverting the surplus water from the Yangtse northwards into the Yellow River drainage basin. It is estimated that each year some 142,000 million cubic metres of water could be diverted northwards and survey teams are now carrying out a first investigation of possible canal routes through the watershed between the two rivers. The linking of the two river systems, following the present expansion of the irrigation network, could, it is argued, finally solve North China's water problem.

It is probably premature to attempt any final assessment of Chinese achievements in the field of irrigation and flood control, though a tentative assessment has been made by the forester S. D. Richardson. Richardson comments: 'In view of the Olympian scale on which water conservancy has been conceived in China, it is only to be expected that problems of coordination will be manifest';[1] like the mass afforestation schemes, many of the water conservancy projects, 'conceived in haste, supervised by poorly trained technicians, and misleadingly reported as successful by over-optimistic and zealous cadres', did not achieve their objectives and this, indeed, has been recognised by the Chinese themselves. Thus, in Richardson's words:

Many of the smaller irrigation facilities were badly planned and were inadequate to meet requirements. For example, 82 per cent of the million small and medium-size reservoirs and ponds in Hupeh province dried up during 1959 . . . , and half the 500,000 reservoirs in the hilly regions of Kiangsu ceased to be of any use by August, 1959. . . . Some projects were started but never completed; others were ineffective because essential ancillary equipment was not available. In 1959 it was reported that the land area under irrigation amounted to 71·3 million ha. but that only two-thirds of the facilities had been completed and that 'much work still remains to be done to increase the efficiency of the completed works'. . . . 'In some cases, wells have been sunk, but water-carrying tools are lacking'. . . . 'In irrigation, the building of reservoirs itself does not mean that the irrigated area indicated in the contruction figures has all actually received the benefits of irrigation. These benefits can only be obtained when the reservoirs are filled, canals and ditches dug, the land is levelled off, and lifting equipment is at hand.'[2]

In the case of the larger water-conservancy projects there have also been problems; these arise largely from the haste with which they had to be undertaken, from imperfect coordination in the earlier years between the various Government departments concerned, and from the

[1] S. D. Richardson, *Forestry in Communist China* (Baltimore 1966), p. 126.
[2] *Ibid.* I have omitted the references to Chinese newspapers and other sources which Richardson cites in this passage.

very magnitude of the programme, a programme which was being implemented 'with unskilled labour the only readily available input factor'.[1]   Some, such as the Hwai River project, were initiated with inadequate hydrological data.   Others, such as the Yellow River project (including the Sanmen project), had to be pushed ahead with before the basic conservation work in the catchment area was more than partially completed; under these circumstances silting of reservoirs may well reduce their effective life.   Given the unprecedented scale of China's water conservancy programme and bearing in mind the difficulties of achieving the best allocation of scarce resources of capital and skilled man-power these problems can not be expected to be banished overnight.   Richardson reminds us that even in the West, where capital and technical skills are plentiful and where the basic knowledge of environmental conditions is much more complete than in China, mistakes in planning or conflicts in land use have not always been avoided.   Chinese planners, he emphasises, have recognised the deficiencies in some of the early projects and 'appear to be making creditable attempts, within the limits of the politico-social structure, to avoid them in the future'.   And the events of the last decade suggest that, even if China has not yet achieved complete mastery over the twin menaces of drought and flood, they are no longer the 'catastrophic deterrents' they have been in the past.   The contribution of water conservancy schemes to the stabilisation and diversification of farming in recent years has already been commented on; the same projects, whether based on river water or on wells, provide also the infrastructure for future progress since they create the moisture conditions necessary if the maximum benefit is to be obtained from the increasing use of artificial fertilisers.   And it is in the stepping-up of unit area yields through use of artificials that the greatest immediate scope for progress lies.

(b) 'Turning the Whole Country Green . . .'

The Chinese living-space has been occupied by men for thousands of years.   Over the centuries the natural vegetation of the plains has been cleared and replaced by a man-maintained vegetation of grain crops or vegetables; the forests on the hills have been relentlessly destroyed by the farmer clearing fields for new upland crops or as a result of the unending quest for fuel.   The aggregate forest area when the present government came to power in 1949 was probably some 90–100 million ha., representing less than 10 per cent of the area of China; locally, however, the area under forest dropped far below the national average, for in the provinces of Kiangsu, Shantung and Hopeh forest occupies less than 0·5 per cent of the provincial area while the timber resources

---

[1] S. D. Richardson, *op. cit.*, p. 127.

of the developing Northwest (Shansi, Shensi and Kansu) are negligible. This widespread deforestation has caused a shortage of fuel and constructional timber; even more important has been the soil erosion which followed removal of the plant cover for this has had a deleterious effect on river régimes and on the agricultural productivity of great areas of interior China.   Because of the obvious needs of an expanding economy for timber[1] and the possibility of creating new resources through afforestation and because of the role of afforestation in soil- and water-conservation programmes there has been a vigorous campaign of tree-planting, with the slogan 'Make China Green'.   The area afforested during the First Five-Year Plan was officially put at 28·2 million acres, made up as follows:

TABLE 9

AFFORESTATION DURING THE FIRST FIVE-YEAR PLAN

Type of Planting	Million Acres
Timber	12·9
Industrial trees[1]	5·4
Shelter-belts	3·7
For soil and water conservation	3·5
Miscellaneous	2·7
TOTAL	28·2

Source: Peking Review, 22 April 1958, p. 15.

In 1958 a nation-wide drive resulted in the afforestation of 69 million acres; in addition, some 30,000 million trees were planted around villages and along roads and riverbanks.   By April 1959 a further 39 million acres had been planted; this meant that, according to official claims, an area almost as large as France had been afforested in fifteen months.   The target for 1968 was to afforest a total of some 260 million acres, thus doubling the forest area of China.

The implementation of the programme has depended on the massive investment of labour; on some communes up to 50 per cent of the labour force was seasonally occupied in this work.   The scale of this mobilisation is indicated by the planting of a thousand-mile-long shelter-belt in northern Kansu; this was carried out by 700,000 workers and two-thirds of the project was completed in one season.   Preparatory work for the establishment of trees has included the construction of contour ditches, contour terraces (level-grade steps), double furrows and, especially on rougher and rockier areas such as the Great Wall country, the 'fish-scale' method of planting (consisting of two or three trees in closely-spaced semi-circular ditches which intercept runoff).   In the

[1] Estimated average annual requirements over the period 1960–90 are 150 M cubic metres; this would exhaust present timber resources (estimated at between 5,400 and 7,500 M cubic metres) in little over a generation.

planting programme the emphasis has been on quick-growing trees
such as poplar and willow, eucalyptus, bamboo and pines, though the
diverse edaphic conditions involved, ranging from dune sands and
saline soils to marsh and mountain soils, has meant that a wide range
of tree and shrub species is being used.[1] Seen from the air these
plantings are beginning to spread a mist of green over some of the
ravaged hills of south and west China and mark the beginning of the

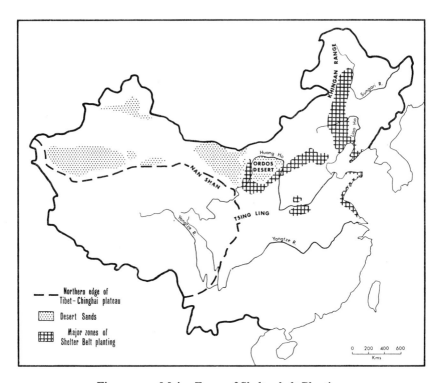

Figure 55.   Major Zones of Shelter-belt Planting.

The major zones are (a) on the western margin of the Manchurian lowland; (b)
on the fringes of the Gobi and Ordos deserts; these are designed to protect the agricultural lands to the east and extend over the Peking lowland; (c) on the coastal
fringes and the edges of the loess country.

The numerous protection plantings (e.g. along the Lan-Sin railway) and the
smaller shelter-belt zones of the arid Northwest are not shown.

transformation of the vegetation cover—and an increasing degree of
control over the erosion which menaces all of upland China.   Equally
striking are the shelter belts which form gridded patterns of the plain
of North China; these latter are, however, dwarfed by the immense

---

[1] These include tung, tea-oil and camphor south of the Yangtse and rubber, coconut and
coffee in the tropical south (apart from Cuba the South China-Vietnam region is the only
tropical region in the socialist world).

shelter-belt plantings on the margins of the deserts of western China, the so-called 'Great Green Wall' which Richardson describes as 'the most ambitious protection-afforestation project ever undertaken'.

The scale of some of the afforestation projects is illustrated by some examples cited by the Chinese press:

1961   700,000 ha. of tree-belts in the 'sand-ravaged' northeast

1961   300,000 ha. of tree-belts to arrest shifting sands in north Shensi

1962   100,000 ha. of shelter belts and one million ha. of barren slopes planted in Kansu

1962   500,000 ha. of dunes stabilised by planting in Inner Mongolia

There can be no doubt of the immensity of the efforts the Chinese are exerting to transform the vegetation cover and thus improve and stabilise the conditions for agriculture. Nevertheless, the success achieved has not always matched the effort expended. This is partly inevitable given the marginal character of many of the environments involved (which include vast areas of unstable sands, erosion-prone mountain soils and soils with a very low nutrient status). Dumont, however, has commented on some of the errors of judgement which in his opinion have marred the programme, notably an excessive emphasis on pines in timber planting[1] and the mistaken attempts to introduce fruit species into ecologically unsuited environments. The absence of adequate care after planting and the wastage caused by faulty management techniques have also reduced the effectiveness of the afforestation drive; Richardson repeatedly emphasises the failure of many of the plantings he observed and estimated that in many areas the survival rate among young trees was a low as 10 per cent. Such heavy losses, due to faulty plantings, and inadequate maintenance of the new plantations, were probably inevitable given the nature of the afforestation campaigns in the 'fifties which were based upon the labour of millions untrained in even the most rudimentary sylvicultural practices; it was also inevitable that, profiting from the experience of this early period, closer State supervision of afforestation work should be fostered.[2]

One-tenth of China, mainly in the northwest, consists of desert sands and the stabilisation and gradual reclamation of these areas has been a major concern of Chinese conservation efforts. As early as 1955 two-fifths of the area afforested was planted to combat sand movement; between 1950 and 1958 3·3 million acres of deserts were afforested and over 4 million acres sown with grass. The afforestation programmes in the areas of desert sands take two forms: shelter-belt plantings to halt the advance of the sand dunes and desert stabilisation plantings. The shelter-belt plantings, which already total some

[1] René Dumont, *La Chine surpeuplée* . . . , pp. 226–7.
[2] S. D. Richardson, *op. cit.*, p. 65.

thousands of miles in length, are planned as individual unities but 'will ultimately form a more or less complete ring around the northern deserts'.[1] The sand stabilisation projects are designed to protect settlements or communication lines from sand encroachment or to increase the capacity of the land for cropping, pastoralism or timber production. A variety of techniques are used—willow or tamarisk plantings along the dune contour if moisture is adequate; brushwood or straw strips across the direction of sand movement with shrubs or trees sown in between; for the protection of crop land 'sand-sealing' which involves the protection of the area by a 50 m. wide tree belt (established with irrigation) and progressive 'sealing' of the sand within the enclosed area by planting of trees in the dune hollows and shrubs and grass on the dune face and by progressive enlargement of the stabilised area. A wide variety of plant species are used including willow, tamarisk and *Artemisia* spp.; a total of some 116 plant species of use in these sand environments has been listed and many of these are of economic value, either because of their medicinal properties, their fodder potential, their edible fruits or their value as providing raw materials for local industries.[2]

The control of desert areas by grass sowing has been greatly aided by the use of the aeroplane; the target for 1959 was to bring some 6 million acres of desert land under control. As part of this programme of stabilisation and expansion of agriculture in the arid west it is hoped to reclaim some 1·6 million acres by irrigation along the upper and middle reaches of the Tarim River; much of this has been developed and is operated by the construction corps of the Chinese army.

The Chinese claim that 'man can not only control deserts but utilise them for his benefit'; their achievements in their Far West, based to a considerable extent on research by the Academy of Sciences, are justifying this claim and providing data and practical knowledge capable of application in desert environments elsewhere in the world.

(c) THE FIVE PLAGUES AND THE FOUR PESTS

The remarkable transformation of rural China's biological environment is perhaps less immediately apparent to the traveller than the dramatic remodelling of the physical landscape; it is, however, an equally important factor in the country's economic advance. China in 1949, says Denis Lambin, was a country where one went with a complete pharmaceutical kit:

> It was the Orient alive with the strangest parasites, with insects that carried germs or viruses, the region whence returning sailors brought back as souvenirs the so-called 'tropical diseases'. China was the

[1] S. D. Richardson, *op. cit.*, p. 122. The summary which follows is based on pp. 120–4 of Richardson's survey.

[2] S. D. Richardson, *op. cit.*, pp. 78–81, gives a list of the principal species used.

country of frequent death, of death from hunger, from lack of hygiene, from epidemic disease—the country where people died also through ignorance.[1]

The conquest of these parasites and of the diseases they carry and of the parasites of animals and plants has been, in Lambin's words:

> . . . one aspect of the conquest and transformation of Nature, of the cultural revolution which will improve the health of the Chinese people and lift them from their backward condition. This struggle is intimately bound up with the improvement of yields and the development of industry and of agriculture, which can develop only with a healthy population.[2]

The elimination of major diseases, such as malaria and schistosomiasis, and the prevention and cure of diseases such as dysentery, typhoid or tuberculosis, figure prominently in the Twelve-Year Plan of agricultural development. This medical emphasis is due in large measure to the fact that the raising of peasant living levels and peasant productivity begins with improved health, and this is especially true in the tropical zone.

The campaign for better health has moved forward on a broad front —improved sanitation and water supplies in village and town, mass immunisation, large-scale training of rural medical staff and the establishment of village dispensaries (see commune details above, pp. 143–68)—backed by a widespread publicity drive.

The campaign has been directed particularly against the five plagues—malaria, schistosomiasis, kala-azar, filariasis and hookworm. These have always been of major importance in the warm and humid South where they dragged down the efficiency of scores of millions of peasants and killed their scores of thousands annually. Schistosomiasis was prevalent over an area of South China inhabited by 100 million people, of whom 10 million were afflicted with the disease. The parasite has a fresh water snail as an intermediate host and the disease is being eliminated by the cleaning of ditches and irrigation channels and by treatment with modern and traditional methods. It has been wiped out in Fukien and Kiangsu and is being eradicated over the rest of South China. Malaria affected 5 per cent of China's population in 1949; by 1960 the figure had dropped to 0·05 per cent and the disease is now significant only in the forest and marsh country of western Yunnan. The campaign against filariasis, kala-azar, hookworm and roundworm follows the same pattern:

> A war of patience which mobilises six hundred million people against the parasites, according to a predetermined strategy and as an integral part of the agricultural plan.[3]

[1] Denis Lambin, 'La Chine propre' in *Cahiers Franco-Chinois* (Paris), Number 3, October 1959, p. 104.
[2] *Ibid.*, p. 106. [3] *Ibid.*, p. 109.

Deep ploughing

Adequate manuring

Irrigation projects

Good seed

The Eight-Point Charter for Agriculture

Like land reform or the control of flood and drought, this revolution in health[1] is lifting a burden from the shoulders of the peasant masses; it is not only adding to the productive potential of the country but eliminating a major cause of suffering and wasted human lives.

The campaign against the 'four pests'—flies, mosquitoes, rats, and sparrows—was partly inspired by considerations of hygiene, partly by the heavy toll on the national larder exacted by these pests. The slogans of the anti-pest drive emphasised this aspect: 'A rat is nine kilos of grain'. 'Half the wheat and rice crops of Hunan and Kirin goes to fill the stomachs of sparrows'. These campaigns have been described by many writers and they illustrate both the strength and the weakness of Chinese rural development policies. They showed, on one hand, what could be achieved in the health field by mass mobilisation of the population and by skilful and patient organisation and education in rural hygiene by health workers and other cadres at the 'grassroots' level. On the other hand, they illustrated the dangers of what Gilbert Etienne has termed 'the unreasonable application of generally reasonable principles'.[2] The classic example of this was the anti-sparrow campaign, for while the sparrow undoubtedly consumes grain it also plays an important role in controlling the various insect

[1] The early stages of this revolution are described by Dr. Brian Maegrith in *The New Scientist* (London) 5 December 1957, and by Dr. T. F. Fox in *The Lancet* (London), 9, 16 and 23 November 1957.
[2] Gilbert Etienne, *La voie chinoise* (Paris 1962), p. 235.

Close-planting

Plant protection

Tools reform

Field management

The Eight-Point Charter for Agriculture

pests which ravage trees and crops; its elimination was in consequence followed by a plague of these pests in some areas.   Here, as in other cases, the excesses of 1958 were followed by a return to a more moderate and rational path . . . and the bed-bug was substituted for the sparrow in the list of pests. . . .   But such errors of judgement should not obscure the reality of the achievement since 1949; the ignorance which formerly left the peasant helpless when confronted by parasites or predators is being eliminated and man is at last beginning to dominate his biological no less than his physical environment.

THE EXPANSION OF AGRICULTURAL OUTPUT

Agricultural development in recent years has been based on the principles set out in the 'Eight-point Charter for Agriculture'; they are: deep ploughing and soil improvement, heavy fertilisation, water conservancy, seed selection, close planting, plant protection, field management and repair of tools.   Few of these are new but each acquired a new content as a result of the agricultural experience since 1949.   At the same time, the need for flexible application of the Charter was underlined by events in 1958 when excessive and often misdirected enthusiasms in applying these principles *en bloc* led to organisational or cropping problems of various kinds; thus, excessive zeal in weed control led to labour shortages on many communes, and

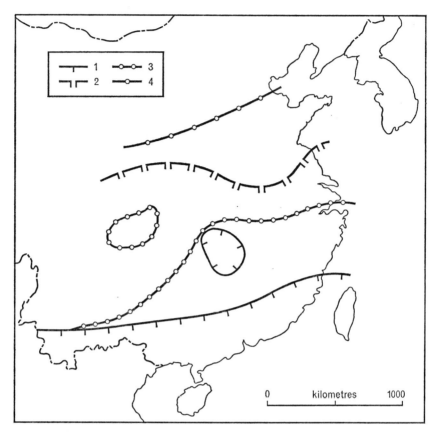

Figure 56.   Northern Advance of Selected Crops.
Two crops of rice a year 1 = 1940; 2 = 1956
Rice and one other crop 3 = 1940; 4 = 1956
(after Dumont)

the indiscriminate use of deep ploughing and close planting often resulted in limited or negative results.

The implementation of the measures set out above was facilitated by the new institutional framework—the commune—whose rise has been described. The success achieved is explained, partly by the liberation of the peasant from age-old prejudices and attitudes, a liberation which expressed itself in a great surge of peasant inventions such as improved tools, new planting techniques, experiments in plant hybridisation and the like; partly by the increasing control over the environment made possible by the extensive water control and irrigation schemes carried out since 1949.

Of these technical developments some, such as the use of improved higher-yielding seed strains on 70 per cent of the crop area, brought an immediate increase of yield without additional labour. Others, such as heavy manuring, close-planting and close tending of each plant, involved an intensification of labour output per unit area.   Intensification on these lines, at a time when massive diversion of labour towards rural industrialisation was taking place, led to acute labour difficulties and to the cry of shortage of labour throughout rural China in 1958. Such a situation serves to underline two things: first, the speed with which the apparent labour surplus in an 'overpopulated' agrarian country can be absorbed; secondly, the fact that ultimately intensification of agriculture and full implementation of the Agricultural Charter depends on some measure of mechanisation, in the shape of irrigation pumps, lorries, and the like, which would permit more effective use of available labour resources.

Meanwhile, mechanisation is still on a small scale.   Many of the communes in North China possess tractors and simple equipment, such as irrigation pumps and improved implements, is beginning to lighten the burden of peasant toil.   The long-term objective of the Chinese is to mechanise all the land that can be ploughed or irrigated by machine by 1969.   By mid-1966, however, mechanised farming was practised on only 10 per cent of the cultivated land and the demands of agriculture for various types of equipment is obviously going to exert a strong pressure on industry.   Heavy use of artificial fertilisers, which revolutionised Japanese farming (in 1957 Chinese rice yields were only half those of Japan), has scarcely begun.   Some 10 million tons were used in 1966 and of this between 8 and 9 million tons were produced in China. This has been supplemented by massive quantities of fertilisers produced by 'native-style' plants on the communes.   Consumption could, however, be greatly increased; thus, to apply chemical fertilisers at the unit-area rate used in Japan to half of China's arable land would call for some 32–35 million tons of such fertilisers.

It will be evident from the above account that the expansion of agricultural output in the last decade has been achieved largely by the intensification and improvement of traditional techniques within the new institutional framework provided by, first, the co-operative and, more recently, the commune.   This is of some considerable importance when we attempt to evaluate China's food problem, for it means that a very significant increase in production, both per unit-area and *per capita*, may be expected when the technical transformation of Chinese agriculture, involving heavy use of chemical fertilisers and widespread mechanisation, gets under way.   Beyond this, there remains the possibility of further increase by expansion of cultivation into the semi-arid and microthermal regions of China's West and Northeast.   Chinese sources give the area of potentially cultivable land as 247 million acres, as against Western estimates of 100 million acres; these figures may be compared with the existing cultivated area of some 260 million acres.   Even if we accept the Western estimate, and

P

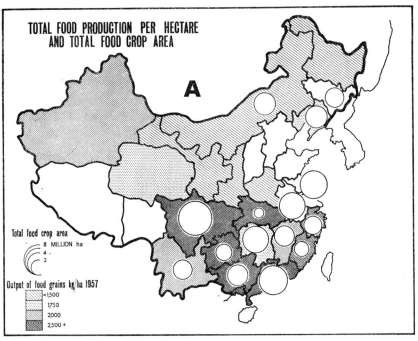

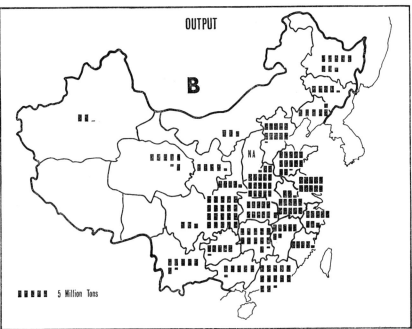

Figure 57.   The Pattern of Food Crop Production, 1957.

Available data for the total area under food crops and for food output per unit area
are shown in Map A; note the significance of the Tsinling Range as a divide between
the high-yielding South and lower-yielding North; note, too, the lower unit-area
production in those southern provinces with extensive areas of poorer upland country.
In Map B the tonnage of food crops produced in each province is shown.   The
dominance of the Yangtse valley provinces, and especially of Szechwan, is obvious.

even if we bear in mind that much of this land may have a much lower crop potential than land already cultivated, it would seem difficult to accept some Western views that China is 'overpopulated' and faces an acute pressure of population on available land resources.

A broad picture of the evolution of agricultural production between 1949 and 1960 is given below:

TABLE 10

AGRICULTURAL PRODUCTION, 1949–60

Crops (million tons)	1949	1952	1954	1956	1958	1959	1960
Food crops	113·2	163·9	169·5	192·7	261·5[a]	281·5[a]	309·5[a]
Rice	48·6	68·4	70·9	84·0	n.a.	n.a.	n.a.
Wheat	13·8	18·1	23·3	25·0	28·9	n.a.	n.a.
Other Cereals	35·8	51·5	49·3	55·3	n.a.	n.a.	n.a.
Potatoes	9·8	16·3	17·0	20·4	n.a.	n.a.	n.a.
Soya Beans	5·1	9·5	9·1	10·2	10·5	11·5	12·5
Cotton	0·4	1·3	1·1	1·4	2·1	n.a.	n.a.
Sugar Cane	2·6	7·1	8·6	8·7	n.a.	n.a.	n.a.
Groundnuts	1·3	2·3	2·8	3·3	n.a.	n.a.	n.a.

Livestock (million head)	1949	1952	1954	1956	1958	1959	1960
Cattle	43·9	56·6	63·6	66·6	65·5	65·4	n.a.
Sheep and Goats	10·3	61·8	81·3	92·1	108·9	112·5	n.a.
Pigs	57·7	89·8	101·7	97·8	160·0[b]	180·0[b]	243·0[b]

[a] Official Chinese statistics; one Western estimate of food crop production in recent years suggests: 1958, 220 million tons; 1959, 200 million tons; 1960, 190 million tons. See *The China Quarterly*, London, Number 6, April–June 1961, pp. 67–8.
[b] Almost certainly an inflated figure (see below p. 213). n.a. = Not available.

CROP PRODUCTION SINCE THE 'GREAT LEAP FORWARD'

In 1958, the year of the 'Great Leap Forward', Chinese official sources claimed that the 1957 output of food crops was doubled and that production reached the figure of 375 million tons. This claim was subsequently drastically revised downwards to a figure of 250 million tons. The reasons for the inflated early estimate do not appear to have been propagandist (the writer was in China at the time the harvest reports were coming in and noted that the reports were accepted at their face value even by Chinese agricultural scientists) but to have arisen from two statistical errors. The first source of error lay in 'the unusually large discrepancy between "biological yield" and "barn yield"', due to the inability of the communes to harvest all the crops and a sharp increase in wastage'.[1]   The second source of error lay in the apparent confusion between yield per unit of crop area and yield per crop hectare; the average grain yield figure (3 tons per hectare) appears to have been based on yield per unit of crop area rather than yield per crop hectare and this would have been higher than yield per crop hectare because of the double cropping of almost half the arable area.   As Yuan-li Wu points out:

> If we take this unit area estimate (i.e. 3 tons per hectare) as yield per hectare of crop area and divide it by the general multiple cropping index of 1·45 reported for 1958, the unit yield per crop hectare would be approximately 2,070 kilograms.   If this figure is then multiplied by the 1958 grain hectare area reported in 1959, or 121 million hectares, the estimated output would be equal to approximately 250 million tons.   This was precisely the revised figure reported in 1959.[2]

Even this figure of 250 million tons is regarded as too high by Western experts who prefer (on the basis of more or less sophisticated guesswork) to place the 1958 crop at between 220 million and 175 million tons; this latter figure, it may be noted, is 10 million tons down on the 1957 crop.

From 1959–60 Chinese production figures get increasingly scanty and the estimates of 'China-watchers' increasingly numerous, increasingly controversial and cumulatively contrary to such estimates as may be pieced together from Chinese sources and to the observations of experts (chiefly French) possessing direct field experience of China.

A sample range of estimates by Western observers is given in the table below:

TABLE 11

FOOD CROP PRODUCTION (Western Estimates) 1957–66

(million tons)	1957	1958	1959	1960	1961	1962	1963	1964	1965	1966
								(181)		
F.E.E.R.	—	193	167	160	166	178	179	(185)	180	175
US est. (H.K.)	185	192	168	160	167	178	179	183	180	175
C.S.	—	193	167	160	167	178	179	—	—	—
Wu	185	175	154	130	140	160	183	—	—	—
Dumont	—	200	—	—	—	—	190	200	—	—
Karol	—	—	—	—	—	—	180	200	210	—
Wertheim	180+	220	—	—	—	—	210	220+	—	—

Notes: F.E.E.R.: *Far Eastern Economic Review Yearbooks*; US est.: estimates of *U.S. Consulate-General in Hong Kong*; C.S.: *Current Scene*; Wu: Yuan-li Wu, *op. cit;*.

[1] Yuan-li Wu in J. L. Buck, O. L. Dawson and Yuan-li Wu, *Food and Agriculture in Communist China* (New York, Washington and London 1966), pp. 77–8.
[2] Yuan-li Wu, *op. sup. cit.*, p. 80.

The increasing divergence in the estimates needs no stressing—by 1964 it was close on 40 million tons; by 1966 American observers were claiming that food production in China had slipped back to the 1961 level, while the Chinese were claiming 'the biggest harvest since Liberation' (interpreted by the West as meaning 'over 200 million tons' but probably in fact of the order of 210–220 million tons).

There is, however, general agreement on the sharp decline in production during the three years 1959–61; in spite of the Chinese claim to have harvested over 300 million tons of food crops in 1960 (see Table 10; the figure is obviously derived from a 10 per cent increase of the preceding year's figure), the actual harvest, according to Chou En-lai, lay 'between 190 and 250 million tons'. This decline was due, in part at least, to the succession of droughts and floods which afflicted the country during these three years. It was also due, as Chinese leaders admitted, to human factors; these, in the opinion of Hong Kong observers, accounted for some two-thirds of the decline though it is obviously impossible to confirm or deny such an estimate. Nevertheless, as Gilbert Etienne suggests, the over-hasty collectivisation of 1958 which provoked an attitude of reserve on the part of many peasants and defects in the administrative structure may have been important contributing factors.[1]

By 1962 Joseph Alsop was advancing his celebrated—or notorious—thesis of 'China's descending spiral';[2] the country was 'caught in a remorselessly descending spiral' and this, if unreversed, 'must eventually reach some sort of sharp breaking point'. Rations were down to 1,300 to 1,600 calories per person daily, population had ceased to grow and is now declining, and the best hope of the Peking régime was, to quote this American expert, to 'just hang on somehow until the Chinese population has been really massively reduced, by something like a quarter or a third, then the pressure on the land will at last be lightened'.[3] Subsequent events, it need hardly be stressed, did not substantiate a prophecy based more on an obsessive dislike of the Chinese Government than on hard realities. . . . By 1962 agricultural production was showing a sharp up-turn and by 1964 the estimates of Western experts returning from China suggested a harvest of between 200 and 220 million tons.

These trends are, however, not reflected in the estimates of Hong Kong observers since 1962, Table 11, and some comment on this is necessary. The first—and obvious—comment is that, relating the Hong Kong estimates to the most generally accepted estimates of China's population growth, it appears that China is somehow managing to feed a population probably 120 million larger than that of 1957 on a food supply smaller by some 10 million tons. This seems an unlikely

[1] Gilbert Etienne, *La voie chinoise* (Paris 1962), p. 209.
[2] Joseph Alsop, 'On China's Descending Spiral' in *China Quarterly*, July-September 1962.
[3] Joseph Alsop, *loc. cit.*, p. 33.

situation, especially in the light of the comments of observers on the relatively high level of grain rations (in 1964 the *minimum* monthly ration was close to 15 kg. of grain)[1] and on the fact that in the last two or three years rations have been so increased that 'most workers do not take advantage of their full ration'.[2]   Moreover, if the estimate of 175 million tons as the 1966 production is accepted, this implies that the very considerable technological inputs of recent years, in the shape of fertilisers and pumping machinery, have had a negligible effect.   The fullest and most recent evaluation of the Hong Kong data is that of Dwight H. Perkins[3] who draws on material presented to the Joint Economic Committee of the United States Congress and on the findings of trained observers such as Robert Guillain.   Perkins comments that 'if these figures (i.e. the Hong Kong estimates) are accurate, then China was in deep economic troubles in 1966 with no obvious way out short of a drastic birth control programme. . . .   The implications of the Hong Kong data', he adds, 'point up the essential implausibility of the estimates.'   Thus a variety of sources, including refugees' reports and the observations of foreign travellers in China, suggests that *per capita* grain rations 'have risen substantially since 1961'.   Furthermore, 'if one believes the Hong Kong figures, it is difficult to avoid concluding that it was not possible for China to raise agricultural output by means of capital investment.   Under these circumstances, one might legitimately wonder why the Chinese Communists were bothering to produce and import more chemical fertiliser'.   In the light of these considerations he comes, reluctantly, to the conclusion that 'the grain estimates reconstructed from statements by Chinese officials plausibly reflect what we know of the performance of agriculture in China since the disasters of 1959–61'. These latter estimates suggest that 'China's post-1960 emphasis has paid off in modest gains, but that her efforts in this direction in the future must be significantly increased if famine is to be warded off'. These 'reconstructed estimates' are as follows:

TABLE 12

OFFICIAL 'RECONSTRUCTED' ESTIMATES
OF GRAIN OUTPUT
(million tons)

1961	*1962*	*1963*	*1964*	*1965*	*1966*
162	173	183	200	200	200 +

[1] W. F. Wertheim, 'La China est-elle surpeuplée?' in *Population* (Paris) May-June 1965, p. 495.

[2] K. S. Karol, *China: The Other Communism* (London 1967), p. 195.   See page 192 above for the range of ration levels in 1966.

[3] Dwight H. Perkins, 'Economic Growth in China and the Cultural Revolution' in *China Quarterly*, April-June 1967, esp. pp. 36–9.

In the present writer's opinion, it is probable that this 'reconstructed' 1966 figure is too low (it is not clear whether the figure refers solely to grains or whether it follows the Chinese practice of including potatoes and sweet potatoes, converted to grain-equivalents); even so, this figure is almost three times the Indian production, for a population only 50 per cent larger than that of India.   This comparison lends added force to René Dumont's description of China, quoted above, as 'the only major Afro-Asian nation emerging so clearly from under-development without the least external aid'.

Appendix 1

SOME AGRICULTURAL DATA FOR 1966

The following additional data is based upon the writer's field-work in China in 1966.   Grain yield appears to be of the order of 2 tons to the hectare, while *per capita* production was cited as 300 kg.; this, it was recognised, is low.   These two figures, for what they are worth, suggest a grain output of 210–250 million tons.   It is recognised that there may be some peasant hoarding but this is not considered a bad thing; it does, however, introduce the possibility that actual production may be in excess of the official figure.   Pigs, critically important as a source of manure, totalled 160 million; this was stated to be the highest total yet reached, from which it is obvious that the totals given in Table 10 have to be scaled down considerably.   Chemical fertiliser production increased 50 per cent over 1965 and lay between 8 and 10 million tons. The area of high-yielding crops was stated to be still low.

Total crop production appears to have increased by rather more than the 5 per cent originally set as the target increase for the year.

Appendix 2

A NOTE ON CHINESE GRAIN IMPORTS

Grain imports since 1961 have been running at about 5 million tons yearly; this represents some 2–3 per cent of the total of food crop production and is sufficient to feed between 15 and 20 million people.   Several arguments have been advanced for the continuation of these imports (which represent 30 per cent of China's total imports) beyond the lean years of the early 'sixties:

1. The economic argument. Wheat can be purchased for £25 per ton but rice sells at £40 a ton; there is thus an economic advantage in importing cheap wheat to free for export more expensive rice. This may be a partial explanation, though rice exports have rarely reached a figure of one million tons.

2. The logistical argument. It is easier to import grain for the northern cities from overseas than to shift it over one thousand miles by rail from surplus grain areas such as Szechwan and Hunan. Viewed thus, the import programme is essentially directed to the feeding of the cities and not to raising *per capita* consumption in the country as a whole.

3. The food-habits argument. Recent years have seen some shift towards wheaten bread at the expense of rice; on the other hand, the major food-producing area and the region where much of the increase in production is concentrated is the rice-growing South (see Table 8, p. 180). The population increase in the subhumid North, the shift towards greater use of wheat and the fact that the climatically marginal wheat-growing areas were more affected by natural calamities than the humid South—all these factors have tended to perpetuate the pattern of wheat imports.

4. The stock-pile argument. China is building up a stock-pile of grain while international conditions allow with the aim of cushioning herself against both climatic and military crises.

5. The provincial-central Government argument. This argument, advanced by Audrey Donnithorne, suggests that 'imports of grain serve to ease relations between the centre and the provinces, as otherwise Peking would be forced to squeeze larger grain transfers out of grain-surplus provinces.'[1] The imported grain, under the direct control of the central Government, strengthens it by making it less dependent on the compliance of the provinces. Viewed thus, grain imports fulfil a function analogous to that of the 'key economic areas' of the past by providing the Government with the grain on which political and military power depends.

There may be a measure of truth in all these arguments. But it may be stressed, while China may be using imported grain to meet *regional* shortages, there seems little evidence to suggest that today these imports are needed to raise *national* consumption levels or to support Dawson's view that the grain imports of 1958–61 'were used to support the rations of favoured groups while the masses were inadequately fed'.[2]

[1] Audrey Donnithorne, *China's Economic System* (London 1967), p. 507.
[2] O. L. Dawson in J. L. Buck, O. L. Dawson and Yuan-li Wu, *op. cit.*, p. 106.

CHAPTER 10

The Industrial Sector

CHINA'S POVERTY and stagnation in 1949 was largely the result of the country's undiversified economy—which meant limited employment opportunities outside agriculture and an agriculture which, because of its lack of diversified cropping, could employ those in the rural sector only a fraction of the year. A semi-employed peasantry, existing on the very margins of survival, with a negligible or non-existent cash income, offered no market for the products of industry, for the consumer goods, or, more important, for the improved implements, the pumps or the fertilisers which would have made possible the stabilisation and expansion of food output. And, in the cities, an under-employed proletariat, existing somehow on starvation wages, offered no real incentive to the expansion or the diversification of food crop production. Rural poverty, urban poverty, in Old China as in most 'under-developed' countries, were thus closely interdependent; neither problem could be tackled singly. Moreover, poverty, hunger, wastage of human life—all these could be eliminated only by eliminating the condition—the lack of a diversified and balanced economy—of which they were but symptoms. . . .

The sweeping social, economic and environmental changes which are creating a new—and diversified—rural sector have been described. No less sweeping have been the changes in the industrial sector, changes which have led to China's emergence as a major industrial nation, changes which reflect the far-reaching reappraisal of China's resource endowment carried through by the People's Government. We must recognise this two-fold transformation—and yet at the same time we should avoid the tendency to think too much in Western terms, of a rural, largely non-industrial, sector on one hand and of an urban, largely industrial, sector on the other. This sharp dichotomy has little relevance in China today; the commune has a range of small industries and the contribution of these to the total output of the commune may be considerable (see p. 239) so the countryman is no stranger to industry; conversely, many cities contain considerable farming areas and a considerable rural population within their boundaries (see p. 273). The Chinese have tried strenuously—and with some success—to avoid the sharp clash of urban and rural interests which bedevils many countries, developed or under-developed; they have tried also to avoid the domination of the country by a handful of giant industrial cities or of the economy by a narrowly-specialised urban-oriented technocracy. Their policies give a distinctive character to the geographic pattern of industry in China and are resulting in a

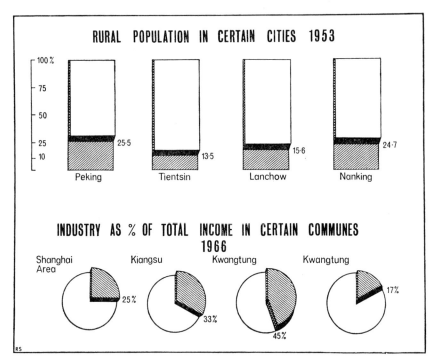

Figure 58.   The Interpenetration of Rural and Urban Life in China.
One of the aims of Chinese planning is to avoid the emergence of a sharp dichotomy between the urban and industrial sector and the rural sector. As the 1953 Census showed, many of the biggest Chinese cities have a sizeable rural element in their population (for the communes of Peking see pp. 143–8); this increased as a result of boundary changes in 1958. And, especially since the development of the commune, industry has become increasingly diffused into the countryside so that industrial activities are an important source of employment and wealth on many communes. The rural component in city populations, coupled with the beginnings of industrialisation in the countryside, means that the sharp distinction between the urban and rural sectors of the country (a distinction typical of the West and of many emerging countries) is largely absent in China. And this contrast between the landscapes of China and those of many other countries may be expected to become more marked as a result of the continued policy of industrial dispersal.

cultural landscape which, because of its interpenetration of agricultural and industrial elements (Figure 58), is very different from that of most emergent countries.   These aspects must be borne in mind when, as in this chapter, an attempt is made to give a broad picture of recent industrial development in China—for in discussing industry separately we are arbitrarily fragmenting the economic and social unity whose creation is one of the major objectives of recent Chinese planning.

POINT OF DEPARTURE

Industrialisation had been hamstrung by the organisation of Chinese society and by the disintegration of Chinese life following the impact of the West.   Much of the production was accounted for by small-scale or handicraft industries, using primitive tools and minute capital investment; out of the 21,000 'factories' enumerated in 1912 only 363 used mechanical power, 93 per cent employed under 50 workers and only 1·1 per cent over 500.[1]   And, if modern forms of organisation such as the joint-stock company are taken as an index of modernisation (and many of such companies, as Feuerwerker emphasises, 'could only formally be counted as modernised') the number of joint-stock companies registered under the Company Law of 1904 totalled, in the decade before the First World War, a mere 227, of which only one-third could be regarded as even medium-scale enterprises.   Isolated examples of modern industry had begun to develop, largely as a result of foreign initiative, but these were confined to the coastal margins.   Here the extra-territorial régime of the Treaty Ports meant comparative security and foreign industrialists could combine relatively modern methods of production with the abnormally cheap labour supply provided by the huddled and impoverished masses of the coast towns.[2] Moreover, such 'modern-style' *Chinese* industrialisation as did take place tended to be concentrated in the same area: 43 per cent of the registered companies were in Shanghai and Kiangsu, another 20 per cent in Chihli (the Peking-Tientsin area) or Kwangtung (Canton).[3] And, with the exception of the heavy industry of Hankow and the Northeast, the industrial sector was dominated by the production of consumer goods—textiles, food processing, cigarette manufacture and the like—but even in the case of some of these consumer goods Old China depended on imports for between one-half and three-quarters of her needs.

Some attempts at industrial expansion had been made under the Kuomintang government but the attempts had only a limited result.[4]

[1] Albert Feuerwerker, *China's Early Industrialization* (Cambridge, Mass. 1958), p. 5.
[2] Feuerwerker (*op. cit.*, p. 245) comments on these advantages; he adds that imperialist domination of the modern sector of the economy tended 'to handicap economic growth within China.'   [3] Albert Feuerwerker, *op. cit.*, p. 7.
[4] One estimate puts the capital invested in modern industry at 5 per cent of the total value of the country's production capital in 1936: Cheng Chu-yuan, *Communist China Problem Research Series*, Vol. 1 (Hong Kong 1958), p. 22.

Above all, little was done to change the distribution pattern and, as late as 1952, almost three-quarters of China's industrial output came from the seven coastal provinces and the cities of Peking, Shanghai and Tientsin; in the interior there was little to relieve the drab and monotonous poverty of a stagnating rural economy. It has been aptly said that large-scale industry in Old China was 'a modern fringe stitched along the hem of an ancient garment'.

This fringe of modern industry was to a considerable extent foreign-owned or -controlled, a fact which emphasised the semi-colonial status of the country. An estimate for 1933 puts the foreign share at 32 per cent; in individual industries the share was much higher: for cotton textiles 42 per cent, for ship-building and repairing 58 per cent, for the tobacco industry 63 per cent. Equally significant was the foreign control of the infrastructure—the communications and power system. Approximately one-half of China's railroad system was under the direct or indirect control of foreign capital; over one-half of the total coal production and four-fifths of the production with modern techniques; 57 per cent of the electricity, gas and water supply systems. Finally, the industrial economy was an incomplete one; heavy extractive industry or light industry dominated and the output of means of production was negligible (only one per cent of the invested capital was in the machine-building industry). Machinery replacements, even for long-established industries such as textiles, had thus to be imported, further underlining the dependent character of China's industry.[1]

Before the Second World War, then, the Chinese industrial economy was retarded, geographically highly localised and partially dominated by outside capital. The war against Japan, followed by the Civil War, reduced this flimsy structure to rubble; by 1949, according to Gross-mann, the effective capacity of the industrial economy was zero. When the Communists came to power in 1949 Chinese society was, in the words of Mao Tse-tung, 'a sheet of blank paper'; as such, it lent itself admirably to receive 'the newest and most beautiful words . . . , the newest and most beautiful pictures'.[2]

DESIGNING THE NEW INDUSTRIAL MAP

The first task of the People's Government on coming to power was to rebuild the country's shattered industrial economy. The initial target was to attain by 1952 the level of industrial production in 1943; by 1952 this was not only attained but total industrial production reached a level some 23 per cent above the 1943 level. From this point the

[1] Yuan-li Wu, *The Economy of Communist China* (New York and London 1965), pp. 116–18; Bernhard Grossman, *Die Wirtschaftliche Entwicklung der Volksrepublik China* (Stuttgart 1960), pp. 28–33.
[2] Mao Tse-tung cited by Stuart Schram, *The Political Thought of Mao Tse-tung* (New York and London 1963), p. 253.

development of the economy proceeded by a series of Five Year Plans; these originally had the aim of transforming China from a backward agrarian country to an advanced socialist industrial nation in the space of three quinquennial plans. An important aspect of Chinese development planning has been its flexibility. Development plans have been continuously reviewed and revised in the light of Chinese conditions. At the end of the First Five Year Plan, for example, significant modifications, such as greater decentralisation and the elaboration of more detailed annual plans, set within the context of the quinquennial plan, were introduced. At the same time, the need for constant readjustment of the economy to remove weaknesses and correct any disequilibrium was reiterated.

This development pattern followed closely the Soviet model; its general features have been summarised by A. G. Ashbrook.[1] They include:

(i) a central economic plan laying down growth rates for various sectors of the economy

(ii) priority to investment once minimum defence and military needs were met

(iii) the principle 'that investments in industry should outrank investment in agriculture and that, within industry, investment in heavy industry should be several times as great as investment in light industry'.[2]

(iv) the policy of running the economy 'at full throttle' so as to achieve maximum output

(v) centralised organisation of production, with each major branch of industry under the control of a Peking-based ministry.

These major features were in large measure a response to the exigencies of the situation the Chinese faced in 1949. To create a diversified and modern economy from the ruins of an undiversified and backward peasant economy implied a heavy emphasis on industrial development. Since, however, agricultural production also had to be greatly increased to provide improved living levels for a growing population and also to provide some of the raw materials and the funds needed for industrialisation, it followed that a very rapid rate of growth in the industrial sector was essential. Moreover, if China was to achieve a balanced and self-sufficient industrial economy, an initial strong emphasis on heavy industry, and especially the machine-building industry (which would provide the basis for future development), was critically important; the textile and other consumer goods industries contributing to the improvement of living levels had to be expanded, though at a slower rate than the heavy industrial sector.

[1] Arthur G. Ashbrook, Jr., 'Main Lines of Chinese Communist Economic Policy' in *An Economic Profile of Mainland China* (Joint Economic Committee, Congress of the United States, Washington 1967) Vol. I, pp. 21–2.   [2] *Ibid.*

This emphasis on the heavy industry sector is typical of the socialist pattern of development and contrasts with the emphasis in the initial stages of development of the older industrial countries; in these latter early development had been based on light industry, especially textiles, and this in turn provided part of the capital resources on which their development of heavy industry was subsequently based.

In some socialist analyses the term 'Group A' is used to refer to means of production, including machine-building; 'Group B' refers to consumer goods. When the Communists came to power the output of means of production represented only 28·8 per cent of the total value of industrial production; under such conditions China was largely dependent on overseas sources for machinery, machine tools and the like. To correct this weak A : B ratio heavy investments in the producer goods industry were essential and in the First Five Year Plan almost nine-tenths of the investment in industry went to the producer goods industry, slightly over one-tenth to the consumer goods industry. This was to give a 17·8 per cent annual increase in Group A, as against a 12·4 per cent increase for Group B. The structural change resulting from this differential growth of the two sectors is summarised below:

TABLE 13

PRODUCER GOODS (A) AND CONSUMER GOODS (B)
as % of total industrial production (by value)

	1949	*1952*	*1957* (*planned*)
Group A	28·8	39·7	45·4
Group B	71·2	60·3	54·6

Source: Lavallée, Noirot and Dominique (1957), p.150

By 1957 actual production figures showed that the two groups were, in fact, approaching parity. Nevertheless, given the need of an expanding industrial sector for more and increasingly complex producer goods the differential rate of growth between Group A and Group B is likely to be maintained for many years. Ultimately, as the economy is consolidated, this disparity will tend to disappear; thus, in the sixth Soviet Five Year Plan the rates of annual growth envisaged were 11·5 per cent for Group A and 10 per cent for Group B.

Two aims of Chinese industrial planning in its initial stages were, then, to revolutionise the country's economy, transforming it from a peasant economy to a modern industrial economy; secondly, to change the character of the industrial sector by a heavy emphasis on the producer's goods sector. The third aim was to correct the imbalance in the geographic distribution of industry by an accelerated development of the interior districts of the country. In creating a new distribution pattern the Chinese have been guided by the general principles of industrial localisation followed by the majority of socialist planners: the siting of new projects near raw material and fuel sources and, if possible, consuming centres in order to cut down transport; the widest possible distribution of industry, thus reducing the differences between industrial and agrarian groups and, more especially, between minority and majority groups; the need to achieve a better balance of industry and agriculture in each major economic region; finally, the strategic need to avoid the exposed and vulnerable coastal regions. The forces shaping the industrial map have thus been quite different from the forces which operated in pre-Communist days and which brought about the excessive concentration of industry in the coast cities.

This policy of industrial dispersion towards the interior took shape with the First Five Year Plan. Existing industrial centres such as Shanghai and the Northeastern Region were strengthened and modernised; their industries played an important role in the accumulation of funds for the construction of new industrial bases in the interior. The main drive of industrialisation was, however, towards the west and northwest. Sixty-eight per cent of the above-norm[1] industrial projects during the First Five Year Plan were constructed in the interior and here output increased 96 per cent between 1953 and 1955, as compared with 55 per cent in the coastal areas. The most striking manifestations of this drive have been the creation of a new iron and steel industry at Paotow in the grasslands of Inner Mongolia; this area has been compared, in its resource setting, to the Urals and will be the centre of a new metallurgical complex; the development of a major industrial complex centring on Lanchow to the northwest; and the intensified development of the oil resources of the northwest and the coalfields of the north. 'It is from these new centres that it will be possible, towards the end of the Second Five Year Plan, to push further the distribution of industry, towards the west and the southwest.'

CONDITIONS FOR INDUSTRIALISATION

The policy of rapid industrialisation rests on three bases: the natural resource endowment of China; the accumulation of funds; and the effective utilisation of the country's vast labour force. Let us look briefly at each of these.

(a) RESOURCE BASIS

The dramatic reassessment of the adequacy of China's resource basis in the last decade is a striking illustration of the validity of Sauer's

---

[1] The 'norm' of investment in capital construction is, for heavy industry, 5–10 million yuan; for light industry 3–5 million yuan.

concept of resources as 'cultural appraisals'. In pre-Communist days the weakness of Chinese science—and more specifically of sciences such as geology—meant that little was known of the country's resource endowment. In the absence of such information it was tacitly assumed that China was relatively poorly endowed with mineral resources and, more especially, that she lacked that broad range of mineral resources needed to build a modern industrial economy. The geological discoveries of the last decade show that this view is no longer tenable.

'The Communist régime fully realises', says a recent American report, 'that the key to China's industrial progress lies in the uncovering and efficient utilisation of its mineral wealth.'[1] Pre-Communist China had less than 200 active geologists; since 1949, some 21,000 'geological workers' and some 400 geologists from the other socialist countries have begun to give us a clearer picture of the country's mineral endowment. Their work has revealed mineral resources 'so extensive that they appear to make China one of the world's chief reservoirs of raw material'.[2] Among the major discoveries is an unsuspected deposit of some 7,000 million tons of iron ore in Kiangsi in Central China and a 3,000 million tons deposit of high-grade ore (50 per cent iron oxide) in Honan. Coal resources appear to be inferior only to those of the Soviet Union and the United States; resources of non-ferrous metals, notably tin, tungsten and nickel, are among the largest in the world. Petroleum production, long a weak link in the economy, has been greatly expanded as the newly-discovered fields in China's Far West came into production. And the energy base is strengthened by the hydro-electric potential of China's great rivers (110 billion kWh. on the Hwang-ho alone). In the words of the American assessment already quoted, China 'has a sufficiently diversified mineral base to become a first rank industrial power'.

(b) ACCUMULATION OF FUNDS

Both the exploitation of the wage-earner and of overseas territories and populations played a significant role in the early industrialisation of northwest Europe. In a country such as China, poverty-stricken, lacking overseas colonies, and with a socialist type of economy, the process of 'breakthrough' to a modern industrial economy was bound to take a rather different form. In the initial stage a temporary source of investment funds was provided by the seizure of Japanese assets, and the property of the feudal and comprador groups. The major source of funds, however, has been the profits of the State industrial sector, of the co-operatives and the sector of State capitalism. The private sector of the economy made an initially significant but declining

[1] *Mineral Trade Notes: Special Supplement, Number 59, March 1960* (U.S. Department of the Interior, Bureau of Mines, Washington 1960), p. 4.
[2] See, for example, the chapters by E. C. T. Chao and K. P. Wang in S. H. Gould (ed.), *Sciences in Communist China* (Washington 1961).

contribution through taxation. The relative significance of these sectors in the early stages of development is indicated below:

TABLE 14

SOURCE OF BUDGET RECEIPTS (%)

	1950	*1952*	*1955*
State enterprises, co-operatives and State capitalist sector	34	60	76·2
Agriculture	29·6	16	11·8
Private Industry and Commerce	32·9	21·2	10·7

A sustained rate of accumulation of investment funds depended obviously on the introduction of improved techniques and the creation of a skilled labour force. Such conditions could scarcely be realised in the initial stages of industrialisation and under these circumstances a strong emphasis was given to maximum utilisation of existing equipment, to rigid economy in operation and emulation drives to increase the efficiency of the individual worker. Combined with the elimination of overlapping and wasteful competition which was made possible by centralised State control and with the pooling of technical data and patents these practices resulted in a significant increase in production from plant inherited from the pre-Communist period. Indeed, it is estimated that seven-tenths of the industrial output during the First Five Year Plan was from such plant, the remaining three-tenths from new or completely modernised enterprises.[1] During the Second Five Year Plan the rising level of technical competence and the increasing role played by large-scale modern enterprises created conditions for a major surge forward on the industrial front. The subsequent rhythm of growth of the total economy and of individual industries is discussed below.

This increasing productivity made it possible not only to achieve a sharp rise in real wages (planned at 33 per cent over the period of the First Five Year Plan) but also to set aside increasing funds for accumulation. The proportions of the national income to be set aside for this purpose as opposed to the proportion made available for personal consumption represented approximately one-fifth of the national income in the later years of the First Plan. And given the immensity of the tasks still confronting the country it is not likely to drop much below this level in the foreseeable future.

(c) LABOUR RESOURCES

China's vast population has traditionally been regarded as a source of weakness and of backwardness; one of the achievements of the present

[1] See, for example, Edwin F. Jones, 'The Emerging Pattern of China's Economic Revolution' in *An Economic Profile of Communist China* (Washington 1967), p. 86.

Q

régime has been to convert it into a factor for progress.   This is especially so in the countryside where 'labour has been converted into capital', in the shape of irrigation works, drainage schemes and other construction projects, on a massive scale.   In the industrial sector likewise the pace of progress is partly explicable by the more effective use of existing labour resources and by the gradual but continuous rise in the level of technical competence.

Between 1953 and 1957 non-agricultural employment rose from 36·5 million to 40·9 million, an average annual increase of 2·2 per cent. This in itself is not a major increase; the overall figures do, however, conceal a significant change in the composition of this labour force— the decline of the traditional handicraft sector and the sharp rise in the modern non-agricultural sector.   The former declined from 20·9 million to 17 million workers; the modern sector rose from 15·6 million to 23·9 million.   Employment in modern industry rose from 5·3 million to 7·9 million; of the increase, four-fifths was in heavy industry, reflecting clearly the direction of the development drive.[1]   This trend towards a more efficient use of labour resources and the emphasis on 'turning labour into capital' increased sharply during the 'Great Leap Forward' of 1958.   But even during the First Five Year Plan industrial policy, with its increasing investment of unskilled labour in lieu of scarce capital and skills to achieve a high rate of growth, prefigured later Chinese policy.   And, at the same time, the initiation of an ambitious scheme of technical education laid the foundations for subsequent development for, in a country such as China where, until recently, virtually the entire population was illiterate and ignorant of any technical skills, a rising level of competence may increase production as effectively as an increase in the labour force.[2]   Even a decade after the 'Great Leap' the size of this unexplored reservior of technical competence is as little known as the size of China's reservoir of mineral resources.

ON THE EVE: An Appraisal of Industrial Development before the 'Great Leap Forward'

'China', says Bernard Martin, 'is a land where the statistician may perish for want of a few figures, where records are more romantic than mathematical.'[3]   The truth of this will have become evident in the section where we attempted to assess levels of Chinese food production in the last decade.   We find ourselves confronting the same difficulties when we attempt to measure Chinese progress in the industrial field;

[1] J. P. Emerson, 'Manpower Absorption in the Non-agricultural Branches of the Economy of Communist China 1953–58' in *China Quarterly* (London), Number 7, 1961, pp. 69–84.
[2] A. Sauvy, 'Evolution récente des idées sur le surpeuplement' in *Population* (Paris), June–July 1960, p. 481.
[3] Bernard Martin, *Strange Vigour: A Biography of Sun-Yat-sen* (3rd edit. London 1967), p. 3.

indeed, from 1958 onwards the gaps in our data, and the discrepancies in the interpretation of such data as we have, are even greater in the industrial field than in the field of agriculture.

We have two sets of data with which to work: the official Chinese figures and the estimates of foreign analysts; the great majority of these estimates are American though they include some French and British estimates. The Chinese data may be flawed by an excessive optimism, the American data flawed perhaps even more decisively by a strong anti-Communist, anti-Chinese, bias. Both sets of data must be used with care though, with the exception of the period 1958–60 when a quality of wild abandon pervaded the formerly cautious Chinese statistical services, it is the writer's opinion that the Chinese data show a closer approximation to reality than the guesses of 'China-watchers' in Hong Kong or the United States.

The Chinese data indicate a five-fold increase in the aggregate output of industry and agriculture between 1949 and 1959, a twelve-fold increase in the gross output value of industry between these dates, and a decisive shift from an agrarian-based to an industrial-based society. By 1959 industry accounted for two-thirds of the gross output value of agriculture and industry, as compared with less than one-third in 1949; the Chinese had thus achieved one of the major objectives of their long march towards modernisation.

The First Five Year Plan set as a target for industry an increase in production of 98 per cent over 1953, involving a yearly growth rate of 14·7 per cent and the achievement of a gross industrial output of some 53,560 million yuan by 1957. This output level was, in fact, passed in 1956, the 1957 output reaching a level of 65,000 million yuan; by that date industrial production represented 43 per cent of the gross output value of industry and agriculture combined.

The growth of production in some of the major sectors of industry between 1952 and 1957 is summarised in Table 15 below; the statistics are based on Chinese official sources:

TABLE 15

PRODUCTION IN SELECTED INDUSTRIAL SECTORS, 1952–57

	Unit	1952	1953	1954	1955	1956	1957
Electricity	Bill. kWh.	7·3	9·2	11·0	12·3	16·6	19·3
Coal	Mill. Tons[a]	63·5	66·6	79·9	93·6	105·9	130·0
Pig Iron	Mill. Tons[a]	1·9	2·2	3·0	3·6	4·8	5·9
Steel	Mill. Tons[a]	1·3	1·8	2·2	2·8	4·5	5·4
Machine Tools	Thousands	13·7	20·5	15·9	13·7	26·0	28·0
Cotton Textiles	Bill. Metres	3·3	3·9	4·5	3·8	4·6	5·0

[a] Long tons.
Source: Grossman (1960), p. 137.

For this earlier period the discrepancies between the official Chinese statistics and the estimates of foreign 'China experts' are not great. The writer of the Foreword to *An Economic Profile of Communist China* observes, almost patronisingly,[1] 'the record of economic achievement during China's First Five Year Plan appeared to be quite good in the opinion of most outside economic observers'. Arthur G. Ashbrook, in his contribution to the same symposium, comments that during the First Five Year Plan, 'the Chinese Communist leadership should be graded high for its economic policy and its economic achievements at this stage of its development'.[2]   Robert M. Field estimates that between 1949 and 1952 industrial production doubled, growing at an annual rate of 27 per cent; during the period of the First Five Year Plan it doubled again, growing at an annual rate of 14 per cent (industry 16 per cent, handicrafts 7 per cent).[3]   For specific sectors the rate of growth was as follows:

TABLE 16

AVERAGE ANNUAL RATES OF GROWTH
BY INDUSTRIAL SECTOR, 1953–57

Electric Power	22
Coal	14
Petroleum	27
Ferrous Metals	31
Textiles	9

Source: Robert M. Field op. cit., p. 273.

Two features may be stressed in considering the First Five Year Plan. First, that the pattern of growth of the economy was the result of a carefully-planned investment policy on the part of the Chinese government; since at this stage the Chinese were following closely the Soviet model of industrialisation there was a strong emphasis on heavy industry and on capital goods and a much lower degree of emphasis on consumer goods such as textiles.   Secondly, the emphasis on large-scale modern industry tended to lead to a high degree of concentration in a relatively limited number of cities; 'virtually all the new construction projects . . . were distributed in some 120 cities, and a majority of the above-norm projects were clustered in 18 cities'.[4]   One of the distinctive features of

[1] *An Economic Profile of Communist China* (Washington 1967), Vol. 1, p. ix.   The obvious comparison is with India.   During the period of the Indian First Five Year Plan industrial production rose 38 per cent (cp. figures for China cited above) and at the end of the Plan the average Indian was, in the words of the *New York Times*, 'still just about the most miserably clothed, fed, and sheltered human being on earth, the most disease ridden, the least literate, the most ground down'.   For a comparison of Chinese and Indian economic performance see W. Malenbaum, 'India and China: Contrasts in Development Performance' in *American Economic Review*, Vol. XLIX (1957).
[2] *Ibid.*, p. 25.   [3] *Ibid.*, pp. 274–5.
[4] Kang Chao, 'Industrialization . . . in Communist China' in *Journal of Asian Studies*, May 1966, p. 383.

development after 1957 was the much wider dispersion of industry—bringing a much more effective diffusion of new technologies and new attitudes among the masses of interior China. This was an essential preliminary if the Chinese were to avoid the cleavage of the new society into, on one hand, a geographically highly localised industrial minority and, on the other, a peasant majority barely touched by new technologies or new attitudes.

'THE GREAT LEAP FORWARD'

The pace of development was greatly accelerated in 1958 and the economy was run flat out with objective (now admitted to have been unrealistic) of overtaking Britain in fifteen years. Mass mobilisation of the population to make good deficiencies in capital, absorption into the economy of those who had remained under-employed, a strong emphasis on ideological motivation as opposed to material inducements—all these were features of this phase. There was a huge increase in non-agricultural employment, which rose in one year from 40·9 million to 58·3 million persons (an increase of 43 per cent). Employment in the industrial sector alone rose from 7·9 million to 23·4 million persons; this, according to Emerson, reflects the policy of making 'very large investments of unskilled labour in lieu of scarce capital and skills in order to achieve the very large target increases in industrial output'.[1] Certainly, large increases in output were achieved; in agriculture, we have seen, there was a 35 per cent increase in food production and, in the industrial sector, Chinese data suggest that the output of coal and pig iron more than doubled, that of machine tools almost doubled, while electricity production increased by almost 50 per cent. Total industrial output, according to an American estimate, doubled during the First Five Year Plan and doubled again between 1958 and 1960.[2] This increase in output was accompanied by a change in the distribution pattern of industry; the processes of industrial dispersion, begun during the First Five Year Plan, were carried much further and 'in 1958 and 1959 the construction work was spread over about 2,100 cities and towns'.[3]

The advance of industry during this period was a many-fronted advance; existing plants were extended, new large- and medium-scale factories established, and the productive capacity of peasant or 'native style' industry was pushed to its limits. A new and specifically Chinese pattern of industrial development began to emerge, with as its essential feature the policy of 'walking on two legs', a policy which created a 'dualistic' industrial economy integrating the most modern and technically-sophisticated capital-intensive forms of industry with the small labour-intensive traditional units.

[1] J. P. Emerson, *op. sup. cit.*, p. 77.
[2] Edwin F. Jones in *An Economic Profile of Communist China*, p. 85.
[3] Kang Chao, *op. sup. cit.*, p. 383.

Thus, a distinctive feature of 1958 was the proliferation of small rural hydro-electric stations, which accounted for almost one-half of the two million kilowatts added to the country's installed capacity in that year. These complement the larger plants, they spread the centres of power supply more evenly, help to speed up the technological revolution in the countryside and help to ease the labour shortages created by the intensification of agriculture and the development of industry. They require only a small head of water, small investment and no very specialised skills for their construction. They could thus be built with local labour and with local raw materials and they could be built rapidly. It was realised that such plants did not in any way represent a final answer to the rural power problem; nevertheless, they supplied the power that was urgently needed and they supplied it cheaply. Even more important, in their construction and operation the peasant acquired experience which would be of major value when larger and more complex hydro plants were built. And, at the same time, work was pushed forward on a series of giant hydroelectric plants such as the Sanmen Gorge project on the Yellow River, the Liuchia Gorge on the upper reaches of the Yellow River above Lanchow, and the Tanchiangkou project on the Han River in Hupeh. These will rank among the world's major power centres.

A similar development could be seen in the iron and steel industry. Here advance was achieved by, on one hand, the creation of large-scale integrated iron and steel complexes of the most modern kind; on the other, the massive experimental development of medium-scale and small-scale 'native-style' blast furnaces, which could draw on seasonally available labour and utilise ore and fuel resources too small to justify the establishment of a major industry.

The existing iron and steel bases at Anshan and Wuhan were extended and modernised. The iron and steel output of the Northeast increased 3·7 times over the period of the First Five Year Plan; in Central China the Number 1 giant automatic blast furnace of the Wuhan steel works came into operation in the autumn of 1958. It was built with Soviet assistance and, with a capacity of 2,500 tons daily, was among the biggest in the world. The third major iron and steel base was created at Paotow, in Inner Mongolia, which will have a steel output of 3 million tons a year. Medium-sized integrated iron and steel works were constructed in many areas. By the end of 1958 plants with an annual capacity of over 600,000 tons had been constructed in Szechwan, Hopei, Shantung and Anwhei; smaller plants with a capacity of over 100,000 tons in Hunan, Hupeh and Chekiang. Perhaps the most distinctive and certainly the most publicised producing unit were, however, the small 'native-style' furnaces. The writer observed hundreds of these all over China—in a park in Canton, in the playground of a Peking school, rising in batches amid the fields of rice and vegetables on many of the communes visited.   They varied in size and design, were built by the local people—peasants or townsfolk—from local materials and used local fuel and ore resources.   By the end of 1958 it was claimed that 2 million of these had been built and that some 60 million people were participating in varying degrees in the mass campaign to produce iron and steel.   The experiment was of short duration; within the next year or so the majority of the peasant furnaces were abandoned and the scheme was dismissed by critics of the régime as a costly failure.

Certainly, the level of output achieved was low—4·2 million tons of pig iron and 3·1 million tons of steel—and the quality was poor.   The significance of the experiment can, however, be assessed only against the wider background of China's industrialisation as a whole.   The long-range objective of this massive campaign was, as Ronald Hsia has pointed out, to speed the pace of industrialisation and its adoption in 1958 represented a triumph for those who held the view that a broadening of the industrial base did not necessarily involve a lower rate of growth, that, indeed, an acceleration of growth was possible.   To quote Hsia:

> To achieve this, they discarded the concept of a balanced growth and envisaged development as a process from balance to unbalance and to a new balance on a higher level, emphasising the temporary, conditional and relative nature of any state of balance.   In this dialectic model, the steel industry was selected to play 'the leading link' to which all other industries became unequivocally subservient in the allocation of materials, labour and transport facilities, and was expected to pull and push forward first the related industries and subsequently all others.   The selection of steel was obviously based on its importance in a developing economy.[1]

Such a mass campaign made it possible to close the gap between steel production and the growing demand for steel in the rural areas much more rapidly and more cheaply than would have been possible by extending existing modern plants; moreover, because of the wide distribution of these small furnaces, the burden on the transport system was reduced to a minimum.   And, with rural needs being met by local production, the higher quality product from modern plants could be used for more important production purposes.

Meanwhile, this pioneer campaign provided conditions under which, in 1959, the transition could be made to larger, more modern furnaces and it left a legacy of real 'steel consciousness' among the people; this is an asset which, as Hsia remarks, 'can be invaluable to an under-developed economy on its path of industrialisation'.[2]   For the future,

[1] Ronald Hsia, 'The Development of Mainland China's Steel Industry Since 1958' in *China's Quarterly*, Number 7 (1961), p. 113.
[2] Ronald Hsia, *op. cit.*, p. 114.   Y. T. Li and W. D. Woo in S. H. Gould (Editor), *Sciences in Communist China*, p. 744, concur with this view.   For a Chinese view of the advantages of the steel campaign see Bernard Grossman, *op. sup. cit.*, p. 154.

the steel industry will 'walk on two legs', one leg being represented by the giant complex on the lines of Paotow, the other by small, widely dispersed, blast furnaces; these may develop in size and degree of mechanisation into medium-scale works of 200,000–800,000 tons capacity or, where conditions are favourable, into bigger integrated steel-works of 800,000–1 million tons capacity.   This policy of 'walking

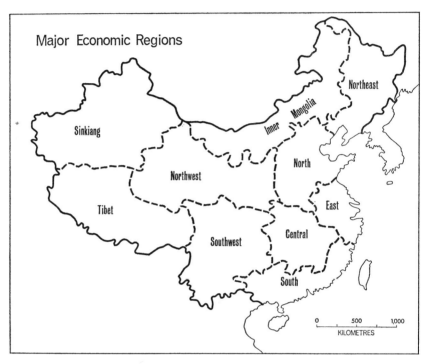

Figure 59.   Major Economic Regions.
These are the basic regions in the economic planning of the country.   The Chinese aim is to build up a diversified and balanced economy within each such region; this implies a balance of industry and agriculture, of light industry and heavy industry and the development within each region of the energy bases on which industry must rest.

on two legs' has enabled the State to concentrate its limited resources on capital and technical skills on the development of heavy industry and has thus contributed to the rapid pace of development in recent years; it is also of major social significance.   As Gatti has pointed out,[1] the creation of a series of giant industrial enterprises on the Anshan or Wuhan pattern would have only a limited impact on a country the size of China; its cultural impact would be small and the great mass of the population would remain cut off from the industrialisation and

[1] Armand Gatti, 'Notes de voyage dans communes chinoises' in *Cahiers Franco-Chinois* (Paris), Number 1, 1959, pp. 34–5.

mechanisation which are the basis of modern life. Decentralisation avoids the creation of a new 'technocracy' in the heart of the peasant masses and makes possible the maximum diffusion of the new techniques throughout the countryside. Under these conditions the Chinese countryside is developing a personality very different from that of the other emergent nations of Asia or Africa.

THE LESSONS OF THE 'LEAP'

By the beginning of the nineteen-sixties the economy, and especially the industrial sector, was running into major difficulties. Chinese statistics of industrial output become fragmentary but the observations of foreign economists who visited China at this period agree that there was stagnation in many sectors and that other sectors were working at only a fraction of their capacity. An American estimate suggests that industrial output declined by 40–45 per cent during the period 1961–63 subsequently recovering to a level 'perhaps 50 per cent over the 1957 level' by 1965.[1]

The crisis arose not only from what Gilbert Etienne has described as the unreasonable and excessive application of what were essentially reasonable and logical techniques of development,[2] but also from miscalculations in several important sectors of the economy. There was undoubtedly a temporary lack of coordination between the various sectors; in the words of Robert Guillain:

> The Leap broke the coordination between various sectors of the economy and overloaded the transport system; it overdeveloped certain sectors of industry such as the manufacture of machine-tools while related sectors tended to lag; it developed other activities, such as hydro-generation or the extractive industries insufficiently.[3]

The planners overestimated the extent to which labour could be siphoned off into urban industry or commune industry without disturbing the balance of the rural economy; they underestimated the extent to which the rapid growth of urban populations would disrupt the normal patterns of communication and trade. Transport seems to have been a bottle-neck in the developed areas of the east (see below pp. 256–7); local industrial development would certainly have reduced the burden on the long-distance transport system somewhat but between 1959 and 1960 freight movements increased 40 per cent and any further intensification of transport facilities came up against the fact that, in extending the road and rail network, there were limits to the extent to which human muscle could replace machinery. Above all, the planners tended to overlook a reality demonstrated by the earlier experience of

---

[1] Edwin F. Jones, op. sup. cit., p. 85.   [2] See above, p. 111.
[3] Robert Guillain, Dans trente ans la Chine (Paris 1965), p. 80.

Europe and evident in most Third World countries today—that successful consolidation of the agricultural base was an essential prerequisite
for successful industrialisation;[1] rather was there a tendency, as Guillain
has commented, to say 'We need such and such an industry; therefore,
we will order agriculture to produce so much'.[2]   The abandonment of
this unrealistic approach is the feature which most clearly distinguishes
contemporary Chinese development from development during the first
twelve years of the People's Government.   And among the human
failures which contributed to the difficulties which followed the 'Great
Leap' are to be listed the lack of 'scientific humility' and the generalised adoption of untried techniques castigated by René Dumont[3] and
the 'massive and enthusiastic hyper-obedience' commented on by Han
Suyin[4] and whose correction has been one of the aims of the Cultural
Revolution.

These errors were aggravated by factors over which the Chinese
planners had little control—the vagaries of climate and of Soviet policy.

The three years following the 'Great Leap Forward' were to prove
years of extreme climatic difficulty with severe drought conditions over
much of the subhumid North (and, in 1960, even the humid subtropical
South), heavy flooding, and typhoon damage in the South and plant
pests ravaging crops in the North.[5]   By December 1960 it was claimed
that three-fifths of the south had been affected by natural calamities of
varying types.   The impact of these conditions in the agricultural
sector had repercussions throughout the entire economy.   It was
precisely at this point that Soviet aid was suddenly withdrawn; as
René Dumont comments:

> The moment chosen for the break (July 1960) was not only that at
> which the pamphlet 'Long Live Leninism' appeared but also that
> when the Russians learned that the Chinese harvest was going to be
> disastrous.   Everything took place as if they hoped, by this stab in
> the back, to force the Chinese to accept their conditions.[6]

They left, taking with them in some cases the plans of the factories
on which they were working and leaving, it is estimated, one half of the
projected industrial enterprises uncompleted; at the same time, the
termination of the supply of heavy equipment and of petroleum by the
USSR inevitably slowed up the pace of Chinese industrial development.
The dislocation of the industrial programme was, however, reduced by

[1] Discussed by Paul Bairoch in *Révolution industrielle et sous-développement* (Paris 1963) and in
Diagnostic de l'évolution économique du Tiers-Monde 1900–1966 (Paris 1967), pp. 115 sqq.
[2] Robert Guillain, *op. sup. cit.*, p. 101.
[3] René Dumont, *La Chine surpeuplée* (Paris 1965), pp. 101–2.
[4] Han Suyin, *China in the Year 2001* (London 1967), p. 78.
[5] For a discussion and maps of the distribution of various types of calamity, see Michael
Freeberne 'Natural Calamities in China 1949–61' in *Pacific Viewpoint* (Wellington) Vol. III,
No. 2, September 1962, pp. 33–72.
[6] René Dumont, *op. sup. cit.*, p. 97.   Some 12,000 East bloc technicians worked in China
between 1949 and 1959; for comparison, in her early development, the USSR, starting from
a higher technological level employed some 20,000 foreign experts.

the swift and energetic Chinese reaction. The dangers of any sort of dependence, any acceptance of 'paternalism' were clearly underscored by the episode; the emphasis was henceforth to be on self-reliance, on the devising of specifically Chinese patterns of development which, even if they entailed delay, provided a sounder basis for the future. As early as 1957 it was recognised by some that 'There is ... too much emphasis on large, modern, mechanised, high-standard construction with no regard to conditions in China'.[1] A reorientation of industrial

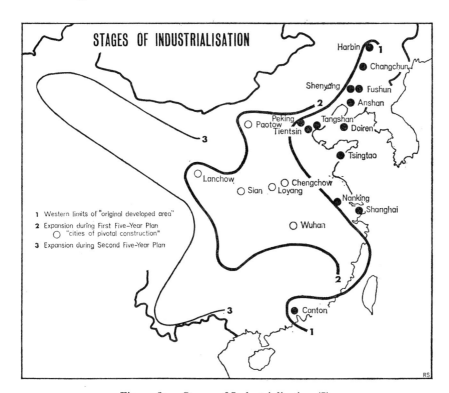

Figure 60. Stages of Industrialisation (I).

Showing the 'original developed area' of the coastal belt and the Northeast, with the major industrial centres; the expansion towards the interior districts of central and north-central China during the First Five Year Plan and the cities of 'pivotal construction' which developed as major industrial bases during this period; and the expansion towards Sinkiang and the Southwest during the Second Five Year Plan.

policies—or a 'readjustment' as the Chinese termed it—was essential; it began in 1961 and continued into 1962 and 1963. The new orientation was indicated by the slogan: 'Agriculture as the base of the national economy with industry as the leading factor.' For a policy of pushing industry, and especially heavy industry, at the cost of agriculture, was

[1] Han Suyin, op. sup. cit., p. 71, quoting Jen Min Jih Pao, 11 April 1957.

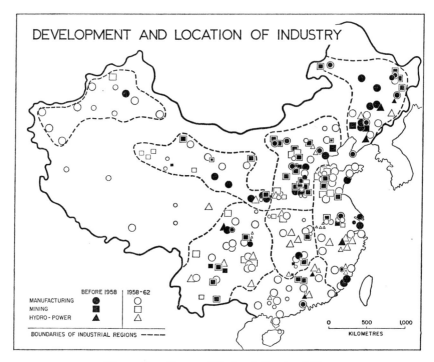

Figure 61.   Stages of Industrialisation (II).

Showing the major industrial enterprises developed before 1958 and the subsequent expansion of industry within the developed area of the East and in the peripheral areas of the West, South and Southwest.

substituted a policy of emphasis on agriculture with the simultaneous development of those industrial sectors most closely related to agriculture, e.g. the fertiliser industry and the production of tractors, irrigation pumps and other types of agricultural machinery. From 1962 the State allocated increasing supplies of raw materials to factories working to supply the needs of agriculture and at the same time began to increase its investments in the rural sector (between 1962 and 1963 these were increased by 26 per cent). It was this process of strengthening the agricultural base of the economy (a process in which the communes played an important part) that made possible the real 'economic take-off' of China; to quote Paul Bairoch:

> This rising productivity has permitted China to pass the threshold at which she faced the danger of being involved in nation-wide famine and has enabled her to embark on a process of industrialisation which, in consequence, has been able to be more rapid than that of the rest of Asia.[1]

[1] Paul Bairoch, *Diagnostic de l'évolution économique du Tiers-Monde*, p. 213.   For a brief account in English of Bairoch's concept of 'thresholds' see Keith Buchanan 'Beneath the Banyan' in *Outlook* (Sydney) August 1968, p. 17.   American analysts seem to be some 2–3 years behind

And, commenting on the wider significance of the Chinese experiment, René Dumont observes:

> China demonstrates to us that *internal efforts alone are necessary for development*; that *one must count first on oneself* and not on foreign aid. The latter brings in its train dependence and can always prove lacking at the moment it is most needed. It makes possible permanent blackmail: that of the USSR on China, that of Europe on Africa or that of the USA on 'their' western hemisphere.[1]

The awareness of these realities—without which an independent economy and a firmly-based industrialisation are impossible—came to the Chinese the hard way; the process of learning may, as American analysts claim, have cost China several years of development—but most under-developed countries have not yet even begun to confront the critical development problems the Chinese have confronted and overcome since the People's Government came to power two decades ago.

THE CHINESE INDUSTRIAL ECONOMY: Its Spatial Patterns

One of the distinctive features of the First Five Year Plan was, we have noted, the *initiation of a policy of dispersal of industry* towards the interior of the country (including the minority regions). The question which confronts us is how far was this policy, with all its implications for the transformation of the Chinese land, modified by the feverish developments of 1958 and by the 'readjustments' of the early nineteen-sixties? The extremely fragmentary character of the official statistical material available since 1960 makes any answer difficult and essentially tentative; the detailed and painstaking work[2] of Professor Yuan-li Wu in combing through a great mass of Chinese newspapers and periodicals, news broadcasts and books has recently provided us with at least a partial answer to this question.

Two general points must be born in mind as background to the question. First, the 'Eurasian perspective' in early Chinese planning; Soviet industry had been expanding from the west eastwards, and the idea of socialist-bloc planning (in the days before the Sino-Soviet split)

in their assessment of recent Chinese development. Thus Alexander Eckstein, after commenting on the return of an atmosphere of quiet self-confidence from 1963 onwards, expresses the view that, given certain preconditions, 'The damage to the economy may gradually be repaired to the point where rapid industrialisation would once more become feasible' *Communist China's Economic Growth and Foreign Trade* (New York and London 1966), p. 84. Paul Bairoch, by contrast, speaks of 'the Chinese success' and points out that, *even on the basis of Western estimates, per capita* income, which was about the Asian average in 1950, was by 1967 40 per cent above this average. Paul Bairoch, *op. cit.*, p. 214. Industrialisation, both small scale and large scale, has obviously played an important role in this increase in income.

[1] René Dumont, *La Chine surpeuplée*, p. 254 (emphasis in original).

[2] Yuan-li Wu , *The Spatial Economy of Communist China* (New York, Washington and London 1967). The great gaps in Western knowledge of China is indicated by the fact that of the industrial cities he lists almost 7 per cent 'cannot be located on the map', *op. cit.*, pp. 292–305.

was for Chinese industry to expand from the eastern, developed regions, westwards, to form a linked Sino-Soviet industrial bloc.[1]   Secondly, as early as 1956, Chou En-lai had emphasised that the 'filling-in' of China's economic living-space must of necessity be spread over a long period of time:

> During the First Five Year Plan, our aim is to utilise the original industrial bases in the east in order to build new industrial centres in the middle.   The cities of pivotal construction are Wuhan, Paotow, Chengchow, Loyang, Sian, and Lanchow, all of which are situated in the central part of China.   Further advance westward must be preceded by the establishment of industrial bases in the centre and the completion of necessary preparations in the western regions. . . . The Second Five Year Plan will have as its goal the construction of industrial bases in the centre and the beginning of construction of industrial bases and some industrial enterprises in the southwest, the northwest, and Sinkiang.   As for the general development of industry in western China, this will have to wait the completion of future Five Year Plans.   *Those who expect the rapid and general establishment of many industrial bases in the far reaches of western China are unrealistic in their outlook.*[2]

A third point arose from the growing Chinese awareness that simply to move industry from coast to interior did not reduce its vulnerability to nuclear attack; only a wide decentralisation, in both coastal and inland sites would achieve this.

Wu's analysis of the urbanisation pattern suggests that 'the locational design of the First Five Year Plan was only partially realised',[3] that while there was a tendency to push ahead with the development of cities (and industry) away from the coast there was also a tendency to concentrate much of the development in the already more-developed areas rather than the less-developed areas.   His detailed analysis of the growth of new industries similarly demonstrated a tendency towards 'a greater emphasis on the establishment of industrial centres in the developed regions *vis-à-vis* the less-developed ones than in the coastal provinces *vis-à-vis* the inland provinces'.[4]   Sixty per cent of the new industrial capacity was located in the large centres, 31 per cent in medium centres and 9 per cent in small centres.   The distribution pattern of Chinese industrialisation is shown in Figures 62 and 63; these maps are based on Wu's data for which the cutting-off point is 1961; so they give no indication of the continuing industrial decentralisation of the last eight years.   The largest number of new major industrial centres is in Central China, followed by Northwest China; this, Wu observes, 'is by far the clearest indication to date of the locational

---

[1] Yuan-li Wu, *The Spatial Economy of Communist China*, p. 23.
[2] *Ibid.*, pp. 18–19 (emphasis added).   [3] *Ibid.*, p. 45.
[4] *Ibid.*, pp. 60–2.   Wu notes that Soviet aid tended to reinforce this general pattern of concentration in the more developed regions.

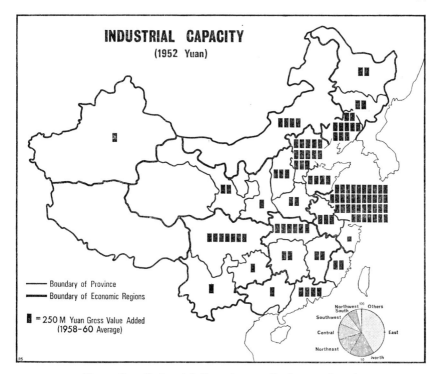

Figure 62. Industrial Capacity *c.* 1960 (by provinces)

Capacity is here expressed in terms of Gross Value Added; the statistical unit is the province. Note the continuing concentration of industrial capacity in the East, North and Northeastern regions; these together contain some seven-tenths of China's industrial capacity. Note, however, the beginning of modern industry in the Inner Mongolian A.R., the Northwestern Region and the Sinkiang A.R. (Data from Yuan-li Wu (1967); for an evaluation of the data see p. 239.)

emphasis in the Communist régime's developmental plans'.[1] If the changes are evaluated on a provincal basis, it appears that, by the beginning of the Third Five Year Plan, Honan, Hunan, and Anhwei had moved from the rank of 'agriculturally developed but industrially under-developed' provinces into the rank of 'agriculturally and industrially developed provinces'; Shansi and Inner Mongolia had moved into the rank of 'industrially developed provinces'; Kansu, Ninghsia, Chinghai, and Sinkiang were in the initial stages of developing a modern industrial economy.[2]

One of the major findings to emerge from Wu's analysis is 'an apparent shift in locational planning' in 1956 from a policy of all-out development of the interior to a policy of developing existing centres and existing economically-advanced regions; this did not, as we have seen, preclude *decentralisation* within such regions. This shift had

[1] *Ibid.*, p. 85.   [2] *Ibid.*, p. 90.

repercussions on the transport situation, for considerable sums (2·37 billion yuan) had been set aside for the construction of new railways in the interior. His data for industrial capacity[1] suggest that, in spite of Communist policy, a high degree of geographic concentration continued to characterise Chinese industry; two-thirds of the total capacity, according to his data, was in Kiangsu, Hopeh, Liaoning, Hupeh, and Szechwan; and nine large industrial centres accounted for about three-fifths of China's total industrial capacity.

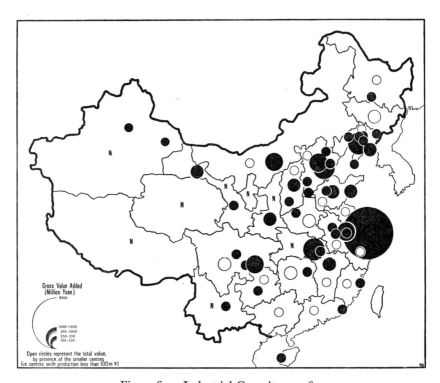

Figure 63. Industrial Capacity c. 1960.

Industrial capacity is expressed in terms of Gross Value Added. Each industrial centre where industrial capacity is over 100 M. yuan in terms of added value is shown; the aggregate capacity of smaller centres, and of centres which cannot be located, in each province is shown by a hollow circle. N = capacity negligible (i.e. under 50 M. yuan). (Data from Yuan-li Wu (1967); for an evaluation of the data see p. 239.)

That there was a shift in locational planning policy away from the early preoccupation with the development of the interior is clear. What is less certain is whether the degree of industrial concentration is in fact as great as Professor Wu claims. And while, in the absence of precise statistics, no final answer to the problem can be given,

[1] Based on plant data weighted by the gross value added.

the following points are worth stressing.   Firstly, his statistical data
terminate around 1961 which means that the industrial capacity (much
of it in small, dispersed, units) added during the last five years of
recovery is ignored; the present writer's observations in China lead him
to believe the aggregate capacity added in some of the formerly
undeveloped regions may be considerable.   Secondly, Wu's preoccupation with urban industry and his neglect of the commune-run
industry in rural areas may result in a considerable underestimate of
the penetration of industrial technology into the rural sector of his co-
called 'undeveloped' regions; these widely dispersed rural industries
may be individually small but their aggregate capacity is far from
negligible (indeed, in 1958, it was claimed that this commune industry
accounted for one-tenth of China's industrial output).   Given the
present Chinese emphasis on narrowing the gap between city-dweller
and countryman, on the social no less than the purely economic
desirability of rural industralisation, commune industry has remained a
critically important sector of the nation's economy (see details for
individual communes given on pp. 143–68).   Bearing in mind these
considerations, it may be hazarded that the degree of industrial
concentration today is less than that claimed by Wu and that the
processes of dispersal and decentralisation may have gone a good deal
further than his analysis suggests.   And, what is more important,
Chinese planning seems to have arrested that widening gap between
city and country, between industrial worker and peasant, which was
typical of pre-Revolution China and which is today the major problem facing most countries of the Third World.

THE CHINESE INDUSTRIAL ECONOMY: *Output and Outlook*

The Chinese planners in 1949 inherited a chaotic and disarticulated
economy; the *per capita* GNP of this Chinese quarter of mankind was
about the average for Asia—and this average was the lowest of any
major sector of the Third World.   Within a decade they rehabilitated
the economy, began the process of creating an integrated economy for
the whole of China and made impressive gains on a broad industrial
front.   Excessive zeal and impatience, manifesting themselves in
miscalculations and errors in plan design, set them back in the early
'sixties; they subsequently recovered to become, in the words of René
Dumont, 'the only large Afro-Asian country emerging so clearly from
under-development without the least external aid'.[1]

Chinese industrial development has been set concisely into its global
context by Alexander Eckstein; says Eckstein:

In spite of the recent setbacks and just by virtue of its sheer size,
China must be ranked among the 10 leading industrial powers in the

[1] René Dumont, *Nous allons à la famine* (Paris 1966), p. 139.

R

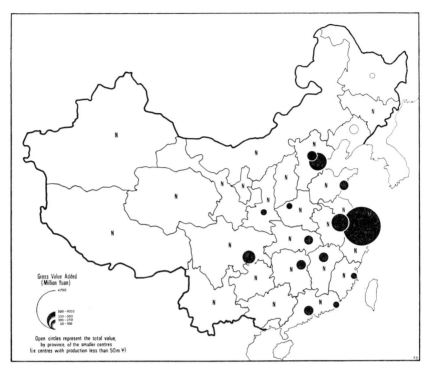

Figure 64.   Light Industry: Capacity *c.* 1960.

Comparison with Figure 63 illustrates the emphasis on heavy industry during the first decade of the People's Republic.   Centres with an industrial capacity, in terms of Gross Value Added, of over 50 m. yuan are shown.   Note the concentration in the Shanghai-Nanking and Peking-Tientsin regions.

Because of the concentration of labour-intensive commune industry in this light industry sector and because the data shown is for large relatively capital-intensive modern units the map gives only a very incomplete picture of the distribution or significance of light industry in China.   (Data from Yuan-li Wu, 1967.)

world.   There is an enormous gap between the size of her industrial establishment and that of the Soviet Union or the United States. On the other hand, the distance between her and Japan, Germany, France, Italy, or even the United Kingdom is much narrower in terms of total industrial capacity, although not in terms of *per capita* product.[1]

Eckstein is concerned with the relevance of this industrial emergence to China's military capacity and her influence in Asia and beyond Asia.   The West is preoccupied with this aspect; that Chinese industry in recent years has been equally concerned to increase the variety and quality of consumer goods is apparent from Barry Richman's comments; says Richman:

[1] Alexander Eckstein, *op. sup. cit.*, p. 85.

There is a surprisingly wide variety of consumer goods of relatively good quality in the stores, even in areas which are seldom frequented by foreigners, such as Wushih and Loyang. The largest Soviet department store—GUM in Moscow—does not come close to the large department stores in Peking, Shanghai, or Tientsin in terms of variety or quality of consumer goods available.[1]

He concludes:

In spite of numerous managerial and technical problems at many of the Chinese enterprises, I am impressed by the wide range of goods that Chinese industry is capable of producing. China seems to be able to produce nearly anything it wants, but often it must produce very inefficiently, and at tremendous cost.[2]

But, as we have stressed earlier (p. 110), the Chinese factory, like the Chinese commune, is not simply an economic unit or even a unit 'where economic performance clearly takes priority'. It is a social, political and educational unit also, a basic 'cell' in the new society the Chinese are striving to create. To quote Richman again:

[the Chinese factory] is a place where illiterate workers learn how to read and write, and where employees can and do improve their work skills and develop new ones through education and training. It is a place where housing, schools, recreational facilities, roads, shops, and offices are often constructed or remodelled by factory employees. It is also a place from which employees go out into the fields and help the peasants with their harvesting.[3]

Leo Huberman and Paul Sweezy see in it 'a socialist rationality' which alone will overcome the social evils which have resulted from the unfettered operation of the free enterprise system. They add—and this observation is of critical importance when we confront the problem of measuring Chinese achievements in the industrial field:

it should be noted that the farther the Chinese depart from bourgeois conceptions of rationality [they are referring to the Western concept of the factory as a highly rationalised production unit. K.B.], the more impossible and meaningless will become quantitative comparisons between their and other countries' levels of income, productivity, etc. . . .[4]

This observation must be borne in mind in any evaluation of the quantitative data presented in this volume; it provides the fundamental background against which the figures of industrial output presented below must be seen.

[1] Barry Richman, 'Capitalists and Managers in Communist China', in *Harvard Business Review*, January–February 1967, p. 72.
[2] Richman, *op. cit.*, pp. 77–78. [3] *Ibid.*, p. 61.
[4] Leo Huberman and Paul Sweezy, 'Understanding the Cultural Revolution', in *Monthly Review* (New York), May 1967. p. 10.

SOME GROPINGS IN A STATISTICAL BLACKOUT...

Since 1960 the Chinese have released few 'hard' statistics on any branch of economic production. The data available—sufficient only for the sketchiest of outlines of industrial progress—consist of figures of percentage change in output (over an often uncertain base) together with percentage figures indicating the degree to which the targets of the economic plan were reached or exceeded; the data is, moreover, extremely fragmentary: in some cases it may refer to a provincial unit, in others to a particular sector of industry, in yet other cases to an individual town or factory. We are driven to groping uncertainly in a statistical blackout; sources hostile to China prefer, in the meantime, to see in this (partly security-motivated) blackout evidence of the stagnation or collapse of the Chinese economy.[1] The Cultural Revolution has made the plight of the Western China expert even more difficult in the last two years, reducing the judgements of 'informed commentators' to straight-out guesswork. The following comments are taken from the *Far Eastern Economic Review 1968 Yearbook*; italicisation is by the present writer:

> 'it *seems very likely* that ... some plants were unable to get their raw materials'
> At Anshan, steel production '*would surely be* much lower in 1967'
> At Wuhan 'it *seems unlikely* that the steel plant was unaffected'
> At Shanghai 'the steel plant *must have been* as much disturbed as the rest of the city'
> 'By mid-1967 *hardly* any plant in China *could be* functioning normally'

The general picture which emerges from this and other Western sources is of confusion, chaos or a collapsing economy. By contrast, on 1 October 1967 Lin Piao was announcing:

> Glad tidings about the successes in our industrial production keep on coming in. In agriculture we are reaping a good harvest for the sixth consecutive year. Our markets are thriving and the prices are stable.[2]

We are confronted with what is nowadays a common enough feature of the political scene—a credibility gap, a continually widening discrepancy between the analyses of the 'China-watchers' and the picture which emerges from Chinese press releases and from the observations

---

[1] The extreme example of this is Joseph Alsop's analysis 'On China's Descending Spiral' in *China Quarterly* (London), July-September 1962 which suggests 'the breakdown of the entire Chinese Communist system' as a 'clear possibility'. More recently, *The Financial Times* (4 July 1967) declared 'the Maoist régime totters inexorably towards final collapse', adding, bewildered, 'the most puzzling aspect ... is the impression that up to now the economy has been functioning fairly smoothly'. This prediction of collapse was made, it is to be noted, two long years ago. . . .

[2] Quoted in *China Trade and Economic Newsletter* (hereafter referred to as *C.T.E.N.*) (London), February 1968, p. 8.

and judgements of those who have recently visited the country. The situation has been summed up in the *China Trade and Economic News-letter*:

> there remains a straightforward conflict of evidence. The Chinese version—which communicates itself to most visiting economists and businessmen—claims that agriculture is booming and that while there have been many weaknesses in industry in the past these are gradually being put right in preparation for a new leap forward. The Hong Kong version is that the situation in agriculture is nothing like so good as the Chinese say it is, while industry in the main is descending into chaos.[1]

On the basis of his limited field work in China and of his analysis of the relevant literature over the last decade, the present writer is inclined to accept the Chinese assessments of their situation. The period of statistical abandon in China ended in the early 'sixties; recent claims of progress have been realistic, measured in their language and increasingly concrete, and these claims add up to a new surge forward in industry. In part, it may be observed, this surge forward is due to

> a new and greater upsurge of invention and determination to master technical problems (which) has followed in the wake of the cultural revolution.[2]

In other words, the very phenomenon which Western observers had described as crippling the economy is proving, according to this source, an important factor in China's industrial progress. . . .

A general impression of the contours of China's industrial economy may be put together from scattered sources; the picture is of necessity incomplete but it indicates the progress achieved in some sectors. With regard to the basic energy sources, coal production is given by *C.T.E.N.* as 250 million tons[3] and may indeed be as high as 300 million tons. Crude oil output reached 7 million tons in 1963[4] and a Western estimate put the 1966 production at 9–10 million tons;[5] this is certainly an underestimate since the Taching field has been developed on a considerable scale since 1963 and production might be expected to have increased by more than 2–3 million tons. In the words of *C.T.E.N.*, in the first eight months of 1968:

> the output of crude oil exceeded the State target by 34 per cent and that of refined oil by 43 per cent . . . Lanchow refinery is said to have doubled its original target for one high-grade oil after having over-fulfilled an earlier quota, apparently for Vietnam.[6]

---

[1] *C.T.E.N.*, February 1968, pp. 8–9.   [2] *C.T.E.N.*, August 1968, p. 2.
[3] *C.T.E.N.*, December 1967, p. 4.   [4] *C.T.E.N.*, October 1968, p. 8.
[5] *Far Eastern Economic Review Yearbook 1967*. The U.S. *Bureau of Mines Minerals Yearbook 1967* quotes the 1966 output of crude petroleum at 13 million tons.
[6] *C.T.E.N.*, October 1968, p. 8.

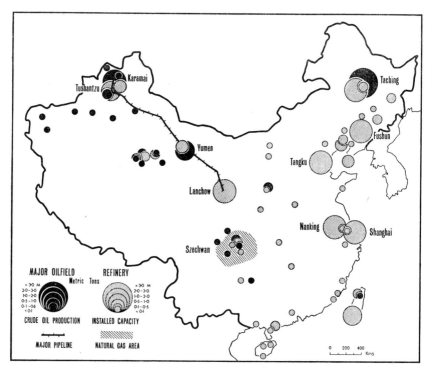

Figure 65.   The Petroleum Industry.

Main producing centres are Karamai (Sinkiang), Yumen (northwest Kansu) and Taching (Heilungkiang); clusters of smaller fields in Szechwan, Chinghai and Sinkiang.   Refining widely dispersed with seven major refineries and some three dozen medium-sized or small-scale refineries to serve local needs.   (Map based on Cheng-siang Chen, 1968.)

For steel, another critical item in the development programme of an industralising country, the *Far Eastern Economic Review* quotes a production of 10–12 million tons,[1] one-half of which came from Anshan; 'the industry seemed in quite good shape' and the variety and quality of production higher than in earlier years.   On this production estimate *C.E.T.N.* (which puts production higher, at probably 20 million tons)[2] comments:

> This conclusion leaves unexplained why, if Anshan is turning out 6,000,000 tons, the three or four other major steelworks which are known to be at any rate half as big as Anshan are not between them producing another 10,000,000–12,000,000 tons.   At least one or two of them were producing around 3 million tons three years ago and were preparing to bring new and more modern plant into use.[3]

[1] *Far Eastern Economic Review Yearbook 1967*, p. 163.   [2] *C.T.E.N.*, May 1968, p. 8.
[3] *C.T.E.N.*, September 1967, p. 4.   U.S. *Bureau of Mines Minerals Yearbook 1967* quotes the Chinese production of steel ingots as 16 million tons in 1966.

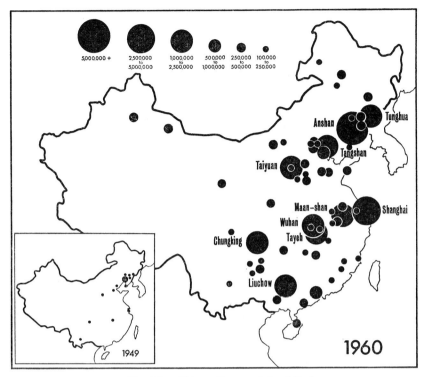

Figure 66. The Chinese Iron and Steel Industry.
Showing capacity of major centres for ingot steel production *c.* 1960. Note the wide dispersion of the major plants (which has been made possible by new ore discoveries) and the multiplicity of small and medium-scale plants which provides one basis for regional economic self-sufficiency.

Changes since 1949 can be judged by comparison with the inset map; on this, the Anshan symbol is on the same scale as the main map but the dots illustrating other centres are for locational purposes only since the aggregate output of these centres was insignificant. (Data from Yuan-li Wu, *The Steel Industry in Communist China.*)

In a field more directly relevant to agriculture eight large modern plants and over one hundred smaller plants were producing at least 9 million tons of (largely nitrogenous) fertiliser in 1966. The smaller and medium plants are widely dispersed; for example, seven were constructed in Shantung and thirteen in Szechwan in 1966; together these hundred smaller units account for 18 per cent of China's output of nitrogenous fertilisers. Another industry catering in part for the needs of agriculture is the plastics industry; factories in fifteen provinces are turning out plastic film (including a new vinyl film made in Wuhan) for the protection of seedlings.[1]

Progress in the field of light industry is indicated by the fact that by 1967 China had emerged as the world's largest exporter of cotton

[1] *C.T.E.N.*, August 1968, p. 6.

fabrics; her total export of these fabrics was close on 1,000 million sq. yards, representing 15 per cent of the world trade in cotton textiles.[1] And the range of products—and the progress—is suggested by the following quotation referring to light industry:

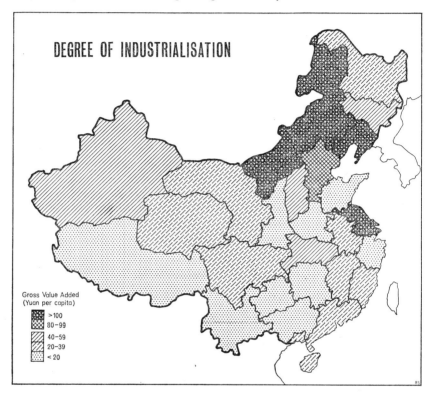

DEGREE OF INDUSTRIALISATION

Gross Value Added
(Yuan per capita)

>100
80–99
40–59
20–39
< 20

Figure 67.   Degree of Industrialisation.

Because of the extremely uneven distribution of population in China (see Figure 7) maps showing industrial output by province may give a misleading picture of the stage (or degree) of industrialisation over the country.   In this map industrial capacity (measured as in Figures 62 and 63) is related to population.

Kiangsu (with Shanghai) is still outstanding (gross value added *per capita* 234 yuan) but the progress in some of the peripheral regions is emphasised.   Gross value added *per capita* for Inner Mongolia is thus 144, for Sinkiang 58; for the older developed provinces of Hopei and Liaoning the figures are respectively 83 yuan and 124 yuan.

Population figures used are those of the 1953 Census; industrial data is from Yuan-li Wu (1967) and subject to the qualifications on p. 239.

The output of all its 'major products' surpassed the State plan for the first half of 1968.   These products include farm implements (except the larger and fully-mechanised types), clothing, metalware and enamel ware, sewing machines, wrist-watches and vacuum flasks, cigarettes and matches, paper, leather, soap, detergents and canned foods. . . .[2]

[1] *C.T.E.N.*, September 1968, p. 3.   [2] *C.T.E.N.*, August 1968, p. 6.

The above statistics are, at the best, merely isolated points of light in the midst of the statistical darkness but they do enable us to establish the general contours of the industrial situation. And the major feature which emerges is the cumulative and many-fronted progress of China to the rank of a major industrial power. There is little evidence that the upheaval of the Cultural Revolution has seriously held back economic development; rather have the new attitudes and new motivations which are being shaped by the Revolution proved a major factor of progress. As E. L. Wheelwright points out, when discussing political education and the study of Mao Tse-tung's works:

> it is easy for westerners to sneer at this kind of political education, and the ritualistic ideology it entails, but a substantial part of it consists of developing the necessary psychological attitudes and approaches to work in a socialist society, for a people which has only just begun to enjoy the benefits of widespread education and which less than a generation ago was mostly illiterate.[1]

And the Chinese emphasis on moral rather than material incentives, on *the kind of life* they are striving to create, introduces a completely new element into industrial society. Seen in its global context, this development in Chinese thinking is politically even more far-reaching in its implications than the nuclear weapons which attest to the growing technological sophistication of the new China. . . .

'WALKING ON TWO LEGS . . .'

The economic dualism expressed in the Chinese development technique of 'walking on two legs' expresses itself in the parallel development of rural-based commune industry and urban-based modern industry and, within the urban centres, in the parallel development of small labour-intensive industry and large scale capital-intensive industry. Examples of commune industry have been given earlier (pp. 143–68); here contrasts within the urban industrial sector are illustrated by four case-studies. These sketches help to emphasise the extra-economic functions of industry referred to above.

(a) MODERN CAPITAL-INTENSIVE INDUSTRY: No. 2 COTTON MILL, PEKING

This complex of three cotton mills was built in 1954 on vacant land. It has a total of 100,000 spindles and 2,400 automatic looms. All the equipment, it is claimed, is Chinese-made. The unit produces on a

---

[1] E. L. Wheelwright, 'Impressions of the Chinese Economy (II)' in *Outlook* (Sydney), August 1967, p. 8. See also C. H. G. Oldham 'Science and Education in China' reprinted from *Bulletin of the Atomic Scientists*, June 1966, in Franz Schurmann and Orville Schell, *Communist China* (Harmondsworth 1968), esp. pp. 478–9.

three-shift basis, with a daily output of 170,000 metres of cloth (serge, taffeta, drill). It employs 5,300 workers; 70 per cent are women and 60 per cent are married; average age is 28 years.

The average wage is quoted as 60 yuan monthly; the wage of the director, a woman, is 150 yuan. Accommodation for a single person costs 40 cents a month; two-roomed accommodation (for a couple with two children) costs 4–5 yuan.

The factory has clinics and four health centres. A thousand children are in nursery schools or kindergartens run by the factory, and 1,400 students are in the elementary school. For older workers there are night schools which take them up to college level; workers studying at an advanced level are entitled to three free periods weekly while teachers will do 2–3 days' physical work each week. The State contribution to the factory's welfare services is about 360,000 yuan monthly; this is expended on such items as schools, nurseries, canteen, and recreational facilities.

A 7½-hour day and a six-day week is worked. Retirement pensions are 60–70 per cent of the worker's wage; in the case of sickness, the full wage is paid for the first six months, after which 60 per cent of the wage is paid.

In 1966 decision-making was a four-stage process:

(1) Production targets, including quality and types of product, were allocated by the State.
(2) These were then evaluated by the factory's Party committee.
(3) They were then discussed by the workers congress of the factory; it was at this stage that any important problems or difficulties were hammered out.
(4) They were finally discussed by the production teams in the factory.

The basic production programme proceeds by these stages to the 'grassroots' level—that of the production team; the modified programme is then transmitted back to the State planning authorities, passing step by step from the production team to the congress and Party committee.

(b) RATIONALISATIONS OF THE TRADITIONAL HANDICRAFT SECTOR: PEKING ARTS & HANDICRAFT FACTORY

This was organised in 1960 from co-operative-groupings of craft-workers which had come into existence after the Liberation. Today it consists of eight departments—jade-working, ivory-carving, lacquer-work, gilt-work, jewellery, cloisonné enamel work, wood-carving, and the making of scenic boxes. It employs 710 workers; of these, one-third are women. The average wage is 60 yuan a month for an 8-hour day, with a range of from 33 yuan to 90 yuan; one or two exceptionally-skilled workers may receive as much as 200 yuan monthly. Medical care for the workers is free and the factory meets one-half of the medical expenses incurred by workers' families. The factory provides canteen facilities, a crèche, a TV room, a reading room and facilities for sports groups. Night schools provide a general education as well as serving as a means of passing on traditional skills.

Dormitory accommodation (each room being shared between three workers) is provided at a cost of 43 cents a month; State-provided accommodation for married couples costs 2–3 yuan a month (these charges and wages can be set into context by comparing with prices of basic foodstuffs; one catty (1·1 lb.) rice was costing 13 cents, one catty of flour, 18·4 cents).

(c) SMALL-SCALE ENTERPRISES DEVELOPED BY LOCAL INITIATIVE

(1) 'BUTTERFLY' SHOE-POLISH FACTORY, TAIYUAN

This small co-operative enterprise employs thirty-four workers; it was originally initiated by eleven women of the area, assisted by four elderly men.

The building housing the enterprise was built by the original core of workers from timber 'borrowed' from nearby factories and bricks from the old walls of the city. Using local techniques of building and the skills of helpers (e.g. the students who put in the electrical wiring) the 'factory' cost a fraction of what a more modern factory would have cost. Today (1966) it has an annual production of 60,000 dozen tins of boot polish with candles and mothballs as a sideline. The products are exported to *inter alia*, Syria, the Republic of the Sudan, Rumania, and Ghana. The value of the daily output of a worker can be estimated at approximately 21s.; wages at an average of 2s. 10d. a head daily.

Wages are, in fact, based largely on needs. The manager, a young woman, receives 45 yuan per month, an older worker with four children, 60 yuan; the average is 28 yuan. The State receives from the factory some 120,000 yuan; the funds accumulated by the factory over seven years amount to 90,000 yuan which is being used to provide housing for the workers and to purchase equipment. Today's wages it might be noted, are four times as high as during the early years of development.

(2) NANKING 'FIRE-FLOWER' GLASS & INSTRUMENT PLANT

This factory was created in 1958 and was originally organised by a production team working under the aegis of the street committee. The capital was only 100 yuan and seven youths were employed, manufacturing test-tubes and pipettes from purchased glass tube. Today a total of eighty workers are employed (75 per cent of the labour force consists of women and 80 per cent is under 25 years of age); the factory now produces, in addition to glassware, a range of electrical control gear, including mercury switches.

Much of the equipment (80 per cent it is claimed) has been built by the workers themselves, and at a fraction of the cost which its purchase would have entailed; the cost of building and equipping the factory is estimated at 17,000 yuan, as against the 100,000 yuan which a modern and complete factory would have cost. Raw materials account for four-fifths of the factory's expenditure, wages and welfare services for one-fifth; of the factory's income, 60 per cent is 'delivered' to the State (which provided funds during the early stages of development), much of this being returned to expand production. Production targets are allocated by the State Precision Instruments Bureau; they are discussed and if necessary modified by the workers and the modified plan is then submitted to the State planning body.

Wages, including those of apprentices, average 28–30 yuan per month, with a range between highest and lowest-paid workers of 54 yuan and 27 yuan; apprentices receive 16 yuan monthly. The factory shares a canteen with another small factory, provides free medical treatment for its workers and, for women with children, a crèche is provided by the street committee. The working day is 8 hours for men, 7 hours for women; this includes study periods which cover both political and technical training.

It will be evident from these sketches that the Chinese factory is much more than a purely economic unit; it is a unit organising welfare and education (including often the training of cadres for other areas), providing housing and political training and, above all, striving to associate the worker with the process of the decision-making in both technical and social matters. Our arbitrary sample confirms Richman's view that the Chinese factory 'is not viewed as a purely economic unit where economic performance clearly takes priority'; the 'emphasis on education, organisation, and ideology' which Bettelheim sees as one of the characteristics of Chinese socialist construction[1] is equally strikingly evident. . . .

[1] Charles Bettelheim, Jacques Charrière, and Hélène Marchisio, *La construction du socialisme en Chine* (Paris 1965), p. 157.

CHAPTER 11

Transport and the Integration of the Chinese Living Space

1. *PERSPECTIVE*

ONE OF the major features of an under-developed economy is, we have seen (p. 103), its disarticulation. This expresses itself in lack of economic integration between the various sectors of the economy; it also manifests itself in the incomplete spatial integration of the nation. A typical under-developed country consists of isolated 'islands' of economic development, often oriented towards an overseas market, separated by a 'sea' of stagnating and self-sufficient peasant agriculture; between these two elements the degree of contact is limited. It is true that many under-developed countries may have a significant rail network (India and Brazil provide examples of this) but, since this rail network was frequently constructed during the colonial or semi-colonial period when the emphasis was on the export of raw materials and the import of manufactures from the factories of the metropolitan country, it was of only very limited use as far as the country's internal economy was concerned; little real attention was given during its construction to the need for those internal lines which would link together the developed areas and open up fully the potential of the 'back country'. These general remarks apply also to the modern road system which was often planned less to facilitate internal circulation of goods and people than to act as a feeder to the railway or as an alternative outlet to the coast cities.

This general picture was certainly valid for pre-Revolutionary China, where the lack of an adequate transport system was a major obstacle to economic development and to the creation of any effective national unity. The country's transport system, if such it may be called, consisted of a series of unconnected links by road, rail or water. The greater part of the mileage was concentrated in eastern China and great sections of the interior were without modern transport of any kind; the northwest and the southwest together had less than 800 kilometres of railroads.   The creation of a national economy was, under such conditions, impossible; the resources of the interior inaccessible and the creation of any real unity between the various peoples (or various regions) of China impossible because of the isolation of many groups. The composite impact of all these factors comes out in Teilhard de Chardin's writings; in 1931, for example, he writes from Peking

> I am going on ahead to the west with two supply trucks.   The 'fleet', which now appears to be 'seaworthy' again is not to set out until the 17th.   A solemn moment—but shall we ever reach Turkestan? There is every sort of political cloud on the horizon, for we are obliged to include in our convoy representatives of the Nanking government, and these are looked on as 'undesirables' in the practically independent provinces.[1]

Elsewhere he comments on recent progress; referring to a journey in Shansi he remarks

> A comfortable journey, too, on the motor road: 48 hours for the 400 miles that before took me a week by mule.[2]

The beginnings of such local (and very relative) progress were, however, wiped out by almost twenty years of war and civil war; at the end of this period the transport system was, over wide areas, reduced to chaos.   In these conditions it was inevitable that the Communist Government should devote a high priority and considerable funds to the creation of an integrated transport network.   One-fifth of the expenditure on the First Five Year Plan was accordingly allocated to the consolidation and modernisation of transport and by the end of the 1950s the broad lines of China's new transport system had been laid down.

THE TRANSPORT INDUSTRY: Traditional & Modern Sectors

The general lines of development of the transport industry can be summarised briefly.   Two main features may be stressed; first, the increasing importance of the modern sector, secondly, the continuing role of the traditional forms of transport.   The former is represented by the network of railways and motorable roads, by the steamships plying coastal and inland waters and the airways; the traditional sector is represented by human and animal carriers, by push carts and other vehicles and by junks and sampans.

An estimate for the early 'thirties, in terms of net value added in the transport sector, suggested that over three-quarters of the net value

---

[1] Pierre Teilhard de Chardin, *Letters from a Traveller* (London 1962), p. 177.
[2] Ibid., p. 163.

added was accounted for by the traditional sector, slightly under one-quarter by the modern sector; in terms of gross receipts the respective figures were 68·3 per cent and 31·7 per cent.[1] At this period the most costly form of transport was by motor vehicle (0·400 CN$/ton-km. as against 0·320 for human carriers and 0·013 for railways). By 1952 the contribution of the traditional sector to the net value added in the transport sector had dropped to 58 per cent, that of the modern sector rising to 42 per cent. As the railway and other developments sketched below will suggest, this decline of the traditional sector will certainly have continued during the last seventeen years.

Two other sets of statistics enable us to get the two sectors of the transport industry into perspective: in 1952 almost 48 per cent of the gross receipts in the transport industry came from the modern sector, slightly over 52 per cent from the traditional sector; 12 per cent only of the employment was in the modern sector and almost 90 per cent in the traditional sector. The inter-relations and juxtaposition of the two was illustrated for the writer by a visit to Wuhan in 1958—the background was that of the giant steel complex with its network of railways, the foreground dominated by groups of workers, lean, cord-muscled and sweating, man-handling heavy castings up a nearby road on flimsy carts. Or close to the Great Wall when the electric train sweeps northwards into a dust-hazed landscape, past the long strings of shaggy Bactrian camels, padding southwards along the edge of the macadamised road on their journey from Mongolia to Peking. In the words of Yuan-li Wu:

'Modern transport was only a part of the total transport plan. No adequate data exist for the traditional sector but its total carrying capacity is estimated to have been as high as 402 million ton-kilometres per day in 1949. On the basis of 300 days a year, the annual volume exceeded 90 billion ton-kilometres, or nearly four times that of the modern transport sector.' He adds, however, 'In practice . . . the effectiveness and potential of the traditional sector were, and still are, probably far smaller than the figures suggest.'[2]

Perhaps these attempts to quantify, along Western lines, are irrelevant and there are obvious dangers in attempting to evaluate separately the two elements in an integrated transport system. And in any case, as the Chinese have stressed, the heavy dependence of the economy on transport by traditional methods, on the use of human and animal muscle, is a transitional phenomenon; the development of the country's oil resources and its growing output of trucks, lorries, railway engines and rolling stock is gradually making the millennial-old burden of the human carrier a thing of the past. . . .

[1] Yuan-li Wu, *The Spatial Economy of Communist China* (New York and London 1967), p. 104.
[2] *Ibid.*, p. 125.

RAILWAYS: 'A Web of Steel'

One of the dominant features of the last two decades has been the extension of the railway system into the formerly inaccessible areas of China's western and southwestern interior. The background of the development is given by Chang Ching-chih:

> Most of the new routes are in the western two-thirds of the country, which only six years ago had virtually no railways; they will help develop the huge resources of these areas. Many of them cross previously unsurveyed deserts and high mountains in the northwest and southwest. Between them, they present probably more new and varied construction problems than have ever been met, at one time, by the railway builders of any one country.[1]

The difficulties include the 13,000-foot high Tsinling Mountains and the gorges of the Kialing River (Paochi-Chengtu Line), the bridging of the Yangtse at Wuhan and later Nanking (a 6,700 metre bridge was recently opened), the sheet floods, alkaline soils and earthquake-liable terrain of the Kansu Corridor (Lan-Sin Line), the shifting sands of the Gobi margin (Lanchow-Paotow Line) and the absence of building materials along long stretches of the two latter lines. These extensions of the rail network into China's western fringe are among the more spectacular achievements of the last twenty years; at the same time, the policy has been to provide multiple tracks on the main trunk routes and to fill in the network of local and transverse lines, thus binding the whole country together with a 'web of steel'.

The main new lines are the Lanchow-Sinkiang (Lan-Sin) line which runs westwards through Sinkiang and which was intended to link up with the Soviet rail system; it has now reached Urumchi and links the northwestern oilfields and Sinkiang with the main centre of population in the east of China; the Lanchow-Paotow line which links up with the rail system of the Mongolian People's Republic and gives access to the Paotow iron and steel complex and the mineral and agricultural resources of Inner Mongolia; the Chining-Erhlien line which links North China with Outer Mongolia and the USSR; and the Paochi-Chengtu line which provides a much needed North-South link across the uplands of Western China. Smaller lines, especially in the south, have opened up the agricultural and mineral resources of the interior and given the South outlets at Amoy, Swatow and the new port of Chanchiang. Some 13,000 kilometres of railways were added to the system between 1949 and 1958 and a further 15,000 kilometres between 1958 and 1963.

By 1963 the Chinese railway system had some 52,000 kilometres of

[1] Chang Ching-chih, 'Nothing Stops the Railway Builders' in *China in Transition* (Peking 1957), p. 171.

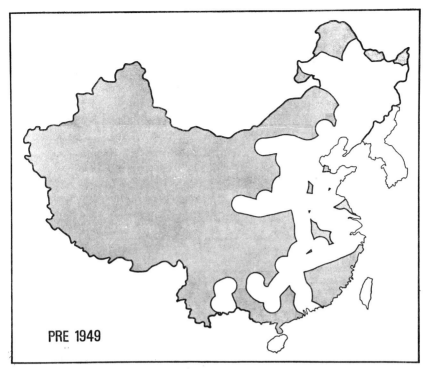

PRE 1949

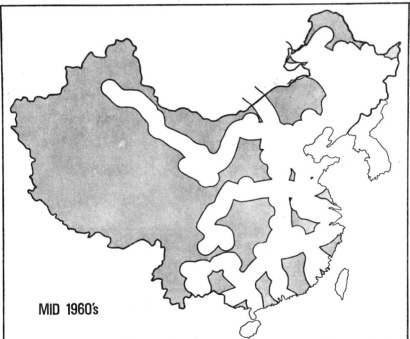

MID 1960's

Figure 68. The Integration of the Economy: Accessibility by Rail, 1949 and 1963.
Note that before 1949 only the Northeast (Manchuria) and parts of the East had a
reasonable degree of accessibility and that in the extreme southwest the line from
Chani via Kunming to Hanoi had no links with the rail system of the rest of China.
By the early 'sixties rail development in the Northwest and Southwest, and the filling
in of the grid elsewhere, had substantially reduced the area with no effective rail
access. With the exception of the Tibet-Chinghai highlands and parts of the
northern steppe fringe the major area still suffering from poor rail access was the hill
and mountain country in western Hupeh and eastern Szechwan. Shaded areas are
those areas more than 100 km. from a railway.

S

trackage, this was made up of 34,235 kilometres of railways in operation, almost 10,000 kilometres of double-tracking and 7,000 kilometres
of new light spur lines. Expressed in terms of kilometres of operating
railways per 1,000 sq. kilometres. the density was highest in the Northeast,
with a density of 13 kilometres, almost double the figure for the Eastern
and Central regions; for the Northwest it was 1·5 and for the Southwest 1. The greatest efforts in railway construction since 1949 have
been in the Northwest and North, followed by the Southwest and the
South; slightly over four-fifths of the new construction has been in the
'less developed' regions.[1]   Yuan-li Wu argues that the emphasis of

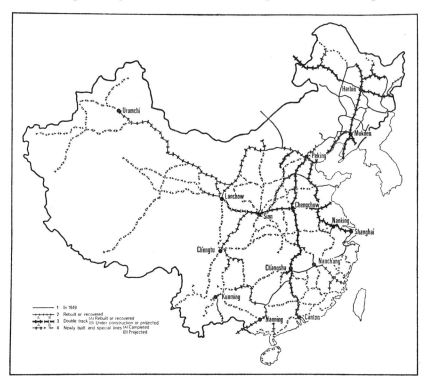

Figure 69.   The Chinese Railway System (mid-'sixties).

Showing the double-tracking of the major routes in eastern China and the new lines,
such as the Lan-Sin line or the Paochi-Chengtu line, which have opened up much
of the northwestern and western interior.   The projected lines 'fill in' the pre-existing
framework, especially in northwestern and southern China.   Note the relatively
well-developed network in the Northeastern Region (Manchuria).

economic planning changed from the development of the hinterland
during the First Five Year Plan to a planning policy which favoured the
more developed areas of the east; under such conditions there may have
been a lack of coordination between the transport policy, which con-

[1] Yuan-li Wu, *op. cit.*, p. 148.

tinued to emphasise development in the interior, and the overall economic plan.[1]   There seems inadequate data to confirm this hypothesis and, in any case, while such may have been the case over the short term, it seems (speaking with the advantages of hindsight) that developments in the Northwest and North (e.g. the Sinkiang oilfields, the Lanchow industrial complex or the Paotow iron and steel base) justified the preoccupation of Chinese planners with the extension of railroad in these regions.

And the rapid overall increase in the importance of the railways is suggested by three sets of data: between 1949 and 1963 the volume of freight carried by the railways increased tenfold (55·89 M. met. tons to 611·13 M.), the volume of freight traffic, measured in billion ton/km., increased sixteen-fold and the number of passengers carried increased five-fold.[2]   These figures indicate the beginning, on a decisive scale, of the integration of the various regions and peoples of China into a coherent national economy.

ROADS & WATERWAYS

China had almost 70,000 kilometres of all-weather roads open to traffic in 1949; this total almost doubled, to 131,000, by 1953 and increased further to approximately 200,000 kilometres by 1960.   The greatest expansion of highway development was in the less developed regions of the country and three-fifths of the total was in the minority regions of the West.   The contrasting pace of development in the various regions is indicated by the fact that, while the length of operating highways increased by one-third in the Northeast, it doubled in the Northwest and quadrupled in the Southwest and Central and South regions;[3] especially in the Southwest and Northwest the new roads have been trunk roads, opening up new regions, rather than 'feeder' roads.   And supplementing this developing national network of roads are the local roads built by the commune for purely local needs; no estimate of the aggregate length of these is available but in all the areas visited by the writer they form a close-meshed network, acting as vital links between the team, the brigade and the commune and the rest of China.

Some of the new roads, such as the Chinghai-Tibet and Sinkiang-Tibet roads, are major engineering feats, crossing difficult terrain over 14,000 feet above sea-level.   Here, and in Yunnan, the development of the road system makes accessible new resources; it also contributes to the effective unification of the State territory.   Full utilisation of this expanded road system hinges obviously on an adequate lorry fleet and here the expansion of China's vehicle production (with major centres at Changchun and Peking) is critically important, while, in the transition

[1] *Ibid.*, p. 206.   [2] *Ibid.*, pp. 181–2, 176.   [3] *Ibid.*, Tables 7–15, p. 159.

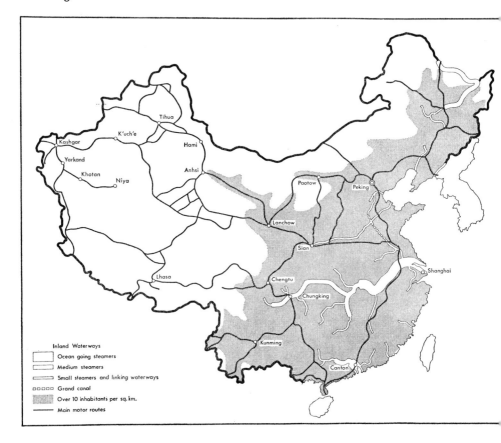

Figure 70.   Roads and Waterways (early 'sixties).
The map illustrates the extensive network of roads developed in the Western Regions and which take the place, along with airways (see Figure 72), of railways in these regions of difficult terrain. In the more closely settled area of the east (over ten inhabitants per square kilometre) only major linking roads are shown. Note the importance of the Yangtse as affording a waterway accessible to ocean-going steamers penetrating deep into Agricultural China.

period to a fully mechanised transport system, traditional forms of transport—5 million mule carts or horse carts and 10 million hand carts —play a vital if humble role. In 1949 this traditional sector was estimated, as pointed out above, to have a carrying capacity four times that of the modern sector.

The great rivers of China—the Si Kiang, the Yangtse Kiang, the Heilungkiang and the Sungari—offer lines of communication in an east-west direction. Together with the complex network of smaller rivers they give China some 168,000 kilometres of navigable waterway (over twice the 1949 total). During the First Five Year Plan 40,000 kilo-metres were opened to navigation by steamer, the navigable channels of

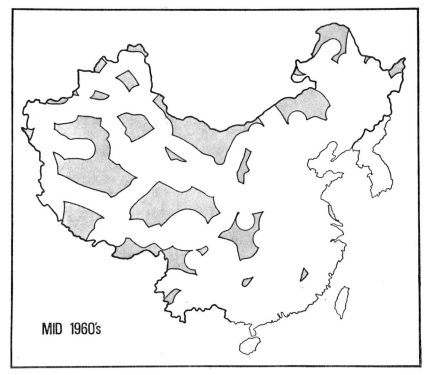

Figure 71.   The Integration of the Economy: Accessibility by Rail, Road and Air
in the Middle 'Sixties.

The development of road communications (e.g. the Chengtu-Lhasa highway) and
of airways is introducing a new accessibility into formerly remote areas of China's
Far West.   The high plateaux and mountains of these areas are girdled by, and
traversed by, new motor roads while airways services link the extreme western fringes
of China with the more developed east.   This increasing accessibility of much of the
country is an important factor in the human integration of China no less than in the
purely economic integration of the State territory.   Shaded areas are more than
100 km. from road, railway or airport.

the Pearl River, the Yangtse Kiang and the Heilungkiang were
dredged, and new harbours opened at Changchiang in Kwangtung and
Yushikou on the Yangtse.   During the period of the Second Five Year
Plan the reconstruction of the Grand Canal was undertaken so as to
provide a major north–south waterway which complements the river
system.   When completed it will link five rivers—the Hai Ho, the
Hwang Ho, the Huai River, the Yangtse Kiang and the Chientang—
forming an integrated water transport system covering almost half of
China; Peking will become an important inland port, connected by
water with cities as far south as Chengtu.   The various large-scale
water conservancy schemes contribute also to the expansion of the
network of internal waterways (Figure 54); to take a single example, in
North Anhwei a carefully planned system of drainage canals is providing

also almost 80,000 miles of waterways navigable to small steamers and junks, linking together all the townships and communes in the area.

AIRWAYS: Bringing Far Places Near . . .

In his study of China published in 1967 Yuan-li Wu states 'No regularly operated routes under Communist control were reported for 1959'. From this one can infer either that China had no regularly operated routes, or that the routes were not 'under Communist control' (operated by Pan-Am or BOAC?) or that the knowledge the West has about the Chinese airways system is either negligible or not accessible to intellectual bodies except the C.I.A. . . .

Wu gives the total of domestic air routes being flown as 16,900 kilometres in the pre-Communist period; by 1958 some 29,000 kilometres of scheduled passenger lines were in operation. The pattern of these and the relative importance of the various routes is shown in Figure 72; this is constructed from the official timetables of the Chinese Civil Airways Administration and shows conditions at the beginning of the 1960s. Between 1952 and 1959 the Chinese claim that the length of civil aviation routes doubled (Wu quotes a figure of 11,400 kilometres for 1950, which would be consistent with this claim). External air routes link China with Moscow, Pyongyang, Hanoi and Rangoon and the flights of Air France and Pakistan International Airways with the Middle East, Western Europe and Japan.

Given the size of China, its difficult terrain and the still skeletal character of the road and rail system in the Far West, air transport is of vital importance. A relatively dense network of air routes had been developed by 1960,[1] with Peking, Wuhan and Sian as the main 'nodes' and with secondary nodes at Urumchi, Chungking and Lanchow. Within China, the aeroplane, more than any other single factor, has integrated the sparsely settled Far West with the remainder of China; distances from Peking to the cities of Outer China—Kashgar, Aksu or Hami—are now measured in hours rather than the weeks which were involved when travel was by land. Services are dependable and comfortable; the main air terminals spacious, beflowered and crowded with Chinese and minority peoples. This greatly increased speed of communication with outlying regions is of major importance in a country developing at China's pace; technicians, blue-prints and delicate precision equipment can be rushed by aeroplane to development areas where other transport might take weeks.

Civil aviation is helping, too, in a wide variety of other fields—pest control, afforestation, the sowing of grass seed, surveying and geophysical prospecting (the central Kiangsi iron ore field was discovered

---

[1] For the initial stages of development of the Peking-Lhasa route see Pan Kuo-ting 'Flight to Lhasa' in *China in Transition* (Peking 1957) pp. 178–182.

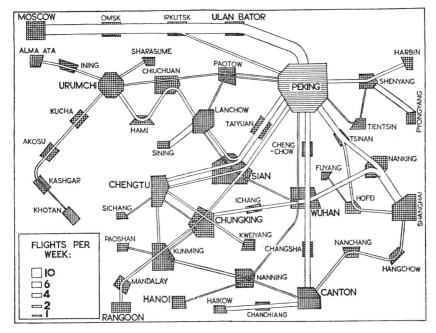

Figure 72. The Chinese Airways Network *c.* 1960.
Thickness of line is proportionate to number of passenger flights per week. Note the main 'nodes'—Peking, Chungking, Sian and Urumchi—and the way in which the aeroplane has made accessible the remotest towns of the Far West. To the Chinese Civil Airways Administration routes shown must be added the links with Western Europe via French and Pakistani airlines.

by aerial prospecting). The aeroplane, in short, has become a vital instrument in the transformation of the Chinese earth; its increasing use is an example of those processes of cultural and technological change which are making possible a complete reappraisal of China's resource endowment.

*   *   *

A comparison of Maps 68 and 71 will show the progress in the development of China's communications network and the extent to which rail, road, water and air routes are knitting together this vast and topographically-divided country. The isolation of even remote rural areas is being overcome so that an area like Tachai, in the Taihang Mountains of Shansi, a classic area for demonstrating what can be achieved in the development of marginal land, is visited by tens of thousands from all over China. Transport is not merely creating an integrated nation in economic terms, but also an integrated nation in human terms.

The development pattern, we have seen, is a dualistic one. Both modern and traditional forms of transport are used though the increasing importance of modern forms of transport has been stressed. And while emphasis has been given, at the national level, to planning which will achieve complete 'articulation' of the economy and integration of the territory, the development of the commune has been followed by labour-investment which has made possible a greatly intensified development of local transport which provides the essential channel for a greatly increased flow of local activities; thus for two sample communes in North and South the density of *local* roads is respectively 600 km. and 150 km. per 100 sq. kilometres of total area.

One final point, and it is a point of contrast with the West. The development of transport in the West was followed by the break-down of local self-sufficiency and by increasing specialisation, the latter manifesting itself in the rise of increasingly single-crop economies. The emphasis of Chinese development is on regional self-sufficiency and the effect of improved transport shows itself chiefly in the development and intensification, even the increasing diversification, of the regional agricultural and industrial economies. The results of the impact of technological change are largely determined by the political and social ideas of the society within which such change occurs; we are often inclined to forget this and to assume, unthinkingly, that the experience of our own Western society must have a global validity. China, at least, demonstrates that this is not so. . . .

CHAPTER 12

Population: Spatial Patterns

THE COUNTRYSIDE

THE BROAD contrasts in population density between various regions of China which were outlined above reflect the diversity of the land utilisation systems and the differing population-supporting capacity of the various environments as evaluated by Chinese farming techniques. The contrasts in spatial patterns, the arrangement of the population in dispersed hamlets, in thinly-strewn or closely-packed villages, in market towns and cities, reflect the influence not only of environmental and agricultural factors (in the narrow sense of the term), they are also a reflection of the social and economic needs of the Chinese peasant. The influence of these needs, extending back over many centuries, shows itself clearly in the spatial arrangement of the rural population, in the distribution of village, market town and regional city, each of which plays a distinctive role in meeting the varied needs of the country-dweller. The socio-economic logic behind the settlement pattern of traditional China has been brilliantly analysed by G. W. Skinner;[1] to ignore this logic and to attempt to impose a new and doctrinaire framework on the life of a rural society as old as that of China (as was attempted in 1958–60) is, as he demonstrates, to court disaster. . . . The marketing community, the market town and the periodic markets form components in a smoothly-working mechanism, evolving always to meet changing rural needs, capable of deliberate modification only within narrow limits—but capable, as history shows, of playing an important role not only in traditional society but in the diffusion of new ideas into that society.

The 'self-contained world of the Chinese peasant' is, Skinner argues, based not on the village but on the marketing community. This is

[1] G. William Skinner, 'Marketing and Social Structure in Rural China' in *Journal of Asian Studies*, Vol. XXIV (November 1964–August 1965), pp. 3–43, 195–228, 363–99. The section which follows is based on this study.

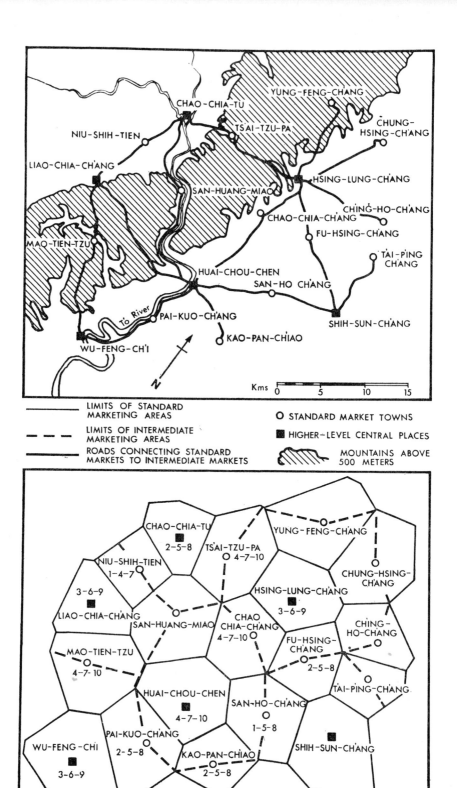

────────	LIMITS OF STANDARD MARKETING AREAS
── ── ──	LIMITS OF INTERMEDIATE MARKETING AREAS
━━━━━━	ROADS CONNECTING STANDARD MARKETS TO INTERMEDIATE MARKETS
○	STANDARD MARKET TOWNS
■	HIGHER–LEVEL CENTRAL PLACES
	MOUNTAINS ABOVE 500 METERS

Kms 0   5   10   15

the population within a 'standard marketing area' which, in broad terms, is the area within walking distance (3·4–6·1 kilometres) of a market town. His analysis of Agricultural China shows that 'in the modal case, marketing areas are just over 50 sq. kilometres in size, market towns are less than 8 kilometres apart and maximum walking distance to the town is approximately 4·5 km. The average (mean) population of the standard marketing community is somewhat over 7,000.'[1] As might be expected, there is a considerable variation in size and population depending on terrain; mountainous and arid regions show marketing areas of 150 sq. kilometres or more, with marketing communities of 3,000 or less, while lowlands of exceptional fertility may show marketing areas as small as 15 sq. kilometres. The model developed by Skinner shows that each marketing area contains eighteen villages; his analysis of *actual* marketing areas in various parts of China shows that conditions approximate closely to this model with a range of from 17·9 to 21·4 villages per market area. The relation between population density and size of marketing area is summarised in the table below:

TABLE 17

Proportion of all Standard Marketing Communities	Range in Average Areas (per km.²)	Range in Densities (per km.²)
5%	158>	<19
15%	97–157	20–59
60%	30–96	60–299
15%	16–29	300–499
5%	15 or less	500>

Source: G. W. Skinner, *op. cit.*, p. 33.

The marketing area and the standard market town are in turn tied into a network of what Skinner terms 'higher level central places'. There results an approximately hexagonal pattern of market towns and higher-level market towns; Fig. 73 illustrates the theoretic standard and

[1] G. William Skinner, *op. cit.*, p. 33.

Figure 73. Spatial and Temporal Pattern of Market Areas in Szechwan.
The region shown lies between 35 and 90 km. northeast of Chengtu; it is an example of an area where each standard market is dependent on two higher level market towns.
Top Map: generalised sketch of area showing market towns and connecting roads.
Bottom Map: abstraction of landscape showing theoretical standard and intermediate market areas; the distribution of market areas follows a broadly hexagonal pattern. Numbers refer to market days within the 10-day cycle (*hsün*); the regular *spatial* pattern of the market centres is paralleled by an equally precise patterning of the market days in *time*. (Maps redrawn, from maps by G. W. Skinner, *op. cit.*)

intermediate marketing areas for a district in Szechwan, together with the reduction of the pattern to a diagrammatic form.

It is to the 'standard' market town that the peasant turns to exchange what he produces for what he needs—soap and matches, candles or oil lamps, needles, thread and looms, in the case of the older peasants, incense and paper effigies for religious rites. In the small market town are also to be found the services needed in a peasant society—the skills of the scribes and the tool-sharpeners, of the barbers and medical practitioners—and also the establishments catering for the recreational needs of the peasant—the tea shops, eating places and wine shops. And so the standard marketing area, the area focusing on such a market town, is a social and cultural unit as well as an economic unit and this aspect is emphasised by the tendency of the villagers to seek wives within the marketing community. The resultant web of kinship relations within the community strengthens the ties created by other social and economic forces.

These 'standard market towns' show a definite patterning in *space*, as is illustrated by Figure 73, while their functions are also interlocked in terms of *time*; their markets, which are periodic, are so spaced that itinerant peddlers of goods and services could pass from one to another, completing a full circuit of the smaller and the intermediate market towns within a given period (usually the lunar *hsün*, i.e. a 10-day period). An example of this patterning in time is given in Figure 73. And the importance of the interlocking of function at different *levels* in the marketing system (standard market, intermediate market and central market) in giving cohesion to Chinese society is well emphasised by Skinner: 'Marketing structures, unlike administrative structures, take the form of interlocking networks. It is the joint participation of standard markets in two or three intermediate marketing systems, of intermediate markets in two or three central marketing systems, and so on, which articulates and unites the little local economies centred on each market town into, first, regional economic structures and eventually into a single society-wide economy. Thus, marketing had a significance for societal integration in traditional China which at once paralleled and surpassed—which both reinforced and complemented—that of administration'.[1]

CHANGES IN THE PATTERN OF THE COUNTRYSIDE

Steady population growth over the centuries, together with the increasing participation of the peasant in market-oriented activities in recent years, led to a steady growth in the number of new settlements and new markets. To illustrate this, Skinner cites the case of four *hsien* in Chekiang province; these had a total of 26 rural markets in 1227

[1] G. W. Skinner, *op. cit.*, p. 31.

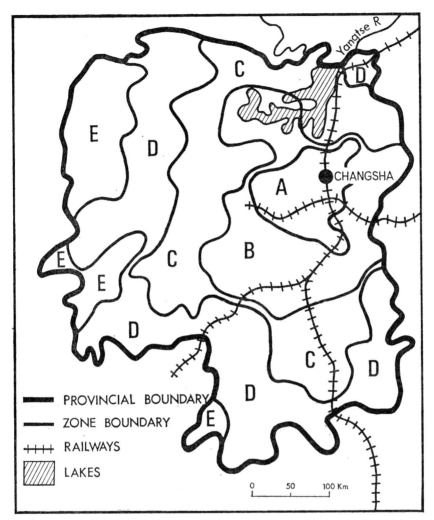

Figure 74. Zones of Modernisation in Hunan, 1958 (based on G. W. Skinner).
Illustrating the progressive penetration of rural China by new forms of economic organisation and new technologies (see p. 268).

Zones are based on the degree of modernisation as measured by size of market centres. Larger populations are regarded as indicating consolidation as a result of modernisation and the closing of smaller markets; on this basis, the percentage of centres *putatively* modernized decreases steadily with increasing distance from Changsha. The size and population of townships by zone is given below:

	Density per km.	Average Township Area	Average Township Population
Zone A	321	44·2 km.	14,168
Zone B	247	53·9	13,325
Zone C	195	64·2	12,508
Zone D	107	81·7	8,729
Zone E	94	70·4	6,619

(*Source:* G. W. Skinner, *op. cit.*, Table 7)

and of these 20 were still functioning in 1877 while 150 new markets had grown up.[1] The process of intensification of rural activities manifests itself, he contends, in two different forms. Within a still *largely traditional* market economy it manifests itself in an increasing proliferation of small marketing centres and this, very obviously, leads to a progressive reduction in the size of the marketing areas. Within a *modernised* economy, with an improved transport system and a growing peasant demand for manufactured goods (before 1949 often imported), there is an increasing tendency for trade to by-pass the smaller (i e. 'standard') market town and to take advantage of the more favourable prices and wider range of goods and services offered by the higher level markets. These begin a process of cumulative development at the expense of the smaller markets; with the decay of the latter their market areas are absorbed by the modernising centre whose marketing area in consequence expands. Yet, while this modernisation leads to *a widening of the social horizon* of the peasant it leads also, because of the very difficulties of coping with the wider unit of some 50–75 villages, to a *contraction of social community* and to a renewed emphasis on the village rather than the marketing community.[2]

The process of modernisation spreads out in what Skinner calls 'successive waves of commercialisation'; the advancing front of these waves is, he notes, 'always well ahead of the area served by modern transport'.[3] Such a process has obviously been greatly aided by the development of transport facilities since 1949, facilities not only for motorised transport but also for traditional forms of transport such as the mule cart or the hand cart. The spatial pattern this process takes may be illustrated from conditions in Hunan; here the proportion of intermediate marketing systems which were modernised by 1958 ranged from some 45 per cent around the regional centre of Changsha to zero in the marginal areas of the province as yet untouched by modern transport (Figure 74). Today, the Chinese see this process of change, of modernisation, spreading out 'like a series of oil-spots' as they put it, from the most advanced communes and production brigades, a series of 'oil-spots' which will eventually coalesce over a modernised country-side. Skinner's analysis gives us an indication of the achievements in this direction between 1949 and 1964 and also an indication of what still remains to be done.

MARKET COMMUNITY & PEOPLE'S COMMUNE

The marketing system of rural China, with its thousands of minor and major market towns (interlocking in space and in the rhythm of their commercial activities) developed slowly over many centuries. It continued to develop, and at an accelerated pace, during the first

[1] G. W. Skinner, *op. cit.*, p. 196.   [2] *Ibid.*, p. 221.   [3] *Ibid.*, p. 214.

decade of Communist rule; by 1958 some 30 per cent of the intermediate marketing systems in rural China had been modernised,
leaving some 48,000 unmodernised standard marketing systems. At
this point, however, and as one aspect of the move towards the consolidation of the emerging system of People's Communes, the régime
decided to dispense with the traditional marketing system and to
replace it by a single supply and marketing department within each
commune. The experiment was a failure for the new mechanisms
proved incapable of fulfilling the functions of the traditional periodic
market system;[1] in consequence, from the middle of 1959 the policy was
abandoned and the reconstruction of the old system was begun.
Skinner sees this abortive attempt to create a new marketing structure
as an attempt to integrate marketing systems with the new administrative and economic unit of the commune; since, however, the marketing
system comprised discrete units only at the lowest level, and consisted
essentially of an interlocking network, whereas administrative units
were discrete at every level, it is 'infeasible to contain or constrain the
interlocked network of natural marketing systems within the bounds
of discrete administrative units'.[2]

The reconstruction of the system was based on intensive field
investigation into the flow-patterns of rural trade; its aim was to
organise the flow of trade according to 'rational economic-area divi-
sions'. By 1964 the old pattern was re-established and the market
town was once again fulfilling its old function. Here the peasants can
market the products of their 'side-line occupations', agents of production teams, brigades and communes make purchases and sales on behalf
of their collective, itinerant traders still make their circuit of the
markets, though in smaller numbers than of old. And with the
subdivision of the communes from 1961 onwards the administrative-
production unit of the commune came to coincide closely in area and
population with the natural marketing community. In 1958 there
were, Skinner estimates, some 80,000 of these, a figure close to the total
of people's communes in 1966 (78,000, see p. 130), while the average
population of the commune today (6,000–7,000 people) parallels
closely that of the standard marketing community (7,000).

THE CITIES

China's total urban population in 1953 was, according to the Census,
77 millions, or 13·2 per cent of the total population; by 1957 it had
reached 92 millions or 14·3 per cent of the total; by 1960 it was 130
millions or 18·5 per cent of the total. If the proportion is low compared

---

[1] The economic disorganisation of the countryside resulting from this policy almost certainly aggravated the difficulties of the 1959–61 period on the agricultural front.
[2] *Ibid.*, p. 374.

to that of many other countries, nevertheless the absolute total of city-dwellers is very large and is exceeded only by the total for the United States and Soviet Union.

Fifty-one million people were, in 1953, living in 420 cities of over 20,000 inhabitants; the distribution of these is shown in Figures 75 and 76; 102 cities had populations of over 100,000, nine of these were 'million cities', with populations of over one million.   These 'million cities' were as follows:

Shanghai	6,204,417
Peking	2,768,149
Tientsin	2,693,831
Shenyang	2,299,900
Chungking	1,772,500
Canton	1,598,900
Wuhan	1,427,300
Harbin	1,163,000
Nanking	1,091,600

Source: Ullman, 1961.

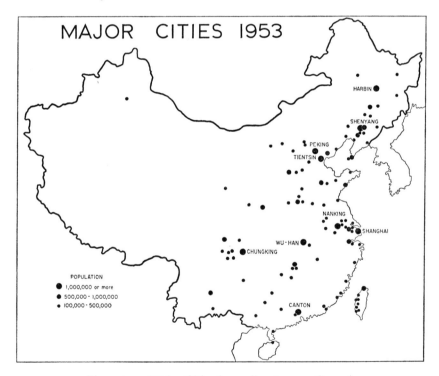

Figure 75.   Major Cities (according to 1953 Census).
Major concentration of cities in the Northern, Northeastern and Eastern Economic regions; urbanisation on any large scale lacking in the thinly-peopled Far West. For the impact of urbanisation during the nineteen-fifties see Figure 77.

These giant cities contained almost one-quarter of the total urban population. At the other extreme, almost one-third of the population classed as 'urban' lived in centres of under 20,000 people. The function and pattern of these small market and administrative centres have been commented on above; they are, indeed, one of the distinctive elements in the Chinese landscape and some 5,100 of them are listed in the 1953 Census. The proportion of urban-dwellers is highest in the industrialised Northeast where it is over 30 per cent; the cities of Peking and Tientsin in Hopeh and Shanghai in Kiangsu raise the proportion of urban dwellers for these two provinces to over one-fifth; otherwise, no provinces show percentages of city-dwellers above the national average. Moderate degrees of urbanisation are shown by the Southeast coastal provinces of Kwangtung and Fukien (12 per cent) and by the far western regions of Tibet and Sinkiang; urbanisation is of least importance (under 5 per cent) in the southern interior provinces of Kwangsi and Kweichow.

THE EXPANSION OF THE URBAN POPULATION

The urban population seems to have increased by over 140 per cent over the two decades 1938–58, the rate of increase being inversely proportional to the size of city; thus, the group of municipalities which had populations of over one million in 1938 shows a 114 per cent increase in the ensuing twenty years as compared with a 362 per cent increase for those of under 50,000 inhabitants.[1] Over the period 1949–60 Kang Shao estimates that the average annual growth rate of the urban population was 7·6 per cent; between 1957 and 1960 it was 12·2 per cent.[2] By the early nineteen-sixties the number of 'million-cities' had increased to seventeen (Figure 77), containing approximately one-third of China's urban population (as compared with one-quarter in 1953).

The growth rate of the smaller towns is probably a reflection of the development and modernisation of the countryside, with the consequent demand for services and the development of small industries. The growth rate of the bigger cities has been largely in response to industrial development and two aspects of Chinese industrialisation have been important in this context. First, the policy of economic regionalisation (see Figure 59 for the major regions) which aims at creating an integrated industrial system, with a heavy industry core and an associated complex

---

[1] Morris B. Ullman, *Cities of Mainland China: 1953 and 1958* (U.S. Department of Commerce, Bureau of the Census), 1961, p. 15. For a shorter period Chinese sources give a different picture: thus, for the period 1952–55 the following growth rates are cited:

Total urban population increased	20%
Population in all cities increased	26%
Population in 10 large industrial cities increased	51%

Cited by Kang Chao, 'Industrialisation and Urban Housing in Communist China' in *Journal of Asian Studies*, May 1966, p. 381.

[2] Kang Chao, *op. cit.*, p. 385.

T

of light and heavy industrial enterprises, and which has tended to 'spread' urbanisation and thus avoid the excessive concentration of development projects in the capital city.[1]   Secondly, the rather different policies with regard to industrial localisation pursued during the First and Second Five Year Plans.   During the First Plan there was a concentration of development in a limited number of cities; as Kang Shao observes 'virtually all the new construction projects . . . were distributed in some 120 cities, and a majority of the above-norm (large) projects were clustered in 18 cities'.[2]   After 1957 a policy of wider dispersion was favoured and in 1958 and 1959 'the construction work was spread over about 2,100 cities and towns'.[3]

Short-range migration from adjoining rural areas has, as indicated above (p. 30), been a factor contributing to this growth and in this migration some Western observers have seen two phases: an earlier phase, prior to 1958, when the 'pull' factor of urban industrialisation was dominant and a post-1958 phase dominated by the 'push' factor and reflecting peasant reaction to the commune system.   The evidence for such a distinction is far from convincing; what is clear is that what was termed the 'blind infiltration' of peasants into neighbouring cities has been increasingly controlled by legislation.   Meanwhile, as a result of greatly improved health measures and the high marriage rate of the Chinese urban population natural growth rates in the cities have certainly been high.   These rates have exceeded 4 per cent per annum (i.e. twice the national growth rate) and in the 'fifties may well, according to some experts, have contributed more to the growth of the urban population than did migration; indeed, in several cities over this period the increase of population through natural growth actually exceeded the total growth, thus implying a loss of population through migration.[4]

A third way in which some of the cities have grown has been by territorial expansion of the municipal area.   Chinese policy has had as one of its objectives the avoidance of the conflict of interests between city and countryside typical of many developed and developing areas. Social and administrative policies involve urban cadres and many urban workers in periods of labour in the countryside; efforts are made to keep the gap in living levels between city-dweller and countryman as narrow as possible; small-scale nodes of industry are diffused deep into the countryside.   The territorial expansion of some of the biggest cities may in part be motivated by this desire to reduce urban-rural differences by creating a series of integrated, more or less self-sufficient, urban-rural units.   Several large-scale changes of this type took

[1] This excessive concentration of resources, skills and new development is described by the French as 'macrocephaly'.
[2] Kang Chao, *op. cit.*, p. 383.   [3] *Ibid.*
[4] Against this background it is difficult to accept Kang Chao's estimate that internal migration probably accounted for close on 100 per cent of the natural growth in China's urban population over the period 1949–60.   *Op. cit.*, p. 386.

place in 1958; Peking, for example quadrupled its area and by the end of 1958 the area under the jurisdiction of Peking municipality was 17,000 sq. kilometres. Even more striking has been the extension of the jurisdiction of Tientsin municipality; by the end of 1958 Tientsin's authority covered an area of 20,000 sq. kilometres (two-thirds the area

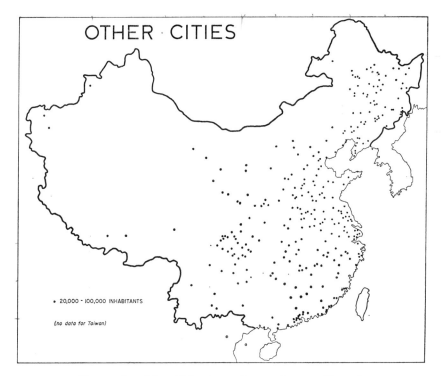

Figure 76.   Other Cities (according to the 1953 Census).
Close scatter of smaller cities, mainly administrative centres and market towns, in Eastern China, contrasting with low degree of urbanisation in arid or semi-arid West.   Some 400 cities of over 20,000 inhabitants are shown; this may be compared with Skinner's estimate, based an city function rather than population size, of some 1,700 'modern central places'.

of the Netherlands) and a total population of 11·4 million (approximately the population of the Netherlands).   These extensions increased the control of the municipalities over the regional transport network and, even more important, over their food supply (notably vegetables, fruit, milk and meat), their water supply (as in the case of Peking), and the supply of construction materials.   Many of the cities had a sizeable rural population at the 1953 Census—Peking, for example, had over 700,000 persons classed as rural, Tientsin 365,000 and Nanking 270,000 (Figure 58)—and these boundary extensions must have significantly increased the size of this rural component and blurred

yet further the distinction between urban and rural populations.
In spite of the enormous absolute increase in the urban population
since 1949 the proportion of the total population who are urban-
dwelling is lower in China than in many other emergent countries.
Nevertheless, the size of the increase *does* pose major problems; at a
time when the creation of a modern economy is demanding full
mobilisation of China's resources of capital, man-power and raw
materials, the planners have been faced with the need to provide urban
housing for an additional 75 million people and to make good an

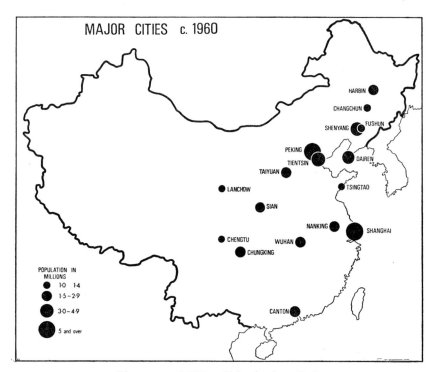

Figure 77.   Million Cities (early 1960s).

Over 40 million people, one-third of the urban population of China, were living in
these seventeen million-cities in the early 1960s.   Note the rapid growth of northwestern cities such as Lanchow and Taiyuan and for the effect of boundary changes
on city growth see pp. 272–3.

estimated 2 per cent per annum depreciation of the existing stock of
housing.   Kang Shao estimates that urban housing increased by some
200 million sq. metres in the decade 1950–60, equivalent to 1·6 sq.
metres of living area for each person added to the urban population.[1]
The overall result of rapid expansion of urban populations coupled with
the relatively low priority given to domestic housing in State and local

[1] Kang Chao, *op. cit.*, p. 388.   See also Kang Chao, *The Construction Industry in Communist
China* (Chicago 1968), pp. 86–109.

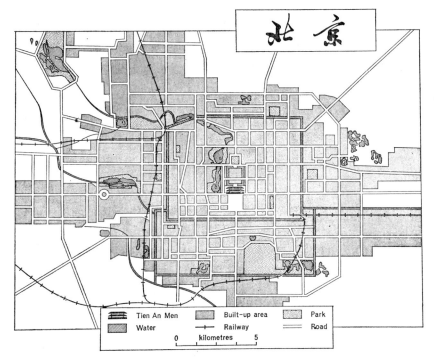

Figure 78. Peking.

Showing the gridded pattern of the Old City, focusing on the Tien An Men gate and the former Forbidden City immediately to the north. The ring of ditches follows the line of the old city walls, beyond which the newer suburbs spread to the west, north and east. The area over which the Peking municipality has jurisdiction was increased in 1958 to some 17,000 sq. kilometres; this gives the municipality a high degree of control over its food supplies (vegetables, fruit, milk and meat). This extension will also have significantly increased the size of the city's rural sector (almost one-third of the population was classed as rural in 1953) and in 1966 the municipal area contained 280 People's Communes.

planning has, he claims, been that the living area per person has halved since 1949. To maintain the initial level of urban housing conditions would, in his opinion, have demanded the construction of a further 700 million sq. metres of living space; this would have meant allocating to housing some 30–35 per cent of the total fixed investment annually.[1] It is difficult to evaluate his conclusions, but there can be no doubt as to the magnitude of the problem. And while, taking the long-term view, the Chinese decision to accord priority to the building of a modern economy is undoubtedly correct, the present writer's impression, based on a dozen or so major cities, is that the Chinese achievement in the field of urban housing is rather greater than the statistics above suggest.[2]

[1] *Ibid.*, p. 395.
[2] There are difficulties posed by the statistics cited by Professor Kang Chao; thus the Chinese living area per person (3·10 m²) is considerably greater than the Czechoslovak area of 1·91 m² (*op. cit.*, p. 393). There are also obvious difficulties in comparing social and domestic

Meanwhile, this expansion of China's urban population finds physical expression in the cultural landscape, in the rapidly extending fringe of factories, dwelling houses and offices around all the Chinese cities, and in the rebuilding, on spacious multi-storied lines, of cities as far apart as Peking and Sian, Lanchow and Kunming. The pace of this redevelopment is remarkable and the juxtaposition of the old and the new (Plates 57 and 60) drives home the progress since 1949; if the new architecture is often severe or unimaginative these effects are softened by the increasing provision of open spaces, by extensive tree-planting in many of the major cities and by the interpenetration of intensive agriculture and urban building on the city margins (see pp. 157–8). And in this redevelopment each city preserves its distinctive personality: Peking, with its massive grey concrete and granite buildings margining the golden roofs of the old Forbidden City, integrates old and new China; the spacious tree-lined avenues which are replacing the old *hutungs* express the spirit of the new régime; Kunming and Nanning are unfolding in similar fashion, but with a warmth and colour in their architecture and their flowering trees which are unmistakably southern; Lanchow is very much a boom town whose population tripled between 1953 and 1960 and where the mud-walled houses of the old caravan city are giving place to the factories, administrative buildings and new residential quarters of a nuclear-age city. . . . The list could be extended, but everywhere the picture is the same—a diversity of personalities, in which the best of Traditional China and the aspirations of New China are interwoven.

indices for a communally-organised society such as that of China with those for more individual-based societies such as those of Japan or India; no city in China, as far as the writer is aware, has slums or squatter settlements to compare with those of Calcutta yet the latter city is quoted as having a living area of 3·7 sq. metres per person (i.e. well above the area for any Chinese city cited).

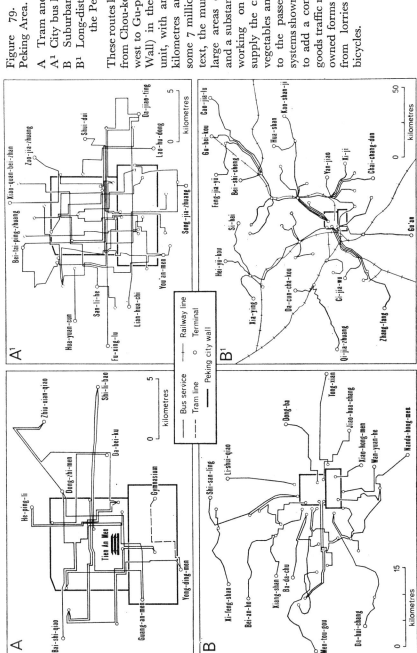

Figure 79. Transport in the Peking Area.

A   Tram and trolley routes
A¹ City bus lines
B   Suburban bus routes
B¹ Long-distance bus routes in the Peking municipal area

These routes knit the whole region, from Chou-kou-tien in the south-west to Gu-pei-kou (on the Great Wall) in the northeast, into one unit, with an area of 17,000 sq. kilometres and a population of some 7 million. As noted in the text, the municipal area includes large areas of agricultural land and a substantial rural population working on communes which supply the city's needs for fruit, vegetables and livestock products; to the passenger traffic on the systems shown on the map we have to add a considerable volume of goods traffic moving by commune-owned forms of transport ranging from lorries to push-carts and bicycles.

CHAPTER 13

China: Over-populated or Under-populated?

La fortune d'une minorité n'a pas de valeur démographique; la possibilité de vie, modeste, mais à perspectives stables ou positives, du plus grande nombre, a au contraire un role décisif . . .—Pierre George.

TO THE historian the Second World War appears as one of the great divides, or watersheds, of human history. To the geographer it is no less significant, for the political upheavals which followed it resulted in the disintegration of the old colonial system and in the emergence, in Eastern Europe and east Asia, of planned societies embracing almost one-quarter of humanity. One of the avowed aims of these societies has been to wipe out poverty and hunger and it is a measure of their success in this field that both geographers and demographers are having to evaluate anew their concepts of population pressure and of the world's resource pattern. These political and social changes have been accompanied by major changes in the demographic field. Vast populations, characterised formerly by negligible or erratic rates of expansion, are entering on a period of massive and accelerating growth as the old checks of famine, disease and political instability have been removed. A paradoxical situation has arisen in which many of the so-called 'under-developed countries' are contemplating without alarm the rapid expansion of their populations while the 'developed countries', with stationary or only slowly expanding populations are haunted by Malthusian ideas.

Nowhere are these changes more dramatically illustrated than in China. China has for long been the classic textbook example of over-population; its total population today approaches, if it has not already passed, 700 millions and is increasing at the rate of some 15–20 million a year. This massive increase is, moreover, regarded by many in China as an asset rather than as a burden—and certainly the developments of the last two decades seem to justify the claim that a socialist society can, by careful planning, achieve a rate of economic growth sufficient to keep production ahead of population growth; that by a series of 'leaps forward' it can speed the transition from agrarian poverty to the higher living levels of a modern diversified economy; and that it can do this even in a society going through a period of rapid population growth.   Nevertheless, strains and hesitations have not been entirely lacking: Ma Yin-ch'u's 'New Population Theory' (1959) stressed that uncontrolled population growth might well delay China's attainment of a true Communist society and the apparent shifts in official attitudes to birth control suggest some official uncertainty as to the consequences of such growth.

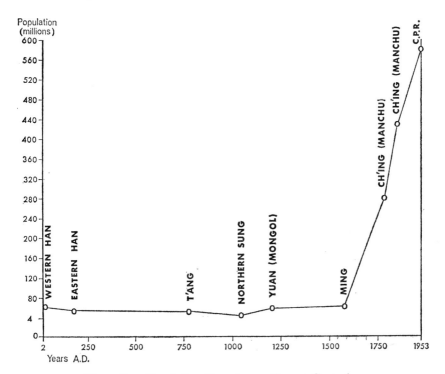

Figure 80.   Population Growth over Recent Centuries.
Note the virtual stability of China's population over some fifty generations and the sudden, sharp, and accelerating increase beginning during the Ming Period; recent population estimates suggest that the upward trend of this graph is likely to be continued for the rest of the present century.

In the pages below an attempt is made to set this problem of population into some sort of perspective.

VIEWPOINTS

Many Western observers have concluded that the 'population problem' of China is insoluble and certainly the data they present on growth rates, peasant poverty and overcrowding, and past decimation by flood, famine or disease seem to confirm their gloomy analysis. Only slowly is it being appreciated that population numbers are not the only variable; that changed political and social conditions can drastically alter the resource balance and thus necessitate a completely new appraisal of the situation; that the quality of a population, no less than its quantity, may change and that a rise in educational and technical levels, which makes possible increasing economic diversification, may also invalidate these gloomy assessments based on a static view of the problem.

Dean Acheson, then United States Secretary of State, presented the 'orthodox' picture in a letter to President Truman. 'The population of China during the eighteenth and nineteenth centuries doubled, thus creating an unbearable pressure on the land. The first problem which every Chinese Government has had to face is that of feeding this population. So far none has succeeded.' William Vogt presented an even more sombre picture and concluded: 'There is little hope that the world will escape the horror of extensive famines in China within the next few years'; since such disasters would cut back population totals he added, 'these may be not only desirable but indispensable'.[1]

Such pessimistic analyses were, moreover, not confined to Western writers; they could be matched by the views of Chinese thinkers. Mencius (c. 372–289 B.C.), for example, wrote, 'An increasing population over a long period of time brings about strife and disorder' and, 2,400 years later, Sun Yat-sen observed, 'At present China is already suffering greatly from over-population which will bring impending danger in its wake ... in time of great drought and famine, many people will starve to death'. The present 'optimistic' view of the Chinese Communist Party is that 'China's huge population [is] a great advantage. ... It is thanks to her vast population that China has been able to create "miracles" and can undertake hitherto unheard of tasks. To wail pessimistically about China's huge population and its high rate of increase is absurd and groundless.'[2] This viewpoint, it is clear, is directly opposed, not only to the views of many Western observers, but also to those of many of the great thinkers of Old China.

THE 1953 CENSUS: Point of Departure

The basis of any modern assessment is the 1953 Census and such subsequent statistics as have been released by the People's Government

---

[1] W. Vogt, *Road to Survival* (New York 1948), p. 238.
[2] Su Chung, 'Facts about China's Population' in *Peking Review*, 1 July 1958.

of China. Like all Chinese statistics since 1949 these have been viewed with some scepticism by Western scholars. G. B. Cressey deliberately chose for his work on China the title 'Land of the 500 Million', thus underlining his doubt of the 1953 Census figure. Dr. N. J. Ling described the Census results as 'more of a political stratagem, skilfully presented under the cloak of statistical authenticity, than a faithful submission of well-ascertained facts'.[1] It is not clear what useful purpose would be served by announcing 'padded' figures of China's population and it seems, from all available evidence, that the People's Government is basing its economic planning on the 1953 figures. After careful examination Dr. S. Chandrasekhar of the Indian Population Institute dismisses the suggestion that the Census figures were a 'political stratagem' and rightly stresses the problems which would arise if the People's Government had 'two sets of figures, a correct one retained for its use and another released for propaganda purposes'.[2] Professor Ping-ti Ho, in his studies on the population of China, points out that, while the 1953 Census was not a census in the technical definition of the term, 'the results seem likely to be closer to the truth than any previous Chinese population figures'.[3] The considered judgement of these two scholars should finally allay the hypercritical suspicion shown to the official population statistics when they were first made public.

The final results issued by the State Statistical Bureau gave the total Chinese population as 602 millions; of these, 11·7 millions were Overseas Chinese and 7·6 millions lived in Taiwan, so the total population under the jurisdiction of the People's Republic of China was 583 millions.[4] Of the total population directly surveyed and registered 51·82 per cent were males and 48·18 per cent females, giving a sex ratio of 107·7 males per 100 females; the legacy of the past, in the shape of female infanticide, is shown in the much higher masculinity rates in the older age groups (age group 7–13 years 115·8 as against 104·9 for age group 0–4). The population is a young one, with 41·1 per cent of the total in the under-18 group, 45·4 per cent in the 18–49 group and 13·5 per cent 50 or over; as such, it has potentialities for very rapid growth once the various limiting factors which operated in the past have been removed.

The Vital Registration Law, passed in 1952, made recording of births and deaths compulsory and, according to Chandrasekhar, 'the country can now therefore boast of registering vital occurrences for almost the entire area, although the registration in rural areas cannot be as accurate as registration in urban areas, particularly the cities'.

[1] N. J. Ling, 'Population Problems of China' in *Contemporary China*, ed. E. S. Kirby, Vol. I, 1956 (Hong Kong).
[2] S. Chandrasekhar, *China's Population* (Hong Kong 1959), p. 33.
[3] Ping-ti Ho, *Studies on the Population of China* (Cambridge, Mass. 1959), pp. 93–4.
[4] This, and following data, from Chandrasekhar (1959).

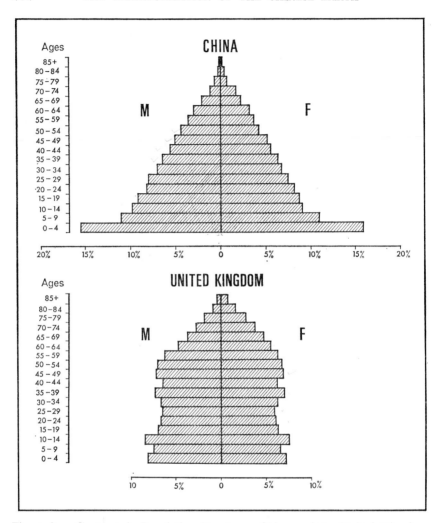

Figure 81. Contrasts in Population Structures: China and the United Kingdom. China's broad-based pyramid, with over one-third of the population aged less than fifteen years (as compared with less than one-quarter in the case of the UK), is typical of countries with a rapidly-expanding population.

Chandrasekhar's data show that, between 1952 and 1957, birth rates dropped from 37 per thousand to 34, death rates from 18 to 11, and rate of increase rose from 19 per thousand to 23. A similar rate of increase had already been recorded in the sample survey of five provinces and one Autonomous Region carried out in 1954; a later table, assembled by Chandrasekhar from various Chinese sources, shows a sharply climbing rate of increase for 1957 and 1958, and these figures, applied to a population of over 600 millions, now yield absolute increases of over 20 millions a year.

TABLE 18

GROWTH OF CHINA'S POPULATION
(Mainland Only)

Year	Population	Increase over Preceding Year Numbers	Percentage
1953	587·9 m.	13·1 m.	2·3
1954	601·7 m.	13·8 m.	2·3
1955	614·6 m.	12·9 m.	2·2
1956	627·8 m.	13·1 m.	2·2
1957	649·5 m.	21·7 m.	3·4
1958	673·0 m.	23·5 m.	3·6

Source: Chandrasekhar (1959), p. 55.

'It is possible', he observes, 'that some 25 million more persons will be added to the population next year (1959). During the last one decade of the new régime the population has increased by more than 130 millions.'

THE DEMOGRAPHIC REVOLUTION: Historical Background & Determinants

This massive and accelerating expansion of population, after long centuries of slow and erratic population increase, serves to underline how effectively the new régime has tackled the 'catastrophic deterrents' which drastically limited the rate of population growth.

Throughout China's history flood and drought have caused untold suffering and, by drastically cutting back population, have maintained a precarious balance between man and food supply. Drought caused the greatest famines; the 1877–78 famine on the loess plateau resulted in between 9 and 13 million deaths, and was equalled by that of 1928 which caused 3 million deaths in Shensi alone. The 1931 Yangtse floods rendered 12 million homeless, those of 1935 affected 14 million people. The classical Malthusian checks have thus certainly operated at many points in China's history; their influence is reflected in past growth rates which between 1779 and 1850 averaged 0·63 per cent per annum, dropping to an average of 0·3 per cent between 1850 and 1953.[1]

It is important to stress that these drastic checks to growth have always been of relative importance and that their impact was greatly aggravated by wars, social disorders or the weakness of the central government. Today, a strong central government, an efficient local administration and a boldly conceived policy of social and economic development are reducing and will eventually eliminate the 'catastrophic deterrents' to population growth. The social and political

[1] Ping-ti Ho (1959), p. 277.

changes since 1949, and above all the development of the commune system, have made possible a vast programme of irrigation and river control and this programme is wiping out many of the old causes of poverty and insecurity.   The events of 1959 to 1961, when the country was affected by unprecedented droughts and floods, showed that the Chinese are achieving a high degree of mastery over their environment and thus over their demographic future.

The commune system has also provided the institutional framework for a nation-wide attack on disease and poor hygiene; indeed, R. Hughes suggests 'that the greatest and most enduring achievements of the organised communes . . . will prove to have been recorded in these basic advances in public health and hygiene . . .'   He goes on: 'In theory, this development of medical care in Chinese villages need not have waited on the development of the commune.   But, in practice, the communes came first: it is as though the harsh regimentation of life was a necessary discipline for the prolongation and protection of life.'[1]

SOME ECONOMIC IMPLICATIONS

The immediate economic problem is that of providing food for a population of over 700 million, increasing at a rate of over 20 millions a year.   Ho observes, 'It seems possible for China even to increase food production at a rate higher than that of her population growth for a limited number of years if advanced agricultural technology is widely introduced.   But the long-range prospect is bound to be far different. In the first place, her present population is already very large and even a moderate sustained growth will be a great strain on her agriculture. Secondly,   more   labour-intensive   cultivation   and   introduction   of advanced agricultural technology cannot in the long run prevent agriculture from reaching the point of diminishing returns.'[2]   In China, however, the success achieved in expanding food production confirms many experts in their view that, with agricultural techniques in a process of rapid transformation, they are very far from even approaching the point at which the principle of diminishing returns begins to operate.   Certainly, the scope for increasing output on the existing (or even a reduced) crop area is very large while from a long-term viewpoint there remains the possibility of pushing the agricultural frontier deeper into the arid and microthermal regions of the West and Northeast and of reclaiming for arable or tree cropping the uplands of Central and South China which were devastated by robber-farming in the seventeenth and eighteenth centuries.   At the present, then, it is difficult to envisage a major food shortage as a limiting factor to population growth in the foreseeable future.

[1] R. Hughes, *The Chinese Communes* (London 1960), p. 71.   See also the views of visiting Western doctors cited by Felix Greene, *What's Really Happening in China* (San Francisco 1960), pp. 11–13.   [2] Ping-ti Ho (1959), p. 195.

The problem of absorbing into the country's economy the increasingly large contingents entering the working age groups is more immediately critical. The annual increase is estimated as 4 million during the First Five Year Plan, 5 million during the Second Five Year Plan and 7 million during the Third Five Year Plan. The cities, it is estimated, can absorb approximately one million industrial workers annually; the residue must be absorbed in the rural areas. Some commentators see the development of the commune system, with its massive investment of labour in major irrigation and flood control projects and its drive for widely dispersed industrialisation, as an attempt to cope with this problem. As Leo A. Orleans writes, 'Almost simultaneously with the abandonment of the birth control policy came the creation of the Communes and the inauguration of the now famous "great leap forward". Whether the timing here was planned or fortuitous is not known, but the effects are indisputable. By utilising millions of men in numerous construction projects . . . an artificial labour shortage was created. But can this conceivably represent a real and lasting solution to the crucial problem of growing over-population, or is it simply a temporary moratorium.'[1]

This paradox of a 'labour shortage' in a country suffering from what Dean Acheson termed 'an unbearable pressure on the land' has been analysed in some detail by the Dutch scholar W. F. Wertheim.[2] Wertheim bases his assessment on field investigations in China in 1957 and 1964 and concludes that, *over the short term*, the Chinese thesis that 'rapid increases of per acre yields in the already intensively cultivated areas should have pride of place in economic planning' is valid. The success achieved in increasing yields and absorbing labour is based, he points out, on the rapid expansion of irrigation and drainage facilities initiated during the 'Great Leap Forward'. At first sight it might seem that the partial mechanisation represented by electric or diesel pumps (instead of man-operated *norias*) for irrigation and by the beginning of tractor cultivation would merely aggravate the problem of under-employment and surplus population. Since, however, these technological changes help to increase the number of crops that can be harvested they effectively create the demand for more rather than less labour. Such labour is needed for the maintenance and extension of irrigation and drainage systems, for transport and for collecting and distributing the very large quantities of manures now being used. Backed by an increasing knowledge of agricultural science and by the possibilities of rational deployment of the labour force within the framework of the commune these new techniques are making possible an

[1] Leo A. Orleans, 'Birth Control: Reversal or Postponement', in *The China Quarterly*, Number 3, July-September 1960, p. 65.

[2] W. F. Wertheim, 'Recent Trends in China's Population Policy' in *Science and Society* (New York), Spring 1966, pp. 129–35. The question is examined in a broader perspective by the same author in 'La Chine est-elle surpeuplée?' in *Population* (Paris), May-June 1965, pp. 477–514.

increase in crop output which, in Wertheim's view, is sufficiently large to keep production well ahead of population growth. He sums up his impressions thus: 'An all-out effort to raise the number of harvests and the yields from the traditional agricultural areas creates a more or less artificial demand for man-power and allows a first step towards mechanisation. At the same time, the surpluses produced help to provide a basis for industrial development, both by the central government and the communes'. He adds: 'The Chinese attack on the agrarian problem can be considered an original contribution to the special type of over-population, characteristic of the irrigated rice areas of southern and eastern Asia'.

Such a solution is, he recognises, a temporary solution only, in that the mechanisation of a wider spectrum of agricultural activities, which is essential if development is to be sustained, will ultimately convert the present labour shortage into a labour surplus. As this point approaches, and once the food base is secure, if Chinese planners wish to 'perpetuate the situation of "lack of man-power" as a precondition to further mechanisation' further diversification of the rural economy—including a programme directed towards the intensification of production in the at present economically-marginal upland areas—and rapid industrialisation will become essential.[1]

Developments in recent years underline the critical need for an increase in the productivity of labour and for the continued diffusion of technical education if such industrialisation and diversification are to make their maximum contribution. From this point of view it may be argued that China's ambitious programme of technical education and the wide diffusion of part-work, part-study schools will play a major role in easing, if not actually solving, her population problem. Sauvy has said that 'an over-populated country is an under-educated country'[2] and has shown how, in Western Europe, the increase in technical competence, by making possible an increasing diversification of the economy, has significantly eased the pressure of population. In a country such as China his concept has an even greater relevance.

It is argued by some that the high rate of population growth makes it difficult for China to accumulate funds and for a country desperately striving to emerge from poverty and to modernise this is a pressing need. A writer in the *People's Daily* (Peking) expressed the view, 'If the speed of our population growth slows down, improvements in the livelihood of our people will quicken correspondingly'. Others, such as Su Chung, have claimed that 'Facts show the opposite. In 1952, 18·2 per cent of China's national income went into accumulation; it rose to 22·5 per cent in 1956.... Accumulation by peasants and co-ops is also rising. In the First Five Year Plan, the sum increased

[1] See Pierre Gourou, 'Notes on China's Unused Uplands' in *Pacific Affairs*, 1948, pp. 227 ff.
[2] A. Sauvy, 'Evolution récente des idées sur le surpeuplement' in *Population* (Paris), June-July 1960, p. 481.

by 47 per cent. . . .'[1] However, it seems clear that the provision of consumer goods and of social services (including schools and housing) must, in the case of a country with a rapidly expanding population, absorb investments which might otherwise have been diverted to strengthening the heavy industry sector of the economy; the result will be a retarded pace of economic development.

'PLANNED BIRTHS' OR 'LAISSEZ-FAIRE'?

The birth control 'campaign'—or, as the Chinese prefer to call it, 'education movement'—appears to have been inspired by the considerations discussed above. Public discussion of the need for population control began in 1954 when Deputy Shao Li-tzu raised the problem before the People's Congress. He stressed that 'his plea for birth control had nothing to do with decadent, outmoded and reactionary Malthusian doctrines. [It] was based on the need for protecting and improving the health of hard-working Chinese mothers and affording better opportunities for their children.'[2] By mid-1955 the official support of these ideas was indicated by Premier Chou En-lai's plea for 'appropriate control in respect of births'. The peak of the campaign was reached in March 1957 when a Birth Control Research Committee was set up 'to coordinate experience and research in contraception'. 'Birth control . . . and planned childbirth', said the Minister of Health, 'are actually indispensable to morality and the State's responsibility to the people.'[3] The more enthusiastic newspapers suggested targets for the campaign—a lowering of the urban birth rate by 30 per cent and of the rural birth rate by 20 per cent; in Shanghai the local newspaper announced that in that city 'over 60,000 people will practise contraceptive methods this year'. Population control was to be achieved by contraception (120 million sheaths were sold in 1957), by clinical abortion, by late marriage or by the sterilisation of either partner. Mass education campaigns in the cities, and pamphlets, contraceptives, and medical advice in the rural areas, spread the new ideas throughout China.

In early 1958 there was an abrupt change in policy. There was strong criticism of those who regarded the population problem as a barrier to economic progress and socialisation, and an increasing emphasis on labour shortages. By the end of 1958 the official line— that a large population was an asset—was firmly re-established. Han Suyin discusses the change in policy and suggests that it was a response to the psychological and practical needs of the situation; that 'it is not correct to speak of China as having reversed its policy . . . what can be

---

[1] Su Chung, *loc. sup. cit.*
[2] S. Chandrasekhar, in *Contemporary China*, ed. E. S. Kirby, Vol. III (Hong Kong), p. 23.
[3] Leo A. Orleans, (1960), p. 61.

U

said is that the government is suspending judgement'.[1]   The psychological need for a re-examination of the situation arose from the necessity of considering peasant reactions.   Any policy of family limitation
might well suggest to the peasant 'that the future was insecure, that a
famine was impending, since the government asked them to have fewer
children'.   That meant the government was frightened there would
not be enough food to go round.   Panic of this kind in China is enough
to paralyse the countryside, to set off extraordinary reactions and to
sap the foundations of the order which the Chinese government was
trying to achieve.   The practical basis for a re-evaluation of the
situation lies in the fact that capital accumulation in China still depends
on the labour of men's hands since machinery is not available and,
in the transition period during which a technologically competent and
scientifically educated peasantry emerges, all the ambitious plans for
the remodelling of the country's economy demand heavy investments of
man-power.   'So many things are being done together, at the same
time, that there is a *shortage* of man-power in all fields of activity.'   This
interpretation, it will be seen, is rather different from the interpretation
of Leo Orleans cited above.   Han Suyin sums up: 'There is, therefore,
no incentive to limit families as a *necessity*; but there remains the incentive to limit the family as a *convenience*. . . .   With a higher standard of
living, and since a large family *is* an inconvenience, the majority of
China's people may demand family planning as a convenience, but at
present this is still a minority.'

THE FUTURE

While the published material available is not sufficiently complete
to make any final appraisal of the situation, it will be apparent from
the account above that official policy on birth control has shown
major shifts; indeed, as Han Suyin remarks, 'There are no such things
as inflexible policies in China, at any time'.   How soon any major
change in present policies will come depends largely on the speed with
which Chinese agriculture is mechanised.   Mechanisation is still a
fundamental goal of Chinese agricultural planning but it is not accorded
the priority it was given at the time of the Great Leap Forward and,
at the time of writing, appears to represent the next stage of development after the current phase of intensification through improved water
control and heavier use of manure and fertilisers.   During this present
phase, the fact that the Chinese have, in Wertheim's words, 'found out
that for the time being a still more intensive cultivation of the fields in
the lowlands produces an increase of yields far greater than the population increase' makes possible a temporary *economic* solution to the

[1] Han Suyin, 'Birth Control in China: Recent Aspects' in *The Eugenics Review*, Vol. 52,
Number 1, 1960, p. 20.

pressure of population. Nevertheless, the *demographic* solution, through various techniques of birth control, is a good deal more in evidence than in 1958. The dissemination—and the use—of various techniques of birth control is evident from the data for some of the communes visited (see pp. 164, 167); what is equally evident is that the growth rate is still high, apparently of the order of 2 per cent per annum.

It was the long-term relationship between mechanisation and population growth which lay at the core of the 'New Principle of Population' enunciated by Dr. Ma Yin-ch'u, President of Peking University, in 1957. He expresses the core of his argument in the extract which follows:

> My Principle of Population is different in stand from Malthus's. I believe that the more developed the Socialist enterprises are, the more expanded will mechanisation and automation become. A thing which formerly required 1,000 persons to accomplish will require only 50 persons. Then, may I ask, what are we going to do with the 950 persons? For this reason I am worried that with more people we cannot become mechanised and automatised at a high speed. One of the reasons for our inability to build any large-size industries and for the necessity of our building more small and medium-size industries is because small and medium-size industries can take in many workers. But since our country is heading towards Socialism, we should build a large number of large-size industries. Lenin also said that without large-size industries there can be no Socialism. However, since our population is too large, it drags down the speed of industrialisation and prevents us from taking the big strides forward. Some people call me a Malthusian; yet I call these people dogmatists and anti-Leninists.
>
> Among the 13-million increase this year, only one million can find jobs in industries, while the other 12 million will have to work in the countryside. But nowadays each peasant can create a wealth of at most some 80 yuan for the State each year, while a worker in a factory, because of modern technical equipment, can create a wealth of over 4,000 yuan for the State each year. The ratio of these two is 1:50. The principal reason for such a huge difference between these two rates of productivity is because industrial production can make use of modern technical equipment while agricultural production can only use draft animals as the main motive power.[1]

The analysis has an *apparent* validity as far as the long-term situation is concerned, but the present writer would question some of the assumptions on which it is based. Thus, the Chinese have, in the last decade, demonstrated that it is possible to build up an expanding network of both small and medium industries *and* large industries. They have shown how, at least in the early stages of rural development, mechanisation, increasing employment and rising levels of living are

[1] Quoted by Chandrasekhar, *op. cit.*, pp. 28–9; see also Orleans, *op. cit.*, pp. 70–3.

not incompatible.   They are showing an increasing awareness of the convenience of smaller families and an increasing willingness to accept some form of family limitation, and this will ultimately show itself in a slackening of population growth rates.   They are, in their rural areas, succeeding in creating a socialist society 'without large-size industries'. Maybe, too, they are less concerned with the questions of relative production levels than was Ma Yin-ch'u and more with the quality of life, with narrowing the gap between the industrial and agricultural sectors. . . . .

But intensification, diversification, the fuller use of at present under-used sections of the Chinese environment no less than mechanisation are going to depend on the existence of a trained and qualified labour force.   Herein, perhaps, lies the major justification for the massive educational drive which was one of the most striking developments following the rise of the communes and for the part-work, part-study schools which may prove to be the most efficient (as well as the most original) technique for creating a politically-conscious *and* techno-logically competent rural and industrial labour force.

CHAPTER 14

Towards a Reappraisal of China's Intellectual Resources

IN EARLIER sections we have outlined some of the ways in which, since 1949, the Chinese have been integrating new resources into the country's economy and striving to achieve full utilisation of resources whose existence has long been known but which, for a variety of reasons, have never been fully utilised. China's population falls into this latter category; under-employment and unemployment emphasised that, even quantitatively, full use of the population resources was far from being achieved, while widespread illiteracy and the lack of any opportunity for technical training meant that even those who *were* employed could contribute only at the simplest and most rudimentary level. Alfred Sauvy has drawn attention to the relationship between lack of education and 'over-population'—and the problems of over-population in Old China certainly stemmed largely from lack of education and technical skills; this prevented the development of a diversified economy and condemned the great majority of the population to a poverty-stricken rural existence. Moreover, illiteracy, by limiting the degree of participation in the social and political life of the nation, meant that this majority was leading a life that was little more than that of half-men.

Against this background the importance of the Chinese Government's drive against illiteracy, its rapid expansion of educational facilities at all levels, its heavy emphasis on technical training and its preoccupation with the full development of the individual as a social being, can be understood. All these developments are necessary if the full utilisation of China's biggest resource—the industry and competence of her 700 million citizens—is to be achieved. They are no less necessary if Chinese development is to be carried beyond the purely economic sphere which obsesses many Western planners and to achieve the avowed Chinese goal of creating 'a new type of socialist man'.

SOME PERSPECTIVES

China, like the countries of the Third World, has been faced with the need to carry through simultaneously a major programme of economic development and modernisation and a far-reaching programme of educational development. The situation she faced has—and this is frequently overlooked—been quite different from that faced by Western Europe during the economic expansion which was ushered in by the Industrial Revolution; in Western Europe the creation of a new economy began in the eighteenth century and was far advanced when education began to be extended to the mass of working folk in the late nineteenth century. The contrast has been explained by Paul Bairoch; says Bairoch:

> If, for the developed countries, economic 'take-off' could be accomplished without being handicapped by the level of illiteracy of the population, it is because totally different conditions existed at the beginning of the nineteenth century; techniques used in industry at that date were unsophisticated and based above all on simple causal relations. Today things are different, science has taken a preponderating place in technique, and, as a result, in economic life and especially in industry. It is for this reason that the question of illiteracy today takes on a form different from that at the beginning of the nineteenth century, and this is the reason why—rightly moreover—the emphasis is today put on this problem in the developing countries.[1]

Jacques Freyssinet goes further and stresses the *increasing* relative importance of trained personnel in the production process:

> technical progress in general tends to reduce the importance of natural resources in the combination of productive forces. More and more it is technical equipment and a highly skilled labour-force which constitute the principal element.[2]

And, he adds, 'it is technical and economic progress which creates natural resources and not the other way round'[3]—which is an economist's reformulation of Carl Sauer's concept of natural resources as 'cultural appraisals'.

The problems which arise from the necessity of carrying through simultaneously an economic and an educational revolution are formidable enough, but they are aggravated by the fact that, in recent years,

[1] Paul Bairoch, *Diagnostic d'évolution économique du Tiers-Monde 1900–1966* (Paris 1967), p. 171.
[2] Jacques Freyssinet, *Le concept de sous-développement* (Paris and La Haye 1966), p. 26.
[3] *Ibid.*

the time gap between the development of new technologies and their application has been growing progressively narrower; countries struggling to modernise are thus, to quote René Gendarme's metaphor, rather like a man running to catch a moving train,[1] for they have to move swiftly from backwardness to the assimilation of new and rapidly changing techniques. . . . Yet, however poor they may be, or however great the difficulties, the developing countries simply cannot afford *not* to run, not to 'attempt to catch the train', not to make the sacrifices necessary to create an increasingly educated and skilled labour force. Indeed, it might be argued that, because of the conditions outlined above, investment in education has become one of the most profitable forms of investment, providing for poor and densely-peopled countries one of the most accessible roads to development.   It does this in three ways: by creating a 'climate of growth' and fostering the basic motivations on whose presence economic development (and social development) depends; by training personnel and inculcating the competences future economic and social development will demand; and by creating a dynamic élite who can fulfil a function analogous to that of the entrepreneur in the Western capitalist system but specifically adapted to the dominant socio-economic system of the country they will serve.[2] One of the first attemps to estimate the economic value of education in a society struggling to modernise was made in the Soviet Union in 1924; there a study made by the Gosplan indicated that, while a year's apprenticeship could increase the productivity of an illiterate worker by 12–16 per cent, four years of primary study would increase his productivity by 79 per cent and nine years of study by 280 per cent.[3] The strictly economic gain is obvious—but a developing country has to confront two problems: first, the sheer magnitude of the cost of an educational programme (especially if modelled on Western lines); secondly, the time-lag between the initiation of an educational programme and the results of the programme, in the shape of qualified students and technicians—at the minimum, five years if traditional patterns of Western education are followed.   The two are interrelated, since heavy investment in education may slow down the investment in other sectors, such as the build-up of capital equipment.   It is partly to meet these problems that the part-work, part-study schools have been evolved in China; these are largely self-supporting financially and their programmes are devised so that the student is, *from the beginning of his training*, integrated into the country's productive system (see below pp. 301–5).

Technical training is, moreover, a 'multiplier of jobs'; this may be illustrated in a very schematic form by taking the example of a group

---

[1] René Gendarme, *La pauvreté des nations* (Paris 1963), p. 473.
[2] See René Gendarme, *op. cit.*, p. 473.
[3] Cited by René Gendarme, *op. cit.*, p. 478.   Several of Gendarme's observations have been drawn on in this section.

of 500 illiterates who, left to themselves, would be engaged in traditional agriculture or unemployed; the introduction of an engineer, even with rudimentary training, makes possible new forms of activity such as the building of bridges or highways or the construction of irrigation systems; each engineer means the employment of, say, five overseers and these in turn make possible the employment of a hundred skilled workers, backed up by 500 untrained workers. The figures are obviously only very crude orders of magnitude, but they illustrate what Gendarme terms 'the cascade of jobs' which is created by education and technical training. We may note, in this context, the critical role of auxiliaries and technicians ('cadres' in the general sense) in multiplying the effectiveness of fully-trained people, and that one of the weaknesses of educational programmes in many developing countries has been the emphasis on training the maximum number of fully qualified people and the relative neglect of the need for technicians who can be trained much more rapidly and in much larger numbers. In medicine, in engineering and in agricultural science (to take the most obvious examples) such partially-trained people can play an important role; they can take over the responsibility for the less exacting tasks, thus making possible the optimum utilisation of the small number of highly-trained experts; and they can play an important role in the rapid dissemination of new techniques deep in the countryside. Few developing countries can afford either the time or the money needed to provide *all* the trained specialists they need; a policy of 'walking on two legs' in educational and technical training is dictated by the social and economic realities of their situation.[1] The progress of China—whether in industry, agriculture or medicine—relative to other 'under-developed' countries is explained partly by the Chinese adoption of such a dualistic programme. Stalin claimed that of all the forms of capital the most precious and most decisive was represented by a country's cadres[2] and, whatever else of Stalin's concepts may have been discarded, this remains, as the Chinese example shows, the golden rule—or the iron rule—of Communist development.

Finally, we may stress that those who are educated—and I use the word in the broadest sense to include those technically trained—not only pass on the 'know-how' of their own special field but also play a critical role in transmitting or reshaping the values of society. It is in the second of these two roles that the greatest weakness of the educational programmes of many emergent countries lies, for only too frequently education—and especially advanced education—merely alienates those who are trained from their own society. The modelling of educational systems in a backward economy on the systems achieved

---

[1] For a brief statement of the policy, see Leo A. Orleans, *Professional Manpower and Education in Communist China* (Washington 1961), pp. 24–6.

[2] Joseph Stalin, *Address to the Red Army Academy*, 4 May 1935, quoted in part in J. T. Murphy, *Stalin* (London 1945), pp. 179–80.

in Europe (and maintained with difficulty) only after two or three centuries of economic development places a major burden on the economy, limits the proportion of the population who can be educated even at the primary level, and is creating a new, educationally-privileged, élite, a new 'mandarinate'. Moreover, since this élite group has often completed its training in the West it returns imbued with Western standards of material comfort and remuneration; as a group it tends to be externally-oriented and the excessive material advantages (in the shape of wage-levels and the like) it succeeds in achieving for itself isolate it completely from the mass of its fellow countrymen. Under such conditions, its impact on the values of society is largely destructive and its role as an agent for the transmitting of new ideas is circumscribed by its isolation. Education is thus in danger of creating what I have described elsewhere as:

> a glaring gap between the reality of the new élites and the quality of the leadership needed to achieve an effective 'breakthrough' in an under-developed country. . . . These groups are the 'new millstones' tied around the necks of the emerging countries. . . .[1]

Chinese educational planners, perhaps partly as a reaction against the mandarin system of traditional China, have striven vigorously to avoid the emergence of new and privileged classes as a result of education and have sought to make education a process which not only disseminates technical know-how but also inculcates a clear awareness of the human values of the new society and of the role of the individual in upholding and strengthening these values. The programme has been ambitious and not without its difficulties (notably the conflict between the 'reds' and the 'experts' in the cadre group),[2] but it has been based on a much clearer understanding of the real needs of an emergent country than is to be found in any other under-developed country.

Because of the increasing scarcity of statistics after 1960, the educational programme of the People's Republic is most conveniently considered in two phases: for the first phase, lasting up to the early nineteen-sixties, we have sufficient statistical data for at least a broad outline of developments; for the second phase, which culminates in the Cultural Revolution, the paucity of statistics means that our account must be impressionistic. This second phase, it may be noted, is characterised by an increasing preoccupation with the content and purpose of the educational programme; education is viewed increasingly as one of the means whereby the new 'socialist man' is fashioned, and there is an

---

[1] Keith Buchanan, 'New Millstones for Old—John Donne and the Economic Stagnation of Africa' in *Comment* (Wellington), July-August 1964, pp. 6–14 and references cited therein.

[2] For an illuminating discussion of this, and of the recruitment and role of the cadre group, see Franz Schurmann, *Ideology and Organisation in Communist China* (Berkeley and Los Angeles 1966), especially pp. 162–72.

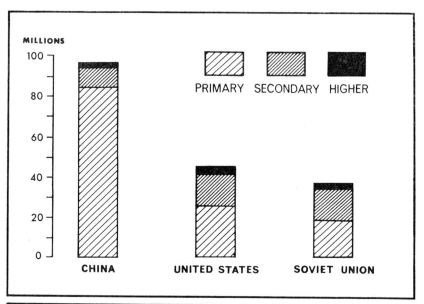

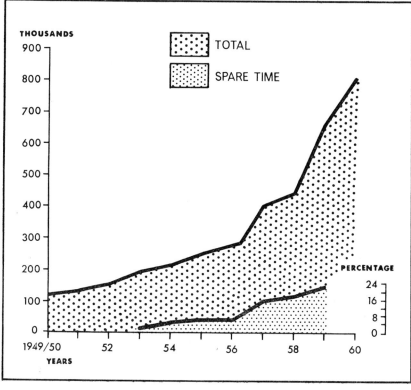

increasing preoccupation with the creation of an educational system specifically suited to the needs of Chinese conditions.

LAYING THE FOUNDATIONS

In 1949 over four-fifths of China's population was illiterate, education a privilege enjoyed by a favoured few, skilled technicians were rare and highly trained scientists and research workers rarer still.   Under these conditions the tasks facing the People's Government in the education field were clear: to teach the masses to read and to write; to expand the school system to bring in as many children as rapidly as possible; to train an increasing number of skilled and semi-skilled workers; and, by the development of advanced education and research institutes, to greatly expand the country's resources of scientific man-power.   Only if these tasks were achieved could the objectives which the Chinese economic planners had formulated be attained; in the words of an American report 'they had to insure the present and future needs of the country with the skilled man-power needed to achieve their objectives'.[1]

The drive against illiteracy aimed at eliminating illiteracy by 1963–64, and in 1958 some 40 million people were attending anti-illiteracy classes and another 31 million were attending spare-time secondary or primary classes.   It is true that the standard for minimal adult literacy was set relatively low—for peasants it meant 1,500 characters and for urban workers 2,000 characters—and with this level of competence it is possible to read only the most simple type of text.   Nevertheless, 'to have raised (by 1957) some 22 million illiterates even to this minimum standard of literacy through spare-time study must be considered a major accomplishment'.[2]   The extension of literacy was facilitated by two important linguistic reforms—the introduction of

[1] Leo A. Orleans, *op. cit.*, p. 5.   [2] Leo A. Orleans, *op. cit.*, p. 51.

Figure 82.   Development of China's Intellectual Resources.

One of the major factors making for progress has been the rapid development of education; this is directed towards wiping out illiteracy and creating a trained and competent work force in industry and agriculture.

The bar-graphs at the top illustrate the size of the problem; in 1958–59 almost 100 million were enrolled in primary or secondary schools or in institutes of higher education.   This total exceeds the combined enrolment of the USA and the USSR and the provision of even modest educational facilities for such a huge student population is a major burden in a country in the process of emerging from decades of exploitation and under-development; only by the large-scale development of various techniques of 'self-help' (see text) is an effective confrontation of the problem possible.

The graph below shows enrolment in institutes of higher education; note the steadily increasing proportion of part-time students.   In the last two or three years the emphasis on part-work, part-study forms of education means that the old distinction between student and worker (as made in this graph) is becoming increasingly meaningless.   (Data from Leo A. Orleans.)

simplified versions of Chinese characters and the experimental introduction of a more or less phonetic romanised script. This policy of
romanisation, however, came up against the difficulty posed by the
diversity of Chinese dialects; only if one dialect (e.g. the Peking
dialect) is taught throughout the country could it succeed. It should,
moreover, be emphasised that the aim of this reform was not to replace
the Chinese characters with the phonetic alphabet but merely to speed
up the learning process. The drive against illiteracy and the creation
of scripts for the minority peoples is referred to above (p. 41).

The progress in the field of formal education is indicated by the fact
that, in less than a decade, enrolment in primary schools increased by
60 millions and in institutes of higher education by 500 per cent. This
rapid increase inevitably involved some sacrifice of quality—in 1956,
for example, two-fifths of the primary school teachers had not completed
their junior secondary education—and this was recognised by the
Chinese who regarded it as a transitional phenomenon. Expenditure
on education has represented in recent years one-tenth of the expenditure in the State budget. The 'Great Leap Forward' in 1958 brought
a rapid increase in numbers attending educational institutions of all
types; it also saw the initiation of a policy of integrating education and
productive work. Universities, secondary schools and primary schools
set up small factories in which pupils received technical training and
which helped, if only on a small scale, to boost output figures and to
defray the cost of the pupils' training. At the same time, there was a
rapid increase in the number of schools operated by factories, by
communes, by street committees and the like. Most of these were of
a spare-time variety, with little equipment and staffed by teachers with
minimal levels of training. These schools were designed to be self-
supporting and to supplement those operated by the State and their
development has enabled the State to pass on to the masses part of the
financial burden imposed by the rapid growth in student numbers.
The policy is described by the Chinese in the following terms:

> We are guided by the principle of the coordination of uniformity
> and diversity, of popularisation and acceleration of standard, and of
> overall planning by the central authorities and delegation of power
> to the localities. We have put into effect a programme with equal
> emphasis on schools operated by the State and those operated by
> factories, mines, enterprises, governmental organs, civic bodies,
> armed forces, people's communes, cities, and street organisations;
> on full-time, part-time, and spare-time education; on popular
> education and vocational education; on school education and self-
> education; and on tuition-free and tuition-paying education.[1]

Looking at the various sectors of the educational system, primary
school enrolments went up from 24 million in 1949 to 90 million in

[1] Quoted by Leo A. Orleans, *op. cit.*, p. 25.

1959–60; secondary general schools increased their enrolment from one million in 1949 to 8·5 million in 1958–59; secondary specialised schools (teacher-training and vocational schools) had 1·4 million students in 1958–59. The numbers enrolled in institutes of higher education rose from 117,000 in 1949 to 810,000 in 1959–60; of these, almost one-quarter were spare-time students.[1] The general fields of specialisation are indicated in the table below:

TABLE 19

ESTIMATED DISTRIBUTION OF POPULATION
WITH COMPLETED HIGHER EDUCATION (1960)

Field of Specialisation	Number (000)	%
Engineering	171·7	27·5
Natural Sciences	38·0	6·1
Medical Sciences	51.6	8·3
Education	134·7	21·5
Agriculture	39·0	6·2
Finance and Economics	69·7	11·2
Law and Social Sciences	66·9	10·7
Liberal Arts	53·4	8·5
TOTAL	625·0	100·0

Source: Orleans (1961), p. 128.

An approximate indication of the progress of China by comparison with some of the other nations of mainland Asia is given by Paul Bairoch; his data,[2] incomplete though they are, show significant contrasts in the educational achievement of the various countries:

TABLE 20

NUMBER OF STUDENTS IN ENGINEERING
AND AGRICULTURE
(per million inhabitants)

India (1962)	220		
Pakistan (1963)	76		
Thailand (1963)	120		
China (1957)	340	(1954	180)

As a result of her educational drive China had, by 1957, a proportion of scientists in training 50 per cent higher than that attained by India five years later, and almost five times higher than the level achieved by Pakistan in 1963. One of the problems in a free-enterprise system —and this applies in most countries of the Third World—is that those

[1] Data from Leo A. Orleans, op. cit.   [2] Paul Bairoch, op. cit., p. 177.

with skills move, like capital, to those regions or sectors of the economy where the remuneration is highest and not to those areas where the social need is greatest.[1] This can be avoided in a totally-planned economy such as that of China where the ultimate placing of graduates is determined by the State Economic Commission in the light of the country's needs. In 1956, for example, 24 per cent of the graduates were to be sent abroad or to advanced research institutes, 25 per cent went to departments and agencies of the Ministry of Heavy Industry and 34 per cent of them to the service of the provinces, the Autonomous Regions or the municipalities.

TOWARDS A NEW CONCEPT OF SOCIALIST EDUCATION

Chinese educational planning has had three major aims: First, to raise the general level of education of the whole population; secondly, to create the technical and administrative cadres necessary for the planned development of the economy; thirdly, to imbue the young with the political and social ideals essential if China is to achieve a true socialist society.[2] The number of children attending school rose from 75 million in 1953 to over 100 million in 1960; the proportion of the school-age population receiving some form of education rose from 60–70 per cent in 1957 to 90 per cent in 1960.[3] And, in a new drive against illiteracy introduced in 1958, it was planned to give some 220 million folk the rudiments of literacy by the end of the Second Five Year Plan (1963).

After the period 1958–60 statistics on Chinese education became increasingly fragmentary; two important reforms initiated in 1958 have, however, been put into practice and the whole educational system has, in consequence, undergone a profound transformation. There has been a widespread development of 'people's schools', run by factories, by communes or by production teams and on either a seasonal or night-school basis; some of these receive varying degrees of State aid, others are financed completely by the collective establishing them. By the early 'sixties half a million of such 'people's schools' were teaching 30 million children.[4] Secondly, and of much greater importance, the schools (and the colleges and universities) were regarded increasingly not only as 'educational' centres where certain theoretical competences were learned but also as production units (see pp. 303–5 below); as such they became to a large extent self-financing and this

---

[1] Thus, in 1966, 46 per cent of the scientists and specialists who migrated to the USA came from the under-developed countries, and of the Asian students working in the USA 80 per cent remain there after completing their studies. Keith Buchanan, 'The Myth-spinners' in *New Zealand Monthly Review*, October 1968, pp. 6–7, drawing on a UN survey made by Professor Ehsan Naraghi.

[2] For a valuable summary of events up to 1964 see Michel Cartier, 'Planification de l'enseignement et formation professionnelle en Chine continentale' in *Tiers Monde* (Paris) April-June 1965 pp. 511–30.

[3] *Ibid.*, p. 523.   [4] Michel Cartier, *op. cit.*, p. 524.

made possible a much wider diffusion of education than would other-wise have been possible. Moreover, the integration of theory and practice, of 'education' and production, was in line with Mao Tse-tung's concept of socialist education as expounded in his lecture *On Practice* as far back as 1937:

> Knowledge begins with practice, and theoretical knowledge which is acquired through practice must then return to practice. The active function of knowledge manifests itself not only in the active leap from perceptual to rational knowledge but—and this is more im-portant—it must manifest itself in the leap from rational knowledge to revolutionary practice.[1]

Such a policy not only makes it possible to break down the barriers which separate the intellectual from the worker; more positively, it gives a new reality to the learning acquired in school or college, since this learning can be constantly tested against the experience the student acquires in the course of his work in the factory or the field and is enriched by the experience of the masses among whom he moves. Moreover, the policy makes it possible for the competence of the student to be used in the reconstruction of his country with the minimum of delay, a factor of major importance in a developing country where skills of all sorts represent one of the major resources. The policy is bringing a revolution in educational attitudes and teaching methods; says Michel Cartier:

> It is essential that the students should be able to use the knowledge acquired as rapidly as possible. It is for this reason that an attempt has been made to associate the students with programmes for the drafting of courses and text books as well as to develop in them a spirit of initiative. To a certain degree, teachers and students take part together in the carrying out of certain scientific pro-grammes and technical projects. The students of the Ching-hua Technical University at Peking have effectively collaborated in the carrying out of several technical projects such as the construction of the dam and the hydroelectric generating station at Mi-yün, near Peking.[2]

These developments are welcomed by the students themselves who claim that after technical training on the well-worn traditional lines they 'needed two years of practical work to get their feet on to solid ground again'[3] and are elements in a complete recasting of the educa-tional system; it was, indeed, attacks on the then existing system which ushered in the 'Great Proletarian Cultural Revolution'. This recasting of the educational system is based upon the Chinese conviction that a

---

[1] *Quotations from Chairman Mao Tse-tung* (Peking 1966), pp. 209–10.
[2] Michel Cartier, *op. cit.*, p. 527.
[3] Quoted by Jean Baby, 'Chine populaire: réduction de la durée des études et fusion avec les masses ouvrières et paysannes' in *Le Monde Diplomatique* (Paris), September 1968, p. 6.

truly socialist society, based on humane values, is by no means an inevitable outcome of an initial success in the workers' revolution; the example of developments within the USSR and the other European socialist states is, they argue, sufficient to demonstrate this.   Rather will it come:

> only as a result of a very long, difficult, and painstaking process of education and the development of a political consciousness, *following* the winning of the battle for control of basic economic (and other) institutions.   The Cultural Revolution is the highest expression therefore in China of this educational process.[1]

What this 'painstaking process of education' means in practical terms was spelled out by the Central Committee of the CCP in its statement made public on 8 August, 1966.   Because this lays down the broad guide lines along which Chinese education is now proceeding the relevant section of the statement is quoted below in full:

> In the great proletarian cultural revolution a most important task is to transform the old educational system and the old principles and methods of teaching.
>
> In this great cultural revolution, the phenomenon of our schools being dominated by bourgeois intellectuals must be completely changed.
>
> In every kind of school we must apply thoroughly the policy advanced by Comrade Mao Tse-tung, of education serving proletarian politics and education being combined with productive labour so as to enable those receiving an education to develop morally, intellectually and physically and to become labourers with socialist consciousness and culture.
>
> The period of schooling should be shortened.   Courses should be fewer and better.   The teaching material should be thoroughly transformed, in some cases beginning with simplifying complicated material.   While their main task is to study, students should also learn other things.   That is to say, in addition to their studies they should also learn industrial work, farming and military affairs, and take part in the struggles of the cultural revolution as they occur to criticise the bourgeoisie.[2]

This decision indicates the general line of development and is not a firm and detailed policy laid down by the Party; indeed, the same document states in forthright terms: 'the only method is for the masses to liberate themselves, and any method of doing things on their behalf must not be used'.

McKelvey, like Huberman and Sweezy,[3] sees in this programme not

---

[1] Donald McKelvey, *Socialist Man and the Chinese Revolution: The Basis of the Cultural Revolution* (Radical Education Project, Ann Arbor, Michigan 1967), p. 2.

[2] 'Decision of the Central Committee of the C.C.P. Concerning the Great Proletarian Cultural Revolution', text given in full in *Peking Review*, 12 August 1966, p. 8.

[3] Leo Huberman and Paul Sweezy, 'The Cultural Revolution in China' in *Monthly Review* (New York) January 1967, pp. 11–17.

only a programme to win the young for the Revolution and its goals but also an attempt to contain and control the growth of the élite group and to ensure that this group does not emerge as a social class with interests antagonistic to those of the masses.   That such an attempt is necessary is clearly evident from the other emerging nations whose political and educational élite constitute a major obstacle to real political and economic development; that this may happen also in a socialist country is suggested by the recent history of the USSR.   The Chinese, it would appear, are satisfied that the country's economy is now strong enough to withstand the disruption and disorder inseparable from the gigantic educational experiment on which they have embarked.   The policy of putting 'politics in command' is regarded with scepticism in the West, if not as a prescription for economic and social chaos on a nation-wide scale.[1]   To the Chinese it implies that 'in economics, participation by the masses and good organisation are more important than machinery—as long as one's goal is building socialism and not just raising production'.[2]   The Chinese Revolution, the war in Vietnam, have vindicated the belief that on the battlefield men are more important, and ideas more decisive, than the most costly and sophisticated machines, and the Chinese are now beginning to demonstrate that truth in the field of peaceful construction.   It may be long years before we are in a position to judge how large a measure of success they achieve, whether by education (in the widest meaning of the word) they *can* transform the mental and emotional landscape of the Chinese quarter of mankind.   But in their implications for the remainder of humanity, in both the proletarian and the wealthy nations, the steps they are now taking are even more momentous than the massive remodelling of their physical environment we have described. . . .

THE PART-WORK, PART-STUDY SCHOOL
'Walking on Two Legs' in Education

The development of the part-work, part-study school has been, as noted earlier, one of the distinctive features of educational development in China in recent years.   Such schools have two major advantages: first, they are to a high degree self-supporting and thus make limited calls on the funds needed for the development of other sectors of the economy; secondly, they help to bridge the gap between worker and intellectual by integrating productive work, whether in industry or in agriculture, into their overall training programmes.   Details are given

[1] Thus most Western sources stress the economic impact of the 'disorders' (which the Chinese, in the 1966 decision of the Central Committee of the CCP concerning the Cultural Revolution, recognised as inevitable); only one source points out that the dislocation on the railways and at the ports was 'hardly on the devastating scale experienced in Britain', *China Trade and Economic Newsletter* (London), February 1968, p. 8.   It's the old case of the mote and the beam in the eye of the observer (or the expert).

[2] Donald McKelvey, *op. cit.*, pp. 1–17.

W

below of two such schools, one located in Peking and geared to the needs of the industrial sector of society, and one in Shansi, geared to the needs of an increasingly diversified agriculture; the details below refer to 1966.

(a) INDUSTRIAL SCHOOL IN PEKING

This was developed as a part-work part-study school from 1965 and in 1966 was one of 110 such schools in the Peking municipal area. It has a total enrolment of 744 students with 32 teachers and 43 technical instructors. The course is a four-year course and the usual age of enrolment is 16–17 years. The training is based on the idea that courses should be such as to serve the present and future needs of the country; that an all-round development of student potential should be aimed at, and that the combination of practical work and study achieves these ends. The courses, it is held, should be few but extensive —so that the student gets the maximum opportunity to weld together theory and practice. The courses include politics, physical training, Chinese, mathematics, physics, chemistry, engineering designing, structural engineering, electronics, welding and general knowledge; in addition, students have a choice of special courses such as basic industrial designing, principles of metallurgy, and machine-tool design. Students are expected to specialise, but at the same time it is recognised the specialisation must rest on a broad general knowledge. The pattern of work in 1966 was one of alternating weeks of study and factory work and this applied to both students and teachers.

The school is completely residential and one-half of the students are girls. There is no charge for schooling or books and students are provided with working clothes; they also receive a subsistence allowance which ranges from 13 yuan per month in the first year to 18 yuan in the fourth year. The working day is 7 hours in the first year (six days a week) and 8 hours in later years. After graduation the students are placed by the People's Council as technicians in various enterprises in Peking; by contrast, students from the technical institutes are trained for work in any part of China.

The combination of work and study achieves one of the CCP's policies—that education should 'serve proletarian politics and train technicians who are both socialistically-minded and proficient in both mental and manual work'. The school appears to be largely self-supporting (a good deal of the equipment is made by the students themselves) and contributes by creating wealth for the State in the shape of machinery, manufactured to meet orders placed by the various Ministries, which can be used in the factories of Peking. Lathes, grinding machines and electrical equipment were among the items recently completed. The school staff stressed that the path of development had not been easy and that many shortcomings had to be overcome; nevertheless, after an initial experimental period of five years, they saw these part-work, part-study schools becoming the dominant instrument of education over much of China. One must add that, at least to a non-technical eye, the finish and quality of the machinery awaiting delivery to the State were an impressive achievement, more especially if the age of the pupils is borne in mind.

(b) Agricultural School in Shansi

This part-work, part-study school developed out of an ordinary middle school in 1965. It has an enrolment of 530 students and 109 staff members and cadres. The school is in a formerly largely monocultural region which, with the development of irrigation, is becoming increasingly diversified in its economy; it offers courses in crop husbandry, animal husbandry and tree crop cultivation. It has approximately 150 acres of land which it farms; one-third of this was reclaimed land and one-third is under orchards. The veterinary station which is part of the school has 25 horses or donkeys and 23 pigs. The grain output from the school's land (wheat, maize, sorghums) was worth £14,000 in 1965; in addition, members earned some £3,000 by side-line occupations such as afforestation or working on the railways. The grain output alone, it may be noted, was sufficient to meet the running expenses of the school for eight months. The school has classrooms, laboratories, a veterinary clinic and dormitories and houses for staff and students. Part of the school is accommodated in what was once a landlord's house; in addition, thirty-three buildings have been constructed (and five wells sunk) since the school was established. The students come from adjoining communes and will return there when trained as technicians. The curriculum includes both lectures and laboratory work and long periods of productive work; the approximate break-up of the year is six months' study, five months' productive work and one month's vacation. The productive work includes work on the school's land or in the communes of the region; students and teachers will go and work in the surrounding countryside six or eight periods of three months during the school's three-year course. During such periods of work in the countryside they advise the peasants on matters of crop production and crop diseases and carry out treatment of, and simple operations on, farm animals. This increasing emphasis on productive work has been made possible by a reduction in the lecture load; this reduction has been, on the average, of the order of one-third.

The multiplication of schools such as this, which are largely self-supporting and whose programmes are closely integrated with the needs of the rural community, is an essential step in creating that pool of cadres and technicians critical to continuing progress in the Chinese countryside.

CHAPTER 15

A Summing-up: 'After the Dust has Settled . . .'

The agents of change in this world are today, as they have always been, those whose battered lives stand most in need of change. The entrepreneurs of social progress are those whose condition requires it. And at bottom, this revolution is nothing but the emergence of competitors who employ the only means of competition available to them. Revolution is the collective free enterprise of the collectively dispossessed.

Carl Oglesby[1]

Whatever China today takes from outside, she undoes and refashions in her own way, as the Romans of old pulled Chinese silk to shreds and wove it afresh into fine gauze for their ladies.

François Geoffroy-Dechaume[2]

ANY SUMMING-UP of the condition of a nation which contains almost one-quarter of humanity presents obvious and inevitable difficulties. These difficulties are enhanced by the 'earthquakes of change' which over recent decades have transformed—and, indeed, are still transforming—Chinese society and by the continuing scarcity of the detailed information upon which any precise assessment must depend. The Chinese experiment is, moreover, one of the most controversial features of our time; it has been attacked, in whole or in part, by both the United States and the Soviet Union and has been the subject of continuous misrepresentation by the politicians, the newspapers and other mass media in both the Western and Eastern bloc countries; only in French publications is there any real attempt to analyse and understand the processes at work and the goals towards which the society of China is oriented. And inevitably any assessment

[1] Carl Oglesby and Richard Shaull, *Containment and Change* (New York and London 1967), p. 111.
[2] François Geoffroy-Dechaume, *China Looks at the World* (London 1967), p. 48.

comes up against the whole question of academic objectivity . . . and this calls for a 'profession of faith' on the part of the writer.

I believe that today academic objectivity is impossible. The Chinese experiment must be seen in its global context, as an attempt by one sector (albeit a critically important sector) of mankind to break out of the stagnation and subhuman conditions in which the great proportion of mankind live out their travesty of a life. The great majority of people in the West disapprove of the means the Chinese are using to forge a modern economy, stressing the human cost of revolutionary change and deploring the sacrifice and austere discipline which alone may make a new society possible. Such folk ignore, conveniently, the sacrifice of two or three generations which alone made possible the industrial emergence of the West, that the affluence they enjoy has, as Frantz Fanon pointed out, 'been built up with the sweat and the dead bodies of negroes, Arabs and Indians and the yellow races'.[1] And, addressing himself to such folk, an English Quaker poses the basic question:

> But what of the pain and violence of No Revolution when poverty, cruel, uncompromising, intolerant of human dignity, is as close to every man and woman as dole and soup kitchen are to workers in an industrial depression; when human relations are conditioned more by want than by love and fellow-feeling, and in beggar and prostitute each man and woman glimpses an abhorrent, but perfectly possible future?[2]

When the issues are posed thus, human (or academic) objectivity is seen to be impossible; if only out of a sense of human solidarity we are—we must be, whether we like it or not—involved. We are either *against* those who are striving to create for their children what they see as a better life (and this does not mean 'better' as we, products of a totally different historical experience, may see it) or we are *for* them, recognising that the very immensity of the tasks they confront will inevitably entail many errors of judgement, that, in the words of Gunnar Myrdal:

> All the underdeveloped countries are now starting out on a line of economic policy which has no close historical precedent in any advanced country.[3]

Recognising, too, that the solutions they find may, and this is surely obvious, have little or no validity as solutions to the problems we in the affluent societies confront. . . .

It may also be underlined (though this should not be necessary) that

---

[1] Frantz Fanon *The Damned* (Paris 1963), trans. Constance Farrington, p. 76. (English edition published by Penguin Books under the title of *The Wretched of the Earth* (1967).)
[2] Peter Townsend, *China Phoenix* (London 1955), p. 13.
[3] Gunnar Myrdal, *Economic Theory and Underdeveloped Regions* (London 1963), p. 102; for some of the differences see the works of Paul Bairoch referred to above (pp. 104–5).

the academic objectivity within which many scholars claim to work is spurious. Robert Engler, writing of social sciences in the West, stresses that 'modes of analysis and tools are never neutral'; he goes on:

> In economics the employment of so-called neutral tools means that the current goals of the economic system are taken for granted. Indeed, the teaching of economics is often a thinly disguised dressing up of business education in a more respectable liberal-arts garb. Growth is good and the gross national product (how apt a label) is a value-free measure. That is, the manufacture of harps and napalm, cigarettes and cancer research, all are dumped on to the same scale to record the onward march of the economy—and incidentally, to justify the way we live and assess priorities.[1]

'Academic objectivity' or academic 'neutrality', of this type—and Engler is describing, not the views of a small minority but the views of nine out of every ten scholars in the Western world today—will clearly find no meaning in a system such as the Chinese are building; a system motivated by moral rather than material incentives can, it will be demonstrated, never work and the Chinese concern with the 'quality of life' rather than material production must be a fraud or a hoax. It will be abundantly evident from what I have written that I lay no claim to this sort of 'academic objectivity'.

*　　　*　　　*

Closing a long review of my earlier short volume on China[2] Professor Frederick Hung comments: 'It will be interesting to see what Buchanan has to say after the dust has settled.'[3] The 'dust' to which Professor Hung refers is the turmoil created by the Cultural Revolution.

I, too, am interested in the character of Chinese society which is emerging, in the cultural landscape—the pattern of agriculture and stock-rearing, mining and industry—which the people of China are creating. Nevertheless, even if I am granted the biblical span of 'three-score years and ten', I doubt whether in these next two decades the dust will have settled sufficiently for anyone to pronounce a final judgement. The Chinese experiment is only just beginning; to date the Chinese have taken but 'one step in a ten thousand-league march' and, in the decades ahead, as they press forward on their journey towards a new society, the dust haze is not likely to lift. Moreover, the present Cultural Revolution is but the precursor of others yet to come; in the words of Mao Tse-tung in December, 1967:

> The present great cultural revolution is only the first; there will inevitably be more in the future. In the last ten years we have said

---

[1] Robert Engler, 'Social Science and Social Consciousness' in *The Dissenting Academy*, Theodore Roszak ed. (New York 1967, 1968), p. 195.
[2] Keith Buchanan, *The Chinese People and The Chinese Earth* (London 1966).
[3] In *Geographical Review* (New York), October 1968, pp. 691–2.

repeatedly that the issue of who will win in the revolution can only be settled over a long historical period. If things are not properly handled, it is possible for a capitalist restoration to take place at any time. It should not be thought by any Party member or anyone of the people in our country that everything will be all right after one or two great cultural revolutions, or even three or four.[1]

The concept of some sort of stability or 'normalcy' in which a final evaluation is possible, and which is implicit in Professor Hung's statement, has little relevance in the case of a country which has embarked on a process of 'continuing revolution' as a means of effecting a total transformation of the mental attitudes of its people and of the physical environment they are shaping. . . . Perhaps, too, it is pertinent to add that if we believe, as many analysts do, that the 'Chinese experiment' can be best evaluated by comparing it with the experience of other countries who are seeking to overcome *their* problems of poverty and under-development, then we confront not only the problem of the 'dust' raised by the Chinese Cultural Revolution but also the murky and chaotic condition of much of the Third World, in Southeast and Southern Asia, in the Middle East, in parts of Black Africa and over much of Latin America. (As I write this, there are riots in Zambia and Mexico City, and war in Nigeria, simmering violence in the Middle East and a Presidential take-over in Brazil.) Meanwhile, in the developed countries, the whole financial system limps from crisis to crisis. If we are to get the Chinese situation into perspective we must see it against a background of a world riven by dissension and shadowed with violence and whose whole financial structure is tottering. Perhaps to someone working in Peking the difficulties of evaluating what is happening in the rest of the world is impeded by the 'dust' raised by *these* outbreaks of violence and simmering unrest. . . . The Chinese are seeing more and more clearly where they are going; can the same be said about the rest of humanity?

*   *   *

Looking back over this volume I cannot but be aware of the extent to which the nature of the source material I have used has shaped the form of my work. Much of the material, especially for the most recent period, was of a generalised nature, lacking in sharp statistical precision. Other material, including some of the material collected in the field, is more detailed and much more sharply focused. This contrast, together perhaps with my own approach and style of writing, results in an overall impression somewhat like that of a Chinese landscape with distant hills, forested or craggy, suggested by a few broad strokes of the brush, and with the figures and the dwelling places in the foreground sharply etched and in painstaking detail. Or perhaps like a painting

[1] Quoted in *Outlook* (Sydney), June 1968, p. 10.

by Chi Pai-shih in which a few careful—yet seemingly careless—washes of colour suggest the leaves or petals above which a gauze-winged dragonfly, perfect in its detail, is hovering. . . . Broad strokes and detail are both essential, though many might wish for more detail, for the carefully-etched and precise picture which, given the tenuous and suspicious nature of the relations between China and the West, it is impossible to present.   My picture is impressionistic, at times selectively so. . . .

Certain broad themes do, however, emerge.   First, the tremendous reappraisal of the Chinese earth which followed the coming to power of the People's Government in 1949.   This reappraisal has changed many of our old ideas about China's resource endowment.   It has demonstrated that the country has the mineral resources essential for the country's development as a major industrial power, has shown that many of the limiting factors to agricultural development, if not yet completely overcome, could be attenuated, and it has begun to release the tremendous yet formerly largely latent energy represented by the intellect of over 700 million people.   This intellectual emancipation is perhaps the greatest single event of contemporary history, an event which will shape the last three decades of this century.   That this type of reappraisal of resources does not follow inevitably on political emancipation is demonstrated by the majority of newly-emergent countries.   The example of China illustrates the importance of breaking the stranglehold of old structures; this is seen most clearly in the agricultural sector where the total destruction of the old agrarian structure, followed by the creation of a new system designed to integrate the peasant into the structure of the new society, is the only way in which real rural development can be got under way.   The example of China illustrates also the importance of dedicated and determined leadership; this was provided initially by the CCP and the core of cadres tempered in a long revolutionary struggle, subsequently by newly-trained cadres to whose formation the Chinese have given a high priority.

Secondly, the Chinese People's Republic is, as René Dumont has stressed, the only 'under-developed' country to begin the process of 'economic take-off' relying almost entirely on its own resources.   Today it has no overseas debts, a satisfactory balance of trade, and a continuing high rate of capital investment, features which make it almost unique among the world's major powers.   It has achieved its present position by a flexible planning policy, increasingly realistic in its recognition of errors and increasingly thorough in their correction, and by the use of its most abundant resource—man-power—as a substitute for scarce capital and scarce capital goods.   It is in its policy of 'turning labour into capital' that China offers its most important lesson to the other emerging countries, and especially the densely-populated Asian countries; in these, one of the most tragic features is the wastage of human abilities resulting from large-scale unemployment and under-employment at all levels in society. The importance of the political factor in development asserts itself again in this context; only if the labour force can be effectively mobilised, only if a sense of dedication among the masses can be awakened, can the dragging burden of a large population be converted into a factor for progress—and to achieve all these things a large and highly-trained body of cadres is essential. A comparison of Chinese and Indian schemes of rural development is instructive in this context.

The third theme I would stress is the Chinese success in developing a 'dualistic' economy or, as they put it, in 'walking on two legs'. The technique of combining agricultural and industrial development, new and traditional techniques, small-scale labour-intensive local industry and large-scale capital-intensive modern industry within a developing economy represents an important achievement of Chinese planners. It is a developmental technique which has proved particularly suited to the conditions of China and could undoubtedly be employed in other emergent countries where similar conditions prevail. Gunnar Myrdal has warned the emergent nations of the danger of swallowing uncritically the scarcely rational economic theories of the West; for such emergent countries China provides not a blueprint but an example of how, relying on one's own resources and relating the character of planning to the specific qualities of the human and physical environments, the problems of development can be attacked. The development of the spirit of self-reliance is an important aspect of the policy of 'walking on two legs'. China is now self-reliant as a nation and this self-reliance reaches down to take in the smallest economic units, for local development, whether of agriculture, industry, mining or the social services, means the encouragement of local initiative, the use of local resources, increasing local self-sufficiency. . . .

The fourth important theme, and one which asserts itself increasingly, is the Chinese emphasis on non-material incentives and their attempt to narrow as much as is possible the 'spread' of wages and other material incentives; with this goes a strong emphasis on 'the quality of life', on the development of 'a new socialist man'. In capitalist society the major incentive to increase production is the material incentive; as E. L. Wheelwright remarks:

Put at the crudest level, this is the 'bribing'—by material means— of individuals to put forth the maximum effort, and acquire the necessary skills. In China this is regarded as 'economism', as contrary to the communist ethos: it is believed to breed inequality and competitive values, and in any case is regarded as unsuitable for Chinese conditions because it would accentuate the differences in living standards between town and country. Hence the Maoist stress on 'putting politics in command', which means developing a socialist morality. This, in essence, is what the cultural revolution is about, *basic human values* . . .[1] (emphasis in original).

Moral incentives are playing an increasing role in the Chinese economy; they seem to be an important factor in the upsurge of production noted by many sources since 1966.[2]

Finally, the Chinese, in the very process of downgrading the importance of material incentives, are, consciously or unconsciously, introducing a vision of the future which is far more realistic than the vision purveyed by the West. The conditions which made possible the contemporary affluence of the West, conditions which included and include the plundering of a great deal of the world, are not going to be repeated;[3] that we should purvey our Way of Life to, that we should imply our levels of wealth are attainable by, the peoples of the emerging countries is either downright dishonest or irresponsibly naïve. The types of development these countries will need are those that will put a sufficiency of food into the belly of each of their citizens and which will absorb all their labour—and this means a pattern of high densities of population, producing their own food, running small factories when they are not working on the land and with a limited number of large capital-intensive modern industrial centres. The Chinese experience in these things is important; even more important is the realism with which they accept that the most that can be aimed for is a meagre and modest level of living . . . no one rich, no one starving. And an affluence attained at the cost of their fellow men, whether in China or elsewhere in the world community, has no place in their thinking or their planning; the sense of human solidarity is, if I may judge from discussions with peasants, workers and intellectuals in many parts of China, a powerful motivating force.

These are some of the major themes in contemporary Chinese society, and it is within the framework of action and thought they encompass that the Chinese are initiating the present—and most decisive—phase in the transformation of the Chinese earth and, we may add, of the 'intellectual landscape' of the country. Whether we applaud or condemn is irrelevant; the Chinese have always been patient, accustomed to a much longer time-scale than we in the West, and they can afford, as Robert Guillain puts it, to 'go their way without worrying what people think about them'.[4]

[1] E. L. Wheelwright, 'Impressions of the Chinese Economy (ii)' in *Outlook* (Sydney), August 1967, p. 8.

[2] See, for example, *China Trade and Economic Newsletter* (London), *passim* and above, pp. 242–7.

[3] On this aspect see Heather Dean, *Scarce Resources: the Dynamic of American Imperialism* (Radical Education Project, Ann Arbor, c. 1966). She quotes (p. 3) the introduction to the survey *Resources in America's Future*: 'It should be pointed out clearly, however, that our conclusion that there is no general resource shortage problem for the balance of the century applies specifically to the United States; it cannot be extended automatically to other countries. In many less developed countries, especially in Asia, Africa and Latin America, population presses hard on available natural resources; for them a sustained increase in living levels can by no means be guaranteed with the assurance it can be for the United States and other more advanced industrial countries'. On this see also Claude Julien, *L'empire américain* (Paris 1968), esp. chap. VI.

[4] Robert Guillain, *Dans trente ans la Chine* (Paris 1965), p. 8.

APPENDIX

THE BASIC UNITS IN THE
ENVIRONMENT OF CHINA

EFFECTIVE ELABORATION of a State plan for the full use of the country's soil and water resources depends to a considerable extent upon a precise classification and evaluation of China's natural environment. Such a classification must integrate in an effective fashion the major elements of the environment—temperature and moisture conditions, soil conditions and relief conditions—giving each its appropriate weight and should rest on bases sufficiently precise statistically to permit increasing refinement and correction as fresh data are accumulated by workers in the various environmental studies. The first draft of such a 'regionalisation' has been completed by the Institute of Geography of the Chinese Academy of Sciences; its main features have been described by Professor Huang Ping-wei[1] and are summarised in the paragraphs below and in Maps 83 and 84.

The major (or higher-stage) units in the classification are based on natural conditions which it is impossible or very difficult to alter (e.g. climatic conditions); the secondary (or lower-stage) units on conditions, such as soil conditions or micro-topography, which are more readily transformed by man. Initially, three primary areas or sectors are distinguished: the Eastern Monsoonal Sector, the Mongolian-Sinkiang Highlands and the Chinghai-Tibetan Highlands; the most important natural features of these three major environments, together with the major manifestations of man's influence on these features, are set out on pages 314–15:[2]

[1] Huang Ping-wei, 'The Complex Natural Zonation of China' in *USSR Academy of Sciences: Geographical Series* (Moscow), 1961, No. 1, pp. 25–39 (in Russian).
[2] *Ibid.*

Percentage of area of country	46%
Major factors defining regional natural differences	Variation in amount of warmth and of temperatures, depending on latitude (northwards from the line of the Tsingling range—river Hwai), also variation in conditions of humidity with varying distance from the sea.
Neo-tectonic movements and topography	Small uplifts; eastwards of the line Chinchow-Chengchow-Peking-Hopei subsidence predominates. Absolute heights over the greater part of the territory are not more than 1,000 m. In the regions of subsidence a large percentage of the area is below 500 m. and there is a spacious plain of accumulation.
Climate	Great influence of summer monsoon, comparatively high humidity.
Hydrography	Surface water predominantly from rain supply, sufficiently abundant ground water.
Exogenous processes	Continual weathering, river erosion and accumulation; abrasion and accumulation along the sea coast; weathering by frost in high-latitude mountain regions, aeolian erosion and accumulation in some regions.
Soils	In comparison with the other two sectors, soil profiles comparatively well developed; mechanical composition relatively fine; high humus content; small quantity of dissolved salts; territorial differences often significant.
Vegetation	Predominantly forests, partially steppes.
Phylocoenoses	Ancient coenoses were destroyed little by the Quaternary glaciation. Flora very varied. Geography of plants very complex.
Natural historical factors	Slight evolution from the Quaternary glaciation conditioned the multiformity of biological species; several plants from the end of the Mesozoic and Tertiary periods have been preserved. Ancient red crusts of weathering distributed very widely south of the river Yangtze.
Influence of human activity	Man's influence very great. Almost all the area fit for ploughing is in use, natural forests have been mostly felled; soil profiles destroyed by erosion. In a varying degree waters, micro-climate and micro-topography have been modified.
Basic problem of land utilisation and transformation of nature	This is the most important agricultural region in China, here agrotechnics are gradually being improved; chemical techniques are being applied; irrigation, mechanisation and electrification of agriculture is increasing. Hills and mountain ranges occupy more than half the territory. A wide development of forestry and animal husbandry is necessary.

MONGOLIAN-SINKIANG HIGHLANDS (part of the Eurasian steppe-desert zone) 27·3%	CHINGHAI-TIBETAN HIGHLANDS 26·7%
Variation in conditions of humidity with varying distance from the sea.	Strong vertical zonation.
Distinct differentiated uplifts. Plains at a height of about 1,000 m. intersect mountain ranges.	Large-scale and recent uplift. Largest highlands in the world. Absolute heights more than 4,000 m. Many mountains above the snow line.
Arid and semi-arid.	Rarified atmosphere, low temperatures, strong insolation, little rainfall, strong winds.
Most have no external runoff. Surface waters, predominantly from rain supply, dry up. Several lakes (principally salty); very important runoff from mountains, formed from snow thaw. Small reserves of ground water.	Most have no external runoff; many glaciers and lakes.
Slight weathering, water erosion and accumulation; strong aeolian erosion and accumulation; glacial exaration and accumulation in mountain regions.	Strong physical weathering, glacial and river accumulation.
Mechanical composition comparatively coarse, small humus content; quite a few soluble salts.	As a consequence of slight chemical weathering mechanical composition of parent material very coarse. Soil profiles poorly developed.
Predominantly deserts, partially desert steppes. High mountains covered with forests and mountain steppes.	Predominantly deserts, steppes and meadowland. Slopes of mountains and mountain valleys forest-covered.
From the end of the Mezozoic, in the process of developing an arid and semi-arid climate, a gradual xerophylisation of the vegetation took place. Flora poor.	Formed after the Quaternary glaciation in the process of upheaval. Apart from Tsaidam, the vegetation of the sector is slightly linked with Mongolian-Sinkiang vegetation. Flora very poor.
In view of low intensity of exogenous processes, the topography, formed by endogenous forces, has been well preserved. In the Quaternary period the climate was comparatively humid; in some places relics of the ancient river systems are very widespread. Above 3,500 m. there are glaciers the Quaternary ice-age.	Widely distributed glaciers of the Quaternary ice-age.
Man's influence comparatively small. Only in Inner Mongolia, in Ningshia, and in the regions where runoff from mountains allows fields to be irrigated, is it more significant.	Influence of man extremely slight.
In irrigated regions agriculture is being developed; in the dry and desert steppes— animal husbandry; in the mountains forestry and animal husbandry. The chief problem is the development of irrigation, making possible stabilisation of the sand and the prevention of salinisation of the soils.	Animal husbandry is the basic occupation of the population. In a few places agriculture and forestry can be developed. The principal problem is the lack of heat, shortage of water, strong winds, and the coarse mechanical composition and small water-holding capacity of the soil.

The more detailed break-up of the country rests initially upon temperature and moisture conditions. As we have seen, if we exclude the Chinghai-Tibetan Highlands, with their marked altitudinal zonation, six major thermal belts, defined in terms of 'accumulated active temperatures', can be distinguished.

Superimposed on these thermal zones, which trend broadly E–W, are the four major humidity zones; these are used in the first stage of regionalisation, for contrasting humidity conditions make it possible to distinguish, within the major thermal belts, four major categories of region: humid, semi-humid, semi-arid and arid (see Figure 83).

The combination of temperature and humidity data makes possible a division of China into eighteen areas or sub-areas; this initial stage in the regional subdivision of the country is illustrated in Figure 83. The pattern is most complex in the northeastern sector where seven areas are distinguished, in contrast to the three major regions of the sub-tropical and tropical southeast; the northwestern arid sector is subdivided into two areas on the basis of temperature and the Chinghai-Tibetan sector into three areas based on moisture conditions (as evidenced by the vegetation cover). These eighteen areas are in turn subdivided into twenty-seven 'zones' and 'sub-zones',[1] each characterised by a distinctive soil-vegetation complex. The basis on which this subdivision rests varies from area to area. Thus, the semi-humid area (2B), semi-arid area (2C) and eastern sector of the arid area (2D) in the temperate belt, the semi-humid area (3C) of the warm temperate belt, and the semi-arid area of the Chinghai-Tibetan highlands (7C) are divided into zones on the basis of distance from the sea (and hence of increasing dryness). Within the semi-humid area of the temperate belt, the boundary between the zonal subdivisions is drawn along the border between leached and typical chernozems (which coincides approximately with the boundary between forest-steppe and steppe); in the steppe-chernozem zone the soils retain moisture badly, are liable to salinisation and drought. A soil boundary is also used to subdivide the temperate semi-arid area and the eastern sector of the temperate arid area. In the former it is the boundary between the dark-chestnut and light chestnut soils; on the dark-chestnut soils the grazing capacity is approximately twice that on the light-chestnut soils and dry-farming gives higher and more stable yields than on the light-chestnut soils. In the temperate arid area a zone of desert steppes (with a xerophilous and grass cover suitable for cattle-rearing) is separated from a zone of grey-brown desert soils with a discontinuous plant cover of limited pastoral value.

By contrast, the zonal subdivision of the subtropical humid area of eastern China (4A1) is based largely on the thermal conditions; the

---

[1] Of the eighteen areas and sub-areas, ten consist of only one zone, the remaining eight of two or three zones.

zonal boundaries thus trend broadly east-west.   In the northern zone the accumulated active temperatures are below 5,000°, which rules out the cultivation of citrus fruits, tung and double-cropping of rice. Humidity conditions are less favourable than further south and less favourable temperature and humidity conditions mean that evergreen broadleaved trees are relatively rare and some of the other trees (e.g. some of the conifers) grow relatively slowly.   In the central zone accumulated active temperatures exceed 5,000° and the summer is warm and prolonged.   Relative humidities are high and winters cloudy.   Citrus trees and tung trees can be grown, as well as tea and camelias and two crops of rice are commonly obtained; the truly 'tropical' crops, such as lichee and lungnan, do not, however, flourish. In the southern zone accumulated temperatures are above 6,000°, the winter warm, the period of low temperatures very short; under these conditions the cultivation of tropical fruits becomes a distinctive element in the economy.

Within the Chinghai-Tibetan sector the semi-arid area is sub-divided, on the basis of climatic and vegetation conditions, into a zone of forests (on the mountains) and meadow-steppes (on the lower-lying areas and plains; the arid area into a zone of dry deserts (e.g. the Tsaidam Basin) and a zone of cold deserts, characterised by low temperatures and high winds which, even where moisture conditions are relatively favourable, preclude the growth of any save the sparsest desert vegetation.

The major areas, sub-areas and zones, slightly simplified, are thus as follows (numbers and letters refer to Map 84):

1 *COLD-TEMPERATE BELT*
   1A Humid area
      1A1 Zone of coniferous forests and of brown podzolised soils

2 *TEMPERATE BELT*
   2A Humid area
      2A1 Zone of mixed coniferous-deciduous forests and podzolised brown forest soils

   2B Semi-humid area
      2B1 Zone of forest-steppe and leached chernozems
      2B2 Zone of steppes and chernozems

   2C Semi-arid area
      2C1 Zone of dry steppes and dark chestnut soils
      2C2 Zone of dry steppes and light chestnut soils

   2D^1 Eastern sector of arid area
      2D^{1}1 Zone of desert steppes and brown soils

2D^{1}2 Foothill zone of desert steppes and grey soils
2D^{1}3 Zone of deserts and brownish-grey desert soils

2D^2 Western sector of arid area
2D^{2}1 Zone of desert steppes and brown soils
2D^{2}2 Foothill zone of desert steppes and grey soils

3 WARM-TEMPERATE BELT

3A Humid area
3A1 Zone of broadleaved deciduous forests and brown forest soils

3B Semi-humid area
3B1 Zone of deciduous forest and leached *korichnevie* soils
3B2 Zone of deciduous forests and forest steppes and *korichnevie* soils

3C Semi-arid area
3C1 Zone of dry steppes and *heilutu* soils

3D Arid area
3D1 Zone of deserts and brown desert soils

4 SUBTROPICAL BELT

4A^1 Eastern sector of humid area
4A^{1}1 Northern zone of mixed evergreen and deciduous forests and of yellow-brown and yellow-*korichnevie* soils
4A^{1}2 Central zone of subtropical evergreen broadleaved forests and red and yellow soils
4A^{1}3 Southern zone of subtropical evergreen broadleaved forests and laterised red and yellow soils

4A^2 Western sector of humid area
4A^{2}1 Zone of subtropical evergreen forests and red soils

5 TROPICAL BELT

5A Humid area
5A1 Zone of tropical rainforests and lateritic soils

6 EQUATORIAL BELT

6A Humid area
6A1 Zone of equatorial rainforests (Nangsha archipelago, not shown on Map 84

7 CHINGHAI-TIBETAN HIGHLANDS

7B Semi-humid area
7B1 Zone of meadowlands and coniferous forests

7C Semi-arid area
    7C1 Zone of forests with meadowlands and meadow-steppes
    7C2 Zone of meadow-steppes and meadowlands

7D Arid area
    7D1 Zone of dry deserts
    7D2 Zone of cold deserts

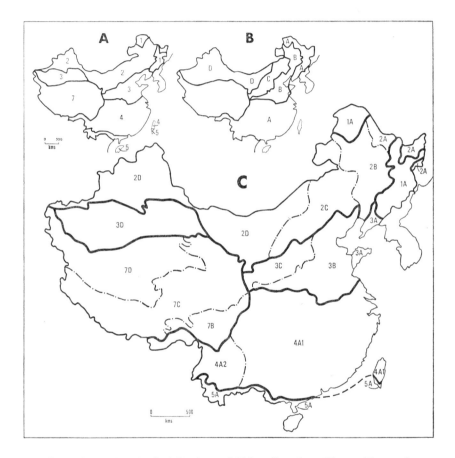

Figure 83. The Physical Regions of China (based on Huang Ping-wei).

Map A shows the major regions based on temperature conditions: 1. Cold-temperate; 2. Temperate; 3. Warm-temperate; 4. Sub-tropical; 5. Tropical; 7. Chinghai-Tibetan highlands (region 6, the equatorial region of Chinese islands in the South China Sea, is not shown).

Map B shows humidity zones: A. Humid zones; B. Semi-humid zones; C. semi-arid zones; D. arid zones.

Map C shows the initial regional break-up based on the combination of these two elements. The Chinghai-Tibetan area is subdivided into humidity zones on the basis of the vegetation cover.

x

These twenty-seven zones or subzones are, at the third stage of regionalisation, subdivided into ninety 'natural provinces'.   This third stage of subdivision 'reflects intrazonal climatic differences' and at this stage the geomorphological pattern becomes important since in some zones topography is the most important factor producing bio-climatic differences.   As a preliminary classification of topography in bio-climatic terms the following categories are distinguished:

1. Plains and hilly plains
2. Hills (relative height under 200 m.)
3. Low mountains (relative height 200–500 m.)
4. Mountains with well-defined intermontane plains and lowlands (occupying not less than 20 per cent of the whole area)
5. Mountains with well-defined vertical zonation and an absolute predominance of one belt or sub-belt (relative height up to 500 m.)
6. Mountains with well-defined vertical zonation and significant development of two or more belts or sub-belts (relative height greater than 500 m.)
7. High mountains and highlands with summits above the snow-line or close to it (relative height greater than 500 m.)

Micro-climatic differences may be of considerable importance in hilly areas and with increasing elevation there is increasing climatic differentiation, manifesting itself in a vertical zonation of soils, vegetation and crops.   Bio-climatic differences, however, are not necessarily conditioned by topography for areas of rather similar topography may show quite different bio-climatic features as a result of different geographic position.   This is implied in Huang Ping-wei's definition of the smallest unit in the present regional classification, the 'natural province'.   Natural provinces, he says, 'are the parts of natural zones with different bioclimatic features, or with different combinations of them, conditioned by a different topography or regional position'.

The major categories of topography and the final subdivision of China into these basic units are illustrated in Map 84.

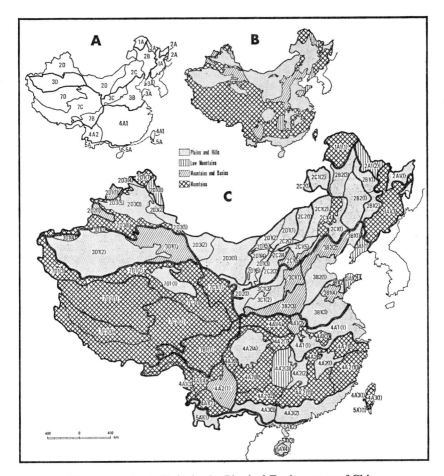

Figure 84.   Basic Units in the Physical Environment of China.

A. Major zones based on combination of temperature and humidity (see Figure 83 above).

B. Major types of land-form.

C. Further subdvision based on soil-vegetation conditions gives a total of 27 zones or sub-zones (see list pp. 317–19) and these, subdivided according to land-form type, give a total of 90 'natural provinces'.

Bibliography

(*The more important books are indicated by an asterisk*)

(i) GLOBAL PERSPECTIVES

* Albertini, J. M., *Les mécanismes du sous-développement* (Paris 1967).
* Bairoch, Paul, *Diagnostic de l'évolution économique du Tiers-Monde 1900–1966* (Paris 1967).
* Bairoch, Paul, *Revolution industrielle et sous-développement* (Paris 1963).
Barraclough, Geoffrey, *An Introduction to Contemporary History* (Harmondsworth and New York 1967).
Carrère d'Encausse, Hélène and Schram, Stuart, *Le Marxisme et l'Asie 1853–1964* (Paris 1965).
de Castro, Josué, *Le livre noir de la faim* (Paris 1961): English translation published as *The Black Book of Hunger* (New York 1968).
Cooper, David (Editor), *The Dialectics of Liberation* (Harmondsworth 1968).
* Dumont, René, and Rosier, Bernard, *Nous allons à la famine* (Paris 1966): English translation published as *The Hungry Future* (London and New York 1968).
Dumont, René, *Types of Rural Economy*, English translation, London 1957.
Dumont, René, *Lands Alive*, English translation, London and New York 1965.
* Fanon, Frantz, *The Damned* (Paris 1963): English translation published by Penguin Books under the title of *The Wretched of the Earth* (London and New York 1967).
Fossaert, Robert, *L'avenir du capitalisme* (Paris 1961).
Freyssinet, Jacques, *Le concept de sous-développement* (Paris and La Haye 1966).
Gendarme, René, *La pauvreté des nations* (Paris 1963).
George, P., *Questions de la géographie de la population* (Paris 1959).
Granick, David, *The Red Executive: A Study of the Organisation Man in Russian Industry* (New York 1961).
* Heilbroner, Robert, *The Future as History* (New York 1959).
Heilbroner, Robert, *The Great Ascent* (New York and Evanston 1963).
Horowitz, David (Editor), *Containment and Revolution: Western Policy towards Srial R evolutio n: 1917 to Vietnam* (London 1967).

Jalée, Pierre, *Pillage of the Third World* (New York and London 1968).
* Jalée, Pierre, *Le Tiers monde dans l'économie mondiale* (Paris 1968).
Johnson, Chalmers, *Revolution and the Social System* (Stanford 1964).
Lacouture, Jean and Baumier, Jean, *Le poids du Tiers Monde* (Paris 1962).
Mus, Paul, *Viet-Nam: Sociologie d'une guerre* (Paris 1952).
* Myrdal, Gunnar, *Economic Theory and Underdeveloped Regions* (London and New York 1963).
Notestein, F., *Demographic Studies of Selected Areas of Rapid Growth* (New York 1944).
* Oglesby, Carl and Shaull, Richard, *Containment and Change* (New York and London 1967).
Roszak, Theodore (Editor), *The Dissenting Academy* (New York 1967).
* Sampedro, José Luis, *Decisive Forces in World Economics* (London 1967).
Sauvy, Alfred, *Le 'Tiers-Monde': sous-développement et développement* (Paris 1961).
* Stone, I. F., *In a Time of Torment* (New York 1967).
Taber, Robert, *The War of the Flea* (New York 1965).

(ii) *CHINA: HISTORICAL SETTING*

Boulnois, Luce, *La route de soie* (Paris 1963): English translation published as *The Silk Road* (London and New York 1966).
Cottrell, Leonard, *The Tiger of Ch'in* (New York 1961; London 1962).
Dawson, Raymond (Editor), *The Legacy of China* (Oxford 1964).
* Eickstedt, E. von, *Rassendynamik von Ostasien* (Berlin 1944).
Feuerwerker, Albert, *China's Early Industrialisation* (Cambridge, Mass. 1958).
* Herrmann, A., *An Historical Atlas of China* (new edition edited by Norton S. Ginsburg and with a prefatory essay by Paul Wheatley) (Edinburgh and Chicago 1966).
* Lattimore, Owen, *Inner Asian Frontiers of China* (Boston 1962).
Martin, Bernard, *Strange Vigour: A Biography of Sun Yat-sen*, 3rd Edition (London 1967).
de Riencourt, Amaury, *The Soul of China* (London and New York 1958).
* Schafer, Edward, *The Golden Peaches of Samarkand* (Berkeley and Los Angeles 1963).
* Schafer, Edward, *The Vermilion Bird: T'ang Images of the South* (Berkeley and Los Angeles 1967).
Shih, Sheng-han, *A Preliminary Survey of the Book 'Ch'i Min Yao Shu'* (Peking, Second Edition, 1962).
Sorre, Max, *Les fondements de la géographie humaine: Tome 1, Les fondements biologiques* (Paris 1943).
Sullivan, Michael, *The Birth of Landscape Painting in China* (Berkeley and Los Angeles 1962).
* Watson, William, *China: Before the Han Dynasty* (London and New York 1961).
* Watson, William, *Early Civilisation in China* (London and New York 1966).
* Wiens, Herold, *China's March into the Tropics*, Office of Naval Research, U.S. Navy (Washington 1952).
Wittfogel, Karl, *Oriental Despotism* (New Haven 1957).

(iii) GENERAL WORKS ON THE ECONOMY AND THE SOCIETY OF CHINA

* Adler, S., *The Chinese Economy* (London 1957).
* Adams, Ruth (Editor), *Contemporary China* (New York 1966).
* Belden, Jack, *China Shakes the World* (London and New York 1952).
* Bettelheim, Charles, Charrière, Jacques and Marchisio, Hélène, *La construction du socialisme en Chine* (Paris 1965).
Buchanan, Keith, *The Chinese People and the Chinese Earth* (London 1966).
Buck, J. Lossing, *Land Utilisation in China*, Chicago 1937 (reprinted, New York 1964).
Buck, J. Lossing, Dawson, Owen L. and Wu, Yuan-li, *Food and Agriculture in Communist China* (New York and London 1966).
Chandrasekhar, S., *China's Population* (Hong Kong 1959).
Chao, Kang, *The Construction Industry in Communist China* (Chicago 1968).
Chen, Jack, *New Earth* (Peking 1957).
* Chen, Nai-ruenn, *Chinese Economic Statistics: A Handbook for Mainland China* (Edinburgh 1967).
China Reconstructs, *China in Transition* (Peking 1957).
Cowan, C. D. (Editor), *The Economic Development of China and Japan* (London 1964).
* Crook, D. and I., *Revolution in a Chinese Village* (London 1959).
* Crook, D. and I., *First Years of Yangyi Commune* (London 1966).
Cusack, Dymphna, *Chinese Women Speak* (Sydney 1958).
Donnithorne, Audrey, *China's Economic System* (London and New York 1967).
* Dumont, René, *La Chine surpeuplée: Tiers-monde affamé* (Paris 1965).
* Dumont, René, *Révolution dans les campagnes chinoises* (Paris 1957).
Eckstein, Alexander, *Communist China's Economic Growth and Foreign Trade* (New York and London 1966).
Elegant, Robert S., *The Centre of the World* (London and New York 1963).
* Etienne, Gilbert, *La voie chinoise* (Paris 1962).
Fitzgerald, C. P., *Floodtide in China* (London 1958).
Fitzgerald, C. P., *The Birth of Communist China* (Harmondsworth 1964; New York 1966).
Fitzgerald, C. P., *China: A Short Cultural History* (London and New York 1965).
Fitzgerald, C. P., *The Chinese View of their Place in the World* (London 1964).
Freemantle, Ann, *Mao Tse-tung: An Anthology of his Writings* (New York 1962).
Fried, Morton H., *Fabric of Chinese Society* (London 1956; New York 1968).
Geoffroy-Dechaume, François, *China Looks at the World* (London and New York 1967).
Gelder, Stuart, *The Chinese Communists* (London 1946).
* Gould, S. H. (Editor), *Sciences in Communist China* (Washington 1961).
Greene, F., *The Wall has Two Sides* (London 1962).
Greene, F., *What's Really Happening in China* (San Francisco 1960).
* Grossman, Bernhard, *Die Wirtschaftliche Entwicklung der Volksrepublik China* (Stuttgart 1960).
* Guillain, Robert, *Dans trente ans la Chine* (Paris 1965).

* Hinton, William, *Fanshen: A Documentary of Revolution in a Chinese Village* (New York 1966).
* Ho, Ping-ti, *Studies on the Population of China 1368–1953* (Cambridge, Mass. 1959).
Hsieh, Chiao-min, *China: Ageless Land and Countless People* (Princeton 1967).
Huard, Pierre and Wong, Ming, *Chinese Medicine* (London and New York 1968).
* Huberman, Leo and Sweezy, Paul (Editors), *China Shakes the World Again* (New York 1959).
Hughes, T. J. and Luard, D. E. T., *Economic Development of Communist China* (London 1959).
Hughes, R., *The Chinese Communes* (London 1960).
Joint Economic Committee, Congress of the United States, *An Economic Profile of Mainland China* (Washington 1967).
Karol, K. S., *China: The Other Communism* (London 1967; New York 1968).
* Kovda, V. A., *Soils and Natural Environments of China*, U.S. Joint Publications Research Service (Washington 1960).
Kuo, Ping-chia, *China* (London 1963).
Kuo, Ping-chia, *China: New Age and New Outlook* (Harmondsworth 1960).
Lamb, Alastair, *The China-India Border* (London 1964).
Lee, J. S., *The Geology of China* (London 1939).
Lethbridge, H. J., *The Peasant and the Communes* (Hong Kong 1963).
Levy, Roger, *La Chine* (Paris 1964).
Lindquist, Sven and Cecilia, *La Chine familière* (Paris 1963).
* Mao Tse-tung, *Selected Works of Mao Tse-tung* (Peking, 1963–), Volumes I–IV.
Mao Tse-tung *On the Correct Handling of Contradictions among the People* (Peking 1960).
Mende, T., *China and her Shadow* (London 1961).
Mitchison, Lois, *China* (London and New York 1966).
* Myrdal, Jan, *Report from a Chinese Village* (London 1965).
* Needham, Joseph, *Science and Civilisation in China* (Cambridge 1954—).
Orleans, Leo A., *Professional Manpower and Education in Communist China* (Washington 1961).
Orr, Lord Boyd and Townsend, P., *What's Happening in China?* (London 1959).
* Pelissier, Roger, *Le troisième géant: La Chine* (Paris 1965).
Petrov, Victor P., *China: Emerging World Power* (Princeton 1967).
* Purcell, Victor, *China* (London 1962).
Richardson, S. D., *Forestry in Communist China* (Baltimore 1966).
Robinson, Joan, *The Cultural Revolution in China* (Harmondsworth, 1969).
Roper, Myra, *China: The Surprising Country* (London and New York 1966).
Rostow, W. W., *The Prospects for Communist China* (New York 1954).
Roy, C., *Into China* (London 1955).
* Schram, Stuart, *The Political Thought of Mao Tse-tung*, revised edition (London and New York 1969).
* Schurmann, Franz, *Ideology and Organisation in Communist China* (Berkeley and Los Angeles 1966).
Sheng, Hu, *Imperialism and Chinese Politics* (Peking 1955).
* Snow, Edgar, *The Other Side of the River* (New York and London 1963).

Snow, Edgar, *Red Star Over China* (New York 1961).
Suyin, Han, *China in the Year 2001* (London and New York 1967).
Torr, Dona, *Marx on China 1853–1860* (London 1951).
Townsend, Peter, *China Phoenix* (London 1955).
Union Research Institute, *Communist China Problem Research Series* (Hong Kong).
del Vayo, J. A., *China Triumphs* (New York 1965).
Winfield, G., *China: The Land and the People* (New York 1948).
* Wu, Yuan-li, *The Spatial Economy of Communist China* (New York, Washington and London 1967).
Wu, Yuan-li, *The Economy of Communist China* (New York and London 1965).
Wylie, M., *The Children of China* (Hong Kong 1962).

(iv) *SOME PERIODICAL ARTICLES*

Alsop, Joseph, 'On China's Descending Spiral', *China Quarterly*, July-September 1962.
Baby, Jean, 'Chine populaire: réduction de la durée des études et fusion avec les masses ouvrières et paysannes', *Le Monde Diplomatique*, Paris, September 1968.
Bettelheim, C., 'The Quality of China's Socialism', *Monthly Review*, New York, June 1965.
Cartier, Michel, 'Planification de l'enseignement et formation professionnelle en Chine continentale', *Tiers Monde*, Paris, April-June 1965.
Central Committee of the Chinese Communist Party, 'Decision of the C.C.P. concerning the Great Proletarian Cultural Revolution', *Peking Review*, 12 August 1966.
Kang Chao, 'Industrialisation . . . in Communist China', *Journal of Asian Studies*, May 1966.
China Trade and Economic Newsletter, London.
Emerson, J. P., 'Manpower Absorption in the Non-agricultural Branches of the Economy of Communist China 1953–58', *China Quarterly*, London, Number 7, 1961.
Fox, T. F., *The Lancet*, London, 9, 16 and 23 November 1957.
Freeberne, Michael, 'Natural Calamities in China 1949–61', *Pacific Viewpoint*, Wellington, Volume III, September 1962.
Gatti, Armand, 'Notes de voyage dans les communes chinoises', *Cahiers Franco-Chinois*, Paris, Number 1, 1959.
Gourou, Pierre, 'Notes on China's Unused Uplands', *Pacific Affairs*, September 1948.
Hsia, Ronald, 'The Development of Mainland China's Steel Industry since 1958', *China Quarterly*, Number 7, 1961.
Huang, Ping-wei, 'The Complex Natural Zonation of China', *USSR Academy of Sciences: Geographical Series* (in Russian), Moscow 1961.
Huberman, Leo and Sweezy, Paul, 'The Cultural Revolution in China', *Monthly Review*, New York, January 1967.
Huberman, Leo and Sweezy, Paul, 'Understanding the Cultural Revolution', *Monthly Review*, New York, May 1967.
Lambin, Denis, 'La Chine propre', *Cahiers Franco-Chinois*, Paris, Number 3, October 1959.

McKelvey, Donald, *Socialist Man and the Chinese Revolution: The Basis of the Cultural Revolution*, Radical Education Project, Ann Arbor, Michigan, 1967.

Malenbaum, W. G., 'India and China: Contrasts in Development Performance', *American Economic Review*, Volume XLIX, 1957.

Needham, Joseph, 'The Past in China's Present: A Background for Contemporary China', *Pacific Viewpoint*, Wellington, Volume 4, Number 2, September 1963.

Orleans, Leo A., 'Birth Control: Reversal or Postponement', *China Quarterly*, Number 3, July-September 1960.

Perkins, Dwight H., 'Economic Growth in China and the Cultural Revolution', *China Quarterly*, April-June 1967.

Richman, Barry, 'Capitalists and Managers in Communist China', *Harvard Business Review*, January-February 1967.

Robinson, Joan, 'Notes on the Chinese Communes', *Eastern Horizon*, Hong Kong, May 1964.

Su Chung, 'Facts about China's Population', *Peking Review*, 1 July 1958.

Suyin, Han, 'Birth Control in China: Recent Aspects', *The Eugenics Review*, Volume 52, Number 1, 1960.

Skinner, G. William, 'Marketing and Social Structure in Rural China', *Journal of Asian Studies*, Volume XXIV, November 1964, August 1965.

Teng, C. C., 'The Demarcation of the Agricultural Regions of China' in *Acta Geographica Sinica* (in Chinese), Peking, December 1963.

United States Department of the Interior, Bureau of Mines, *Mineral Trade Notes: Special Supplement, Number 59*, Washington 1960.

Wertheim, W. F., 'Recent Trends in China's Population Policy', *Science and Society*, New York, Spring 1966.

Wertheim, W. F., 'La Chine est-elle surpeuplée?' *Population*, Paris, May-June 1965.

Wheelwright, E. L., 'The Cultural Revolution in China', *Monthly Review*, New York, May 1967.

Wheelwright, E. L., 'Impressions of the Chinese Economy (11)', *Outlook*, Sydney, August 1967.

Yuen Ren-chao, 'The Languages and Dialects of China', *Geographical Journal*, August 1943.

(v) *POETRY, NOVELS AND SOME WESTERN TRAVELLERS*

Ayling, Alan and Mackintosh, Duncan, *A Collection of Chinese Lyrics* (London and Nashville 1965).

Birch, Cyril (editor) *Anthology of Chinese Literature* (Harmondsworth 1969).

Bodde, Derk, *Peking Diary* (London and New York 1951).

* Buck, Pearl, *Shui Hu Chuan (Water Margin)* translated by Pearl Buck as *All Men are Brothers* (New York 1937).

* Buck, Pearl, *The Good Earth* (numerous editions).

Buck, Pearl, *The Mother* (numerous editions).

Bynner, W., *The Jade Mountain* (New York 1964).

Davis, A. R., *The Penguin Book of Chinese Verse* (Harmondsworth 1962).

Fraser, Ronald, *Lord of the East* (London 1956).

Hersey, John, *A Single Pebble* (London 1956).
* Hsu Kai-yu, *Twentieth Century Chinese Poetry: An Anthology* (New York 1963).
Hua, Su, *Ancient Melodies* (London 1953).
* King, Evan, *Children of the Black-haired People* (London 1956).
Kazantzakis, Nikos (translated by G. C. Pappageotes), *Travels in China and Japan* (Oxford 1964).
Kuo Mo-jo and Chou Yang, *Songs of the Red Flag* (Peking 1961).
Lu Hsun, *Selected Works* (Peking 1956–).
Merwin, Samuel, *Silk* (Harmondsworth 1942).
Payne, Robert, *Chungking Diary* (London 1945).
* Payne, Robert, *The White Pony* (New York 1960).
Teilhard de Chardin, Pierre, *Letters from a Traveller* (London and New York 1962).
Suyin, Han, *Destination Chungking* (London and New York 1953).
Thai, Vinh, *Ancestral Voices* (London 1956).
Wong, Man (trans.), *Poems from China* (London and Hong Kong 1950).
Wong, Man (trans.), *Poems of Mao Tse-tung* (Hong Kong 1966).

(vi) *ILLUSTRATED WORKS*

Cartier-Bresson, H., *China* (New York 1964).
* Cartier-Bresson, H., *China in Transition* (London 1956).
Forman, W. and B., *The Face of Ancient China* (contains some superlative photos of *modern* China) (London 1960).
Glimpses of China (Peking 1958).
Hajek, L., Hoffmeister, A., and Rychterova, Eva, *Contemporary Chinese Painting* (London 1961).
Myrdal, Jan and Kessle, Gun, *Chinese Journey* (London and New York 1965).
Peoples Communes in Pictures (Peking 1960).
* Schulthess, Emil, *China* (London and New York 1966).
(*See also Pelissier, Roger, cited above.*)

Index